Sexuality:
Existential perspectives

Editor
Martin Milton

First published 2014

Reprinted with new cover, 2021

PCCS Books Ltd
Wyastone Business Park
Wyastone Leys
Monmouth
NP25 3SR
UK
Tel +44 (0)1600 891 509
www.pccs-books.co.uk

This collection © Martin Milton, 2014

The individual chapters © the authors, 2014

All rights reserved.

No part of this publication may be reproduced, stored in a retrieval system, transmitted or utilised in any form by any means, electronic, mechanical, photocopying or recording or otherwise, without permission in writing from the publishers.

The authors have asserted their right to be identified as the authors of this work in accordance with the Copyright, Designs and Patents Act 1988.

Sexuality: Existential perspectives

A CIP catalogue record for this book is available from the British Library

ISBN 978 1 906254 70 4

Cover designed by Moffat & Taylor
Printed in the UK by CMP, Dorset

Contents

Acknowledgements	vi
Foreword *Dr Elena Manafi*	ix
Introduction – Sexuality: Debates and controversies *Prof. Martin Milton*	1

Part 1: Existential perspectives on sexuality

1 – Being sexual: Reconfiguring human sexuality *Prof. Ernesto Spinelli*	21
2 – Being-in-the-world sexually *Dr Hans W Cohn*	62

Part 2: Drawing on the philosophers: Merleau-Ponty and Sartre

3 – Merleau-Ponty and existential sexuality *Dr Paul Smith-Pickard*	79
4 – Sexual expression, authenticity and bad faith *Richard Pearce*	92

Part 3: A gay essence?

5 – The freedom to be fixed: Can I be a homosexual please? *Dr Marc Medina*	119

Part 4: Existential perspectives on affirmative therapy

6 – Gay affirmative therapy: A critique and some reflections on the value of an existential-phenomenological theory of sexual identity *Prof. Simon du Plock*	141
7 – Gay affirmative therapy: Recognising the power of the social world *Prof. Darren Langdridge*	160

Part 5: Contemporary concerns

8 – Being sexual: Childhood and sexuality — 177
Prof. Ernesto Spinelli

9 – Open non-monogamies: Drawing on de Beauvoir and Sartre to inform existential work with romantic relationships — 198
Dr Meg-John Barker

10 – Trans and existential-phenomenological practice — 217
Christina Richards

Part 6: Sexuality and the consulting room

11 – A dangerous methodlessness: Sexuality in the therapeutic relationship — 233
Marcia Gamsu

12 – Individual therapy and Foucault's dark shimmer of sex — 251
Dr Paul Smith-Pickard

Part 7: Existential contributions to specific modalities

13 – Existential group therapy: Hell is other people? — 265
Christina Richards

14 – Existential sex therapy — 285
Dr Meg-John Barker

15 – 'Three's company, two's a crowd': Existential couple therapy — 305
Prof. Simon du Plock

16 – Family therapy and sexuality: Liminal possibilities between systemic and existential approaches — 324
Dr Alex Iantaffi

Epilogue *Prof. Martin Milton* — 336
Contributors — 338
Index — 343

Dedication

In memory of Jean Inglefield (1938–2014)

She lived life to the full with love and courage

Acknowledgements

As editor I would like to acknowledge all the hard work that contributors have undertaken in order for this book to come to fruition. The enthusiasm and interest throughout the process – from approach to delivery – has been very much appreciated and it has been an honour to work with such committed and courageous colleagues. I would also like to acknowledge the hard work and effort of so many colleagues in this field, in particular my colleague and friend Adrian Coyle, who helped me get started on this road and instilled in me a trust in the importance of this book; colleagues on both the University of Surrey and Regent's University London courses who have encouraged, tolerated and facilitated my thinking and the space in which to work; and trainees in my classes, those with whom I have worked as research supervisor, my thinking is enriched by all your hard work.

Christina Richards re Chapter 10: I would like to thank my colleagues at Charing Cross GIC as well as around the globe for their invaluable expert work on trans. I would also like to thank the activists and workers outside of the established fields of academic and applied endeavour who work tirelessly and often with little financial reward to move the field of gender forward. Lastly, I would like to thank my clients for sharing their lives and knowledge with me.

Christina Richards re Chapter 13: I would like to thank Professors van Deurzen and Tantam for their tuition in existential group therapy as well as Consultant Psychologist Dr Penny Lenihan and Consultant Psychiatrists Dr James Barrett and Dr Andrew Davies for their expertise as co-facilitators. Lastly, I would like to thank the various group members from whom, as ever, I have learned so much that cannot be found in expert texts.

Meg-John Barker re Chapter 14: I would like to thank the fantastic multi-disciplinary team at Guy's Sex and Relationship Therapy Clinic for introducing me to the world of sex therapy and for support and discussions. I am very grateful particularly to the clients who agreed that I could share their stories in my writing. Thanks to my tutors and fellow students at the New School who helped me to apply existential ideas to these issues, and to my academic colleagues in critical psychology whose research has informed my work in this area. Finally many thanks to all at COSRT (College of Sexual and Relationship Therapists) for making me so welcome in the world of sex and relationship therapy.

Permissions

Thanks to Sage Publications for their kind permission to reprint 'Being-in-the-world sexually' (Chapter 2 of this volume, pp. 62–75). Reproduced by permission of SAGE Publications, London, Los Angeles, New Delhi and Singapore, from Hans W Cohn, *Existential Thought and Therapeutic Practice: An introduction to existential psychotherapy*, July 1997. (© SAGE Publications, 1997)

Thanks to Taylor and Francis Ltd for their kind permission to reprint 'Existential sex therapy' (Chapter 14 of this volume). It was originally published as Barker, M (2011) Existential sex therapy. *Sexual and Relationship Therapy*, 26, 33–47.

Thanks also to Palgrave Macmillan for their kind permission to include an extract from 'Therapy with Couples Presenting with Issues of Addiction' by Simon Du Plock from E van Deurzen & S Iacovou (Eds) *Existential Perspectives on Relationship Therapy*, 2013, Palgrave Macmillan, in Chapter 15 of this volume (pp. 305–23). Reproduced with permission of Palgrave Macmillan. The full published version of this publication is available from: http://www.palgrave.com/products/title.aspx?pid=544833 on www.palgrave.com

Foreword

– Dr Elena Manafi –

Depending on one's attitude in living and experiences, existential philosophy is seen as pessimistic, nihilistic, absurd or an exaltation of human passion, freedom and responsibility that affirms life in the midst of inevitable suffering, loss and the certainty of death. There is no doubt that existential philosophy creates disquiet. We feel stripped of our omnipotence and self-understanding and come face to face with the void, our vulnerabilities, and sense of lack. Slowly or abruptly – with an aphorism – we witness a relentless critique of what we have so far taken for granted, of what we hold most dear to our hearts. Nevertheless, our need for control, security, certainty, stability and autonomy and our search for meaning, power, continuity and happiness are affirmed but always in the presence of their polarity. Nietzsche said, 'Happiness and unhappiness are brother and sister – or even twins who grow up together' (Nietzsche, 1882/1974, § 338: 270) and Camus pointed out that 'There is no sun without shadow, and it is essential to know the night' (Camus, 1942/2000: 110).

(Human) existence becomes a perpetual dialectic, a movement that ceases with death or destruction. Tranquillity is bound to be interrupted, as existence – being in general – is the expression of a tension or at best a dance between polarities. Existential philosophy embraces a position that unites rather than dichotomises opposites (i.e. the plethora of binary oppositions inherent in most medical, psychological and psychotherapeutic discourses). The either/or stance is replaced by an and/with attitude that introduces paradox, ambiguity, uncertainty and therefore anxiety, an emotion that is inevitable and with which we need to coexist if we are to dare to live rather than merely survive. Kierkegaard encapsulated this when he said, 'Whoever has learned to be anxious in the right way has learned the ultimate' (Kierkegaard, 1844/1980: 153).

Numerous other dictums such as Nietzsche's (1882/1974), *God is dead*, and Sartre's (1944/1989), *Hell is other people*, provoke and 'force' us to question long-held assumptions. When we read existential literature, our cherished notion of the self as an autonomous, rational, fixed, inner entity, collapses right before our eyes. Our identity and character cease to be personal possessions; like everything else they become dynamic concepts that denote the unitary phenomenon of being-in-the-world-with-other-people (hyphens indicate the interdependence of 'self' and other, 'self' and world, 'self' and existence). We are temporal, embodied, embedded, relational and historical beings subject to the givens of existence.

Quite rightly you might be asking 'where is sexuality in all this'?

As Cohn (Chapter 2) noted, 'Sexuality has been strangely neglected by writers on existential psychotherapy'; it is an omission noticed by both practitioners and trainees. So the answer to the question is: This is it! You are holding it. A pioneering piece of work, an enormous, daring act by all authors, who combine their philosophical and theoretical expertise, their personal and clinical experiences, their passion and despair, to give 'flesh and bone' to a long-held silence.

This book is not just about sexuality; you will not witness a detached stance of scholars who are writing dispassionately behind their academic desks, aiming at constructing a unified, existential discourse on sexuality. Such attempt would indeed be an oxymoron as it only takes a look around us to realise – sometimes with uneasiness and fear and other times with excitement and intoxication – that existence cannot be unified. Being is inherently dynamic and fluid in nature (Spinelli, Chapter 8); we can never predict with accuracy what, when and how something will emerge. Our very human attempts to control and predict our modes of being (be it sexual or other) at some point fail; the question is what we do then. Do we stay with whatever perplexes us and revise our precious theories, or do we label the 'inconvenient' phenomenon as abnormal, a perversion and then proceed with its alteration, isolation – or even worse – eradication. The Otherness of the other scares, infuriates, or fills us with compassion because the Other is closer than we think, it can sometimes feel as if it is within (Pearce, Chapter 4). That's the terror and beauty of an embodied, relational existence.

This book will not give you a universal theory about sexuality and I doubt that you will feel secure and at ease with everything that is written.

Some forms of sexual expressions of our being are still a taboo; they are far from being welcomed and accepted. Yet the fact remains that what you and I might consider perverse is for someone else their everyday, lived, sexual experience. The book is written by mortals, like the rest of us, and like the rest of us, the authors are exposed to the multiplicity of sexual existence. Unlike some of us however, they are all-embracing and giving voice to the complexity, uncertainty, ambiguity, diversity, and plurality of the most intimate and at the same time public aspect of our being – namely, our being-in-the-world sexually. All chapters go beyond the 'what' of sexuality and embrace the 'how' of our 'being-sexual-in-the-world-with-other-people'. Definitions will of course be given and comparisons to other modalities will be made but the commitment to the existential-phenomenological stance prevails. Each chapter approaches sexuality from a relational, embodied vantage point that does not reduce it to a mere act but unveils the intricate ways in which 'sexuality permeates human existence and vice versa' (Merleau-Ponty, cited in Smith-Pickard's Chapter 3). There are ample examples, sometimes personal, often clinical, bringing to light the struggle, the pain, the shame, the frustration and pleasure that emerges out of a sexual existence that is far from straightforward. In this sense the book addresses a much wider audience than clinical practitioners and academics in the field.

Oscar Wilde is thought to have once said that everything in the world is about sex, except sex. Sex is about power (Dempsey, 2012; Stotts, 2013). Power liberates but it can also oppress; it all depends on which side of the 'fence' we find ourselves. Being-sexual is an embodied interrelational engagement; sex is one of the many modes of expressing this. As all relational acts it is imbued with power and Pearce (Chapter 4) offers a humanising, Sartrean account of the continuous interplay of the dominance and submission, freedom and objectification so often encountered in sexual relationships.

The power of the (sexual) 'norm' has created a lot of grief and has given rise to endless debates that have entered social and political arenas (Milton, Introduction). Breaking the boundaries of sexuality as a seemingly 'private affair' has led to a number of movements and specialised forms of psychotherapy for 'sexual minorities' under the ethics of non-discriminatory practice. The recent development of *affirmative therapy* is critically discussed in two chapters (du Plock, Chapter 6 and Langdridge, Chapter 7) that together form a thought-provoking argument, which highlights the pros and cons of an area of specialisation that is not unproblematic in itself.

The book approaches the multiplicity of our sexual 'landscape' from philosophical, therapeutic, developmental, systemic, cultural, social and political vantage points. For an excellent sketch of this 'landscape' and contents of the book turn to the editor's introduction.

I will bring this foreword to an end with a continuation of Spinelli's joke (Chapter 1): in my opinion, he rightly noticed that, 'the gods of psychotherapy bequeathed psycho-analysis with sex while the existentialists got death'! This book bridges the gap. So let me pay tribute to the existential attitude by bringing the polarities of Eros and Thanatos together and leave you all with a wish:

Enjoy – in whatever shape or form – because it's later than you think!

Greece
September 2013

References

Camus, A (2000) *The Myth of Sisyphus*. London: Penguin Books. (First published 1942)

Dempsey, BJ (2012) *The Many Shades of BDSM: A safe and scintillating entry into the escalating pleasure of BDSM*. Iola, WI: Adams Media.

Kierkegaard, S (1980) The concept of anxiety. In H Hong & E Hong (Eds) *The Essential Kierkegaard*. Princeton, NJ: Princeton University Press. (First published 1844)

Nietzsche, F (1974) *The Gay Science* (W. Kaufmann, Trans). New York: Random House. (First published 1882)

Sartre, J-P (1989) *No Exit, and Three Other Plays*. New York: Vintage Books. (First published 1944)

Stotts, A (2013) *No Angels in Montmartre*. Bloomington, IN: iUniverse.

Introduction

Sexuality: Debates and controversies

– Prof. Martin Milton –

There is a long history of scholarly interest in sexuality across a range of disciplines and we have bodies of knowledge in such areas as economics, education, health, law, sport and sociology (Black, Sanders & Lowell, 2007; Boehmer, 2002; Donovan, 2006; Epstein, 2000; Moon, 2008; Morris-Roberts & Gilbert, 2013; Sherrod & Nardi, 1998; Strand, 1998). Of course, as well as it being an area of scholarly and professional interest, sexuality is an area of personal importance for many of us – particularly in our intimate lives, but also in the more social domain. We live in, what Barker calls, 'a sex-saturated culture' (2011, and this volume); sexuality peppers our everyday talk and this is the case across cultures and contexts. For readers of this book of course, sexuality is also represented in the fields of psychology, psychotherapy and philosophy.

This introduction considers the wider landscape related to sexuality before going on to focus on specific issues and concerns that affect the profession and practice of the psychotherapies. Following on from this, issues related to a specifically existential contribution to understanding sexuality will be considered. This introduction will end by orienting the reader to the rest of the book and the specific contributions that existential thinkers have to offer this area.

The landscape

As the topic of sexuality has such a long history of scholarly interest, some might assume that this array of insights, theories and perspectives means it is a well-understood area of human life – a case of 'seen it all before' maybe and that we can be confident that we actually understand it. Experience and the views of the contributors to this book suggest otherwise though, as sexuality and its various forms, practices, relational styles and identities, remain charged and difficult topics for us – societally, personally and politically.

Sexuality in the social domain

As noted above, sex and sexuality remain key features of everyday talk whether it's in people's relationships, 'banter' or on television, in film and the arts and through our growing technologies. You see it on the sports fields and in the school yard, in the high street and in the academy. Some of this is evidently fun, a source of vitality and life affirming, with people enjoying flirtation, desire and appreciation.

Sexuality though is often more complicated than this. Individuals, families and the public can react with confusion and outrage when sexuality is not as expected. One example from popular culture may illustrate this. When JK Rowling was in New York discussing the much loved character, Professor Albus Dumbledore, she commented that she 'always thought of Dumbledore as gay'. The news was apparently met with thunderous applause (Pugh & Wallace, 2008) but it then also gave rise to disbelief, concern and outrage from religious and conservative groups (*Daily Mail*, 2007). This was a very split reaction as is often seen on sexuality-related topics.

We are also seeing a more destructive and aggressive side of our responses to sexuality in the social domain. As with gender, we see the media and new technologies being used in service of extreme heterosexist and hetero-patriarchal stances, such as threats of rape and murder on the social networking site Twitter; we also see young people being bullied and stalked due to their non-conforming expressions of sexuality.

A specific area of the social domain is the political and we see sexuality continuing to be a key focus here.

Same-sex sexuality as a political 'hot potato'

In the political domain, we often see the understanding of sexuality being considered by way of a focus on 'non-normative' expressions of desire, relationship and identity. This is evident in the degree to which same-sex sexuality has become a topic with which politicians are engaged. Even a brief review of headline-hitting political events in the first half of 2013 allows us to see how widespread this debate is.

The United Kingdom saw controversial debates occurring in Parliament in the run-up to the passing of the 'Marriage (Same Sex Couples) Act 2013'.

The United States similarly saw debate after debate as different states considered equal marriage. And in January, President Obama was the first US President in history to mention sexual minorities in a Presidential inauguration. He stated that: 'Our journey is not complete until our gay brothers and sisters are treated like anyone else under law – for if we are truly created equal, then surely the love we commit to one another must be equal as well' (Trotter, 2013).

Less favourably, in his 2013 re-election campaign Zimbabwe's President Robert Mugabe undertook a campaign against sexual minorities. He is quoted as pledging 'hell for gays' if he was elected and stating that he wants to change laws to ensure LGBT (lesbian, gay, bisexual and transgender) people 'rot in jail' for life (*Daily News Live*, 2013).

Russia has seen an escalation in what has been termed 'anti-gay violence' as Pride marches and gay activists have been physically beaten and incarcerated under the new Russian laws which make it an offence to provide information on homosexuality to people under 18 (BBC, 2013).

Uganda has passed its Anti-Homosexual Act (2014), dropping the death penalty proposed in favour of life imprisonment and extending punishment to people involved in 'promoting' homosexuality (BBC, 2014).

There are of course many more examples, but a comprehensive account of global political stances to sexuality is not necessary for the purposes of this chapter. While sociologists and political scientists might understand this phenomena in their own ways, there are two specific aspects that are relevant to this book. The first is that understandings of sexuality are played out in the social world and not just in one's personal and private world. Second, the choices available to an individual about expressing themselves fully will vary depending on whether the self that is being expressed is subject to such threatening responses from the world in which he or she exists.

Another consideration is the way in which political factors overlap with professional bodies of knowledge. Possibly the most relevant for this book is that of psychiatry, where the sexual and political overlap.

Psychiatry: Another key cultural influence

Sexuality has long been considered a topic worthy of psychiatric attention and, indeed, psychiatry labelled 'homosexuality' as a disorder for a period of time. In fact it was included in the *Diagnostic and Statistical*

Manual (*DSM*) system up until 1980. When drawing on a colleague's constructionist discourse analysis of 'abnormal psychology' texts, my colleagues and I noted that until the:

> revision of the classification system in 1980, homosexuality was included in the *DSM* as a category of mental disorder, which served to reaffirm the moral and cultural sanctions against non-heterosexual behaviour. Contrary to the predictions of the 'scientific project', Kutchins and Kirk (1997) argue that science, scientific fact and research findings were not the key factors in deciding whether or not to include or exclude this particular diagnosis in the *DSM*; it was a 20-year debate about beliefs and values. This adds weight to social constructionist claims that classification systems and their use to classify 'abnormal' functioning are products of their time and place.
> (Milton, Craven & Coyle, 2010: 62)

Even though 'homosexuality' as a disorder in itself has been removed as a diagnostic criteria, psychiatry remains engaged with sexuality-related issues as they present in the clinic; for example, sexual dysfunctions may be treated pharmacologically before being referred for sex therapy (see Barker, this volume). Also, of course, the fact that LGBT populations experience minority-related stress (Bidell, 2012; Bridget, 1995; D'Augelli & Hershberger, 1993; Head, 2013; Institute of Medicine (IOM), 2011; King et al, 2008; Rivers, 1997; Rotherum-Borus, Hunter & Rosario, 1994) also means that they may be referred to psychiatry.

At this point it is useful to turn more directly to what our own profession has to offer us in our attempts to try to understand sexuality.

Psychotherapy, sexuality and sexual minorities

The various psychotherapy literatures have bodies of knowledge which psychotherapists (and others) can draw upon in their efforts to understand people and also to inform their practice. While there is some useful literature there, a great deal of the material that has existed historically in relation to sexuality has been problematic.

The first problem has been that much of the thinking and writing on sexuality has tended to construct a normative and 'compulsory' heterosexuality (Kitzinger, 1987) and with this, normative constructions of gender have also been taken to be 'truths' (see Barker, 2012; Richards, this volume). The assumptions therefore being that sexual attraction is a norm; it has a particular presence and focus; is always between men and women;

that men and women inevitably play set roles to accommodate specific, known and predetermined desires. In addition it assumes that terms such as 'man' and 'woman', 'heterosexual' or 'lesbian' are clear, understandable and capture everyone's experience of gender or sexuality.

There are other strands of literature that look at non-heterosexuality. Much of this literature has seen same-sex sexuality as a perversion or as pathology. This is particularly evident in psychoanalytic literature, where same-sex sexuality is constructed as examples of incomplete development or as indicators of psychological immaturity (Freud, 1977). Also, this is not just an historical phenomenon as a recent study by Bartlett, Smith and King (2009) highlighted. It seems that many practitioners remain of the opinion that same-sex sexuality is somehow pathological or at best sub-optimal, views upheld by the theories of Limentani (1994), Rayner (1986) and Socarides (1978). This is, of course, in debate, the broader face of psychoanalytic practice – the British Psychoanalytic Council (BPC) and the American Psychoanalytic Association are advocating a changed perspective through public statements and conferences that assert a non-discriminatory position. The BPC state 'The British Psychoanalytic Council opposes discrimination on the basis of sexual orientation' (BPC, 2011). There has been discussion as to the degree that a public statement by an organisation reflects updated attitudes and evolved theory for all the members of those organisations (see Knowlson & Milton, 2012). While this dilemma is present in psychoanalytic circles, it is also evident in the experiments of the behaviourists (Milton, Coyle & Legg, 2002) and in the writing of Medard Boss (1966) and so other schools of thought cannot simply assume that this style of homonegative thinking is an issue for psychoanalysis alone. What this introduction is aiming to point out though, is that a common response to non-heterosexuality has been to (a) single it out as distinct and (b) to problematise it.

There is another literature which has problems of its own. It too singles out different forms of sexuality but instead of problematising same-sex sexuality, this literature takes the opposite stance which is to ignore lesbian and gay experience, assuming it has no distinct qualities that require attention. This is evident in those approaches that assume a universal methodology (such as CBT and humanistic therapies).

> The method of practice inherent in these models is, in cognitive behavioural training, to learn the methods correctly (Beck, 1976), or in humanistic models to develop the ability to provide the 'core

conditions' (Rogers, 1951) – the implication being that these skills can then be applied in the same way to all clients, a claim which is debatable ... By taking this stance difference can be ignored and the distinct experience of 'the other' is denied.

(Milton & Coyle, 1999: 44)

The problematic nature of much of the available literature on working with lesbian and gay clients was one of the influencing factors that led to the British Psychological Society (BPS) Division of Counselling Psychology study *Issues in Psychotherapy with Lesbians and Gay Men: A survey of British psychologists* (Milton, 1998) being undertaken. It was of course also a factor in the production of the recent BPS *Guidelines and Literature Review for Psychologists Working Therapeutically with Sexual and Gender Minority Clients* (2012). The British Psychological Society has also come out with a position statement on therapies that attempt to change sexual orientation (2013).

Another, more recent, development is that the psychotherapy profession has developed a literature that discusses what is known as affirmative psychotherapy (see Davies & Neal, 1996; Gonsiorek, 1985; Greene & Herek, 1994; Hitchings, 1994; Milton, 2000; Milton & Coyle, 1999; Milton, Coyle & Legg, 2002). When the reader looks at this field they will see that once again, there is no single perspective or consensus. As with the literature mentioned above, two distinct viewpoints can be discerned in this body of work. One is that affirmative therapy is a technique-oriented and distinct way of working, with particular stances that must always be taken (Davies, 1996).

The second viewpoint is that:

> lesbian and gay affirmative practice is a non-discriminatory, contextually aware attitude that can be incorporated into mainstream psychotherapy theory and practice. The challenge is thus to 'update' our models or develop further models that attend to the diversity of experience that exists.
>
> (Milton & Coyle, 1999: 45)

For readers interested in these different perspectives Part Four of this volume will be of particular interest as the chapters by Langdridge and du Plock offer insights into these different perspectives and the contributions that an existential perspective has in helping us take critical stances to them.

As broad and useful as all of these developments are, we should not be too confident in the breadth of our knowledge, as this literature also highlights a lot of what we do not understand. We long ago moved beyond trying to figure out why a specific 'category' of sexuality *exists* to trying to learn more about the wide array of people's experiences. Currently while there is still a lot of interest in some topics we know quite a lot about (for example, topics such as heterosexual, lesbian and gay experiences), there is also an awareness that we have a rather impoverished understanding of other forms of gender and sexuality such as asexuality, bisexuality, trans experiences, and polyamorous relationship forms to name just a few (Barker, 2012). Our understanding remains limited due to our knowledge being based on assumption and the application of knowledge from incompatible areas.

Now that the landscape has been described, we can turn our attention to the specific contributions of an existential perspective.

Existential theory and practice: Debates, controversies and contributions

At a meeting of the Society for Existential Analysis in 1996, Prof. Ernesto Spinelli wryly commented that when dividing up the topics of interest, psychoanalysis had gotten sex and the existentialists had gotten death. He then went on to present his paper 'Some hurried notes …' (Spinelli, 1997). As Medina (this volume) reminds us, Spinelli wasn't the only one of this opinion. Medina quotes Smith-Pickard and Swynnerton (2005) as saying that the area had 'barely been explored' and notes that Cohn wrote that the topic was 'strangely neglected' (1997). People might be forgiven for thinking that this 'split' has been absolute but, as this book demonstrates, things have changed and more recently existential theorists and practitioners are offering a variety of perspectives to facilitate debate and assist us in clarifying and understanding human sexuality more fully.

Existential authors have long added critical perspectives to a range of topics that psychotherapy engaged with; for example, some of the challenges pertain to the notion of psychiatric classification (Szasz, 1960, 1997), understandings of the self (Heaton, 1995; van Deurzen-Smith, 1995, 1996), supervision (van Deurzen & Young, 2009) and the foundational stances of psychoanalysis (Cohn, 1997; Spinelli 1994), humanistic therapies (Spinelli, 1994) and CBT (Spinelli, 1994). It is unsurprising then, that as well as this outwardly challenging stance, when it came time to consider existential understandings of sexuality, theorists and practitioners have also engaged critically 'in-house' and we see some useful debates and controversies on a range of topics. The foci have varied widely, but they include the following selection of topics.

Definitions and meanings of the term 'sexuality'

As will have been gleaned, the term 'sexuality' is one that is used to describe a range of different phenomena and as such will inevitably fail to capture the specifics of much of these experiences. Of course, the multiplicity of things to which the term relates – desires, practices, relationship statuses and identities – means that there is much to debate. In covering the range of topics that they do, contributors to this book start to fine-tune different dimensions of sexuality and draw our attention to the embodied, emotional and interpersonal phenomena that infuse sexuality.

Construction or essence?

There is a debate as to whether we should understand sexuality as a construction (and therefore somewhat fluid) or as a 'solid' experience, an essence. Some authors have taken the notion of choice and freedom and considered the ways in which sexuality has enormous variations between people and for individuals across time, very often drawing on the work of Merleau-Ponty and Sartre as Paul Smith-Pickard and Richard Pearce do in this volume. While others, including Medina (this volume), have highlighted the 'givens' of existence and the experience of people who claim to only know themselves in a relatively stable, solid manner. These seemingly contradictory experiences give rise to interesting ideas and understandings of the nature and meaning of the different aspects of sexuality.

The ontic and the ontological dimensions

The above-mentioned contributions – and those in this book – often give rise to discussions that suggest a key confusion is whether the analyses being made in any specific texts are considering sexuality as an ontic expression of an *individual* or sexuality as an ontological feature of *being*. My own reading of the literature is that the omission of such a clarification is often behind the differences between authors and I am therefore glad to see contributors such as Spinelli and Medina considering this issue in an explicit fashion.

The possibility of an affirmative stance for existential thinking and practice

The notion of an affirmative stance to existential practice has been hotly contested in recent literature. There are some authors who seem happy to consider an affirmative stance to therapy as being consistent with an existential-phenomenological approach (see Langdridge, 2007; Milton, 2000); others have questioned this, noting some difficulties (see du Plock, 1997; Goldenberg, 2000).

The debate about an affirmative stance is closely linked to the other debates listed above and one question that arises is as follows. If an existential perspective privileges the constructed and ontological dimensions of sexuality (or any other experience for that matter) are there times when you may deny your client's experience of themselves as a stable, unchanging entity? How do we understand this situation?

It follows that this raises questions of attunement and 'technique'. While the phenomenological method requires us to bracket understanding, and sometimes to ask clients to do the same thing, if we challenge the experience of an identity, especially when compounded by a client's experience of rejection or bullying in the social domain, the client may well, and quite reasonably, experience us as trying to diminish their experience, blame the victim or overwrite their experience, rather than fully attest to social oppression and inequality of experience.

A focus on the personal and/or the contribution of the social world

A different stream of existential thinking that relates to the various experiences of sexuality mentioned above is that of our 'situatedness'; the fact that we exist in the world. Different aspects of sexuality are manifest in relation to the self, in relation to the other and to the world more generally. While we often find ourselves in debates about whether it is this or that aspect, phenomenon A or phenomenon B, existential thinking reminds us that multiple meanings coexist and therefore personal desire may well relate to social discourses. This in turn may contribute to a wider sense of ease or unease when attempting to live authentically in the world. I am delighted that contributors such as Langdridge and Richards engage with these issues in this volume.

'Pure' existentialism or contributions to a pluralistic understanding?

Some of the areas of consideration mentioned give rise to a tension between how we might *understand* an issue or situation and the separate issue of how we might *act* in relationship to it. It is the difference, for practitioners, between formulation and therapy, or case conceptualisation and intervention.

The contribution that existential thinking can make, to a myriad of issues, is always tempered by the context and the meaning the understanding may have for those it is developed with or offered to. The contexts will include the contributions of other theoretical frameworks and other contextually specific bodies of professional, social and legal knowledge. Also relevant to the issue of sexuality are the ways in which existential thinking has to engage with religious, cultural and health service assumptions about it. In some health services people will only be seen if their difficulty can be translated into a diagnosable condition, such as a 'sexual dysfunction' (Barker, 2011, this volume) or 'gender identity disorder' (Bouman & Richards, 2013). This may also be the case if the client wants to take advantage of the medical insurance cover.

The integration of existential thinking into other frameworks or contexts is not always easy. We have seen that existential thinkers have long highlighted the limitations and absurdities of many positivistic assumptions; many practitioners find themselves having to engage with these ideas in order to undertake their professional roles. And of course, it isn't only existential practitioners that may find this task difficult (see Fletcher, 2012; Milton, 2012) but due to its relational understanding it may well be one that existential practitioners cannot avoid if they work in these contexts. Contributors to this book have risen to this challenge and engaged with a wide variety of other perspectives that include dynamical systems theory (Spinelli, Chapter 1), family systems theory (Iantaffi, Chapter 16), the NHS (Richards, Chapters 10 and 13) and psychiatric diagnosis (Barker, Chapter 14).

A challenge to reductionism

As the reader will no doubt have seen, much of the broader thinking on sexuality has taken either a problematising or a liberal stance to forms of non-heterosexuality – usually focusing on lesbian and gay experiences. The assumption was initially that the concept of 'heterosexuality' was a comprehensive term that satisfactorily captured the various aspects of human sexuality. When this was critiqued, thinking moved to understanding heterosexuality to be just one of a number of identifiable forms. This is a form of reductionism. A reductionist stance may help with many things, for example, managers needing to develop services, or epidemiologists that need to survey rates of infectious disease and calculate how much vaccine a country may need, may find it appropriate to use broad categorisations that ignore the complexity and fluidity of individual experience of a phenomenon. But for psychotherapists, reductionist thinking is a problem as it cannot offer us the wider awareness that human science needs and existential thinking can contribute to. When a client enters therapy they are not generally wanting a label but to understand themselves.

Reductionist understandings take attention away from what an experience is actually like. For example, we all think we know what heterosexuality is, looks like and feels like. But, when we move beyond the stereotypes what does it actually look like? Reductionist thinking assumes that there are definite states of being, experiences or meanings attached to having a particular form of expression or a particular identity. In doing so, it means that we fail to consider other experiences. The debates and arguments about other assumed static forms of identity and expression, for example, lesbian and gay experience, were the first to come to the fore and have taken a long time to engage with. While huge advantages have come out of these debates, it is important therefore that we remind ourselves that questions about sexuality are not only about forms of experience and expression we can label as lesbian or gay – to do so would continue to be reductionist and, as Cohn notes, 'unphenomenological' (1997, this volume). Whether we assume 'heterosexuality', 'gay' or 'lesbian' … we remain guilty of reducing a variety of experiences down to single terms that simply do not capture the person's lived experience or the range of different experiences that people have.

The reductionist stance is also there when we assume that it's only adults that have a sexuality, that only certain types of behaviours occur, that there are right and wrong identities and so forth. One of the key characteristics of the existential approach is that it has steadfastly refused to simply adopt these assumptions and instead has developed ways in which we might look beyond assumption to engage with experience in an open and authentic a manner as is possible. And I am delighted to say that this has been a central concern of the contributors in this volume too.

This book

This introduction has drawn the reader's attention to the fact that sexuality has been, and remains, a source of scholarly, personal and political interest over a very long period of our history and yet in some ways we remain lost in reductionist assumptions and biases a great deal more than would be thought necessary. It shows though that existential theory is no longer just stuck with 'death' as a topic of interest. We are well involved in the attempt to clarify understandings and to explore new and creative formulations as the debates above testify. It is with delight therefore that I invite the reader to consider this book and the knowledge, challenges, debates and controversies it contains.

Sexuality: Existential perspectives contains two reprinted seminal chapters as well as contributions from a range of existential psychologists and psychotherapists on the topic of human sexuality, its practices, forms and meanings – with of course an eye for the ways in which it is related to human joy or distress and the role that sexuality plays in psychotherapy. The contributors have not shied away from the need to take a questioning and challenging stance towards our own (and each other's) existing knowledge. This therefore means that the reader will see contributors disagree with philosophers, with each other and with others in the wider field of psychotherapy. Furthermore, in my view, this is how it should be. After all, these authors are trying to attend to fluid and complex phenomena that are meaningful in the ontic and ontological realms, the personal and the social, individual and socially discursive too. So it is right to notice when our own ideas have limitations, and of course over time existential authors have been as much a victim of their time as Freud, Klein or any other contributor to this field. As Paul Smith-Pickard notes 'from where we stand today the perspective of sex and sexuality in the post-war existentialists seems entrenched in heterosexist and phallocentric images of sexual behaviour that run alongside their ontological perspectives' (This volume: 258). I am delighted to see that the contributors to this volume have not overlooked that challenge.

The book itself is structured into seven parts.

In Part 1, Ernesto Spinelli engages with some of the wider epistemological issues and challenges that existential phenomenology present to us in understanding this rich and varied area. I am also delighted to have permission to reprint Hans Cohn's seminal chapter that made an enormous contribution to this field.

Part 2 offers Paul Smith-Pickard and Richard Pearce's insights into the work of Merleau-Ponty and Sartre respectively and the way that these are helpful in their understanding of issues related to sexuality.

In Part 3 Marc Medina considers the experience of sexuality being (or at least feeling) like an essence and offers some insights into the dilemmas that we face in understanding the tension between the ontic and the ontological, the theoretical and the lived experience.

As mentioned above the notion of affirmative therapy has been influential in the field of psychology and psychotherapy for several decades now and this book would have been woefully incomplete if we were not able to engage with this framework and to consider how existential therapy might add to this debate. So Part 4 outlines two different perspectives on this – one from Simon du Plock and one from Darren Langdridge.

Part 5 shifts focus and considers some concerns that seem only now to be being given the attention that they warrant. In this section Ernesto Spinelli looks at childhood and sexuality, Meg-John Barker looks at open non-monogamous relationships and Christina Richards looks at our understanding of transgender experiences.

Part 6 turns our attention to the consulting room and Marcia Gamsu and Paul Smith-Pickard both consider the issue of sexuality in the therapeutic relationship itself.

The final part explores ways in which existential thinking might fruitfully engage with ideas and practices that originate in other fields. Simon du Plock gives us an insight into working with couples, Christina Richards writes on existential group therapy, we have permission to reprint Meg-John Barker's important paper on sex therapy and are delighted to have Alex Iantaffi consider the ways in which existential perspectives may be helpful to family systems therapists – and vice versa.

There may be an advantage to reading the book from Chapter 1 to Chapter 16 as the order guides the reader through a number of overlapping areas. But equally there may be an advantage of not following a preset pathway. The book was constructed so that readers may 'dip' into chapters one at a time as the material guides them, as the authors all have their own particular area of interest or expertise and were asked to ensure that their contribution could act as a stand-alone contribution. However you decide to engage with this book, the contributors and I hope it is a useful and thought-provoking book that will help in developing your ideas and concepts for the benefit of the clients we work with and the profession as a whole.

References

Barker, M (2011) Existential sex therapy. *Sexual and Relationship Therapy, 26*(1), 33–47.

Barker, M (2012) *Rewriting the Rules: An integrative guide to love, sex and relationships.* London: Routledge.

Barker, M (2014) Existential sex therapy. In M Milton (Ed) *Sexuality: Existential perspectives* (pp. 285–304). Ross-on-Wye: PCCS Books.

Bartlett, A, Smith, G & King, MB (2009) The response of mental health professionals to clients seeking help to change or redirect same-sex sexual orientation. *BMC Psychiatry, 9*(11).

Beck, AT (1976) *Cognitive Therapy and the Emotional Disorders.* Harmondsworth: Penguin Books.

Bidell, M (2012) Addressing disparities: The impact of a lesbian, gay, bisexual and transgender graduate counselling course. *Counselling and Psychotherapy Research: Linking Research with Practice, 1,* 8.

Black, DA, Sanders, SG & Lowell, J (2007) The economics of lesbian and gay families. *The Journal of Economic Perspectives, 21*(2), 53–70.

Boehmer, U (2002) Twenty years of public health research: Inclusion of lesbian, gay, bisexual, and transgender populations. *American Journal of Public Health, 92*(7), 1125–30.

Boss, M (1966) *Sinn und Gehalt der Sexuellen Perversionen.* Bern: Huber.

Bouman, WP & Richards, C (2013) Diagnostic and treatment issues for people with gender dysphoria in the UK. *Sexual and Relationship Therapy, 28*(3), 165–71.

Bridget, J (1995) Lesbian and gay youth and suicide. Presentation at National Children's Bureau conference on *The Needs of Gay and Lesbian Young People.* April, London.

British Broadcasting Corporation (BBC) (2013) Russian Duma passes law banning 'gay propaganda'. Retrieved 6 August 2013 from http://www.bbc.co.uk/news/world-europe-22862210

British Broadcasting Corporation (BBC) (2014) Uganda's President Yoweri Museveni signs anti-gay bill. Retrieved 26 April 2014 from http://www.bbc.co.uk/news/world-africa-26320102

British Psychoanalytic Council (2011) Retrieved 6 August 2013 from http://www.psychoanalytic-council.org/about-us/bpc-policies-and-statements

British Psychological Society (2012) *Guidelines and Literature Review for Psychologists Working Therapeutically with Sexual and Gender Minority Clients.* BPS: Leicester.

British Psychological Society (2013) *Position Statement Opposing Sexual Orientation Conversion Therapies.* BPS: Leicester.

Cohn, HW (1997) *Existential Thought and Therapeutic Practice.* London: Sage Publications.

Cohn, HW (2014). Being-in-the-world sexually. In M Milton (Ed) *Sexuality: Existential perspectives* (pp. 62–75). Ross-on-Wye: PCCS Books.

Daily Mail (2007) Retrieved 6 August 2013 from http://www.dailymail.co.uk/news/article-490261/JK-Rowling-US-Bible-belt-outing-Dumbledore-gay.html

Daily News Live (2013) Retrieved 5 August 2013 from http://www.dailynews.co.zw/articles/2013/08/05/gays-fear-crackdown-after-mugabe-win

D'Augelli, AR & Hershberger, SL (1993) Lesbian, gay and bisexual youth in community settings: Personal challenges and mental health problems. *American Journal of Community Psychology, 21,* 421–48.

Davies, D (1996) Towards a model of gay affirmative therapy. In D Davies & C Neal (Eds) *Pink Therapy: A guide for counsellors and therapists working with lesbian, gay and bisexual clients (pp. 24–40).* Buckingham: Open University Press.

Davies, D & Neal, C (Eds) (1996) *Pink Therapy: A guide for counsellors and therapists working with lesbian, gay and bisexual clients.* Buckingham: Open University Press.

Donovan, JM (Ed) (2006) *Sexual Orientation and the Law: A research bibliography selectively annotating legal literature through 2005.* Buffalo, NY: William S. Hein & Co.

Du Plock, S (1997) Sexual misconceptions: A critique of gay affirmative therapy and some thoughts on an existential-phenomenological theory of sexual orientation. *Journal of the Society for Existential Analysis, 8,* 56–71.

Epstein, D (2000) Sexualities and education: Catch 28. *Sexualities, 3,* 387–94.

Fletcher, R (2012) Introduction: Dealing with diagnoses. In M Milton (Ed) *Diagnosis and Beyond: Counselling psychology contributions to understanding human distress* (pp. 1–12). Ross-on-Wye: PCCS Books.

Freud, S (1977) *On Sexuality.* Harmondsworth: Penguin.

Goldenberg, H (2000) A response to Martin Milton. *Journal of the Society for Existential Analysis, 11*(1), 102–5.

Gonsiorek, JC (Ed) (1995) *A Guide to Psychotherapy with Gay and Lesbian Clients.* New York: Harrington Park Press.

Greene, B & Herek, GM (Eds) (1994) *Lesbian and Gay Psychology: Theory, research and clinical applications.* Thousand Oaks, CA: Sage Publications.

Head, S (2013) *UK Therapists' Experiences of Working with LGBT Clients Who Have Experienced Intimate Partner Violence: An interpretative phenomenological analysis.* Unpublished PsychD Portfolio. Guildford: University of Surrey.

Heaton, J (1995) The self, the divided self and the other. *Journal of the Society for Existential Analysis, 6*(1), 31–60.

Hitchings, P (1994) Psychotherapy and sexual orientation. In P Clarkson & M Pokorny (Eds) *The Handbook of Psychotherapy* (pp. 119–32). London: Routledge.

Institute of Medicine (IOM) (2011) *The Health of Lesbian, Gay, Bisexual and Transgender People: Building a foundation for better understanding.* Washington, DC: The National Academies Press.

King, MB, Semlyen, J, Sharon, ST, Killaspy, H, Osborn, D, Popelyuk, D & Nazareth, I (2008) A systematic review of mental disorder, suicide and self-harm in lesbian, gay and bisexual people. *BMC Psychiatry, 8*(1).

Kitzinger, C (1987) *The Social Construction of Lesbianism.* London: Sage Publications.

Knowlson, T & Milton, M (2012) Some of my best friends are psychoanalysts. *Psychology of Sexualities Review, 3*(1), 89–94.

Kutchins, H & Kirk, SA (1997) *Making Us Crazy.* New York: Free Press.

Langdridge, D (2007) Gay affirmative therapy: A theoretical framework and defence. *Journal of Gay and Lesbian Psychotherapy, 11*(1-2), 27–43.

Limentani, A (1994) On the treatment of homosexuality. *Psychoanalytic Psychotherapy, 8,* 49–62.

Milton, M (1998) *Issues in Psychotherapy with Lesbians and Gay Men: A survey of British psychologists: Division of Counselling Psychology Occasional Papers, 4.* Leicester: British Psychological Society.

Milton, M (2000) Is existential psychotherapy a lesbian and gay affirmative psychotherapy? *Journal of the Society for Existential Analysis, 11*(1), 86–102.

Milton, M (2012) *Diagnosis and Beyond: Counselling psychology contributions to understanding human distress.* Ross-on-Wye: PCCS Books.

Milton, M & Coyle, A (1999) Lesbian and gay affirmative psychotherapy: Issues in theory and practice. *British Journal of Sex and Marital Therapy, 14*(1), 43–59.

Milton, M, Coyle, A & Legg, C (2002) Lesbian and gay affirmative psychotherapy: Defining the domain. In A Coyle & C Kitzinger (Eds) *Lesbian and Gay Psychology: New perspectives* (pp. 175–97). Malden: Blackwell Publishing.

Milton, M, Craven, M & Coyle, A (2010) Understanding human distress: Moving beyond the concept of 'psychopathology'. In M Milton (Ed) *Therapy and Beyond: Counselling psychology contributions to therapeutic and social issues* (pp. 57–72). Chichester: Wiley Blackwell.

Moon, D (2008) Culture and the sociology of sexuality: It's only natural? *The Annals of the American Academy of Political and Social Science, 619*(1), 183–205.

Morris-Roberts, C & Gilbert, K (2013) *Jockocracy: Queering masculinity and sport.* Champaign, IL: Common Ground.

Pugh, T & Wallace, DL (2008) A postscript to 'Heteronormative heroism and queering the school story in J K Rowling's *Harry Potter* series'. *Children's Literature Association Quarterly, 33*(2), 188–92.

Rayner, E (1986) *Human Development: An introduction to the psychodynamics of growth, maturity and ageing* (3rd ed). London: Routledge.

Richards, C (2014) Trans and existential-phenomenological practice. In M Milton (Ed) *Sexuality: Existential perspectives* (pp. 217–30). Ross-on-Wye: PCCS Books.

Rivers, I (1997) Lesbian, gay and bisexual development: Theory, research and social issues. *Journal of Community and Applied Social Psychology, 7*, 329–43.

Rogers, CR (1951) *Client-Centered Therapy.* London: Constable.

Rotherum-Borus, MJ, Hunter, J & Rosario, M (1994) Suicidal behavior and gay-related stress among gay and bisexual male adolescents. *Journal of Adolescent Research, 9*, 498–508.

Sherrod, D & Nardi, PM (1998) Homophobia in the courtroom: An assessment of biases against gay men and lesbians in a multiethnic sample of potential jurors. In GM Herek (Ed) *Stigma and Sexual Orientation: Understanding prejudice against lesbians, gay men and bisexuals* (pp. 24–38). Thousand Oaks, CA: Sage Publications.

Smith-Pickard, P & Swynnerton, R (2005) The body and sexuality. In E van Deurzen & C Arnold-Baker (Eds) *Existential Perspectives on Human Issues: A handbook for therapeutic practice* (pp. 48–57). Basingstoke: Palgrave Macmillan.

Socarides, CW (1978) *Homosexuality.* New York: Jason Aronson.

Spinelli, E (1994) *Demystifying Therapy.* London: Constable. (Republished 2006, PCCS Books)

Spinelli, E (1996) Some hurried notes expressing outline ideas that someone might someday utilise as signposts towards a sketch of an existential-phenomenological theory of sexuality. *Journal of the Society for Existential Analysis, 8*(1), 2–20.

Strand, DA (1998) Civil liberties, civil rights and stigma: Voter attitudes and behaviour in the politics of homosexuality. In GM Herek (Ed) *Stigma and Sexual Orientation: Understanding prejudice against lesbians, gay men and bisexuals*. Thousand Oaks, CA: Sage Publications.

Szasz, T (1960) The myth of mental illness. *American Psychologist, 15*(2), 113–8.

Szasz, T (1997) *The Manufacture of Madness: A comparative study of the Inquisition and the mental health movement*. Syracuse, NY: Syracuse University Press.

Trotter, JK (2013) The text of Obama's inaugural address. Retrieved 6 September 2013 from http://news.yahoo.com/text-obamas-inaugural-address-165950611.html

Van Deurzen, E & Young, S (2009) *Existential Perspectives on Supervision: Widening the horizon of psychotherapy and counselling*. Basingstoke: Palgrave Macmillan.

Van Deurzen-Smith, E (1995) Ontological insecurity revisited. In HW Cohn & S du Plock (Eds) *Existential Challenges to Psychotherapeutic Theory and Practice* (pp. 82–94). London: *Journal of the Society for Existential Analysis*.

Van Deurzen-Smith, E (1996) The survival of the self. *Journal of the Society for Existential Analysis, 7*(1), 56–66.

Part 1

Existential Perspectives on Sexuality

1

Being Sexual: Reconfiguring human sexuality

– Prof. Ernesto Spinelli –

Some years ago, in my capacity as the then Chair of the Society for Existential Analysis, I focused the annual talk from the Chair on the question of human sexuality as might be viewed from the perspective of existential theory and practice. I chose to discuss human sexuality because, surprisingly, contemporary existential authors had said little on this enormous topic. Jokingly, I suggested that this might be because the 'gods of psychotherapy' bequeathed psychoanalysis with 'sex' while the existentialists got 'death'. My talk and its subsequent published versions (Spinelli, 1997a,b, 2001, 2006, 2009) received a good deal of attention and critique within the existential community (Acton, 2010; Crabtree, 2009; du Plock, 1997; Joseph, 2009; Medina, 2008; Milton, 2000; Pearce, 2011; Sears, 2010). This chapter revisits the original arguments in the light of the subsequent comments and critiques. Its aim is to challenge several of our society's current dominant concerns surrounding being sexual. The questions it raises focus upon various pivotal themes centred principally around issues of biology, normality and identity – all of which are, of course, crucial concerns of existential phenomenology.

Such issues surrounding sexuality highlight an increasingly unpalatable realisation for psychotherapists: our culture's discourse on being sexual presents the single most telling counter-argument to our profession's most foundational injunction: that it is 'good to talk'. We do talk, and talk incessantly, about being sexual. Among other things, psychotherapy has taught us a particular way to talk about sexuality. It is, I believe, a way whose multitude of limitations reveal a pervasive set of values and assumptions that are themselves the source to the majority of our society's sexual confusions and discontents.

In contrast to this, existential phenomenology proposes an alternative mode of discourse, a different way of talking and thinking about being sexual. In this, it is indebted, as with so much else, to the ideas of Martin Heidegger who, in his series of dialogues with groups of psychiatrists and psychologists, reminded them that it is not so much *what* we talk about but rather *how* we talk about it that is pivotal to the possibilities of change (Heidegger, 2001). With Heidegger's injunction in mind, I have sought to present the outlines of ways of talking about being sexual that question several seemingly 'natural', culturally embedded assumptions that were elaborated as key elements of modern sexology from its beginnings during the mid-nineteenth century. Throughout, my argument will be to demonstrate the limitations of such perspectives with regard to the lived experiences of being sexual that we all share and enact.

However, before I can begin to develop this critique, I must alert readers to a more basic, if no less challenging, dilemma: what is human sexuality and how might it be best defined? As will be discussed below, there exists no simple or straightforward reply to such questions.

Defining human sexuality

Recently, Tamara Sears has highlighted the recurring confusion generated by writers who have employed the term sexuality to mean both sexuality per se and as the means to describe some thing or act that is sexual (Sears, 2010). This confusion is encapsulated in a quote by Jeffrey Weeks: 'The more expert we become in talking about sexuality, the greater the difficulties we seem to encounter in trying to understand it' (Weeks, 2003: 1, as cited in Sears, 2010: 20).

Sears' research expands upon this confusion. She discerns that the very term 'sexuality' was first defined only in the nineteenth century. When comparing various dictionary definitions given to the term, several meanings emerge, including:

1. the quality or state of being sexual
2. the condition of having sex
3. sexual activity
4. the expression of sexual receptivity or interest especially when excessive.

Such definitions, as well as being somewhat limited (i.e. sexuality is the quality or state of being sexual), also have a tendency to consider sexuality as both a verb (a way of being or doing) and a noun (the 'thing' that is experienced or done) thereby highlighting the elusive quality of the topic under focus. Similarly, Paul Smith-Pickard and Richard Swynnerton argue that:

> In ordinary, everyday language, sexuality is often used to indicate predilections and behaviours in various groups and individuals …. Sexuality thus becomes reified as a defining characteristic of an individual rather than remaining at the level of description of a fundamental aspect of intersubjectivity.
> (Smith-Pickard & Swynnerton, 2005: 50)

This shift from the abstract to the concrete bedevils all discourse on sexuality. At the same time, it seems to me that this self-same shift is a definitional requirement. If, as Sears concludes, the best definition regarding sexuality that we can arrive at is 'being or doing something sexual' (Sears, 2010: 65) then it must be asked: how is the 'sexual' in 'being or doing something sexual' to be identified? What – or who – determines that it is, or is not, sexual? All this is very reminiscent of the famous exchange between Alice and Humpty Dumpty:

> 'When I use a word,' Humpty Dumpty said, in rather a scornful tone, 'it means just what I choose it to mean – neither more nor less.'
> 'The question is,' said Alice, 'whether you can make words mean so many different things.'
> 'The question is,' said Humpty Dumpty, 'which is to be master – that's all.'
> (Carroll, 2007: 104)

And who are the 'masters' who determine the meanings to be attributed to sexuality? In one sense, we could point to the 'experts' – be they scientists or religious leaders. But, more truthfully, it is all of us. Sexuality is what we say it is.

Maurice Merleau-Ponty who, as we shall see below, is existential phenomenology's most significant contributor to the debate on human sexuality warned that theorists 'must be careful not to overextend the term otherwise it will become meaningless' (Smith-Pickard & Swynnerton, 2005: 51). At the same time, it seems to me that he, too, is challenged by it. On the one hand, he writes that sexuality is 'always present like an atmosphere'

(Merleau-Ponty, 1962: 168, as cited in Smith-Pickard & Swynnerton, 2005: 51). This would suggest that sexuality is indistinguishable from existence itself. Yet Merleau-Ponty is at pains to reject this conclusion. He writes that 'sexuality permeates existence and vice-versa' (Merleau-Ponty, 1962: 169, as cited in Smith-Pickard & Swynnerton, 2005: 51).

How is one to understand this distinction? I suspect that what Merleau-Ponty is hinting at is that sexuality, like existence, cannot be 'pointed to' in any direct way. To do so, would be to encase it into a structure, to 'thing-ify' it. If, on the other hand, we de-structure sexuality, so that it becomes more verb-like, or process-like, 'like an atmosphere' in other words, then all that we have available to us to address or point to it are its manifestations through the myriad ways that we think, feel and act sexually. Behaviours, thoughts and feelings which we label as sexual are aspects or expressions of sexuality, just as all beings are expressions of Being. It seems to be the case that in any discourse on sexuality, all that the discourse can truly address in any direct, reflective fashion, are the *expressions* of sexuality – that upon which we imbue – or impose – a sexual meaning.

How then are we to define sexuality? Sears' definition is as good as anything I've come across. But it remains evident that, simply in the attempt to define sexuality, its 'atmospheric' principle is restricted, limited by the constraints of language and the necessary structuring or 'thing-ifying' of being that language demands. We need to consider our words with care. Even so, whatever words we settle upon to define sexuality will only point out what, like Humpty Dumpty, we have declared sexuality to be rather than illuminate the 'being' of sexuality.

In an attempt to minimise this persistent confusion, I have adopted a position that seeks to address concerns raised by human beings' sexual experiences rather than make any claims toward their clarification and demarcation as some 'thing' that we label as human sexuality. As such, from this point onwards, I will, wherever possible, avoid the use of the term human sexuality and replace it with that of 'being sexual'.

An existential critique of three foundational assumptions regarding being sexual

Various assumptions and biases have dominated Western thought regarding being sexual since its modern day 'invention' (or reinterpretation) that began during the Victorian era (Foucault, 1979; Weeks, 1985). This way of considering the issues has been led by a specifically biological focus through which questions and assertions of sexual normality/abnormality, aim, drive and identity have been made possible and, as well, have created many of the disputes and discontents that persist within our culture's understanding and experience of being sexual. Nineteenth-century sexology (as with much of contemporary sexology) was primarily concerned with the issues of 'doing' sexuality. Nonetheless, the focus on 'doing' led to assumptions and decrees regarding matters of 'being' sexual. Out of these views, emerged three key assumptions that continue to dominate contemporary thought:

1. that being sexual can only be understood as a biological activity whose originating aim is that of reproduction and hence serves as the key mechanism for the survival of our species

2. that seen in this way, it becomes possible to identify 'normal' or 'natural' expressions of being sexual which can be contrasted with 'abnormal' or 'unnatural' deviations from, or perverted expressions of, being sexual

3. that being sexual is a key component of a person's identity, such that who one is as a person can to a significant degree be described, labelled and judged by what one does or does not act out in sexual relations. This third point also holds numerous corollary assumptions regarding the 'fixedness' of one's identity and, through it, the 'fixedness' of one's sexual orientation as well as debates as to whether such 'fixedness' is predominantly inherited biogenetically or acquired through lived experience.

Each of these three key points can be challenged from an existentially informed perspective.

Being sexual and biology

With regard to the first dominant assertion, it is evident that the human desire to engage in sexual activities is not solely, nor even primarily, dictated by biological 'cycles' linked to reproductive drives in the service of species survival. Human beings' willingness and inclination to pursue sexual possibilities reveals that nothing so straightforward as reproductive cycles can provide sufficient rationale for their range, scope and frequency. The desire to reproduce may be one instigator to sexual behaviour, but it is rarely the primary one.

Even if one were to argue that the desire to enact non-reproductively focused sexual relations serves as a preparatory 'testing out' or 'bonding' process for any eventual reproductively focused sexual activity, this claim would still fail to address a multitude of instances of human sexual behaviour, not least the frequency of masturbatory activity. Furthermore, to argue that any form of non-bonding sexual activity or of bonding activity that cannot lead directly to the possibility of reproduction is a 'deviation' of the sexual drive or aim simply reveals a circularity of argument: the second assertion (i.e. that it is possible to distinguish normal and abnormal expressions of being sexual) is presented as evidence for the first assertion (i.e. that being sexual can only be understood as a biological activity whose originating aim is that of reproduction), while at the same time the first assertion serves to provide the a priori basis upon which the second assertion is imbued with its explanatory worth.

It is in the work of the French existential phenomenologist, Maurice Merleau-Ponty that existential phenomenology sets out its counterargument. For Merleau-Ponty, the issues regarding being sexual must be placed within the broader concerns of the body as a whole and its relation to consciousness. His starting point is to critique all views that disengage mind and body. Instead, his stance makes plain that human consciousness is always an *embodied* consciousness. Human beings inhabit and are living expressions of an 'incarnate principle ... of Being' (Merleau-Ponty, 1968: 139) which he refers to as 'the flesh'.

The flesh is 'the formative medium of the object and the subject' (Merleau-Ponty, 1968: 138). That is to say, with regard to the body, human beings are conscious that we both *have* a body and *are* a body. Furthermore, our embodied consciousness of both being and having bodies places us in an inescapable (and irreducible) relation (what Merleau-Ponty refers to as *intersubjectivity*) wherein the awareness that I both am and have a body is always simultaneous with the awareness of others being and having bodies (Merleau-Ponty, 1962). Merleau-Ponty's biology of the flesh removes the duality of self and other (as well as that of mind and body), both being coexistent principles (or 'polarities') of an inseparable and irreducible totality.

Considered from this primordial grounding of interrelatedness, being sexual provides a crucial configuration through which embodied beings reveal, explore and engage with embodiment itself. Being sexual expresses our enacted response to embodied consciousness. Our sexual encounters provide us with a pivotal means with which to express simultaneously both our own presence and the other's presence as revealed during the interaction. Even in solitary sexual activities such as masturbation, the presence of 'the other' – be it an imaginary 'other' distinct from the subject, or an internalised 'subjective other' who is exposed or freed through the act – is inevitable. In both instances the self and other that are temporarily present may be surprising, disturbing, as expected or as desired (Wooler, 2012, personal communication). In all instances, being sexual serves to reveal each particular being's way of engaging with, and being engaged by, the perceived other. This engagement might be welcoming or rejecting of either self or other or both, it might be curious or fearful, fixed and stilted or ambiguous and open toward any and all, or only to one, or none of its intersubjective possibilities. Whatever the case, it remains primarily an engagement focused upon the existential 'given' of relatedness and all of the uncertainties and experiences of anxiety (be they positive or negative, exhilarating or debilitating, ecstatic or joyless) that are its lived expression.

In summary, the investigation initiated by Merleau-Ponty seeks to clarify being sexual as it is revealed in its intersubjective dimensions. Its importance lies in its ability to 'awaken' each of us to our interrelational being. 'This ... is the origin of sexual desire, of the unknown but known sense of ourselves as sexual beings, the desire is an expression of a yearning to know ourselves through the other' (Pearce, 2011: 238).

Although Merleau-Ponty can be said to present a view of being sexual that remains significantly biologically attuned, the biology being revealed here is of a distinctly different kind to that which dominates contemporary Western sexological theories. Rather than be considered from a reductive, reproductively driven stance, this alternate embodied view places issues of relatedness as expressed through a flesh-consciousness at the heart of being sexual. In doing so, this stance frees us from the need to explain all the varied manifestations of being sexual in a fashion that must ultimately reduce them to any bioreproductive exclusivity. No longer can any 'natural' manifestation of being sexual be addressed as separate to, or a precedent for, its cultural conditions for expression. The biology being proposed no longer separates consciousness and body matter. Human sexuality becomes *the consciousness of being sexual* – be it imagined or behaviourally expressed, and in becoming so, being sexual can no longer be the singular concern of species reproduction. It can certainly include such, of course, though not as some mindless predetermined drive or species imperative.

Being sexual: Issues of normality and abnormality

It is the last point above that provides the basis for an existential-phenomenological response to the second dominant assertion. With regard to any assumptions concerning questions of normality and abnormality, such terms must be reconsidered from a standpoint that places their sociocultural construction/interpretation on par with, and inseparable from, any avowedly fixed, reproductively focused 'givens' of being sexual. Acknowledging that all cultures impose their views of appropriate and inappropriate, or 'normal' and 'perverse', forms and expressions of sexual behaviour, the challenge becomes that of exposing the error in the tendency to make such pronouncements from the exclusive primacy of their assumed bioreproductive imperatives.

In adopting this stance, it becomes far more problematic to determine just what may constitute either 'normal' or 'abnormal' expressions of being sexual. If we can no longer rely solely upon some assumed universally bio-driven 'natural' predetermined basis upon which to make our pronouncements, all that we have available to us is something far more tenuous, and, as well, far more revealing, of our interpersonal and socioculturally constructed biases. Cultures vary in their dictates and preferences as to what is and is not acceptable sexual behaviour. Just as significantly, that which any given culture views as appropriate or perverse at one point in time can, and often does, alter at another. The consequence of this awareness, of course, forces us to acknowledge the plasticity of that which we label as either acceptable or transgressive and which is subsequently either wholly or partially sanctioned or is entirely proscribed.

This conclusion, it seems evident, is not easy for societies to acknowledge. Nor is it the case that the implications discerned from it are likely to be overly gratifying. Nonetheless, in acknowledging their sedimented power, the means by which fixed beliefs and biases can be challenged shifts the debate towards issues of sociocultural values and aspirations rather than remaining at the level of questionable assertions expressing the dictates of either nature or super-nature. Via such a shift, it becomes possible for investigations and theories to coincide more adequately with people's actual lived experiences of being sexual.

One unambiguous example of a challenging shift has been put forward by the British consultant psychiatrist, Chess Denman. She has proposed that all discourse regarding the range of sexual activities and preferences enacted between two or more participants should be stripped of its psycho-moral jargon and instead be reconsidered solely from the standpoint of whether it is coercive or mutually agreed (Denman, 2003). This proposal has a great deal of merit even if, on consideration, it becomes apparent that what determines an act to be coercive is not always unproblematic. Legal criteria may be straightforward but in instances of BDSM (bondage and discipline, sadism and masochism), for example, the criteria may be complex and remain uncertain (Wooler, 2012, personal communication). Even so, acknowledging these possible limitations, Denman's suggested shift in emphasis to a more legal focus and attitude would significantly alter notions of normality and abnormality in sexual relations between partners (be they 'real' or 'virtual') while still serving to protect the great majority of those whom society considers to be at risk.

A further example that encompasses a critique of both the first and second assumptions can be found in the novel, if still controversial, reconsideration of a major aspect of evolutionary theory that has been developed by Joan Roughgarden (2009). Roughgarden's challenges to our understanding of the biology of being sexual reveal conclusions whose convergence with the above critiques is striking.

The theory of natural selection provides the most powerful and well-established account of how species have evolved. The subsidiary theory of sexual selection clarifies the mechanism that permits natural selection. At its centre lies the assumption of competition that encourages the survival of the fittest. Males compete to fertilise as many females as possible, while females compete to select high quality mates for reproductive purposes. But how is a male's 'high-quality' to be discerned? Through secondary characteristics – size, shape, colour and so forth. The classic example evoked to clarify sexual selection is that of the peahen's choice of the peacock with the most dazzling train of feathers.

Roughgarden's research and her subsequent hypothesis challenges sexual selection as it is most commonly understood. For one thing, the evidence from observations of species behaviour often contradicts the theory. For example, Roughgarden highlights research from 2008 which suggests that, in contrast to what has been assumed, peahens disregard male plumage in making their mating choices (Roughgarden, 2009). Instead, she proposes, that far more important than sexual selection is what she terms *social selection* – the development of relationships between members of species whose intent is to create and maintain a stable infrastructure for raising offspring to reproductive age. Social selection places at least equal importance on strategies of cooperation and negotiation as it does on competition. In like manner, it is not the fittest individual (or gene) but the fittest cooperative organisation whose survival chances are improved. If sexual selection emphasises the number of offspring produced as a basis for evolutionary success, social selection instead focuses on the degree to which the rearing of offspring is deemed successful with regard to survival opportunities. Reproduction per se is the critical spur to sexual selection;

but for social selection, reproduction is just one of several critical factors relevant to species survival.

Roughgarden's theory highlights two key limitations within sexual selection theory that are relevant to this discussion. First, in its overwhelming emphasis on gender-specific universal sex roles, sexual selection cannot account for the compelling and abundant evidence of sex role reversal. Second, other than view it as a genetic defect or a maladaptive aberration, sexual selection theory cannot account for the continuing presence of same-sex or bisexual behaviour in species. With regard to the second point, Roughgarden's research (which closely corresponds to Bruce Bagemihl's pioneering studies (Bagemihl, 2000) documents evidence for recurrent same-sex and bisexual behaviour in some 450 different invertebrate species – from all-male 'orgies' by giraffes, bottle-nose dolphins and killer whales, to persistent female same-sex mounting by Japanese macaque monkeys, to the same-sex societies and sexual behaviour of male longhorn sheep.

Roughgarden argues that same-sex and bisexual behaviour, viewed from the perspective of social selection theory, emerge as being as natural as heterosexual behaviour. In removing sexual behaviour from the exclusive 'natural imperative' of reproduction, as assumed by sexual selection theory, social selection provides an explanation of the diversity of being sexual that centres upon an emphasis of the development of cohesive relationships and social interaction patterns that enhance survival strategies. Further, she proposes that the more complex and sophisticated the social system is, the more there will be an intermixing of heterosexual, same-sex and bisexual behaviour. Being sexual from this standpoint is expressive of far more than simply reproductive mating. Being sexual provides the experience of socialisation and intimacy that, in turn, enriches experiences of cooperative and coordinated behaviour as well as communal bonding.

Being sexual and identity

The third major contention – the relation between being sexual and identity – continues to provoke the greatest interest and debate.

The Victorian sexological project permitted a radical transposition of an act or practice into a statement of inner experience and identity. Via this shift in focus, the description and labelling of any sexual act became the primary means with which to identify, label and pronounce upon the psyche of the person who engaged in that act. In doing so, a crucial process of internalisation occurred: the act became the person. From this point on, and still to the present day, statements regarding sexual behaviour became inseparable from statements regarding personality and identity. The continuing sexological interest in categorising sexual acts has permitted, in parallel, the construction of sexual categories of identity (Foucault, 1979). As Foucault highlights:

> Homosexuality appeared as one of the forms of sexuality when it was transposed from the practice of sodomy onto a kind of interior androgyny, a hermaphrodism of the soul. The sodomite had been a temporary aberration; the homosexual was now a species.
> (Foucault, 1979: 43)

An example of Foucault's argument can be seen in the shift of emphasis in British society from discourse on the behaviour of those men who frequented so-called 'Molly Houses' to their being labelled male homosexuals. Eighteenth-century 'Molly Houses' were typically specified taverns or private rooms where men congregated either to cross-dress or to engage in same-sex relations involving various forms of sexual behaviour, both legal and illegal (since the 1533 Buggery Act anal intercourse, whether hetero- or homosexual, had been declared illegal in Britain) (Gelder, 2007). Such activities were just that – activities rather than expressions of identity. It was only with the invention of the term 'homosexuality' in the nineteenth century that several of these behaviours were declared to signify a different sort of being whose identity and consciousness could be contrasted – pejoratively, to be sure – with heterosexual identity and consciousness.

One critical consequence of this shift, as Foucault reminds us, is that the way in which we structure our thoughts will alter the thoughts themselves. Contemporary sexological theory continues to adopt this shift in thinking: how an individual expresses (or fails to express) him- or herself sexually provides a pivotal means with which to identify who that individual is (and is not) and, how 'healthy/stable/normal' he or she is (or is not).

In contrast to this, an existential-phenomenological perspective argues that it becomes immediately evident that the correlation of sexual acts with the construction of a 'sexual identity' (be it heterosexual or LGBT)[1]

---

1. Where necessary, I employ the initials LGBT (lesbian, gay, bisexual and transgender) which are intended to emphasise the diversity of alternatives to being sexual hetero-sexually. I am aware that this descriptor is ever-expanding such that 'Q' (for queer or questioning), 'I' (for intersex), 'A' (for asexual), 'P' (for pansexual) and a second 'T' (for transvestite) are becoming increasingly common additions. For the sake of brevity, I

imposes significant restrictions and divisions upon the human experience of being sexual. Such terms serve as labels that permit often rigid definitions of self and other. Indeed, with regard to these particular terms, it is evident that each requires the other in order to provide itself with any substantive meaning. But, it must be asked, just how valid are these demarcations of identity? What purpose do they serve? In brief: 'with all these categorisations comes the paradox: they control, restrict and inhibit whilst simultaneously providing comfort, security and assurances' (Plummer, 1981: 74).

This view, first put forward by Kenneth Plummer, places the issues within the wider perspective of 'the self-construct' (and, more recently, the worldview) that I have proposed in other writings (Spinelli, 1994/2006, 2007). This argument holds that in order for the self-construct (or the wider worldview) to be maintained over time so that it retains its meanings, values and behaviours, such a construct must, of necessity, impose fixed, or *sedimented*, limitations upon what lived experiences it can (or must) acknowledge, identify with, or 'own' as its defining features and qualities. As a consequence, it must also *dissociate* or 'disown' those experiences that provoke challenging contradictions or alternatives to the sedimentations (Spinelli, 1994/2006, 2007). For example, to identify oneself *exclusively* as heterosexual or LGBT requires the maintenance of a rigidly sedimented construct as well as the experiential dissociation from any life challenges or contradictions that would threaten its de-sedimentation.

This interweaving of being sexual with identity is not the outcome of a 'natural' determined set of circumstances, nor does it reveal genuine 'hard-wired' differences between the various constructs (nor, indeed, as will be argued below, between the wider gender constructs of 'male' and 'female'). Rather, the basis for the maintenance of such constructs is nothing more, or less, than *existential choice*. Likewise, more generally, the existential argument being presented raises implicit critiques surrounding matters of *essence* and its possible 'fixedness' with regard to assumptions surrounding alternatives to being sexual heterosexually as well as to debates surrounding *otherness* as well as *gender differences*.

Not surprisingly, these conclusions have raised several significant concerns (Acton, 2010; Crabtree, 2009; du Plock, 1997; Medina, 2008). For example, Simon du Plock has written:

---

have elected to keep to the most commonly employed abbreviation though my hope is that it will be seen to embrace all possibilities.

> I found myself intellectually convinced [by the paper] ... but emotionally felt troubled and rather angry. I was particularly struck by [its] assertion that [heterosexual and LGBT relations express the very same intersubjective desires]. My gut reaction was that homosexuality – *my* homosexuality – had somehow been explained away, diminished.
>
> (du Plock, 1997: 66–7)

And later:

> Sexual orientation was being presented as a choice. My sense, though, is that sexuality may not feel like a choice – may not be available to consideration by us in the way that we are used to choices being available – for the simple reason that it is a choice of a different type, a part of an individual's fundamental project.
>
> (du Plock, 1997: 67)

Raising similar concerns, Marc Medina has written: '... an individual may experience their sexual preference as a natural given and furthermore something that has always been and will always be fixed' (Medina, 2008: 13, see also this volume).

More broadly, such concerns reveal two central assumptions surrounding alternatives to heterosexual ways of being sexual. Namely that alternatives as expressed via the acronym LGBT reveal unique and distinct expressions of sexuality such that comparisons between them or with any other expression of sexuality – and heterosexuality in particular – are at best misleading and at worst further heterosexist attempts to deny their equal standing; and second, that such alternatives do not express a choice one makes but a foundational way of being.

These views reveal a recurring sense of unease with an existential approach to being sexual as I have sought to present it, at least insofar as it pertains to issues surrounding being sexual homosexually. I want to respect that unease and, further, want to make it clear that, given the history of mistreatment, exclusion, demonisation, torture and outright murder of men and women simply on the grounds of their ways of expressing being sexual, such unease seems to me to be entirely appropriate. That those who engage in or seek to validate LGBT relations today continue to be similarly abused in many parts of the world should make evident why such unease persists. Even though substantial changes in legal, social and interpersonal acceptance have occurred in most Western countries over the last thirty years, much remains to be achieved. As but one example of this, the current responses by some interpreters of both the Bible and the Koran to the establishment of same-sex marriage unveil persistent deep-rooted rejective responses even in the most libertarian of cultures. Given such circumstances, it is hardly surprising that any minority group whose continuing demarcation by the majority is one of 'otherness' and 'difference' should itself adopt those self-same defining characteristics not as acknowledgement of error or weakness but as primary means towards the experience of personal and mutual affirmation, pride and empowerment.

Accepting all this, if we are committed to an existential-phenomenological exploration of such issues then we are also committed, as Karin Knorr-Cetina reminds us, 'to turn the obvious into the problematic' (Knorr-Cetina, 1981, cited in Kaye, 1995: 30). What begins to present itself as problematic is precisely centred upon a number of key existential concerns including the issue of choice and the precedence of existence over essence, and because many of the concerns expressed, I would suggest, arise out of a critical misunderstanding of major aspects of existential theory, it is necessary to elaborate and clarify its position.

Being sexual: Existential choice

Critics of the existential stance regarding choice have raised the question as to why would anyone 'choose' to adopt a problematic construct that has the potential to threaten not only the social status and liberties of the individual who adopts it, but which can also become the means for a culture to exclude and abuse that individual as well as, in the most extreme circumstances, to demand an end to his or her continued existence. The question is valid. But ... is this what existential choice argues?

Sartre made it plain: choice is more accurately a condemnation than it is a matter of celebration. Every choice made has its pay-off and its price and which is which in many of the choices either willingly undertaken or forced upon us is not readily predictable or foreseeable (Sartre, 1956). Even the best, most desirable and fulfilling choice will provoke some degree of regret since every choice confronts us with what has been lost to us as a result of having made that choice. From the standpoint of existential phenomenology, choice is understood in the following ways:

1. Choice is a condition of relatedness. Existential choice is not at the separate individual or subjective level, but is always grounded in intersubjectivity. The 'I' who chooses is not an isolated,

exclusively self-defining 'I' but rather an 'I' whose uniqueness, individuality and reflective existence is a consequential expression of relatedness. In this way, 'my' choice is not mine alone to make. Nor is its impact and consequence directed solely to, or for, me.

2. Choice is not at the level of origination. Existential choice makes no claim that persons have the capacity or ability to control or determine the plethora of event stimuli that occur at any and every moment. Like the Buddha's teachings, existential thought argues that 'You are not the Do-er'. Human existence is always situated in a set of 'thrown' conditions. Within such conditions, existential choice concerns itself with the significance and meaning given to them, the interpretation made of any given event, the attitude taken toward it, the affective and behavioural responses to it. Ultimately, *the way a being is in relation with the presenting conditions is that being's choice.* Facticity, or that which is preset or determined, such as our time and place of birth, our nationality and so forth, is not a separate set of conditions, nor is it an obstacle to freedom and choice. Our freedom and choice *includes* facticity. If a tension exists, it is not between freedom/choice and facticity per se, but rather between a stance toward freedom and choice that includes facticity or one that excludes it.

3. The choice available to construe meaning is not always, nor even often, at a multi-optional level. The given conditions of embodiment, temporality, spatiality and historical context may well impose a *single-option choice* as to the meaning ascribed to any particular experience of being. As Heidegger puts it, my choice '*is* only the choice of *one* possibility – that is, in tolerating one's not having chosen the others and one's not being able to choose them' (Heidegger, 1962: 331, as cited in Cohn, 2002: 97; emphasis in the original). Existential choice, and the possibilities that emerge through it, rests on the choosing or embracing of that choice that is there, already present, rather than adopting an inauthentic stance that assumes or insists that *something other* than that one choice can be, and in some sense is already, present. Although a single-option choice might not, at first, appear to be a choice at all, this argument is critical to the understanding of existential theory's stance on choice. Consider the following example: I am in a room that I cannot leave. Inside the room, loud grating music is playing which I cannot turn off. As far as I am concerned, harming or

killing myself in order to escape the noise are not options worthy of my consideration. I am faced with a single-option choice: can I choose to accept my circumstances as they present themselves to me? Of course, I can invent all manner of multi-option choices but these are only available to my imagination. Nonetheless, I could convince myself, or claim that, even so, any of these imaginary options is actually available to me. And if I do so, and act on this imaginary choice that is not an actual choice I am all too likely to add to my sense of misery or provoke an even greater tragedy. How? Either because I act as though the imaginary choice achieved the desired actual consequences and create all manner of unwanted and unexpected consequences that arise as a result of this false premise, or because the imaginary choice fails to fulfil my project and confronts me with my failure and the regret that accompanies it. Instead, if I embrace the one actual choice that is available to me, to remain in the noise-filled room, the experience may still be miserable, perhaps even tragic, but in accepting the one actual choice my *relationship* to the event conditions alters even if the event conditions remain the same. At its most basic, in taking this stance, I am no longer a victim to my circumstances. This stance, too, may well provoke regret (as all choices will) but it is the regret that emerges from the making of the choice available to me rather than the regret of avoiding that choice and deceiving myself into believing and acting as though 'something other' is there for me.

This view of choice makes plain once again how, existentially speaking, choice is not solely, or even primarily, a pleasant or desirable enterprise. Indeed, the attempt to abdicate from or deny choice may provide a desired reduction of tension as well as an escape from the regret arising from the often difficult and uncertain demands which existential choices present. Further, this existential view of choice discloses how many of the disruptions and tribulations that provoke such pain and unease can be seen to arise when we insist upon claiming the ability to choose that which is not open to our choosing. Faced with the choice of 'A or A', many of us insist that it remains possible for us to choose the non-existent option of 'B' and then act out its consequences.

In differing ways, du Plock and Medina, as well as later writers (Acton, 2010; Crabtree, 2009; Pearce, 2011), appear to have responded to the question of existential choice from standpoints that approach choice in a more 'everyday' sense or Husserlian 'natural' attitude, rather than from its phenomenological attitude and existential focus. From that everyday perspective, their concern is more than justified. Such views of choice are all too often the assertion of those whose vested interests maintain assumptions of abnormality or 'unnatural behaviour' and who seek to provide any number of 'treatments' for such. It is also obvious that, from an everyday standpoint, the assertion that same-sex expressions of being sexual are not a choice but a set of predetermined conditions, or 'givens', can have significant impact not least at a socio–political level – regarding the acceptance of those who express that 'given'. Therefore, it is important to acknowledge the potential danger in the misuse of terms like 'being heterosexual/LGBT is an existential choice' and to be clear just what the statement intends to express. Let me be specific: existential choice viewed from the perspective of being sexual argues that:

1. Labels such as heterosexual or LGBT are grounded in a set of relational conditions. They are not 'owned by' or 'bequeathed to' any one group or individual in isolation. They are labels that make sense not as intrapsychic, isolated definitions of self, but as particular statements of relational meaning whose worth and limits still require much greater analysis. Although somewhat glib, the sound-bite employed by a media advertising campaign for Orange mobile phones from 2008: 'I am who I am because of everyone' encapsulates this argument.

2. Being heterosexual or LGBT is an interpretative response to a combination of 'givens' such as embodiment, temporality, spatiality and historical context, all of which are within both general and particular – as well as ever-dynamic – cultural conditions. In this sense, these labels and their associated meanings, values, affects and behaviours are constantly open to reinterpretation and extension be it at a personal or a wider cultural level.

3. To choose 'being heterosexual or LGBT' does not suggest a multi-option view of choice. Instead, existential choice regarding being sexual expresses the willingness, or lack thereof, to acknowledge 'that which is there for me' as opposed to 'what is imaginable but not present'.

The implications of existential choice, particularly with regard to the last point, should become more apparent, and pertinent, in the discussion that follows.

Being sexual: Existence precedes essence

Sartre's (in)famous summary of existential thought, 'existence precedes essence' (Sartre, 1948: 28) is derived from a sentence in Heidegger's *Being and Time:* 'The "essence" of Dasein lies in its existence' (Heidegger, 1962: 67). For the issues surrounding an existential view of being sexual, this primal statement is of immense significance not least because the debate regarding existential choice is often confused and conflated with the concerns regarding matters of *essence*. For example, a recurring view raised by authors such as Marc Medina has been to argue in favour of an essentialist perspective wherein 'homosexuality is an existential given that may in the future be proved to be a biological reality' (Medina, 2008: 132). It seems evident that Medina's project seeks to propose homosexuality (and, implicitly LGBT in general) as a different ontology that is only understandable to those who share that ontology. Essentialist arguments place significant reliance upon biology. It is not biology in general or per se that is the issue but, rather, it is the particular *way* of biologising being sexual. Before turning to an existential view on this issue, it is important to ask: do any other alternatives to an essence-dominant perspective on being sexual exist? Yes, indeed they do.

Queer theory

Queer theory emerged in the early 1990s as a critical approach developed through a combination of both feminist and lesbian/gay studies. Its central challenge has been to dispute the notion of stable or fixed identity categories of gender and sexual expression. Its view is that identities are made up of so many factors and components that to emphasise any one characteristic is both absurd and false (Halley & Parker, 2011). As Darren Langdridge has summarised:

> In brief, queer theory is concerned with providing a challenge to fixed identities: heterosexual, bisexual and homosexual alike. The notion of a stable sexual subject is contested and traditional identity politics are challenged as forms of disciplinary regulation ... Instead it is argued that identities are always multiple and unstable.
>
> (Langdridge, 2007: 42)

Queer theory's challenges to dominant essentialist perspectives on being sexual, and on identity in general, are often resonant with existential phenomenology. In *Queer Theory,* Annamarie Jagose writes:

> Queer is a way of pointing ahead without knowing for certain what to point at – rather, it describes a horizon of possibility whose precise extent and heterogeneous scope cannot in principle be delimited in advance – Queer is always an identity under construction, a site of permanent becoming ...
>
> (Jagose, 1996: e-text)

David Halperin states the issue even more succinctly: 'Queer is ... identity without an essence' (Halperin, 1997: 62).

Sexual fluidity

In recent years, a good deal of compelling evidence from both quantitative and qualitative research has emerged pointing to the conclusion that, far from being 'fixed' in biology, our sexual identities rely far more upon constructivist variables that are influenced by any number of psychosocial factors such as conformity, locational circumstance and peer pressure (Butler, 2006; Fine, 2010). Lisa Diamond's influential text, *Sexual Fluidity: Understanding women's love and desire* (2008) provides a compelling case for sexual fluidity. Rather than view heterosexual or LGBT identities as rigid 'hard-wired' traits, Diamond argues that they are more adequately understood as fluid conditions that remain dependent upon a wide number of interrelational and sociocultural contextual factors. Sexual fluidity encompasses three key ideas:

a) the non-exclusivity in attraction to either gender
b) the open possibility of change in the focus of attraction
c) that attraction is directed toward the person, not the gender.

Over a ten-year period, Diamond's research followed the experiences of being sexual of 100 women who at the start of the study had labelled themselves as either lesbian, bisexual or 'unlabelled'. During that time period, two-thirds of the women altered their initial identity labels, one-third of them doing so at least twice, and of the new labels adopted, the most common new label was that of 'unlabelled' (Diamond, 2008). Later research has indicated that women, more than men, appear to behave more openly to the uncertain possibilities of sexual fluidity. Male sexual fluidity is more likely to be apparent in settings such as prisons and military compounds and under circumstances such as wartime conditions, where male-with-male bonding is often the only option and/or is the primary means to a reasonable level of stability under stressful circumstances. In all cases, however, the degree of sexual fluidity – or lack thereof – correlates with the ability to focus more on the person or the sexual activity rather than upon gender.

The acceptance for sexual fluidity provokes a radical challenge to a person's identity stability. Because sexual fluidity disputes essentialist stances on being sexual, it has been criticised by both heterosexual and LGBT theorists who promote such views. In reply, Diamond has written:

> Perhaps we are reluctant to accept the notion of sexual fluidity because of the social and scientific implications of the phenomenon. Shifting away from sexual determinism and toward a more flexible understanding of sexuality … entails notable changes in the way we think about sexuality. Some people will embrace such changes because they involve more expansive understandings of all individuals' sexual possibilities. Others will reject them out of fear that they might trigger a conservative backlash against lesbian/gay/bisexual individuals and jeopardize hard-won progress toward social acceptance.
>
> (Diamond, 2008: 236)

Taken together, these arguments offer significant challenges to essentialist-dominated perspectives of being sexual. Existential phenomenology, too, raises similar concerns which are most obviously encapsulated via the existential assumption that 'existence precedes essence'. What the assumption proposes would appear to be self-evident; however, it continues to be expressed in ways that confuse the issue and which, however inadvertently, imply its opposite. An example of this confusion can be found in the recent text, *Skills in Existential Counselling and Psychotherapy*, by Emmy van Deurzen and Martin Adams. Van Deurzen and Adams rightly highlight the above assumption as a key principle of existential theory (van Deurzen & Adams, 2011). They write: 'What [existence precedes essence] means is that the fact *that* we are is more basic than *what* we are. We *are* first and define ourselves later. Moreover we are always in the process of becoming something else' (van Deurzen & Adams, 2011: 9).

Unfortunately, although they claim to be promoting the view in question, this clarification confuses matters and emerges as yet another declaration of the precedence of essence. The problem lies in van Deurzen and Adams' emphasis on the subject, be it 'I' or 'we', as that which both *is* existentially and *becomes* as essence. This primacy fails to clarify that, from an existential standpoint, the very subject that reflects upon its existence and essence *is itself an essence*. That is to say, the 'I' (or 'we' in their statement) is already a reflective construct attempting to clarify its own construction. In brief, to argue that 'that I am' precedes 'what I am' is, at best, a limiting dilution of the existential argument. Why? Because the issue is not concerned with 'I' (or 'we') but with being per se. As such, the argument that existence precedes essence is more accurately an attempt to clarify that being precedes any particular form or structure – such as 'I' – that being might adopt.

The point being made here is not simply a matter of semantics. While it is the case that human language cannot but essentialise or 'thing-ify' lived experience, it remains crucial to avoid the false foundational primacy of the 'I' (or 'we' as in the case of the above quote). *That* being is (or, more accurately, that being continually becomes) precedes *what* being is (which is to say, both *what* structure being adopts and *how* being is expressed through it).

With regard to the issue of essence as viewed from the standpoint of being sexual, an interpretation of 'existence precedes essence' from the standpoint of a foundational 'I' (that I am) paradoxically elevates an essentialist position such that one could conclude, for example, that being heterosexual or LGBT expresses *that* which I am as opposed to *what* I am. What is lost in this stance is the revolutionary claim being made by existential theory which, from the standpoint of being sexual can be rephrased in the following way: *Being sexual precedes whatever form, structure or expression that being sexual chooses to adopt.*

Even at the more everyday level of subjectivist-dominated language, the radical shift being proposed by the argument 'existence precedes essence' can be partly (if still problematically) expressed in the following way: The statement 'I *am* heterosexual/ LGBT' is not the same as the statement 'I *am being* heterosexual/LGBT'. The former expresses a viewpoint that is mired in its primacy of essence. The latter at least approaches the dynamic of an ever-becoming being by seeking to express a view that acknowledges that being as reflected through the structure 'I' is labelling itself as heterosexual/LGBT. Clumsy as it may be linguistically, this latter statement admits at the very least a potential fluidity, an awareness that 'being is (becoming)' prior to any subjective statement asserting its own essence (that I am) or identity (who or what I am).

Being sexual: Otherness

Underpinning the essentialist arguments surrounding being sexual lies a related concern: to essentialise permits the appeal (or accusation) of *otherness*.

As was previously raised, the views of various authors have insisted that to not view being sexual homosexually as a unique and distinct expression such that comparisons with any other expression of being sexual – and being sexual heterosexually in particular – is at best misleading and at worst a further example of heterosexist attempts to deny the equal standing of being sexual homosexually. In a related fashion, it has been asserted that '[being sexual homosexually] is constructed in very different ways to heterosexual identities and experiences' (Milton, 2000: 94). Furthermore, in her paper *Rethinking Sexual Identity*, Catherine Crabtree argues that these differences in labelling ways of being sexual have 'significant implications for the meanings which individuals ascribe, and which are ascribed to, particular sexual feelings, acts and relations, and thus for the way in which sexual identity is experienced' (Crabtree, 2009: 250).

Once again, it seems to me that such perspectives are valid if one adopts a fundamentally essentialist stance. From an existential stance, however, they are far more problematic. Of course, one can argue that differing structures provide different modes of expressing, and experiencing, being. But this is not, as I see it at least, the existential argument. Instead, what existential theory argues is that being sexual (however expressed) is the common human baseline through which all the different structures and expressions of being sexual emerge. The differences only arise out of the shared human foundation of being sexual. To emphasise and elevate only the emergent differences takes us to positions and arguments that make little sense within an existential perspective.

More to the point, all such statements reveal an appeal to an alien and inevitably unbridgeable 'otherness'. Existential theory also posits the ultimate mystery of 'the other'. But this existential 'other' is not just, or even principally, the external other who is but one of a world of others with whom the 'I' is contrasted. The existential 'other' resides as much 'within' as 'without'. Indeed, existentially, 'I am (an) other'. This sense of otherness is, therefore, both intra- and intersubjective. It's not that the dominant have no label for themselves; their label cannot truly be separated from that placed upon the other.

Labelling

Gore Vidal has noted that 'heterosexuality [is] a weird concept of recent origin and terrible consequences' (Vidal, 1995: vii). He goes on to argue that with the invention of heterosexuality, 'there had to be another word to denote the opposite, and thus 'homosexuality' was invented … The division has led to endless trouble for many men and women' (Vidal, 1995: ix).

Today, we typically understand the terms 'heterosexual', 'homosexual' and 'bisexual' to refer to opposite sex attractions, same-sex attractions and varying degrees of attractions to either sex. As Pierre Tremblay and Richard Ramsay have argued however, until recently 'sexual orientation has been perceived in the traditional form of the 'binary'. One was to be either homosexual or heterosexual' (Tremblay & Ramsay, 2004: e-paper). The introduction of subsequent distinct labels such as 'bisexual' has made it obvious that 'the prior dominant categories of homosexual and heterosexual create false binaries and therefore give us inadequate information and impression' (Leck, 2000: 332). Such additions and challenges to labels associated with being sexual reveal that rather than having a fixed and firm foundational meaning, labels are constantly open to redefinition, extension and re-evaluation.

A telling example of this flexibility of labels can be seen in how the term 'heterosexuality' has shifted in meaning from something denoting a perversion to its current association with notions of normality. In *The Invention of Heterosexuality*, Jonathan Katz's research revealed that the terms 'homosexual' and 'heterosexual' were both invented at the end of the nineteenth century (Katz, 1995). Further, prior to the 1930s, the primary associations made with the term heterosexuality were linked to states or behaviours designated as abnormal.

> Heterosexuality [had not] yet attained the status of normal. In 1901, Dorland's Medical Dictionary, published in Philadelphia, continued to define 'Heterosexuality' as 'Abnormal or perverted appetite toward the opposite sex.' ... [The] 1923 Webster's defined 'heterosexuality' as a 'Med.' term meaning 'morbid sexual passion for one of the opposite sex.' Only in 1934 does 'heterosexuality' first appear in Webster's hefty Second Edition Unabridged defined in what is still the dominant modern mode. There, heterosexuality is finally a 'manifestation of sexual passion for one of the opposite sex; normal sexuality.' Heterosexuality had finally attained the status of norm.
> (Katz, 1995, cited in Tremblay & Ramsay, 2004: e-paper)

Once established, the binary terms took on a fixedness of meaning whose rigidity did not easily allow for the acknowledgement of further labels. Until relatively recently, there was major resistance, for example, to the acceptance of bisexuality as a valid label.

In gay and lesbian communities, the general response to bisexual individuals has been to negate their existence because they were perceived to challenge the belief that only heterosexual and homosexual people existed. Tisdale (1998) writes:

> Many gay activists see any talk of bisexuality as diluting the coherence of the community, particularly damaging in a time of attack ... Others simply don't believe in bisexuality ... As a result, there were great abuses by gay and lesbian identified individual (and professionals with similar beliefs, including therapists) of individuals daring to assert that their sexual attractions included both sexes.
> (Cited in Tremblay & Ramsay, 2004: e-paper)

Viewed from a cross-cultural perspective, this rigid adherence to preferred labels can be seen to become even more problematic. Holt Parker has concluded:

> Our division of hetero versus homo ... is a parochial affair ... [I]f we impose our categories on another culture, we are making a crude mistake. When it comes to 'talking sex', we are at best speaking with an atrocious accent. At worst, we are speaking incomprehensible gibberish.
> (Parker, 2001: 348)

Nonetheless, once established, the power of labels to confirm and assert a classificatory divide is all too evident. If in significant ways one's sense of oneself is dependent upon the validation of the label and, through it, the delineation of difference, then all manner of questionable 'evidence' intended to maintain the label can be called into play. One such example can be seen in the claims regarding the presence and/or discovery of 'the gay gene'.

The ever-elusive 'gay gene' was initially thought to be located in the X-linked DNA segment (Hamer, 1994; Le Vay, 1996). Although it generated a good deal of initial excitement and media coverage, further research has found no evidence whatsoever to support the idea of a 'gay gene' (Wilson & Rahman, 2005). In similar fashion, claims to have identified anatomical differences between male heterosexual and gay brains have failed to be supported by any reliable evidence. Here, too, following an initial claim for the evidence of such, further research has strongly disconfirmed such views (Tremblay & Ramsay, 2004).

Once again, the power of the label, rather than that to which the label seeks to allude or clarify, is the key to the issue. If we consider the significance of labels relating to ways of being sexual, we can see that such labels not only have come to designate difference but have also been bequeathed with judgemental authority. It is in the interest of all who at least accept these claims of difference to locate the avowed differences in some sort of 'essentialist given' such as genes or brains. But further, such differences are also ascribed with positive or negative core values. The subsequent social and personal impact of these strategies can be seen to be of major significance in terms of how one is to be identified and treated within a society. With this, the power of the differentiating label is further magnified by all concerned. Under such essentialist circumstances, the claim on all sides must be 'I have always been' rather than 'I became' or 'I am being'.

If the labels were merely attempts to categorise difference, the persistent allegiance to essentialist perspectives on being sexual would not be so rigid. It is the plethora of value judgements associated with such label differences that maintain their divisive power. It is not difficult to understand the appeal of essentialist arguments not only for those who employ such in order to diminish and ostracise but as well for those who have been, and continue to be ostracised. It is the consequences that such arguments can generate that raises concern.

Essentialising being sexual permits self and group identification but also demands differentiation. Significantly, it provides the means to divide and to mystify. To belong to one group in this way allows its members to claim knowledge or awareness that belongs only to that group and which cannot be shared by members of alternate groups. This argument would have it, for example, that 'being sexual homosexually' is a distinct 'given' that can be fully discernible only to those who are so identified. Similar arguments, of course, have been made by those who wish to impose an unbridgeable divide between assumptions of difference between male and female consciousness, as well as differing forms of consciousness between races (e.g. Caucasian versus African versus Asian) and cultures (e.g. Semitic versus Aryan). In the exact same way as these, the assumed evidence for such relies upon disputable claims of biological 'proof', whether existent or forthcoming. For some, the identification of a 'gay gene' would resolve crucial issues surrounding the label of homosexuality once and for all. Perhaps naïvely, it does not seem to occur to these authors that the subsequent agenda for many of those parties most interested in discovering such a gene would be to promote the development of new ways of genetic restructuring whose intent would be to either eliminate or restrict the passing on of such a gene.

Nonetheless, as Stuart Wooler has expressed to me in a private communication (Wooler, 2012), what still remains as an issue is what might be termed as an 'experiential divide' – for example, that inability on the part of a heterosexual male to 'get' the delight in running his hands over another man's body. Such instances appear to many as touchstones for unmediated essence. On reflection, however, as research on sexual fluidity indicates, under different personal, social and cultural circumstances or environments what appears to be the essentialist basis for this divide is not truly so. Nonetheless, the power of experiential divides needs to be recognised and acknowledged. However, this does not mean that its presence should lead us to assume its essentialist basis. But let me present the issue from a different angle.

Left-handedness

Not so many years ago, in most Southern European countries, to be born left-handed immediately imposed all manner of pejorative perspectives upon the person so defined. Parents feared the onset of such a disturbing possibility. Experts of one sort or another made multiple and fearsome pronouncements regarding the dangers – physical, moral, developmental, intellectual, social and emotional – surrounding this labelled problem. Equally, they theorised as to its basis and origins – some ascribing it to inbuilt biological dictates, some to very early (and implicitly abnormal) life experiences. Further, they provided various prescriptions for its control and possible elimination – some of these bordering upon, if not full-blown examples of, interventionist forms of torture. The adult who had not been prevented from maintaining and developing this problematic tendency was viewed as a social outcast at best, a mental, moral (quite literally 'sinister') and emotional degenerate at worst. Labels and nicknames were devised to identify offenders and such terms became powerful insults to employ in moments of anger or vexation serving to humiliate those so named.

In the example of left-handedness, we find something all too similar to what has been argued above. The power of the label here, as before, is not only to demarcate and distinguish, but to impose additional – and typically negative – qualities of being upon those so labelled. Had the continuing stridently negative views regarding left-handedness remained, or perhaps even intensified, it would not be surprising that such differences would generate all manner of personal, interpersonal and sociocultural divergences between the labelled groups. Left-handed people might, for instance, begin to meet in specially designated 'left-handed locations' where they could engage with other 'left-handers' or carry out any number of activities in ways that did not ostracise, and might even permit a celebration of their left-handedness. Perhaps, as well, views regarding a distinct 'left-handed consciousness', understandable only to those who were left-handed, might begin to emerge and provide the means to link left-handedness to identity in profound ways and, through such, raise justifiable demands for sociopolitical legal standing, equality, and respect for members of the left-handed minority in a right-handed majority society.

But none of this occurred. For whatever reasons, society's fears of left-handedness dissipated. Yes, left-handed and right-handed people today might well continue to acknowledge genuine differences in behaviours such as those related to the manipulation of objects. But the idea that such differences either suggest or reveal distinct, generalisable modes of consciousness accessible only to members of either group and which, more importantly, provoke altogether different foundational expressions of being seems at best, a remote and somewhat laughable proposition.

What makes it so unlikely is that the acknowledged differences between the two groups suggest nothing that is linked or related to notions of natural or unnatural, normal or abnormal, healthy or unhealthy, and the like. It may be a 'given' that humans may engage with the self, others and the world from a right-handed or left-handed – or even ambidextrous – mode of being. That should not lead us to suppose that this difference in mode can – or should – lead us to generalise significant foundational variants in psyche and identity exclusive to each group alone.

This is not to minimise nor deny the great many problems, confusions, dangers and complexities that can and do arise for all – and in particular for those whose way of being sexual is linked to notions of differences that are in turn associated with acts of exclusion and statements of degeneracy. What *is* being suggested is that the significance in these differences is not in the differences themselves. Rather, from an existential perspective, the resulting differences can be seen as mutually construed expressions of relatedness rather than inevitable conditions of an exclusivity that is indicative of a foundational essence, or 'given'.

Being sexual: Gender

Many of the arguments focused on the previously discussed issues of existential choice, existence/essence and otherness are reprised in gender-focused concerns regarding being sexual. Meg-John Barker, in their paper,

De Beauvoir, Bridget Jones' Pants and Vaginismus, raises the question: 'Perhaps the reason for the lack of consideration of gender within existentialist philosophy and therapy is the fact that existentialists do not believe in any natural differences between different groups of human beings, such as men and women' (Barker, 2011: 204). Developing a similar critical perspective, Aloysius Joseph in his text, *An Inquiry into Sexual Difference in Ernesto Spinelli's Psychology: An Irigarayan critique and response to Ernesto Spinelli's psychology,* argues that:

> while existential phenomenology ... acknowledges the social, political, historical and cultural engendering of the subject, it ... fails to recognize that the factors constituting our lived experience are themselves derivative of a collective and shared discourse that is framed by a phallocentric economy of relations.
>
> (Joseph, 2009: 18)

Further, he asserts that:

> Existential phenomenologists describe intersubjectivity as if it is constituted through our embodied subject's interaction with another embodied subject of the same kind, overlooking the sexually specific differences of the two subjects – both sensory and morphological.
>
> (Joseph, 2009: 12–13)

Much of Joseph's thesis, as the subtitle to his book attests, is derived from arguments developed by the philosopher and psychoanalyst, Luce Irigaray. Irigaray's challenging views are complex and continually evolving which does not make it an easy task to provide a summary that sufficiently respects their originality and power. Be that as it may ....

Irigaray argues that female subjectivity has not, as yet, been identified because it continues to be assimilated to male subjectivity. Being female is associated with issues of unthinking matter and nature, but there is not, as yet, a genuinely distinct female subjectivity. Irigaray contends that women are only truly defined through their role as 'mother' (whether they are or are not themselves actual mothers) such that their identities arise only through that role. Society values this role, protects it, and recognises its dependence upon it but the price for women is nothing less than that of failing to become their own subjects in the world. In contrast to men who are their own subjects, women are 'the other' in relation to male subjects (which is to say that their role is to support male subjectivity). Only when women achieve their own subjectivity will there be the emergence of genuine sexual difference. Until then, sexual difference does not exist other than from the biased perspective of male subjectivity (Irigaray, 1985).

When any discourse occurs between men and women (or, indeed, between men and men or women and women) the discourse is currently always and only one of male subjectivity. This argument provides the basis for Joseph's critique of both my own 'psychology' (as his title over-generously puts it) and of existential phenomenology in general. For, as therapists engaged in discourse with our clients, we fail to at the very least understand the phallocentric nature of our way of talking, hearing and thinking with and about them (and ourselves), thereby severely limiting the existential project's aim to respond to clients (and, most obviously, female clients), and to engage in relationships with them (be they male or female) as truly subjective others.

Irigaray's project has been to first critique phallocentric subjectivity, then to set out the conditions that would define a second subjectivity, and third to develop and define a relationship of subjectivities rather than relationships where only a single (male) subject exists or can be defined. To enter into this last possibility, Irigaray asserts, requires new modes of thinking and speaking. 'Inventing a new relationship is fundamentally the same as inventing a new socio-cultural order ... For me sexual difference is a fundamental parameter of the socio-cultural order ...' (Irigaray et al, 1995: 105).

I wish to neither minimise nor dismiss all of the above arguments. They express carefully considered perspectives and conclusions that demand serious consideration. Nonetheless, several concerns remain. First, as Barker argues, the question of gender is not typically seen to be a 'given' within existential-phenomenological theory. In part, this is due to an existential wariness in over-generalising differences into unsuitable categories of division. In general, with regard to gender, de Beauvoir's conclusion that 'one is not born but rather one becomes a woman' still dominates much of existential theory (de Beauvoir, 1949: 295 cited in Barker, 2011: 204). Perhaps most importantly, however, as Barker herself acknowledges, is the concern that 'gendered roles vary across dimensions such as culture, class, generation, sexuality ... it is worth approaching each client with curiosity about the way such messages may play out in their world' (Barker, 2011: 213–14). That being sexual is experienced and expressed in a variety of ways – or even in constructively derived unique ways, undoubtedly acknowledges differences in meaning and experience.

The dilemma is whether it makes sense to categorise those differences into fixed and generalised 'givens' such as gender.

Current Western cultural perspectives perceive gender from the standpoint of binaries – male and female. But such binaries are open to reconsideration. In her book, *Gender Trouble*, Judith Butler argues that although earlier feminists had rejected biological narratives of gender, they had nonetheless maintained a binary view of it. Instead, she proposes that rather than being a fixed 'given', gender is more appropriately viewed from the perspective of variable fluidity whose shifts express its response to, and relation with, differing contexts. 'There is no gender identity behind the expressions of gender; … identity is performatively constituted by the very 'expressions' that are said to be its results' (Butler, 2006: 25). For Butler, gender is, more accurately, a performance – an act of gendering, or of being gendered – it is what is done, rather than who one is.

Culturally derived gender configurations may become so fixed within a culture that they not only appear to be 'natural' but also serve to define crucial biases and assumptions within that culture. But this should not obscure their origins or flexibility. By creating 'gender trouble' – which is to say, by altering the form which a gender performance adopts – traditional, seemingly 'essentialist' assumptions of gender can be subverted.

In similar fashion, Joan Roughgarden's work (briefly discussed on pp. 29–30 of this chapter) highlights the diversity and flexibility of gender roles and expression based on changes in social and environmental circumstances. Under such conditions, reversals of gender roles are not uncommon in many species. Roughgarden also highlights the existence of 'gender multiplicity' in many species which reveals differing typologies of gender extending beyond the more 'natural' binary of male and female (Roughgarden, 2009). In human gender studies focused upon the biological bases to gender differences, the predominant evidence reveals no significant link between gendered behaviour and either differences in hormonal levels or activity (Fine, 2010), or in more general brain functioning (Jordan-Young, 2011). Physiological differences as the source of essentialist divisions of gender appear to have no basis in scientific research; gender emerges as a sociocultural construct.

That the essentialist basis to gender remains, at best, a question for further debate, should in no way invalidate the various concerns raised regarding the acknowledgement of differences. Differences may well be so seemingly fixed along sociocultural divides that, as Butler highlights, they appear to all within that culture as 'natural' and, hence, shared by all in a roughly equal or similar fashion. Nor is it the case that existential phenomenology proposes, as Catherine Crabtree wonders, that 'different identities/orientations can be freely chosen at will' (Crabtree, 2009: 254). Rather, as was discussed above, existential choice is not always, nor frequently, about the selection of alternatives. Rather it is concerned with the acknowledgement or acceptance as that which presents itself as a single option from the standpoint of 'I am being' rather than from the fixed stance of 'I am'. This shift in stance permits a novel experience of relatedness that opens previously unforeseen possibilities within the identified condition. Further, it highlights that the issue of difference cannot be so easily demarcated along clear-cut generalised sociocultural divides such as gender and sexual identity. Perhaps most significantly, this view of difference acknowledges the inseparability of difference and sameness.

Existentially speaking, if each of us is different (or unique), that difference can only be experienced because of a foundational set of shared constituents or 'givens'. As was stated in my original paper, differences in gender or identity:

> express the very same intersubjective desires ... as can be ascertained in all other – manifestations. That such may be the chosen means by which an individual both expresses and avoids intersubjective anxieties, that such may both allow and prevent particular forms of self/other dialogue, that they may be dependent upon interpretational distinctions as to what form of dialogue is acceptable or desirable with reference to particular categories of 'others', reveals nothing that is not similarly revealed in any other form of ... relation, such that to distinguish [any particular expression of difference] as inherently different [i.e. a difference of kind or essence] ... must be challenged.
> (Spinelli, 1997a: 13)

Although several commentators took exception to this argument, I continue to stand by it. It seems to me that their concerns are valid only if one adopts a non-relational understanding of difference. Of course, it is vital to acknowledge difference and to be clear, perhaps particularly when working therapeutically with issues of difference such as gender and identity, 'of to the possibility that discrimination may well still be part of ... [clients'] ... lived reality' (Crabtree, 2009: 255). But such an attunement, it seems to me, ought to be ever-present in *all* encounters with clients, and others in general.

This takes me to the views and concerns expressed within the work of Luce Irigaray. While I continue to prize the perspective and challenges she brings through her analyses, I retain a degree of unease with what seems to me something approaching a circularity of argument that is to be found in many psychoanalytically influenced conclusions. If Irigaray is correct and all current discourses on subjectivity are phallocentric, then it must be the case that her own discourse is as well. It may be critical of phallocentrism but, by her own analyses, how can one know with certainty that it has somehow evaded phallocentrism's restrictive grasp? There seems to be no way out of this dilemma. How can one know, for example, that a separate female subjectivity has emerged without maintaining a suspicion that it may be yet one more expression of phallocentric subjectivity? And if such is the case, then what remains is a conclusion that no matter what the expression of subjectivity, it might yet still be phallocentric. But if so, then how can we speak of, or postulate, difference in the way that Irigaray wishes to?

Might not this conundrum only be broken if we reject its essentialist assumption of foundationally inherent gender differences? If we were to do so, we would still be able – indeed, obliged – to address matters of difference. But these would be expressed from a perspective that acknowledged such differences as interpretative variations arising out of a shared grounding. This view would in no way diminish the significance of dominant modes of thought and language that restrict, inhibit, and proscribe. Nor would it encourage the denial of the 'otherness of the other' – however that 'other' self-defines or is defined.

The acknowledgement of that which *unites* persons in their diverse experiences of difference and power permits a view of greater complexity regarding these very same issues – not least by providing a dynamic perspective wherein difference and power are seen to be fluid, revealing shifting patterns of conditions and relations between beings as well as within the boundaries of any particular being's sense of self and other.

Being sexual as an expression of aesthetics: An imaginary alternative

As a final way of challenging the various assumptions regarding being sexual that have been explored in this chapter, I want to reimagine the history of inquiry into human sexual being. My purpose is to demonstrate that our currently dominant perspectives on being sexual reveal deep-seated sociocultural biases that have been so profoundly ingrained in our perspectives on being that they have come to be seen to be 'natural' rather than interpretative. Further, I want to propose that alternative perspectives, such as the one being proposed, offer us novel and usefully apposite ways of considering recurring dilemmas, doubts and dangers regarding being sexual.

So, let us reimagine the history of sexology such that when its modern inquiry began in the nineteenth century, the group of 'experts' called upon to examine the various issues and concerns regarding being sexual were not predominantly from the medical profession but, rather, were theorists and critics concerned with matters of *aesthetics* whose focus became that of *'the aesthetics of being sexual'*.

Theories of aesthetics originated from dominant sociopolitical biases surrounding the availability of the experience of beauty and perfection. Nineteenth-century theories of aesthetics linked aesthetics to morality such that moral propriety or goodness corresponded to the ability to recognise, appreciate and express beauty. These views on aesthetics typically posited that the ability to appreciate and exemplify beauty, and hence reveal moral goodness, particularly when focused upon artistic expression, could only reside within those persons who were morally capable of an aesthetic appreciation – namely, males belonging to the aristocracy, some females from the upper classes and various exceptionally suitable male representatives from the growing middle class. Indeed, the aesthetic experience was utilised as a powerful way of defining class and of providing the 'upper' levels of class with the evidence of their own superiority over 'lower' classes. Aesthetics was seen as a higher order faculty reserved only to those who had moved beyond the baser demands and necessities of living (Sheppard, 1987).

Problems with this view began to arise when examples of aesthetic expression and appreciation were acknowledged to have been originated by those who, it was claimed, were not equipped to recognise and appreciate aesthetic beauty – those such as 'primitives' from non-Western societies ,as well as male and female creative thinkers and artists who did not come from the appropriate class background. These challenges eventually forced the reconsideration of theories of aesthetics which, in turn, provoked substantial confusion and often acerbic disagreement between experts with regard to how to define beauty, whether its link to moral values could be maintained, and which of the manifold claims to its expression (as in music or art) were to be recognised as examples of beauty and aesthetic achievement as opposed to rubbish and filth. Eventually, the ability to appreciate beauty as well as to create expressions of it began, somewhat grudgingly, to extend to the positing of a more general, or universal, human quality (Rancière, 2006). In doing so, however, aesthetics became increasingly imbued with uncertainty.

For instance, the uncertainty as to the aesthetic worth and quality of artistic expression continues to this day. Debates persist as to what is and is not an example of art, what should be venerated and what should be dismissed. The debates, by and large, arise through the ever-more extreme extension of the boundaries of aesthetics. For example, the furore regarding the aesthetic worth of works of art that were categorised as examples of Impressionism has been repeated with the appearance of Abstract Expressionism, Cubism, and Pop Art. An all-too similar furore presents itself today in debates surrounding Conceptual Art and Found Objects. But what is most interesting and significant for the concerns of this paper is that with the appearance of each new challenge, the previously disturbing 'challengers' lose much of their perturbing effect, are typically re-evaluated as appropriate, potentially even 'sublime' expressions of beauty and, as a consequence, are embraced ever further into the mainstream of acceptability.

Let us now consider the impact that theories of and perspectives on aesthetics might have on the experience of being sexual.

An aesthetically focused sexology arose during the nineteenth century as a means to circumscribe the sorts of ways of being sexual that were to be appreciated as expressions of beauty and moral goodness. Those expressions that failed such tests were to be dismissed or denied of any aesthetic worth. Being sexual for the sake of reproduction provided a necessary 'baseline' unconscious aesthetic that could be recognised and expressed by one and all. But true, consciously attuned, aesthetics belonged only to those who could recognise genuine expressions of beauty and goodness and who could enact such sexually through appropriate ways and means. Those who persisted in being sexual in unaesthetic ways, or who championed such as being novel expressions of aesthetics, were to be criticised, shunned and/or segregated so as to avoid the spread of their morally corrupt claims of beauty and, if necessary, imprisoned or executed so as to protect those whose curiosity or inability to distinguish might well lead them to be sexual in ways that debased genuine expressions of beauty and goodness.

However, over time, the power to define (and limit the definitions) of being sexual in aesthetically appropriate ways was challenged and extended both by those who had initially been excluded as experts but had now found the means to greater acceptance as well as by those who had always had the recognition but who, through their own experiences or through those of respected others, sought to expand the horizons of what should and could be recognised as aesthetic expressions of being sexual. In short, the power to define was no longer as secure or as certain as it had been before.

How did this occur? In part, the process was set into motion through the very identification of an aesthetic expertise in being sexual. Both the expertise and its focus became talking points, arenas for discourse and theory. Various ways of being sexual aesthetically and unaesthetically were demarcated, labelled, named. Theories of, and disputes surrounding such labels, and whether or not they revealed or were bereft of aesthetic qualities entered the public imagination. Prior to this, in their unacknowledged and unnamed state, many aesthetically transgressive and proscribed attitudes and expressions of being sexual had been contained within select groups via their secrecy and affiliation to underground movements who championed a novel expression of aesthetics that was appreciated only by that clandestine minority. Now, however, having become the focus of discourse and debate, much of their mystique and 'otherness' began to dissipate. In doing so, they moved into the open, gained increasing acceptance and subsequently became established as novel and desirable expressions of the dominant perspective of aesthetics. In some cases, they even became so generally embraced that they became the standard bearers of a safe and secure normality. Consider, for example, how both oral and anal intercourse moved from the inappropriate and illegal to the ordinary. Or how pornography has shifted so rapidly from the hidden and suppressed to the open terrain which it inhabits today. Or how, at least in some cultures, being sexual homosexually has gone from the unnameable and criminal to levels of acceptability than even a couple of decades ago would have seemed inconceivable. Or how the current interest in sado-masochistic ways of being sexual has been aroused through the phenomenal success of a best-selling novel. Ways of being sexual that not so long ago would have been seen as transgressive or at least unusual and undesirable – to be appreciated and enacted only by those who inhabited an aesthetically dubious sexual underground – can be seen to shift rapidly into the domain of the mainstream, to the everyday and expected norm – the ordinary.

Viewed in this way, the aesthetic imagination regarding being sexual, just like its artistic counterpart, must out of necessity constantly seek out novel transgressive ground from which to challenge dominant contemporary notions of acceptability and definability. It cannot stand still. Once invoked, the aesthetic boundaries of sexual expression cannot remain fixed and stable. If imagination is to survive, it must continue to imagine and, via its acts of imagination, it must challenge its current boundaries, most often by extending them. In doing so, not only can it transform that which was once scorned or even demonised so that it becomes 'normal' or, possibly, even an elevated expression of sexual aesthetics, it also, of necessity, brings ever closer to the fold that which was once at the furthest reaches of the proscribed and unacceptable. Every underground movement has the potential to journey toward the surface of the mainstream. Just as past transgressive acts and behaviours have become 'ordinary and acceptable', so too will those acts and behaviours that are currently deemed to be transgressive or even repugnant move increasingly toward becoming absorbed into the 'ordinary' of the future. My own best guess, given its increasing appearance in the humour and innuendo so characteristic of sitcoms and advertising, is that bestiality (being sexual with animals other than human beings) will prove to be the next instance of this unrelenting movement from the underground to the overground. Time will tell.

Might not this aesthetically informed perspective on being sexual, as strange and artificial as it might initially appear to be, offer a valid potential alternative to our dominant perspectives – if only insofar as it weakens their reliance upon claims to 'naturalness' or to an unproblematic obviousness. And is it not the case that, much more clearly than does our dominant view, the aesthetic alternative enjoins us to reconsider the issues surrounding being sexual within a wider terrain that exposes many of the confounding and confusing dilemmas that both dominate and define our current culture as expressions of the mainstream's uneasy flirtation with that which it continues to deem as taboos? And by so doing, does not this alternative prevent us from so easily distancing ourselves from the those ways of being sexual such that they can no longer be labelled as incomprehensible or belong *only* to an alien 'other'?

Conclusion

My arguments throughout this chapter have been focused on an existential critique of dominant assumptions regarding being sexual. With Heidegger's injunction in mind, it has sought to present the outlines of ways of talking about being sexual that question our more 'natural' culturally embedded assumptions. This questioning has sought to challenge sedimented biases that were initially elaborated by Western culture at around the time of the invention of sexology during the mid-nineteenth century. Throughout, my argument has been to demonstrate the limitations of such premises with regard to the lived experiences of being sexual that we all share and enact. Following the impetus of many others, I have sought to reconfigure the issues surrounding being sexual such that they are no longer so dominated by stances and conclusions based upon essentialist-dominated perspectives.

Instead, I have opted for a critique, derived from existential phenomenology, that has focused critically on the issues of choice, essentialism, otherness and gender. In doing so, I have attempted to demonstrate that existential thought provides viable alternatives to challenge rigidified ways of thinking about being sexual.

Nonetheless, as valid or challenging or worthwhile as these arguments may be, it is unlikely that they can, in themselves, impact significantly upon our *experiences* of being sexual. For example, a good deal of my argument has attempted to dispute essentialist assumptions of difference. But, even if the points I have made are convincing, they do not, nor do they intend to, diminish or remove the sociocultural conditions that generate much of that continuing sense of difference. So what is the point? For me, it is this:

As I understand it, the greatest challenge that an existential perspective provides on questions of being sexual (as well as on questions of being in general) is that we are not victims. Not to nature. Not to nurture. We can, and do, convince ourselves of such in all manner of ways and not least when it comes to our ways of being sexual. The existential challenge to lived experience is steeped in paradox: rather than enjoin us to attempt different ways of experiencing being sexual (or experiencing being in general) it, instead, urges us to truly embrace that way of being as and when it is being experienced. In doing so, such challenges can reinstate a felt sense of 'ownership' and connectedness to that experience such that although the experiential circumstances may remain the same, our relationship to them can shift. Specifically, the relationship has become one that includes us as active agents of our lived experience rather than as victims to possessive forces. In this, our facticity becomes a constituent of our choices rather than an obstacle to them. Being sexual existentially takes us away from the certainty and security of an imposed 'I am ...' and places us in the uncertain terrain of 'I am being ...'.

Without doubt, the challenge of an existential perspective on being sexual is accompanied by its own fears and insecurities. Viewed as expressions of relatedness, the multiple experiential possibilities of being sexual are inevitably placed within a context of uncertainty and anxiety. Is such a trade-off any sort of improvement to that which currently exists as the dominant mode of discourse? Insofar as it can begin to challenge recurring dilemmas centred upon essence, choice and difference as expressed via concerns surrounding gender, identity, and normality, I believe that existential theory offers a more adequate set of principles with which to clarify the human experience of being sexual. This chapter has offered a possible step towards such an enterprise.

The conclusion which we are left with strikes me as being all too similar to another I proposed some time ago: existential perspectives on being sexual provide substantially different, yet still coherent, alternatives with which to challenge dominant orthodoxies. For now, it must be admitted that the impact of this existential stance remains akin to 'a voice crying in the wilderness'. But at least, and thankfully, it remains a voice nonetheless.

References

Acton, H (2010) I am what I am: Existentialism and homosexuality. *Existential Analysis, 21*(2), 351–64.

Bagemihl, B (2000) *Biological Exuberance: Animal homosexuality and natural diversity.* London: Stonewall Inn Editions.

Barker, M (2011) De Beauvoir, Bridget Jones' pants and vaginismus. *Existential Analysis, 22*(2), 203–16.

Beauvoir, S de (1997) *The Second Sex* (HM Parshley, Trans). New York: Vintage. (First published 1949)

Butler, J (2006) *Gender Trouble: Feminism and the subversion of identity.* London: Routledge.

Carroll, L (2007) *Through the Looking Glass.* London: Penguin. (First published 1872)

Cohn, HW (2002) *Heidegger and the Roots of Existential Therapy.* London: Continuum.

Crabtree, C (2009) Rethinking sexual identity. *Existential Analysis, 20*(2), 248–61.

Denman, C (2003) *Sexuality: A biopsychosocial approach.* London: Palgrave Macmillan.

Diamond, L (2008) *Sexual Fluidity: Understanding women's love and desire.* London: Harvard University Press.

Du Plock, S (1997) Sexual misconceptions: A critique of gay-affirmative therapy and some thoughts on an existential-phenomenological theory of sexual orientation. *Journal of the Society for Existential Analysis, 8*(2), 56–71.

Fine, C (2010) *Delusions of Gender.* London: Icon Books.

Foucault, M (1979) *A History of Sexuality Volume 1: An introduction.* London: Allen Lane.

Gelder, K (2007) *Subcultures: Social histories and social practice.* London: Routledge.

Halley, J & Parker, A (2011) *After Sex? On writing since queer theory.* London: Duke University Press.

Halperin, D (1997) *Saint Foucault: Towards a gay hagiography.* Oxford: Oxford University Press.

Hamer, D (1994) *The Science of Desire: The search for the gay gene and the biology of behavior.* New York: Simon & Schuster.

Heidegger, M (1962) *Being and Time* (J Macquarrie & E Robinson, Trans). New York: Harper and Row.

Heidegger, M (2001) *Zollikon Seminars: Protocols–conversations–letters* (F Mayr & R Askay, Trans). Evanston, IL: Northwestern University Press.

Irigaray, L (1985) *This Sex Which Is Not One* (C Porter, Trans). New York: Cornell University Press.

Irigaray, L, Hirsch, E & Olson, GA (1995) Je – Luce Irigaray: A meeting with Luce Irigaray. *Hypatia, 10*(2), 93–114.

Jagose, A (1996) Queer theory: An extract. *Australian Humanities Review.* Retrieved 9 December 2013 from http://www.australianhumanitiesreview.org/archive/Issue-Dec-1996/jagose.html

Jordan-Young, R (2011) *Brain Storm: The flaws in the science of brain differences.* London: Harvard University Press.

Joseph, A (2009) *An Inquiry into Sexual Difference in Ernesto Spinelli's Psychology: An Irigarayan critique and response to Ernesto Spinelli's psychology.* Saarbrücken, Germany: VDM Verlag.

Katz, JN (1995) *The Invention of Heterosexuality.* London: University of Chicago Press.

Kaye, J (1995) Postfoundationalism and the language of psychotherapy research. In J Siegfried (Ed) *Therapeutic and Everyday Discourse as Behaviour Change* (pp. 29–59). Norwood, NJ: Ablex.

Knorr-Cetina, KD (1981) *The Manufacture of Knowledge.* Oxford: Pergamon Press.

Langdridge, D (2007) Gay affirmative therapy: A theoretical framework and defense. *Journal of Gay & Lesbian Psychotherapy, 11*(1/2), 27–43.

Leck, G (2000) Heterosexual or homosexual? Reconsidering binary narratives on sexual identities in urban schools. *Education and Urban Society, 32*(3), 324–48.

Le Vay, S (1996) *Queer Science.* Cambridge, MA: MIT Press.

Medina, M (2008) Can I be a homosexual please? A critique of sexual deliberations on the issue of homosexuality and their significance for the practice of existential psychotherapy. *Existential Analysis, 19*(1), 129–42.

Merleau-Ponty, M (1962) *Phenomenology of Perception* (C Smith, Trans). London: Routledge & Kegan Paul.

Merleau-Ponty, M (1968) *The Visible and the Invisible* (A Lingis, Trans). Evanston IL: Northwestern University Press.

Milton, M (2000) Is existential psychotherapy a lesbian and gay affirmative psychotherapy? *Journal of the Society for Existential Analysis, 11*(1), 86–102.

Parker, H (2001) The myth of the heterosexual. *Arethusa, 34,* 313–62.

Pearce, R (2011) Escaping into the Other: An existential view of sex and sexuality. *Existential Analysis, 22*(2), 217–43.

Plummer, K (1981) *The Making of the Modern Homosexual.* London: Hutchinson.

Rancière, J (2006) *The Politics of Aesthetics* (G Rockhill, Ed & Trans). London: Continuum.

Roughgarden, J (2009) *The Genial Gene: Deconstructing Darwinian selfishness.* London: University of California Press.

Sartre, J-P (1948) *Existentialism and Humanism* (P Mairet, Trans). London: Methuen.

Sartre, J-P (1956) *Being and Nothingness: An essay on phenomenological ontology* (M Warnock & H Barnes, Trans). London: Routledge.

Sears, T (2010) *A Phenomenological Critique of how Sexuality is Understood in Existential Thought.* Unpublished MA Dissertation, London: School Of Psychotherapy and Psychology, Regent's University.

Sheppard, A (1987) *Aesthetics: An introduction to the philosophy of art.* London: OPUS.

Smith-Pickard, P & Swynnerton, R (2005) The body and sexuality. In E van Deurzen & C Arnold-Baker (Eds) *Existential Perspectives on Human Issues* (pp. 48–57). Basingstoke: Palgrave Macmillan.

Spinelli, E (1994) *Demystifying Therapy.* London: Constable. (Republished 2006, PCCS Books)

Spinelli, E (1997a) Some hurried notes expressing outline ideas that someone might someday utilise as signposts towards a sketch of an existential-phenomenological theory of sexuality. *Journal of the Society for Existential Analysis, 8*(1), 2–20.

Spinelli, E (1997b) Human sexuality: An existential-phenomenological inquiry. *Counselling Psychology Review, 12*(4), 170–8.

Spinelli, E (2001) *The Mirror and the Hammer: Existential challenges to therapeutic orthodoxy.* London: Continuum.

Spinelli, E (2006) Human sexuality: Existential challenges for psychotherapy. *BPS Psychotherapy Section Review, 40,* 17–29.

Spinelli, E (2007) *Practising Existential Psychotherapy: The relational world.* London: Sage Publications.

Spinelli, E (2009) Human sexuality: An existential perspective. *Psychotherapy in Australia, 15*(4), 16–23.

Tisdale, S (1998) Second thoughts. *Salon Magazine. September 11.* Retrieved February 2013 from www.salon.com/1998/09/11/tisd/

Tremblay, PJ & Ramsay, R (2004) The social construction of male homosexuality and related suicide problems: Research proposals for the twenty-first century. Presentation at Gay Men's Health Summit. July, 2000. Boulder, Colorado. Retrieved 9 December 2013 from people.ucalgary.ca/~ptrembla/homosexuality-suicide/construction/gay-youth-suicide-san-diego.htm

Van Deurzen, E & Adams, M (2011) *Skills in Existential Counselling and Psychotherapy.* London: Sage Publications.

Vidal, G (1995) Foreword. In J Katz (Ed) *The Invention of Heterosexuality* (pp. vi–xi). New York: Dutton.

Weeks, J (1985) *Sexuality and Its Discontents: Meanings, myths & modern sexualities.* London: Routledge & Kegan Paul.

Weeks, J (2003) *Sexuality* (2nd ed). London: Routledge.

Wilson, GD & Rahman, Q (2005) *Born Gay: The biology of sex orientation.* London: Peter Owen.

2

Being-in-the-World Sexually

– Dr Hans W Cohn –

Sexuality has been strangely neglected by writers on existential psychotherapy. The theme has also remained unfocused in existential thinking. Heidegger does not seem concerned with it. Sartre, in *Being and Nothingness*, states that sexuality is not determined by biological instincts but by one's 'upsurge ... into a world where "there are" others' (Sartre, 1958: 407) and he characterises the sexual relationship as 'a double reciprocal incarnation' (Sartre, 1958: 391). This is an evocative phrase but we also know that in Sartre's description relationships tend to slide into a sado-masochistic mode where the battle for superiority and the invalidation of the other is paramount.

It is, not surprisingly, Merleau-Ponty who devotes a chapter in his *Phenomenology of Perception* to our sexual existence, saying that 'in his sexuality is projected [man's] manner of being towards the world, that is, towards time and other men' (Merleau-Ponty, 1962: 158). Madison, in his book on Merleau-Ponty, comments: 'sexuality never functions as an autonomous physiological mechanism. It is already penetrated and transformed through and through by personal attitudes, and conversely personal existence always has a sexual meaning or coloring' (Madison, 1981: 47–8).

Merleau-Ponty sees sexuality as an intrinsic aspect of existence in a way that other writers fail to do. But just as 'Being-in-the-world' means implicitly 'Being-with-others', 'Being-towards-death', 'Being-in-the-body', it also means 'Being-sexually'. We are all sexual beings and our sexuality, like all existence, has 'given' aspects. It is our responses to these 'given' aspects that vary. An existential-phenomenological approach needs to explore what these 'givens' are and the ways in which we respond. Such an exploration may not be easy but we need to attempt it if we wish to understand the spectrum of sexual difficulties that our clients present to us.

It is interesting to reflect that psychoanalytic therapy had its origin in Freud's speculations on the nature and transformations of the sexual drive, and for some time critics of his theories focused on what they called his 'pan-sexualism'. If writers on existential psychotherapy seem to neglect the sexual aspects of human difficulties – with the exception of Medard Boss who, as we shall see, in dealing with sexuality abandons his phenomenological stance – there may be in this an element of opposition to the psychoanalytic emphasis on the sexual drive.

Sexual difference

Anatomically and physiologically, men and women find themselves in the realm of the 'given'. But anatomical and physiological differences have given rise to sociocultural assumptions which do not necessarily follow. These assumptions may present themselves as 'givens' when, in fact, they are not. The danger that biology is seen as 'destiny' is always with us, in spite of feminism's untiring opposition. In Western culture, for instance, men are considered to be more active, more aggressive, more reasonable than women; being a woman implies being more passive, less aggressive, more emotional. Such a view proposes unilinear causal connections between our anatomy and physiology and our way of being which entirely ignores context and history. It is, therefore, unphenomenological.

It is interesting to consider Freud's views on this matter. Freud has often been accused, and rightly, of being ambivalent and confused in his approach to sexual difference, but he could also be astonishingly open-minded. In his *Three Essays on the Theory of Sexuality* (published in 1905) he proposed that the sexual drive is always masculine, in both boys and girls. But in a footnote, written ten years later, he explains that it is difficult to distinguish what the terms 'masculine' and 'feminine' actually mean. Pure masculinity and femininity cannot be found, there is always a 'mixture' (Freud, 1905: 219–20 [7: 141]). In *Civilization and Its Discontents*, Freud asserts that man has an 'unmistakably bisexual disposition'. Anatomically, maleness and femaleness can be clearly characterised, but not psychologically (Freud, 1930: 105–6 [12: 295–6]). Freud, in his papers on sexuality, frequently returns to the notion of constitutional bisexuality, which stands like a question mark on the margins of those aspects of his theories which tend to polarise femininity and masculinity.

Such a polarisation of masculinity and femininity arises from the concept of the Oedipus complex where anatomy seems indeed to become destiny. This complex, briefly summed up, implies that the boy's desire of mother and envy of father leads to a fear of castration which can only be held at bay by renunciation of mother and identification with father. Here the fear of the loss of the penis, the agent and symbol of masculinity, is central to the progress of male development. This identification with father becomes the basis of the formation of the super-ego. Initially Freud thought that the process he called the Oedipus complex applied to women as well. When it came to a closer understanding of the psychological processes involved, Freud felt at a loss and said so quite openly. Ernest Jones reports him saying once to the psychoanalyst Marie Bonaparte: 'The great question that has never been answered and which I have not yet been able to answer. Despite my thirty years of research into the feminine soul, is "what do women want?"' (Jones, 1961: 474). As late as 1926, in *The Question of Lay Analysis*, Freud wrote: 'We know less about the sexual life of little girls than of boys. But we need not feel ashamed of this distinction; after all, the sexual life of adult women is a "dark continent" for psychology' (Freud, 1926: 212).

Eventually Freud admitted that the same theory that applied to men could not be applied to women. There could not be a threat of castration when castration has already taken place, so to speak. So what is the little girl's reason for renouncing father? And why did she turn away from mother and towards father in the first place? Freud proposes the following sequence of events: the little girl discovers that she has no penis; she holds mother responsible for this lack which she resents and turns to father. 'She gives up her wish for a penis and puts in place of it a wish for a child; and *with that purpose in view* she takes her father as a love-object' (Freud, 1925: 256 [7: 340]). But the girl is disappointed once more: 'One has an impression that the Oedipus complex is then gradually given up because the wish is never fulfilled' (Freud, 1924: 179 [7: 321]). Freud does not clearly state what happens in the end: 'It must be admitted that in general our insight into these developmental processes in girls is unsatisfactory, incomplete and vague' (Freud, 1924: 179 [7: 321]).

What happens to the formation of the super-ego in these circumstances? Freud knows that he is treading on thin ice when he says:

> I cannot evade the notion (though I hesitate to give it expression) that for women the level of what is ethically normal is different from what it is in men. Their super-ego is never so inexorable, so impersonal, so

independent of its emotional origins as we require it to be in men.
(Freud, 1925: 257 [7: 342])

These theoretical constructions seem, to some extent, far-fetched despite their undoubted ingenuity. But constructions are not phenomena – they remain inexperienced, do not 'meet the eye'. Why do I devote space to them? The fact that Freud experienced such difficulties in imposing his rather inflexible schema on the ever-changing spectrum of what we call masculinity and femininity illustrates very strikingly the difference between intellectual explanation and experiential perception. (One has to read Freud's various attempts to 'explain' gender differences offered in the papers he produced throughout his life to appreciate his difficulties!)

But for psychotherapists, an examination of the Oedipal schema is particularly important if they wish to assess the psychoanalytic contribution to the question of homosexuality.

Homosexuality

Freud's attitude to homosexuality was ambivalent throughout. Though he clearly denied it was the 'disorder' it is still considered to be by a number of psychoanalytically oriented therapists, his theories nevertheless contributed greatly to the common assumption that it is developmental arrest. This is, in fact, what Freud called it himself in the famous letter he wrote answering the enquiries of the mother of a homosexual man. This letter is entirely sympathetic, speaks of the 'great injustice to persecute homosexuality' and mentions Plato, Michelangelo and Leonardo da Vinci as great men who had been homosexuals. But it also calls homosexuality 'a variation of the sexual function produced by a certain arrest of sexual development' (Jones, 1961: 624).

Clearly this statement has its roots in the concept of the 'negative Oedipus complex', which finds its solution in the identification of the boy with his mother and the girl with her father. In other words, there is a 'normal' development – the identification with the parent of the same sex – which makes its alternative 'abnormal'. Another assumption of this theory is that identification with the parent of the other sex implies the search for a partner of the same sex, which does not follow. As therapists we frequently see clients who are over-involved with the parent of the other sex and are nevertheless heterosexual. (Psychoanalysts would perhaps say that they are homosexual but do not know it.)

On the other hand, in *The Ego and the Super-ego*, Freud – returning to his proposition that all human beings are basically bisexual – stresses constitutional elements: 'In both sexes the relative strength of the masculine and feminine sexual dispositions is what determines whether the outcome of the Oedipus situation shall be an identification with the father or with the mother' (Freud, 1923: 33 [11: 372]). But how can a development be called arrested when it depends on constitutional disposition? In the same passage, Freud wonders whether we should not assume the existence of a:

> more complete Oedipus complex which is twofold, positive and negative, and is due to the bisexuality originally present in children: that is to say, a boy has not merely an ambivalent attitude towards his father and an affectionate object-choice towards his mother, but at the same time he also behaves like a girl and displays an affectionate feminine attitude to his father and a corresponding jealousy and hostility towards his mother.
>
> (Freud, 1923: 33)

In other words, a clear developmental distinction between heterosexuality and homosexuality cannot, in fact, be made. In writing this, Freud is much nearer to a phenomenological view of sexual difference than in his psychoanalytic speculations.

It would, of course, be absurd to say that psychoanalytic theory is responsible for the widespread hostility which homosexuality arouses in our culture. It is more likely that the theory mirrors the culture. The reasons make up a web of many strands and to follow their ramifications would take us beyond the scope of this book. But at the centre of this web is a concept of 'nature' which is a system of arbitrarily fixed sociocultural rules. A primitive biological view – which to some extent is also reflected by some religious beliefs – sees the exclusive aim of sexuality as procreation. Homosexuality cannot be 'natural' because it cannot lead to childbirth. Thus sexual feelings and acts that are not directed towards procreation are necessarily 'unnatural'. Such a view, of course, restricts severely the occasions on which heterosexuality can be called natural. An existential-phenomenological perspective cannot accept the imposition of such an inflexible sociocultural grid – without any regard for interaction, history or context – or existence.

Early on, in his *Three Essays on the Theory of Sexuality*, Freud contradicted this biological view of homosexuality by denying its innateness. 'Under a great number of conditions and in surprisingly numerous individuals, the nature and importance of the sexual object recedes into the background' (Freud, 1905: 149 [7: 61]). In a footnote, added in 1910, Freud illustrated this view by the example of ancient Greece where the sexual drive was considered more important than its aim: it was sexual passion that counted and not in the way in which it manifested itself (Freud, 1905: 149 [7: 61]). Ten years later, in another footnote to the *Three Essays on the Theory of Sexuality,* Freud wrote: 'Psycho-analytic research is most decidedly opposed to any attempt at separating off homosexuals from the rest of mankind as a group of special character (Freud, 1905: 145 [7: 56]). However, by suggesting that homosexuality was due to a 'negative' solution of the Oedipus complex, Freud contributed to this very 'separating off' of homosexuals which he said he opposed.

Phenomenologically, the attempt to find a particular 'cause' to explain an imprecisely defined area on the wide spectrum of sexuality is quite meaningless. It is obvious that no single cause could account for a spectrum of sexual behaviour that stretches from the permanent choice of a partner of the same sex throughout life to an occasional choice, covering instances of homosexuality suggested by circumstance (as in prison or the army), as well as a turning away from a long-time partner of the same sex to one of the opposite sex, and vice versa. There is, of course, also actual bisexuality for which psychoanalysis has no explanation – except for Freud's conviction that it is the constitutional basis of all sexuality.

For the existential psychotherapist, homosexuality is not a 'condition' brought about by specific factors, but a way of being in which whatever is 'given' is most delicately intertwined with our responses. One could say that there is no such thing as 'homosexuality' as such, rather there are infinite ways of 'being-in-the-world' homosexually. It is a way of being which can only be understood phenomenologically with a descriptive exploration of as wide a context as possible. Whether and when such an exploration is needed is, of course, a question in itself – one to which we shall return. Singling it out for exploration would imply the very thing which is here denied – that it is an extraordinary, even pathological state.

In light of this, it is regrettable that Medard Boss, one of the few existential psychotherapists to have written on homosexuality, includes it among the 'perversions' (Boss, 1966). It needs to be said, first of all, that in the use of this term Boss does not imply dismissal or condemnation. He sees the various sexual 'perversions' as attempts to achieve loving relationships in situations where the capacity to realise them fully is inhibited or crippled. Nevertheless the 'perversions' are seen as deficiencies, and there is the implication that heterosexuality is the only sexual mode in which the potential for loving can be fully realised. A norm is set from which homosexuality deviates. An existential-phenomenological approach has no place for 'norms', as van Deurzen-Smith puts it: 'Existential therapists are fundamentally concerned with what matters to the client. He or she avoids making normative judgements, and renounces any ambition to, even implicitly, push the client in any particular direction' (van Deurzen-Smith, 1996: 192).

The reason why Boss sees heterosexuality as a norm is that only in a heterosexual union are masculine and feminine potentialities brought together. This is a surprisingly simplistic assumption. It implies that there are definite masculine and feminine potentialities, and that we know how to define them. Also it takes for granted that whatever is called 'masculine' is present only in men, and what is called 'feminine' is present only in women. This assumption seems to me to be neither phenomenological nor existential.

From what we have seen it is clear that homosexuality, as such, is neither a developmental arrest that needs to be unfrozen nor a psychological disorder that needs to be alleviated or 'cured'. Homosexual people, however, have difficulties like anybody else, and some of their difficulties may concern their sexuality – as do some of the difficulties of heterosexual people. Homosexual people are, of course, especially vulnerable in a situation in which they are targets of persecution. In this case an existential therapist will explore the context of their sexuality, as she or he would whenever there are sexual difficulties.

Illustration

Rod came to see me because he is gay and wishes to marry and have a family. He has tried to have sexual relations with women but did not succeed. He had read that homosexuality was due to childhood events, and that their exploration might lead a homosexual person to become heterosexual. Rod had no permanent partner, and though he enjoyed frequent sexual encounters he found his loneliness intolerable.

I went along with his wish to explore his childhood and we found that he was smothered by a powerful mother whilst his father played only a small part in his life. This is, of course, the childhood situation seen by many therapists as giving rise to a boy's identification with the mother rather than the father and preparing the way for homosexual behaviour. These therapists tend to forget how often we find dominating mothers and absent fathers in the childhood of heterosexual clients!

Rod made a few more unsuccessful attempts to relate sexually to women and eventually the theme of our talks shifted from relating sexually to relating as such. It seemed that he had always been a loner, distrustful of other people, very uncertain of what he had to offer, and therefore afraid of being cheated and exploited. Gradually he came to see that his isolation had nothing to do with his sexual choice, but that it was a protective barrier which he was afraid to dismantle. He had constructed this barrier as a defensive response to a number of threatening 'givens' among which his dominating mother and indifferent father certainly played a part. Eventually he risked a breach in this barrier and has now been living for some time with another man – a new development in his life.

Perversions

To understand the psychoanalytic approach to perversions we need to take a brief look at Freud's theory of drives. Freud distinguishes between the source, the aim and the object. The source is a bodily stimulus, the aim is the release of the tension which stimulation – once it has reached a certain degree which Freud calls 'pressure' – has built up, and the object is the means by which this tension is discharged. In the case of the sexual drive, the source is the excitation of certain bodily areas (not necessarily the genitals) including 'the production of sexual excitation by rhythmic mechanical agitation of the body' (Freud, 1905: 201 [7: 120]). When discussing infantile sexuality Freud, interestingly, also mentions 'affective processes' as sources of excitation. He says 'that all comparatively intense affective processes, including even terrifying ones, trench upon sexuality' (1905: 203 [7: 123]) – a comment that raises the difficult question of the connection between terror and sexuality which transcends mere biology. The aim of the sexual drive is often the same as the source – mouth, anus, genitals (the 'erotogenic zones'). In the adult, however, it is said to be the union with a person of the opposite sex with which the earlier objects ('component drives') have merged.

This is the point where Freud's belief in the biological existence of a variety of possible 'objects' has given way to the 'normality' of one embodied in heterosexuality. Thus, in *The Language of Psychoanalysis,* Laplanche and Pontalis characterise 'perversions' as a 'deviation from the "normal" sexual act when this is defined as coitus with a person of the opposite sex directed towards the achievement of orgasm by means of genital penetration' (Laplanche & Pontalis, 1973: 306). They continue with a summary that distinguishes three kinds of perversion:

1. orgasm is reached with other sexual objects: homosexuality (which Freud originally called 'inversion'), paedophilia, bestiality
2. orgasm is reached through other regions of the body, for example the anus
3. orgasm is possible only when certain extrinsic conditions are present: fetishism, transvestism, voyeurism, exhibitionism, sado-masochism. At times these conditions can, by themselves, bring about sexual release.

It is important to note that we do not talk about 'perversions' in children. As Freud sees it, children are naturally 'polymorphously perverse' (Freud, 1905: 191 [7: 109]). Thus it becomes questionable to talk of perversions as 'unnatural'. Also, most of the various types of behaviour called perverse are found as part of so-called 'normal' heterosexuality and are called perversions only when they become predominant.

In a famous saying Freud called neuroses *'the negative of perversions'* (Freud, 1905: 165 [7: 80]). Neurotic symptoms are the result of a repression of the wishes that perversions express freely. But this non-judgemental openness is undermined by the concept of development: if heterosexuality is the aim, then the return to earlier stages is inevitably a regression. 'Development' literally means 'unfolding' and implies the emergence of something new from what is already there. It has acquired the meaning of a move from a less to a more desirable and 'mature' stage and thus gives rise to criteria of normality. Phenomenologically the butterfly is different from but not superior to the caterpillar.

Existential-phenomenologically there cannot be a process like regression, as this implies a linear view of time. If the past is always an aspect of our present experiential capacity, there is no need to 'go back' to it. The reappearance of strands of infantile sexuality in adult sexual behaviour is not surprising. In the light of the simultaneity of temporal modes, it seems unnecessary to separate 'earlier' from 'later' components.

Problems can arise when clients feel that a desired sexual activity becomes difficult or impossible. Clients may feel that masturbation takes the place of sexual relations with others, or that orgasm is dependent on wearing certain kinds of clothes. Such activities become problematic for clients because they feel they are 'not normal' by the rules of their sociocultural context – even though they are in fact quite happy with the way that they experience sexual satisfaction. But it can also be that they would prefer a different way of sexual activity which appears to them more meaningful. Such clients will go to a therapist for help, and the existential therapist will explore with them the different aspects of their sexuality and their feelings about it. The important point is that it is they who are dissatisfied, and not the therapist who judges them to be 'immature' or 'inadequate' and in need of being 'sorted out'.

Illustration

Tim was only sexually aroused when the woman he wanted to make love to wore leather gloves. Without them Tim was impotent. Leather gloves were his 'fetish' – the magical object that gave him the capacity to be sexually active. In fact, the mere presence of leather gloves, even without a woman, could bring him to sexual arousal.

Psychoanalytically, the fetish represents the mother's lacking penis: the boy has never accepted its lack because it conjures up the threat of castration (Freud, 1927: 147–57 [7: 351 ff]). This is a complicated and, in my view, rather a far-fetched explanation. A more behaviouristic approach would link the leather gloves with early sexual experiences involving such gloves in one way or another.

An exploration of his relations with women showed that he had on the whole avoided sexual contact with them, and had been fully potent even with the help of his fetish on only a few occasions. He felt he had to keep women at bay – he craved for their care but feared their power. There were a number of powerful but unstable women in his family, including his mother whom he rarely saw. At the same time such women had had a magnetic attraction for him throughout his life. The development of his experiential pattern which led to his 'fetishism' never became clear. He came to see that he both needed women and was afraid of them. His 'fetish' regulated, so to speak, his relation to them. This eased his mind considerably, though we never discovered the origin of his sexual behaviour.

Sexuality and violence

The consideration of perversion brings us to the difficult question of sexual acts which involve the violation of others. This covers a wide spectrum of behaviour, from imposing the view of genitals on an unprepared spectator to child abuse, rape and sexual murder. The question of consent is, of course, fundamental though by no means always clear in actual situations. In sado-masochistic acts the claim of consent can be a controversial issue. Most people would agree that the sexual use of children is always a violation whether they 'consent' to it or not.

We are facing the central problem of the nature of human destructiveness. This is a contentious and many-layered area, and within the framework of this book my considerations are bound to be sketchy. Erich Fromm, in his *Anatomy of Human Destructiveness* (1974), gives a lucid and comprehensive account of many of the relevant issues. In an interesting exposition of Freud's 'theory of aggressiveness and destructiveness', Fromm explores an earlier view where destructiveness is seen as a component of the sexual instinct and at the same time as independent of it. In his earlier writings, Fromm points out that Freud talks about the aggressive side of the sexual drive as manifesting itself as the wish for incorporation and mastery of the loved object. But at the same time Freud proposes 'aggressiveness as being independent from the sexual instinct, as a quality of the ego instincts which oppose and hate the intrusion of outside stimuli and obstacles to the satisfaction of sexual needs and those for self-preservation' (Fromm, 1974: 584).

In 1920, Freud's *Beyond the Pleasure Principle* replaced the old dichotomy between sexual and ego instincts with a new one – that of libido (which he also called 'Eros') and the death instinct. Fromm quotes Freud's explanation of this new duality:

> besides the instinct to preserve living substance and to join it into ever larger units, there must exist another, contrary instinct seeking to dissolve those units and to bring them back to their primaeval [sic], inorganic state. That is to say, as well as Eros there was an instinct of death.
> (Fromm, 1974: 585–6, quoting Freud, 1930: 118–9 [12: 309–10])

Originally the 'death instinct' seemed to be the origin of self-destructiveness but eventually Freud saw destructiveness, as such, as the death instinct turned outwards. Fromm shows clearly that the original meaning of the death instinct does not, in fact, lend itself to such a transformation. He asks: 'is there any evidence or even reason for this identity of the tendency to cessation of all excitation and the impulse to destroy?' Fromm does not think so and insists rightly, I think, that 'life's inherent tendency for slowing down and eventually to die' has nothing to do with 'the active impulse to destroy' (Fromm, 1974: 599). Most psychoanalysts did not accept Freud's concept of a death instinct. But, as Fromm says, 'they transformed the death instinct into a "destructive instinct" opposite to the old sexual instinct. They thus combined their loyalty to Freud with their inability to go beyond the old-fashioned instinct-theory' (Fromm,

1974: 601). This polarisation of instincts still governs a great deal of psychoanalytic theory and its understanding of the connection between violence and sexuality.

Fromm's position is different. He believes that in man 'instinctive determination has reached its maximum decrease' (Fromm, 1974: 301). In other words, our responses are only to a small extent instinctively determined: 'Man's irrationality is caused by the fact that he lacks instincts, and not by their presence' (Fromm, 1974: 353). Human destructiveness is the result of a choice. In an approach that comes at times quite near to that of existential phenomenology, Fromm sees destructiveness as 'one of the possible answers to psychic needs that are rooted in the existence of man' (Fromm, 1974: 294). He says that 'the need for relatedness can be answered by love and kindness – or by dependence, sadism, masochism, destructiveness' (Fromm, 1974: 340). The existential phenomenologist would describe relatedness not as an existential need but as an existential 'given', to which there can be loving or destructive responses.

The important view which Fromm and the existential phenomenologist share is that destructiveness is not an aspect of sexuality itself. Fromm distinguishes 'benign' from 'malignant' aggression. Benign aggression is the ability to move 'forwards towards a goal without undue hesitation, doubt or fear' (Fromm, 1974: 256). This is the original meaning of the Latin verb *aggredi*. Some people see this moving forward as an inevitable component of a sexual approach. But this form of 'aggression' would be considered benign by Fromm; its aim is not to overpower or destroy. (The Latin word is intransitive!) The various forms of sadism illustrate what Fromm calls 'malignant' aggression. Freud came to see sadism as a blending of Eros and the death instinct turned outward towards others. Fromm rejects such an instinctual interpretation and asserts that the core of all manifestations of sadism is 'the passion to have absolute and unrestricted control over a living being' (Fromm, 1974: 384). Fromm sees this 'passion' as rooted in the very 'limitations of human existence' – sadism being the 'transformation of impotence into the illusion of omnipotence' (Fromm, 1974: 386). Life's uncertainty and unpredictability can give rise to feelings of anxiety and powerlessness. A possible response is a compulsive search for absolute power, manifesting itself in the wide-ranging spectrum of sadistic practices.

Once destructiveness is no longer seen as an aspect of sexuality itself, it is possible to distinguish between a sexual and a non-sexual sadism. Sexuality is one of the intrinsic aspects of our 'Being-in-the-world', and as such can be one of the ways it can affirm or destroy existence.

Summing up Fromm's arguments and emphasising their existential-phenomenological relevance, we can say the following about the relation between sexuality and violence:

a) Violence is not an aspect of sexuality itself which has made itself independent of its context.

b) Rather sexuality can be the potential channel which carries a destructive response to existential 'givens'.

c) One of these 'givens' can be relatedness itself – which can become the target of rejection, distortion and destruction.

d) Another 'given' is life's uncertainty and unpredictability which can lead to feelings of panic and powerlessness. These in turn may give rise to the compulsive need to overpower and destroy others sexually.

An existential phenomenologist may wish to add: if 'Being-in-the-world' is always 'being-with-others', and existential relatedness is the mutual openness of human beings to each other, the sexual violation of the other deprives him or her of their subjectivity, turning them into objects, and there is the destruction of existence itself.

References

Boss, M (1966) *Sinn und Gehalt der Sexuellen Perversionen* (3rd ed). Bern: Huber.

Freud, S (1905) *Three Essays on the Theory of Sexuality*. S. E. VII. London: Hogarth Press. (Pelican Freud Library. Vol. 7. Harmondsworth: Penguin Books.)

Freud, S (1920) *Beyond the Pleasure Principle*. S. E. XVIII. London: Hogarth Press. (Pelican Freud Library. Vol. 11. Harmondsworth: Penguin Books.)

Freud, S (1923) *The Ego and the Super-ego*. S. E. XIX. London: Hogarth Press. (Pelican Freud Library. Vol. 11. Harmondsworth: Penguin Books.)

Freud, S (1924) *The Dissolution of the Oedipus Complex*. S. E. XIX. London: Hogarth Press. (Pelican Freud Library. Vol. 7. Harmondsworth: Penguin Books.)

Freud, S (1925) *Some Psychical Consequences of the Anatomical Distinction between the Sexes*. S. E. XIX. London: Hogarth Press. (Pelican Freud Library. Vol. 7. Harmondsworth: Penguin Books.)

Freud, S (1926) *The Question of Lay Analysis*. S. E. XX. London: Hogarth Press.

Freud, S (1927) *Fetishism*. S. E. XXI. London: Hogarth Press. (Pelican Freud Library. Vol. 7. Harmondsworth: Penguin Books.)

Freud, S (1930) *Civilization and Its Discontents*. S. E. XXI. London: Hogarth Press. (Pelican Freud Library. Vol. 12. Harmondsworth: Penguin Books.)

Fromm, E (1974) *The Anatomy of Human Destructiveness*. Harmondsworth: Penguin Books.

Jones, E (1961) *The Life and Work of Sigmund Freud* (Ed and abr L Trilling & S Marcus). Harmondsworth: Penguin Books.

Laplanche, L & Pontalis, JB (1973) *The Language of Psychoanalysis*. London: Karnac.

Madison, GB (1981) *The Phenomenology of Merleau-Ponty*. Athens, OH: Ohio University Press.

Merleau-Ponty, M (1962) *Phenomenology of Perception* (C Smith, Trans). London: Routledge & Kegan Paul.

Sartre, J-P (1958) *Being and Nothingness* (H Barnes, Trans). New York: Philosophical Library.

Van Deurzen-Smith, E (1996) Existential therapy. In W Dryden (Ed) *Handbook of Individual Therapy* (pp. 179–208). London: Sage Publications.

Part 2

Drawing on the Philosophers: Merleau-Ponty and Sartre

3

Merleau-Ponty and Existential Sexuality

– Dr Paul Smith-Pickard –

Sexuality but not as we know it?

Any discussion around sexuality is inevitably problematic because it is often difficult to find a consensus of meaning or indeed meanings about what sexuality actually is.

More than half a century ago Merleau-Ponty recognised this problem when he said that, 'the question is not so much whether human life does or does not rest on sexuality, as of knowing what is to be understood by sexuality' (Merleau-Ponty, 1996: 158).

In the *Phenomenology of Perception* Merleau-Ponty attempts to provide us with a description of sexuality from an existential perspective whilst at the same time revealing the problematic nature of such a venture. 'How can we identify a content of consciousness as sexual?' he asks. 'Indeed we cannot. Sexuality conceals itself from itself beneath a mask of generality, and continually tries to escape from the drama and tension which it sets up' (Merleau-Ponty, 1996: 168). So when we embark on a discussion of sexuality we should be mindful that we are entering a labyrinth of meaning, difficulties and contradictions. This is no less true within the specialised field of psychotherapy than it is in everyday life, and yet the issue of sexuality is a prominent feature of our lives despite, or perhaps even because of, its problematic status and meaning.

So why is it so difficult to pin down this elusive and flexible signifier that seems so central to our lives? A large part of the problem here is that our use of the word and our collective perceptions about sexuality are contextual, and being historically located they change over time and within different social groupings. Even within the pages of the *Phenomenology* it is easy to be confused by the normalising images of heterosexuality seemingly at odds with Merleau-Ponty's phenomenological approach and later ontology of sexuality.

So what is to be understood by sexuality in this chapter? In my previous work I have used the phrase 'existential sexuality' (Smith-Pickard, 2006, 2009) rather than simply 'sexuality'; and this begs the question why should I feel it necessary to make the distinction at this time when others in the past, including Sartre, Merleau-Ponty, de Beauvoir, Foucault and Laing, have not done so? The phrase is an attempt to reduce the level of confusion and cultural prejudgement that appeared previously when I used the term 'sexuality' in an unqualified way. This confusion is in part due to divergent images of sexuality in various modalities of psychotherapy as well as a range of colloquial meanings.

In everyday language, the term 'sexuality' is frequently used as a defining characteristic of an individual connected to images of selfhood, identity, sexual acts, and cultural expression relating in one way or another to our sexual lives. In colloquial use, sexuality has become gender focused, individualised, and located primarily in the genitals. Within this colloquial appropriation sexuality becomes an object of differentiation and individualism where we talk about a person's 'sexuality' in much the same way that we talk about their occupation or education. This prompts Foucault to suggest that 'the homosexual was now a species' (Foucault, 1990: 43). That is not to say that the colloquial meanings of sexuality are in any way incorrect or invalid compared to other meanings, but that what one group sees as sexuality may differ from another group and the normative images within a society can create prejudice and alienation. Sexuality has become a portmanteau word that avoids direct or obvious meanings and as Merleau-Ponty suggests, it hides behind a 'mask of generality' (Merleau-Ponty, 1996: 168).

In contrast to some of the colloquial significations, existential sexuality describes an ever-present mode of primary relatedness that we experience as unique existents caught up in an inevitable involvement and struggle with other sexual beings; 'the for-itself' says Sartre, 'is sexual in its very upsurge in the face of the Other and through it sexuality comes into the world' (Sartre, 1996: 406). What Sartre is describing here is sexuality as an interpersonal phenomenon rather than a defining characteristic of a person.

The description of existential sexuality that I am presenting is one of inter-experience based upon ideas and images taken from thinkers over the past 70 years or so who have been influenced by the work of Maurice

Merleau-Ponty (1908–1961), along with ideas that influenced him. In this description, sexuality is presented as an ever-present phenomenon revealed in the interrelational space of embodied encounter occurring throughout the life span extending beyond mere sex or sexual behaviour.

For Merleau-Ponty sexuality is the basic and primordial way in which we project ourselves into the world and towards others. He sees it as a fundamental element of encounter and intersubjectivity, describing it as the 'mute and permanent question which constitutes normal sexuality' (Merleau-Ponty, 1996: 156) that we pose in our attitude towards being with others that is 'always present like an atmosphere' and 'spreads forth like an odour or like a sound' (Merleau-Ponty, 1996: 168) where, 'as an ambiguous atmosphere, sexuality is co-extensive with life' (Merleau-Ponty, 1996: 169).

In order to unpack these sound bites from Merleau-Ponty's description of sexuality from the *Phenomenology*, I will look at the similarities and the differences between him and Sartre in their understanding of sexuality and human relationships. But before doing this I will identify other influences on his thinking, in particular the intellectual and ideological context of post-war Paris, and how this might help us gain a better understanding of Merleau-Ponty, the 'bricoleur', and how this contributed to his ideas about sexuality.

Twentieth-century bricoleur

The term *bricoleur*, first introduced by the structural anthropologist Claude Levi-Strauss, describes a style of thinking where a creative assemblage and synthesis is made of diverse ideas that happen to be available at the time. Merleau-Ponty is arguably the ultimate twentieth-century bricoleur creating a synthesis of internal relationships between existentialism, psychoanalysis, Gestalt psychology, structuralism, Marxism and phenomenology. These were a group of synchronously emerging intellectual fields where the external relationships between them frequently appear in stark opposition to each other but whose internal structures complement each other and whose influence is traceable in Merleau-Ponty's existential account of sexuality.

Dutch philosopher Douwe Tiemersma (1987) claims that we can see the whole of Merleau-Ponty's philosophy as a field theory, whilst Claude Levi-Strauss described Merleau-Ponty's final posthumous publication *The Visible and the Invisible* as a synthesis of structuralism with phenomenology.

More recently Beata Stawarska provides evidence that throughout Merleau-Ponty's work there is a weaving together of the seemingly divergent worldviews of phenomenology and psychoanalysis where, 'both disciplines become transformed in relation to the other, and so are internally rather than externally related' (Stawarska, 2009: 58).

In the early part of his career Merleau-Ponty had close associations with Sartre and de Beauvoir, indeed it is even impossible to refer to the early work of Merleau-Ponty without some reference to Sartre, and despite all the other influences he absorbed into his philosophy from the cultural milieu of his time Merleau-Ponty's philosophical project remains embedded in French existentialism. Merleau-Ponty's existentialism is also influenced by Husserl and Heidegger; he was also strongly influenced by the ideas of Marx, Freud, and de Saussure. He had close friendships with structuralist anthropologist Claude Levi-Strauss and with psychoanalyst Jacques Lacan, both of whom were also inspired by the structural linguistics of Ferdinand de Saussure.

In order for us to come close to his perspective on sexuality it is helpful to recognise a recurring fundamental theme within intellectual developments of the mid-twentieth century. This theme was of the present but undisclosed world, a hidden world behind the readily accepted and taken-for-granted world. The project within this theme was to discover how this hidden undisclosed world can be revealed, and how it is structured. For example the theme of the undisclosed world is one that Merleau-Ponty found in the work of Freud where the project of psychoanalysis was to reveal the unconscious, unveiling those processes that are not transparently known and seemingly without a purposeful intentionality. The theme is also evident in the structuralist anthropology of his close friend Claude Levi-Strauss who sought to uncover the structurally unconscious dimensions of human life and culture.

Merleau-Ponty's philosophy is littered with references from Gestalt psychology, and he frequently used the phrase 'field of existence', an image where figure emerges from a generalised holistic and unified field or ground. His interest in language and the structural linguistics of Ferdinand de Saussure brought him into contact with the anonymous system of language (langue) and the embodied language of speech (parole) that brings about a world through expression and gesture where the perceived world is transformed into the spoken word and things acquire significance by being named. De Saussure's theory of language also provided the structural dimension for Lacanian psychoanalysis that considered the unconscious to be structured like a language.

In post-war Paris the other major influence on intellectual life besides existentialism was Marxism. In the Marxist analysis of ideology there is an attempt to disclose and reveal the hegemony of common sense that blinds us to the structures and workings of the dominant ideology that we would otherwise take for granted.

Merleau-Ponty's phenomenology, as laid out in the preface to the *Phenomenology of Perception*, can be seen as a fusion of Marxism, with structuralist semiology, along with aspects of Husserl's later work. In the preface we find a phenomenological reduction that rejects the anti-existential image of the transcendental ego and attempts a subversion of the concealed ideology of common sense in our taken-for-granted viewpoint in order to bring both it and the relationships it supports into the open and into question in a Marxist-imbued phenomenology:

> It is because we are through and through compounded of relationships with the world that for us the only way to become aware of the fact is to suspend the resultant activity, to refuse it our complicity … not because we reject the certainties of common sense and a natural attitude to things – but because, being the presupposed basis of any thought, they are taken for granted, and go unnoticed, and because in order to arouse them and bring them into view, we have to suspend for a moment our recognition of them.
> (Merleau-Ponty, 1996: xiii)

Merleau-Ponty was witness to the newly emerging ideas of Structuralism based on de Saussure's linguistics where we find the deconstruction of the sign in semiology and the search for meaning in the denotative and connotative elements of signification. Furthermore, the idea of bringing things to light, of things being revealed, is a dominant feature of the phenomenology of both Husserl and Heidegger. As Heidegger says: 'For us phenomenological reduction means leading phenomenological vision back from the apprehension of a being … to the understanding of the being of this being (projecting upon the way it is unconcealed)' (Heidegger, 1988: 21).

When Merleau-Ponty tells us that sexuality spreads forth like an odour or a sound and that it is always present like an atmosphere, we may realise that he is talking about sexuality as background field or primordial structure where manifestations of sex and sexuality have the potential to emerge as figure against ground. Or we might also understand that sexuality is always present like a Freudian unconscious atmosphere with an underlying dynamic potential or that the real meaning of sexuality is masked by colloquialisms, cultural taboos and genitalia. In Merleau-Ponty's synthesis and reinterpretation of these worldviews or intellectual fields we have a recurrent theme of first-person experience set within a structural context. This structural context is both the 'ambiguous atmosphere' as a sort of ubiquitous background presence, as well as the system of structural articulations through which sexuality comes into the world.

Sexuality permeates existence

In their seminal chapters on sexuality in *Being and Nothingness* and *Phenomenology of Perception* both Sartre and Merleau-Ponty recognise sexuality as a fundamental aspect of Being with an ontological significance throughout our lifespan beginning at birth and ending in death. This means that sexuality is not simply focused or dependent on sex or sexual actions but is coextensive with life with a broader significance for interpersonal engagement. However, as Merleau-Ponty warns us, we must be careful not to extend the meaning of sexuality to being synonymous with existence or to make our meaning of it so broad as to be meaningless. Rather to understand that 'sexuality permeates existence and vice-versa' (Merleau-Ponty, 1996: 169). Similarly, Sartre sees the phenomenon of sexuality as paradigmatic, the 'skeleton' on which all concrete relations with others are hung. He suggests that an understanding of sexuality will provide us with a foundation and a blueprint for the structural articulation of all human relations.

Like many of their generation Sartre and Merleau-Ponty were drawn to the ideas of psychoanalysis and whilst they both rejected the cognitive and mechanistic theories of mind and theories of instinct, they drew inspiration from other aspects of Freud's theories that they reinterpreted in their own idiosyncratic fashion. For instance in speaking about sexuality Sartre points out that he is not referring to an instinctual 'libido' that slips in everywhere, but to an understanding of sexuality and desire that will provide us with an understanding of how all our relationships are articulated (Sartre, 1996: 407).

As for Merleau-Ponty, he claims that: 'for Freud himself the sexual is not the genital ... the libido is not an instinct' (Merleau-Ponty, 1996: 158), and that sexuality is a generalised intentionality towards the world we find ourselves placed in and living through. It is, 'what causes a man to have a history. In so far as a man's sexual history provides a key to his life, it is because in his sexuality is projected his manner of being towards the world, that is, towards time and other men' (Merleau-Ponty, 1996: 158).

Feminist critiques of both Sartre and Merleau-Ponty challenge heterosexist images in their phenomenological descriptions of sexual behaviour or sexed embodiment. The heterosexual normative bias is perhaps glaringly obvious in *Being and Nothingness* but Judith Butler rightly accuses Merleau-Ponty of importing 'tacit normative assumptions about the heterosexual character of sexuality' (Butler, 1989: 86).

Despite feminist misgivings, Merleau-Ponty's focus on the lived experience of the body has been strongly influential in the development of 'corporeal feminism' of the 1990s. Likewise we cannot ignore his privileging of the body as the site of experience and the fundamental locus of intentionality in his discourse on, and our understanding of, sexuality where he attempts to overcome the Cartesian split of mind from body with his holistic image of the 'body-subject' with its ambiguous personal, pre-personal and interpersonal status.

There are times in *Phenomenology of Perception* and *Being and Nothingness* when Sartre and Merleau-Ponty seem to be speaking with one voice. This is not so surprising given their close connection at the time and their collaborative roles in the publication of Sartre's radical journal *Les Temps Modernes* (1945–1952). At times their sentences are virtually interchangeable when they invoke neo-Hegelian images of master and slave into images of intentionality and subjectivity. This is particularly evidenced when they speak about bringing the other's consciousness into the body and thereby attempting to capture the consciousness of the other through a process of objectification. However this was also an important point of divergence in their thinking demonstrated by their contrasting views of the intentionality of the body in the ambiguous image of 'double sensation'. This notion allows Merleau-Ponty's thinking to develop into a philosophy of ambiguity and a thesis of reversibility that takes him far away from Sartre's view of human relationships.

Double sensation and reversibility

The point of departure between Merleau-Ponty and Sartre becomes clear at the level of the sensing body and their respective accounts of one hand touching the other hand. This is a powerful metaphor for how they individually regard relationships in general and sexuality in particular.

Sartre sees touching and being touched as two radically distinct species of phenomena and refutes the notion of 'double sensation'. Whereas Merleau-Ponty, through his insistence on the primacy of perception, where I can only perceive the world with the realisation that I can also be perceived, sees these phenomena as ambiguously and irrevocably linked. For him the term 'double sensation' means that my body is always both ambiguously subject and object for me. It alternates, can both touch and be touched, see and be seen, in a mutual and reversible relation to a world where I coexist with things and other embodied subjects. This radical image of reversibility is described in the following manner:

> When I press my two hands together, it is not a matter of two sensations felt together as one perceives two objects placed side by side, but of an ambiguous set-up in which both hands can alternate the roles of 'touching' and 'being touched'. What was meant by 'double sensation' is that, in passing from one role to another, I can identify the hand touched as the same one which will in a moment be touching.
> (Merleau-Ponty, 1996: 93)

Sartre however views this situation as a direct trajectory of intentionality and objectification, where he sees the active grasping hand turning the other hand into a thing:

> the hand which I grasp with my other hand is not apprehended as a hand which is grasping but as an apprehensible object. Thus the nature of our body for us entirely escapes us to the extent that we can take upon it the Other's point of view.
> (Sartre, 1996: 358)

Whilst Sartre's view is archetypically that of the ejaculatory male focused on a direct trajectory of intentionality, Merleau-Ponty's view is more reciprocal and focused on the perceiving and perceivable experience of the body as the site of all perception. 'Our own body', he says, 'is in the world as the heart is in the organism: it keeps the visible spectacle constantly alive, it breathes air into it and sustains it inwardly, and with it forms a system' (Merleau-Ponty, 1996: 203).

The system he is talking about here is not simply about the subject/object ambiguity of our own bodies but one of mutual reciprocity that leads to a fluid resonating relationship between people. This is interestingly captured by Merleau-Ponty in this following statement that reflects the complexity of sexuality as a relational ontological phenomenon of reversibility:

> Since sexuality is relationship to other persons, and not just to another body, it is going to weave the circular system of projections and introjections, illuminating the unlimited series of reflecting reflections and reflected reflections which are the reasons why I am the other person and he is myself.
>
> (Merleau-Ponty, 1996: 230)

Perhaps this quotation, in fact a re-reading of Freud's sexual aggressive impulse whereby Merleau-Ponty sees the sexual as our way of living our relationship with others, will make more sense to us if we look at it not in isolation but in the context of earlier descriptions of the phenomenon of sexuality by Merleau-Ponty and the role of desire in human relationships.

Desire

Merleau-Ponty regards sexuality as the basic way in which we project ourselves through desire into the world aiming at an incarnation of consciousness. Desire brings us into the primacy of the body. 'What we try to possess,' says Merleau-Ponty, 'is not just a body but a body brought to life by consciousness' (Merleau-Ponty, 1996: 167). In other words erotic desire aims not simply at a sexual act or orgasmic pleasure or even the objectification and domination of the other. Instead desire aims to make a difference to the other by capturing their consciousness and what we desire is to be desired. To be able to make a difference to another, to be desired by them, is to be existentially validated by them. In desire the self realises itself through the reactive body of the other. I make a difference to you and know that I am.

In our attempts to make a difference to another, to be existentially validated by others, to be desired by others, we use existential sexuality to capture their consciousness as a form of enchantment. We learned to do this in varying degrees of sophistication or even desperation from earliest childhood in a basic and primordial need for the other.

Sexual desire presupposes the existence of other unique existents in a shared world where the image and presence of the 'Other' is constantly with us as a horizon of our existence. The 'Other' ambiguously both poses a threat to our existence and an affirmation of our existence. It also presupposes a mutual embodiment, as only embodied beings can express the fundamental intentionality of sexual desire as a troubling moment of self-consciousness, an upsurge of the world that reveals our embodied presence to both ourselves and to the world.

Desire is not necessarily sexual desire in the sense of aiming at sexual physical contact. Such is the case with sexual attraction where we may desire sexual contact but mostly what we desire is a reciprocal response from the other that they also find us attractive or have a level of sexual interest in us. The mutual reciprocity of desire forms the basis of many if not the majority of our interpersonal relationships. This is so even when the possibility of sex is completely absent from the relationship.

Desire presents itself as a pre-reflective apprehension that is prior to reflective comprehension where according to Merleau-Ponty; 'There is an erotic "comprehension" not of the order of understanding, since understanding subsumes an experience, once perceived, under some idea, while desire comprehends blindly by linking body to body' (Merleau-Ponty, 1996: 157).

Desire links us through a shared body-to-body experience reflecting the body-subject's ability to direct itself towards, and place itself in relation to, a world and as such desire and existential sexuality can be seen as the ground of our co-existence in a shared world.

As the linking of body to body in desire does not presuppose physical contact or sexual/orgasmic intention, we might ask what is the relationship between sex and existential sexuality?

Sex and existential sexuality

Obviously sex and existential sexuality are connected in some way and the relationship can probably be best described as one of figure to ground, where sex emerges out of the ever-present ground of existential sexuality, which is why Foucault asks; 'Is "sex" really the anchorage point that supports the manifestations of sexuality, or is it not rather a complex idea that was formed inside the deployment of sexuality?' (Foucault, 1990: 152).

He clearly believes the latter and writes about sex being an aspect of sexuality in a similar way to both Sartre and Merleau-Ponty who both reject the primacy of sex and regard sexuality as having intelligibility and a significance that goes beyond an engagement with sex. For them sex is made necessary by the operation of sexuality. Indeed sexuality refers to the sexual in our lives but sex is simply an aspect, a significant point on the spectrum of existential sexuality. We have access to Merleau-Ponty's understanding of sexuality through his philosophical work, which is often cryptic and ambiguous.

One of the significant differences between Merleau-Ponty and Sartre is that the latter also wrote plays and novels to illustrate his ideas and make them available to a wider public audience. So if we want to access Sartre's understanding of phenomenology we can turn to his novel *Nausea* where we find incredibly graphic phenomenological descriptions by way of visual metaphor. We can also turn to another writer with an existential perspective who wrote about the spectrum of sexuality at the same time as Sartre and Merleau-Ponty but on the other side of the Atlantic. In his 1947 novel *The Wayward Bus,* the American novelist John Steinbeck parallels and mirrors the ideas of the French existentialists of how consciousness is experienced bodily and how we attempt to capture the consciousness of another person through their bodily awareness or their induced self-consciousness.

He uses the events of a seemingly ordinary bus ride through the back roads of the Californian countryside as an arena to articulate the complex relational activities of a group of strangers. This simple story, about a journey both actual and metaphorical, is shot through with existential sexuality, revealed through interpersonal relations. The main focus of the story is the world-weary Camille who seems to have the unfortunate ability to trigger men's desire by the transparency of her sexual being. Her power ebbs and flows. She is both person and sexual object as she negotiates the interpersonal territory between isolation and engulfment. Steinbeck examines and describes everyday relational aspects of existential sexuality in men and women, amplified by the context of strangers on a journey of misadventure, like so many hothouse flowers being forced to unfold. Here existential sexuality is presented by Steinbeck as a multi-layered, ambiguous, omnipresent experience, shared as a basic and fundamental way of being in a world with others. The narrative touches on shame, fascination, sadism, enchantment, desire, pleasure, the bodily presence of others, as well as the sexual act itself. And yet it is not simply a story about sex but about existence infused with existential sexuality, of embodied inter-experience where desire and sexual attraction can existentially validate and where the lack of it can feel like a negation of one's whole being.

As we have already seen whether through the philosophical works or through novels, existential sexuality is a mutual system that attempts to capture or appropriate the awareness or consciousness of the other person through bringing that awareness into bodily felt sensations. At the same time we offer our own body into that intersubjective space of the encounter to allow the other person to also make a difference; they impress themselves upon us. In other words we receive the resemblance and otherness of the other person as a bodily felt experience even without physical touch.

What I am describing here as existential sexuality is a system of reciprocity whereby we fascinate and are fascinated by each other, we appropriate and are appropriated by each other, and what we desire is that the other person should desire us in return in a mutual reciprocity. As far as Merleau-Ponty is concerned it is the very ground of our existence; 'There is no explanation of sexuality which reduces it to anything other than itself, for it is already something other than itself, and indeed, if we like, our whole being' (Merleau-Ponty, 1996: 171).

If existential sexuality permeates all aspects of our existence, the challenge for psychotherapy is to find functional and ethical ways to engage with the primary relatedness that is existential sexuality within the therapeutic encounter. There is much that we can learn perhaps from this formulation of existential sexuality about how we engage and disengage with clients, along with a recognition that however much we may choose to deny it or reframe it with concepts that attempt to distance the therapist from its influence, existential sexuality is inevitably present in the consulting room.

References

Butler, J (1989) Sexual ideology and phenomenological description: A feminist critique of Merleau-Ponty's phenomenology of perception. In J Allen & IM Young (Eds) *The Thinking Muse: Feminism and modern French philosophy* (pp. 85–100). Bloomington: IN: Indiana University Press.

Foucault, M (1990) *The History of Sexuality: Vol.1: An introduction.* (R Hurley, Trans). London: Penguin. (First published 1976)

Heidegger, M (1988) *The Basic Problems of Phenomenology* (A Hofstadter, Trans). Bloomington, IN: Indiana University Press.

Merleau-Ponty, M (1996) *Phenomenology of Perception* (C Smith, Trans). London: Routledge & Kegan Paul. (First published 1945)

Sartre, J-P (1996) *Being and Nothingness* (HE Barnes, Trans). London: Routledge. (First published 1943)

Smith-Pickard, P (2006) Transference as existential sexuality. *Journal of the Society for Existential Analysis, 17*(2), 224–37.

Smith-Pickard, P (2009) Existential sexuality and the body in supervision. In E van Deurzen & S Young (Eds) *Existential Perspectives on Supervision* (pp. 68–78). Basingstoke: Palgrave.

Stawarska, B (2009) Psychoanalysis. In R Diprose & J Reynolds (Eds) *Merleau-Ponty: Key concepts* (pp. 57–69). Stocksfield: Acumen.

Steinbeck, J (1947) *The Wayward Bus.* New York: Viking Press.

Tiemersma, D (1987) Merleau-Ponty's philosophy as a field theory: Its origin, categories and relevance. *Man and World,* Vol. 20 (pp. 419–36). Dordrecht: Nijhoff.

4

Sexual Expression, Authenticity and Bad Faith

– Richard Pearce –

> For I believe that a man can always make something out of what is made of him. This is the limit I would accord to freedom: the small movement which makes of a totally conditioned social being someone who does not render back completely what his conditioning has given him.
> (Sartre, 2008: 35)

Issues around sex are certainly prevalent in the therapy room, either explicitly or implicitly, and my concern in this chapter is to unravel something of the complexity that underlies this prevalence. I am not concerned here with the techniques that might characterise an existential approach, but rather with elucidating the understanding of sex (and therefore therapeutic concerns that might be present) that is consistent with such a philosophical perspective.

I take, as a starting point, the premise that we are meaning-making beings. Above all we seek to make sense of our lives in the context of our finitude. We seek to give our lives purpose and value in a way that makes our lives meaningful. At the same time, the being that makes meaning is both transient and contingent. Transient in that our sense of ourselves is in a constant state of change, is never still or known entirely as we perceive an object to be known; and contingent in so far as our choices are always, to a degree, conditional on our context and past experience, as well as the choices of others. The being that makes meaning, therefore, is continuously in a state of change, of becoming.

The term 'being' as used in this chapter requires some clarification. The approach followed here attempts to follow Sartre's ontology. This might be encapsulated by the expression 'singular universal' which implies that an understanding of the abstract universal (such as existence or being), can only be approached and understood through the particular, through the ontic expression of that universal; and that the two (the ontological and its expression) are in a perpetual state of interaction and change (Catalano, 2005). The notion of 'being', therefore, can only be understood through the manifestation of 'a being'; one that describes 'universal' characteristics that are attributes of humanity and are made known through 'singular' expression, through what Sartre described as 'lived experience' (1981).

If our lived experience is such that it is consistent with this sense of becoming, then it is more possible for us to feel comfortable with ourselves, to feel authentic. Lived experiences that cause us to be in conflict with that which gives meaning, or to render such meaning inaccessible or thwarted, cause us emotional discomfort or pain and lie at the root of the many surface pathologies that are described in the proliferating literature on psychological 'disorder'.

But if we are meaning-making beings, who seek to find purpose and value in our way of being-in-the-world, and accept at the same time the observation that a very prominent source of emotional discomfort for many concerns sexual expression, then we must ask the question: what purpose or meaning do we attribute to sex, what role does it play in our lives that is consistent with our way of being-in-the-world? Further, stemming from this, to what do we attribute the ubiquitous nature of this subject in the therapy room?

In the process of attempting to answer these questions, this chapter illustrates discursive argument with vignettes derived from the author's experience as a therapist.[1] The first section locates the focus of discussion in the arena of authenticity, reviewing, through reference to the work of Sartre, the way in which this concept and the associated concept of 'bad faith' are rooted in our search for ourselves, to live in accordance with our 'fundamental project', and the fruitless paradox of such endeavour. It is here, in the arena of freedom and responsibility that we encounter the possibility of bad faith.

The second section extends the framework by considering the ground of our awareness, and the association between this and our unrequited desire

---

1. In order to protect the confidentially of client identity the vignettes taken from therapeutic experience are in all cases composites based on a number of clients' experiences rather than the experience of individuals. Additionally, variables such as age, gender, sexual orientation and cultural background are also changed where appropriate to ensure anonymity. The essential features of the experience are then presented in a way that preserves the essence of that experience while disguising its source.

to know, and be comfortable with, ourselves; the uncertainty this vain pursuit engenders and the consequent ease with which we fall into 'bad faith' or inauthenticity. It is appropriate however, to consider the 'being' that is seeking to make meaning of existence; in particular, we then consider the question of what it means to 'be' sexually. We identify humans as having sexual potential, whose underlying physiology, while informing our natures, also leaves room for freedom and choice in our sexual expression.

The chapter then proceeds to consider our fallibility in recognising and acting on our freedom in the way we relate to others, and reveal a potential, if not a tendency, to act in bad faith, to manifest an inauthenticity in the way in which we express ourselves sexually. The chapter then elaborates on this tendency implicit in the Sartrean 'fundamental project', before moving on to a more direct discussion of sex and authenticity, and the ease with which a search for intimacy can lead to its opposite.

A second theme of the chapter attempts to take this paradox of individual authenticity into the arena of human society. Drawing on Sartre's later work (1981, 1992, 1960/2004), the chapter considers first the way in which the human individual and her preferences are both determined by, and determining of, the wider social and historical context; a process that informs sexual, as well as other, modes of expression. We review the Sartrean concept of totalisation, and the implications of this for our 'fundamental project', and the role that sexual expression plays in this. The following section elaborates this concept, considering the way in which sex can be understood as a vehicle for social as well as individual expression.

Finally, the conclusion attempts to draw together the various threads of the chapter, weaving together the role that sexual activity plays in our search for ourselves through others: the 'singular universal' in our encounter with the paradox of authenticity.

Authenticity and bad faith

The Sartrean concept of 'bad faith' appears early in *Being and Nothingness* (1943/1956), suggesting that for the author it was a precursory concept, one that was necessary for the coherence of much of what follows.[2] The

---

[2]. See Sartre (1956: 47–70). See also Weber (2011) for a discussion of this theme and an elaboration of the concept of bad faith and the conceptual link to that other well-known Sartrean notion of 'the look'. Weber also demonstrates implicitly an ethical basis for authenticity. A clear and helpful analysis of 'Bad Faith' is provided by Morris (2008, Ch. 4).

term 'bad faith' describes a condition whereby we live in denial of our 'true nature', and our essential freedom. However much he qualified the scope of human freedom in his later years (as exemplified by the opening quote of this chapter), a central feature of Sartre's existential philosophy is that humans are essentially free beings. There is always room for manoeuvre, a possibility of choice, no matter how constrained or circumscribed the context. It follows that our (intentional) actions carry with them responsibility, since it is ourselves both within, and outside of, awareness that choose among alternatives. Bad faith ensues when we deny that choice, and therefore choose not to accept the responsibility (and uncertainty) that goes with our choosing. We act as though we are a determined object, a confusion of transcendence and facticity (Rae, 2009; Weber, 2011). The expression also applies when we deny the choices of others, when we see the other as an object, rather than another subject, free to choose as we are.

There are well-known descriptions of bad faith in Sartre's work, but underlying them all is the absence of a god, or a moral authority: take this away and we have no guiding principle for choice (the moral dilemma that inhabits Western culture). The word 'faith' in the expression is important in this respect. 'Faith' implies belief in the absence of proof, and belief always entails an element of doubt, of uncertainty. But, as suggested above, to be human is to be uncertain of our existence, but this is hard to live with, hard to accept. It is easier to deny the uncertainty of who we are, of our existence and therefore our choices, so that we can avoid the responsibility of our freedom. 'Good faith' then, would be a (pre-reflective) acceptance of the indefinable and unrealisable nature of self, of constant ambiguity, of the uncertainty that choice brings.

For Heidegger, the word 'authenticity' implies the notion of 'becoming one's possibilities'. Losing sight of these, taking what might appear as an easier option meant 'falling' into inauthenticity, into the 'they'. In Sartre's work this same notion is developed in his discussion of bad faith, with the latter providing an elaborated understanding of inauthentic choice. Our choices and actions are embedded in a network of 'projects'. We project towards the future in our freedom, with each choice potentially congruent or incongruent with what he describes as our 'fundamental (or original) project'. That congruency in turn describes our potential for authenticity or bad faith.

Sartre coined the term 'fundamental project' to describe the expression of an authentic sense of self, and recognised the impossibility of knowing this in an objective, concrete sense. It is a sense of ourselves that we both hold and strive towards. It most of all reflects our 'desire for being'. It is a reflection of our values and is a notion, I suggest, that we carry with us as a pre-reflective, pre-cognitive sense of who we are in the world. We 'feel' through our bodies this sense of who we are (Mirvish, 1992; Mirvish & Rechtin, 1999; Morris, 2008; Wider, 1997). It underpins also our sense of authenticity. Whether we form, early in our lives, a sense of ourselves and our destiny that describes this, or whether it is more appropriately perceived as a more dynamic concept is less relevant here, what matters is that such attempts to frame a self-concept are fundamental to our sense of 'being-in-the-world' (Borchers, 2005; Jopling, 1992).

The fundamental project, however, is not a static position or state of nature, rather it is a 'totalised' expression of our non-reflective consciousness: a dynamic entity, but still one that reveals 'the original choice of our being'; one that provides the framework for our being-in-the-world. But each network of projects, and our fundamental project, are premised on the realisation of 'self', of knowing oneself in terms of an objectivity. Each project is therefore unrealisable. To act in denial of that is to act in bad faith, to be inauthentic. To be authentic, for Sartre therefore, is to be 'in despair'; to be accepting of the failure of realising what is intended by our actions, but nevertheless to act or choose regardless of this acceptance (Sartre, 1940/1984). Sartre talks of the 'despair' of authenticity in his *War Diaries* (Sartre 1940/1984), notes which are reminiscent of his later work on 'being for others' and 'bad faith', and also foreshadow his concerns with regard to love and relations between individuals in the *Notebooks for an Ethics* (Sartre, 1992).

Underlying this analysis of authenticity, therefore, is a sense (or denial) of what it entails to be a self. To elaborate this point: in the development of each and every one of us we become aware of a world that is separate from ourselves. This becoming aware creates a distance between ourselves and other entities in the world, both in a particular and a general sense. Precisely when this awareness kindles and grows is controversial, but how we handle this emerging and developing sense of separateness may be the most significant characteristic of each human life, outside of the context within which that life is played out.

One consequence of this sense of separateness concerns how well it is received. We may find this state too threatening, too uncertain and unsafe, and seek to overcome this portending isolation through merger with the world, with the group, or with another. There are many ways we may attempt to achieve union with the world: we may seek to merge into the background, and live our lives in the shadows of existence where uncertainties are minimised. One manifestation of this may be the desire to be 'at one with nature', to be absorbed by the natural forces that surround us, free from the uncertainty of human relationships, which appear more threatening than the apparently random vagaries of nature.

Alternatively, we may seek to shelter in the social, to avoid standing out, to be anonymous in the security of conformity. More particularly, we may take refuge in the group: class, ethnicity, kinship or family provide the 'safe place' or nest through which we try to escape our aloneness and view the world from the secure base of mutually agreed and reinforced rules of engagement, a relative anonymity, a refuge within a social and economic capsule masked by a veneer of cultural distinction, the diminution of the other, of the separate, through collective association (Sartre, 1940/1984). The reciprocal nature of our interactions with the 'world' in which we find ourselves is the underlying theme of Sartre's *Critique of Dialectical Reason* (Sartre, 1960/2004), which provides the theoretical underpinning for later themes in this chapter.

As individuals there is also a strong desire to escape from the sense of isolation that comes with separateness. Through our relations with others we find solace from the overwhelming sense of uncertainty that our separateness brings. While it is through these relations that we first come to know our separateness, and through which we constantly seek to construct a more concrete sense of our separate selves, it is through them also that we seek to escape from the tyranny of aloneness. We desire 'closeness' to others in order to escape from both the threat of others and from ourselves. The greater the degree of 'closeness' the more possible this escape appears. But of course this desire for 'escape' is paradoxical. The 'other' represents at the same time a vehicle of escape from our isolation, from a sense of self, as well as the means through which we seek to know and construct this sense of self through difference.

Awareness of others, therefore, brings with it a paradox of seeking to find what we are simultaneously seeking to avoid. In our relations with others we are seeking to know ourselves, to grasp our subjectivity as object through experiencing ourselves as the object of an other's perception. But what is it we are seeking to grasp? And what is the intentionality behind such seeking. The dilemma of the self-construct is well documented; the existential tradition has ably demonstrated the impossible goal of self-knowledge that we are constantly striving for, a goal only realisable in death; but why is this goal so important to us?

To grasp our subjective sense of who we are and concretise or objectify this sense, implies we know who we are, we are certain of our selves. This sense of certainty implies knowledge of how to be in the world; since I am that, I cannot be any other way. I can accept myself as that, and be accepted as that by others. If I do not feel accepted as that, then I can change into something more acceptable; I can know my acceptability and can be in the world in a way that is certain and acceptable to those with whom I relate.

But, my subjectivity is not graspable, it is a subjective awareness that cannot be an object, and to grasp it through the subjectivity of another is impossible because that would mean appropriating the other's subjectivity. Without being the other, I am not able to do this. So I remain uncertain of my 'self' and of my acceptance by others, my being-in-the-world is characterised by uncertainty. This uncertainty that characterises my being-in-the-world, my existence, is the core of existential anxiety, and of being human. It is a relational anxiety, and we might try (at times) to escape it through eschewing human contact, possibly through immersion in the 'natural' or supposedly non-human world. We might also try to deny our uncertainty through assuming a spurious certainty derived from a contrived sense of self. Both of these forms of escape from, or denials of uncertainty, have been described as manifestations of inauthenticity or bad faith.

If uncertainty lies at the heart of existential anxiety, and if in seeking to reduce that uncertainty we look to others, to various ways of relating, to the use of others in attempts to give meaning to our lives, it may be that we seek intimacy. We seek a pre-cognitive sense of being known by, and knowing another. 'Intimacy': a common word in the therapy room, usually used in the context of unfulfilled desire, of a lack which can only be provided, it is imagined, through sex, or alternatively through the closeness that is implied in mutually enjoyed sex even, as in the case of friendship, when there is no sexual desire. So there are gradations of intimacy, and perhaps the potential, mutual self-revelation and the abandonment of self associated with sexual arousal and orgasm provide for many a sought-after archetype of intimacy. Certainly the frequency with which the words 'intimacy' and 'sex' are used interchangeably in the therapy room bears witness to the extent to which sexual activity is idealised as part of a search for intimacy, and perhaps from escaping from oneself, and that dark pit of existential uncertainty, through merger with another.

But it would be naïve to suggest that sexual desire is only about such a search for intimacy, even if that is often prominent amongst those in therapy. For many, existential anxiety, the uncertainty of self, takes a different route. For example, where relationships with humans are too threatening, too evoking of past pain or where the uncertainty of outcome is somehow unbearable. Here it is not intimacy that is sought through sex, but possession and control: a form of relationship, but one that is made 'safe' by denying the possibility of reciprocal awareness, of being known and 'seen'. The 'other' is perceived as a threat to one's own subjectivity: better to bear the pain of existential anxiety than to risk (or bear the uncertainty of) the greater pain of being known and shamed by others. It is possible to identify a wide range of sexual practices as being manifestations of such motivation, from the relatively harmless (for example, the practice of mutually agreed promiscuity or 'fuck buddies') to those that cause serious physical or psychological damage to others (such as rape or paedophilia).

The contingency of encounter and the origins of intimacy

Before exploring further the authenticity of our sexual responses to others, I will elaborate on the felt context of encounter that is the awareness of others. An awareness of being held in mind by another has been described by Sartre's account of 'the look'. Many commentators agree that Sartre's 'look', while a valuable and informative analysis, captures only one extreme end of the continuum of possible responses to an awareness of another. It is a response based on shame or on pride, both of which arise from a sense of being reduced to the object of the other's subjectivity. The other becomes, as a result, a threat, and a focus of competition and anxiety. There is a thread, in *Being and Nothingness*, from this initial encounter with the other to Sartre's analysis of sexual relations (and human relations in general) as being characterised by conflict, and expressed sexually through a combination of sadism and masochism.

The inadequacy of this analysis as a complete explanation of human relations is accepted, but it provides, nevertheless, a very powerful explanation of an aspect of these relations, and a useful basis for elaborating a less partial approach to what happens when we encounter another.[3] In addition, the physicality of 'the look' as portrayed by Sartre cannot be denied. The sense of shame can be appreciated physically as well as conceptually. The notion of being 'held in mind', of being present to another, whether encompassing a visual glance or an imagined presence, is perhaps first sensed in our

---

3. Martinot (2005) develops this theme with reference to the importance of dialogue, however Mirvish (2002), in an important article, summarises other commentators' contributions while adding his own invaluable commentary, drawing on Sartre's *Notebooks for an Ethics* as source of Sartre's attempts to deal with the possibility of non-conflictual relations (see also Mirvish, 1984). A further important contribution also drawing on the *Notebooks* comes from Anderson (1993).

bodies, or in our embodied pre-reflective consciousness, prior to becoming known through reflective consciousness. This is not to suggest a dichotomy between bodily (physical) senses and reflective (mental) consciousness, but to posit that, if there is no Cartesian split, we think with our entire bodies, not just with our brains (Johnson, 2007).

Introducing 'Jenny'

As an illustration of the varying possibilities of encounter, I introduce my patient Jenny, a young woman in her mid-twenties, presenting with severe depression and a history of suicide attempts. Although probably a beautiful young woman according to popular criteria, she loathed her body and felt her looks to be repellent to others. She was living increasingly as a recluse, and occasionally self-harmed. The origins of her predicament are not relevant here, although this was the main focus of our work together. In addition, though, we agreed that she would try to 'get out' of her room at least once each day, to go for a walk to the local park and back. Initially, she avoided eye contact with anyone on her walks. She described the felt sense of being seen by another as something she dreaded, something that would confirm her feeling of worthlessness. Slowly, however, she managed to exchange looks with people, and then gradually to greet some of the people she passed. Of course, many would pass her by without looking, but she noted that as she felt more able to engage in returning the glance of those who looked, she would consequently feel more at ease with herself, more attuned to 'being-in-the-world'. These walks, and the developing engagement, proved very important in her gradual acceptance, and letting go, of past embedded experiences. Perhaps the process was most captured by her description of a chance encounter as she set out on her walk one morning:

> I was crossing the road and this woman was coming the other way. I had never seen her before, but we looked at each other as we passed. Not for long, but perhaps for fractionally longer than usual. I felt her looking at me, and I knew she felt me looking at her. And it was all OK. That was all, and I went on to the park. I didn't see her again, and I am not sure I would recognise her if I did, but it meant something to me. I am not sure what, but it was like she was telling me it was OK to be me, and I was telling her it was OK to be her. Like we both knew that.
>
> (Jenny)

This was a very pivotal event for Jenny. Of course, it did not occur in isolation, it was not a sudden epiphany, but a chance encounter that occurred in the context of a process of opening out. But the significance of this glancing exchange bears more detailed scrutiny.

How we experience the presence of another is conditioned by the embodied (pre-reflective) consciousness that prevails in the context, and the sense, of the other, which is in turn conditioned by the embodied response of the other as (in this case) manifested in the fleeting gaze exchanged. With respect to Jenny, she found in the felt presence of the other woman something receiving and accepting that helped her to be more accepting of herself. The pre-reflective exchange of presence told a story of familiarity and comfort, a story of knowing and being known, a story of potential intimacy.

It was hard for Jenny to move to a place where she could experience not only a sense of shame and avoidance in the presence of another, but also potential acceptance. The potential reciprocity of acceptance was not overtly affirmed or stated, but was something that Jenny experienced in her felt sense of the other's look. Of course, in this instance it was only potential, but that was what was significant for her: the knowledge that there was potential for a reciprocal and accepting experience of knowing and being known, an exchange of subjectivities. What was also apparent in Jenny's story was that such a potential was contingent: the encounter of two people who possibly found in the glance they exchanged the potential for a shared world, a potential that existed as a result of the coming together of two receptive embodied consciousnesses.

In our encounter with the other we move on a continuum between shame and acceptance, between a retreat into withdrawal and fear, and a desire for intimacy. How we meet the other will be contingent on a felt response, which is in turn contingent on the proximities of two lives and the context in which they cross; a matrix of possibilities where individual choice, while constrained by past histories and current context, has a limited but significant part to play in the tapestry of a life. It is the choice between the possibility of defence, of retreating into the safe haven of isolation and certainty, and acceptance of the uncertain outcome of mutually conceived knowledge and merger. We are pulled in both directions: to retain the safety of separateness or to embrace the possibility of intimacy.

Being sexually: Sexual potential and sexual expression

This chapter has so far focused on drawing out the meaning of authenticity from an existential perspective, one that is contingent on our contact, our coming up against, the world that meets our perceptions. As sentient, meaning-making beings we seek ourselves most of all through our engagement with other sentient beings. At the same time, meaning arguably arises first as a sense, a pre-reflective presence that is only later interactive with language and reflection. We feel, and know it in our bodies before we 'understand' it in our discourse (with ourselves or others). It follows, therefore, that our first knowledge of ourselves is also part of that felt sense, the pre-reflective awareness that we carry constantly with us.

Given the ubiquitous presence of sexual concerns in the therapy room, however, it is pertinent to ask how sex fits into the equation. If we describe ourselves as 'beings with sexual potential', what does this mean and what are the implications of such a statement? Merleau-Ponty more than all existential philosophers described the intrinsic nature of sex in our relations with others. For him, our sense of presence was permeated by an awareness of sexual potential (Merleau-Ponty, 1962).

Sexual potential occupies a significant space in our physiology, our facticity. It is described by our anatomical distribution of erogenous zones and the chemical processes that express through hormonal activity the potential for sexual activity. Even though the fostering of our reproductive capacity may have been the evolutionary reason behind the development of these physiological characteristics, this bears little or no relation to sexual activity in human beings (see also Spinelli, Chapter 1, this volume). But this capacity, this scenario of sexual potential remains part of our bodies, part of our pre-reflective awareness that is as much a part of our sensory matrix as feeling and breathing, it evanesces (sometimes) from our pores. In this sense it is a characteristic that describes human existence, we exist sexually, sexual potential is an expression of our ontology. But, unlike breathing, the extent to which this potential remains nascent or latent varies considerably between individuals and with time and context. It is apparent that the strength of these chemical or physiological processes varies between individuals. Experiences in the therapy room provide ample evidence that some individuals seem disinterested in sex, while for others it is a major preoccupation. It is no doubt true that sexual activity can wane with age, and changes in the hormonal structure. The significant number of ageing men who bring to therapy the loss of interest in sexual activity from their partner following childbirth or menopause, and claim this as justification for infidelity, pornography or paying for sex, might appear to confirm age-old prejudices that men have greater, more diverse, and more persistent sexual interests than women. From this perspective sexual potential remains rooted in the physiological; there is no place here for the notion of potential and choice. But this is a sociocultural stereotype: there is always anecdotal evidence of unevenly waxing or waning of sexual interest within both male and female same-sex partnerships. In addition, it is not uncommon for gender roles to be the reverse of that described, where women's sexual interest is felt to be unmet by more passive and disinterested male partners. It may be true that hormonal activity reaches a peak early in life, and tends to decline thereafter, and sexual activity can be observed to follow this pattern. But it is always possible to cite cases where the pattern of sexual behaviour does not accord with the hormonal pattern; a sudden increase in sexual activity in the so-called 'mid-life' years is a frequent testament to this.

So while the physiological processes that engender sexual potential are a part of us, part of our facticity, the frequently observed departures from biological determinism suggest that we respond to our sexual potential in diverse and non-biological ways. We manifest a set of sexual preferences that appear to be rooted both beyond and within our bodies. How we use our sexual potential is much more complex than a mere reflection of physiological processes. The use of our sexual potential, our sexual expression, I suggest is an ontic expression, our way of 'being-in-the-world'. In a more formal sense, existence (or 'being') for humans implies sexual potential, a potential that is only known and understood through expression. A further characteristic of humans is that expression carries with it the inevitability of choice, even if that choice is constrained, as suggested in the opening quotation of this chapter.

Sex and authenticity

So how might the concept of bad faith assist in the understanding of sexual expression? In *Being and Nothingness* Sartre was very pessimistic about human relationships in general and sexual relationships in particular, suggesting them to be underpinned by conflict, with any possibility of reciprocal acceptance becoming unsustainable. This pessimistic analysis was prefaced by a discussion of the 'sense' or presence of the other described by 'the look': as discussed, a notion underpinned by the notion of bad faith, and inauthenticity.

Lack of intimacy is a very common subject in therapy; it highlights a lack, a sense of being made separate from, an absence of closeness. In the context of sexual relationships it reveals an unrequited desire for a sense of 'oneness' with another, for merger. These feelings described by three very different clients are symbolic of many.

Rosie, Ashley and Charlie: The search for intimacy

Rosie had suffered much and felt that no one could hear her story; the lack of intimacy in her sex life was a source of real distress: 'I want sex to be about creating an understanding through a complete knowing of each other; but for him it seems like it's a way of avoiding knowing me or himself, of avoiding being intimate with me.'

Ashley, a promiscuous, and impatient young man, sometimes consumed with guilt, told me he was looking for something in sex he couldn't seem to find: 'I want to be so close to someone, like I am inside their head, and them in mine ... I know it's not possible, but I want to be as close as I can get.'

Charlie, lonely in his middle-aged relationship: 'He is just so self-contained, so self-sufficient, there is no room for me ... and I want to reach out ... to share ... to be curious and open.'

The lack of authenticity in the sexual relationships described by these three clients is apparent. The sexual expression for each takes place in a context of bad faith: for two of them, Rosie and Charlie, there is no mutual acceptance of subjectivity with objectivity, their partners able to see them only as 'other'; Ashley, on the other hand, uses sex in his search for intimacy, but in so doing turns his sexual partners into objects, unsuspecting vehicles in his misguided search for himself.

These three clients are typical of many who bring sexual issues to therapy. The common element amongst them is the association of sex with intimacy, and the identification of a lack of intimacy with sexual dissatisfaction. This is not to say that a search for intimacy is the only driver in sexual expression, we are hormonal beings, but, as suggested above, we are also relational beings, and it is the search for intimacy, the discovery of self through another, that provides in the context of our physiology, the motivation for authentic sexual expression.

Of course, many clients manifest their sexual concerns around issues other than intimacy. I would argue, however, that these concerns almost always stem from the same source: the feelings of a lack of fulfilment, a lack of connection, that is engendered by a failure of sexual expression to provide a pathway to a sense of meaning, to a sense of ourselves that is in tune with our 'fundamental project'.

Perhaps sexual dysfunction is the most common presenting issue in this category. A typical example of which concerns men with erectile dysfunction brought about by an overwhelming desire to 'perform', to please or satisfy their partner, and a consequent fear of failure. The underlying sense is of themselves as objects, bodies-for-the-other. This sense is echoed in many women in therapy, who see themselves as 'frigid' and as failures because they are unable to enjoy sex, unable to be an object for the other. The emotional pain that is concomitant with both of these manifestations of bad faith is often severe.

That is not to say that sexual relations practised in bad faith necessarily cause levels of anxiety sufficient to bring people to therapy. Most manifestations are likely to go by unnoticed other than a sense of unease or lack of fulfilment. Frequently, such unease may lead to attempts at substitution; to other potential avenues of attachment be it alcohol or other drugs, various preoccupations with consumption, whether of food or materials, and often to a rejection of sex or intimacy as something either undesirable or unobtainable: a withdrawal behind the veils of safety and isolation. This may be accompanied by a retreat into the pursuit of sexual expression alone, often through the use of pornography or fetishes; surprising preferences are often disclosed in the therapy room.

The withdrawal from the possibility of intimacy, of good faith in sexual expression, is often accompanied by hostility towards the other, particularly the other as sexual object. Sexual promiscuity can be an example of the use of sex as a weapon (often an addictive one), although more often it displays a curiosity and search for something not recognised. More extreme displays of hostility, however, such as rape and sexual harassment reveal a deep fear and loathing of the 'other' or, in many contexts, of the 'stranger'. The case of Martin captures the way in which our experiences, our contingency, may render it difficult to either accept or know intimacy, yet seek it in impossible pathways using sexual activity as an expression of bad faith.

Martin's pain

Martin is in his late twenties. He works in 'marketing'; not a well-paid position he tells me, but 'it's enough to get by'. He told me how he had never felt 'safe' at home, and at school was bullied and 'always felt an outsider'. He was 'thin and scrawny', and 'didn't fit in'. 'I was a long-distance runner, not a team player.' He remembers adolescent sexual fantasies about other boys and 'came out' when he was 16: 'It felt like a reason and justification for being who I was.' After this he slowly began to feel better about himself, coming to terms with his gay identity. When he first came to therapy he had been living with his partner Will for three years, in what he describes as a 'loving relationship'. Although he had few real friends apart from Will, he was outwardly sociable; and exuded good looks and superficial charm.

Martin came to therapy after he had begun to visit gay clubs looking for casual sex. Will was often travelling for his work, and this provided Martin with an opportunity to explore what he described as his 'fantasies' in secret. While he became weighed down by guilt and self-dislike, he was also dependent on the challenge and thrill of 'seducing as many men as possible'. He had begun to feel that he was 'not doing his job', unless he was pursuing another sexual conquest. I had the impression that Martin was searching, in his promiscuity, for an intimacy that was lost. The perception developed of someone who wanted to be recognised and affirmed.

This was Martin's description of this part of his journey:

> It was an easy decision for me to accept myself as gay; it made sense of my life and somehow gave me an identity, a feeling that I was a whole person ... I always had this uneasy feeling that I was not good enough, that I never felt good enough, although I didn't know what for ... When I met Will it all seemed OK for a while, I could be myself and it was OK. But somehow, after a while, I began to feel trapped, like he didn't really know me ... I realised that something was still missing; and I felt I had to test the boundaries, to break out, to discover who I was, who I could be ... maybe it wasn't the best way to do this, but it seemed like a way, the only way I could find ... it was like searching for something without knowing what it was.

During therapy, Martin soon dropped what he describes as his 'cruising obsession', but remained melancholic and confused. Eventually he told his partner of his activities, and after a brief separation they reconciled.

I believe Martin's desire to continually 'seduce other men', to dominate them, stemmed from his distrust of intimacy and the paradoxical need to be affirmed and recognised. At the same time he knew that he was making himself unhappy, but felt unable to do anything about it. His sexual relations with Will had become quite infrequent as the trust between them eroded, and he increasingly sought solace and affirmation by sexually dominating others. His rupture and subsequent reconciliation with Will came after he had been able to recognise and 'let go' of his sense of distrust, and feel comfortable enough with himself to be open and accepting of both himself and others; he no longer needed to 'capture' others to make himself safe. He was able to explore the possibility of a more authentic relationship.

Moving beyond the individual: The singular universal

The analysis so far has focused on the individual and the paradox of authenticity in sexual relations that emerges in the individual's engagement with her world. This reflects Sartre's early thinking. In order to elucidate a rationale for the interaction between an individual and her world, however, I draw on the work of the later Sartre, the Sartre that attempted to integrate individualistic, post-Renaissance, Western Man, with the social perspective of twentieth-century Marxist political economy. A brief excursion here into a Sartrean dialectic clarifies this point. His later philosophical approach was premised on what he described as the regressive-progressive method.[4] This method is a way of perceiving human behaviour that considers the way in which individuals receive their experiences: a process first of 'interiorisation' that involves the absorption and expression of their world. Their 'world' in this case, or their facticity, embraces the totality of the social, cultural, physical and personal (relational) environments in which they reside at any particular moment. An experience is received and in some way held (interiorised). Individuals then respond to what is interiorised, interaction with their 'world' is both changed by the interiorisation and changes that world.

For Sartre, both these processes are dialectical processes. The dialectic implies a process of change through which interacting forces are changed by the encounter, each containing the influence of the other in a new synthesis. An experience of the 'world' changes, through absorption, the recipient, whose response changes in the same way the 'world' within which she is situated.

---

4. This approach encapsulates Sartre's later work, from the *Critique of Dialectical Reason* to *The Family Idiot*. It is outlined in the *Search for a Method* (Sartre, 1968). The dialectic is a central component of his later work, most elaborately discussed in Sartre (2004). Very useful discussions of this can be found in Catalano (1986) and Morris (2008), while Ally (2010) provides a synthesis of Sartre's unpublished or unfinished works that demonstrate the significance of this method.

I have discussed the encounter with the other in terms of responses to a pre-reflective, embodied felt sense; that the idea of an embodied mind carries with it the cognitive consequences of physiological data. While we are feeling and reflective beings, we are also a series of chemical processes. Embodiment implies that we are a totality of emotional, cognitive and physiological processes that are interacting dialectically and constantly, to produce the constantly changing entity we manifest at each moment in time.

Referring back to the process of interiorisation, our embodiment implies that our encounters with another contain the potential for chemical (or hormonal) responses that may influence that encounter. But this is merely potential, and the extent to which these sexual responses are present will depend on the elements of the encounter. The encounter that Jenny experienced crossing the road did not (as far as we know) elicit any sexual response, but it still contained the potential for such a response. The look of the stranger was interiorised and responded to. A process occurred that changed her interaction with her world.

This rationale describes the manner in which an individual experiences the world in context, albeit a constantly changing one. That context is described by the sum of the economic, cultural, and natural environments that obtain at any point in time. The being that experiences that world is an embodied mind that has potential, a latency described by genes and physiology. Part of that latency is sexual potential, the hormonal resonance that occupies our bodies. The experience of 'being-in-the-world' is, on one level, a totalisation, an interaction of interior and exterior worlds that is only what it is, and what Sartre describes as the 'practico-inert'. Our 'being sexually in the world', therefore, is at any moment a totalisation, a particular configuration, and an expression of our sexual potential.

There are several dimensions to this 'sexual potential'. An interior dimension describes the way in which we feel our sexual potential at any point in time. We have a sense of our 'sexualness' that is a part of our pre-reflective, pre-cognitive, intuitive state of being: part of our overall sense of ourselves that is manifest in our 'project' or authentic way of being-in-the-world. But the interior is not a given, or a fixed entity, rather it might be seen as a continuing or resonating interaction of the felt sense and the parameters of that felt sense, a constant dialogue between feeling and that which feels. This might be described as an interaction between facticity and preconscious awareness, but these expressions imply a separateness which is not intended.

An exterior dimension describes the world in which the interior exists, and there are many aspects to that which are external to the being that is in the world; all manifestations of that which is other, or separate from the individual entity fall into this category. In terms of our sexual potential: this will, of course, be influenced by cultural norms and prejudices, social expedient and economic necessity. For example, heterosexual women, lesbians and gay men might express their sexual potential very differently in twenty-first-century Western societies than in many other contemporary societies or Western cultures of 100 years ago. This is not to say, for example, that people feel more 'free' in current urban Western societies than in, say, an isolated rural community in North Africa, merely that cultural and social norms born of perceived economic necessity provide the parameters within which people feel, and choose to express themselves sexually. There are countless examples of how major changes in economic circumstance influence acceptable sexual behaviour, although not, of course, in a straightforward and linear pattern, but rather in response to, and in concert with, a complex socioeconomic dialectic.

We are, at any moment, a totalisation of these interior and exterior forces. We live in a context which permeates us through a dialectical interaction, so that there is always movement. Our interior potential, born of what we are given and what we make of it, meets and is met by the exterior. This implies that our physicality in all its manifestations, together with our life experience, forms a potential that is, in turn, shaped and expressed through interaction with the social, cultural and physical environment that constitutes our exterior; in a relationship that is always reciprocal, although the degree of reciprocity is often unseen.

Sartre described this contextualised individual as a 'singular universal' (Sartre, 1981). Each individual expresses the universal, epochal energies of their time, but by interiorising also changes them in that process. We are individuals moulded by, and in turn moulding (albeit usually unseen and unsung) a constantly interacting array of social and economic contingencies and histories. Our sexual behaviour, our perceptions, preferences and choices, is an expression of this 'singular universal'.

The concept of totalisation allows a broader interpretation of the notion of the fundamental project. Nevertheless, the original construct arising from our 'desire for being' is helpful in framing a notion of our 'sexual potential'. The latter manifests as an expression of that construct, an immanence of sexual presence. But this implies that our sexual disposition is engendered not only from the interior manifestation of this being, but also from our exterior. Our felt sense of our sexual selves, the choices and desires that ensue, are always to an extent a reflection of the contexts in which we live and have lived.

Sexual expression and social expression

By the term 'sexual expression' I refer not only to choices regarding sexuality, but also how, within those broad choices, preferences and fantasies are felt and sometimes practised through actions. As a therapist I am aware that such 'expressions' are sometimes highly individual, so much so that it would not be possible to relate them here without loss of confidentiality. Most often they are commonplace and adhere to specific cultural perceptions of 'normality'. But always the manifestations are current felt responses to the myriad of individual and social influences described.

It is apparent that the later Sartre defined the self-construct as a broader entity than in his earlier work, one with more dynamic potential. 'Praxis' describes not only action, but also a capacity to challenge; to move beyond the accepted order or social configuration (the practico-inert) if that is in conflict with the felt sense of the fundamental project. In terms of sexual behaviour this might manifest in the struggle to express the (interiorised) felt sense of a sexual proclivity that runs counter to socially accepted behaviour. For example, Western societies witnessed a struggle for the social acceptance of male same-sex relationships over the latter half of the twentieth century, a challenge to the pervasive order that is now open, but still ongoing in such societies. In other sociocultural contexts this struggle is currently becoming increasingly dangerous and difficult as it contends with the rise of religious conservatism. One can make links here between the efficacy of that challenge and the stability of socioeconomic conditions: in periods of relative certainty the social acceptance of changes in individual expression is greater, difference is more easily countenanced. Uncertainty spawns fear of the 'other' and behaviour that is conceived as 'other'. The de facto social conservatism of the 'revolutionary' movements of the twentieth century are witness to this, in spite of rhetoric that sometimes ran counter to such conservatism.

This is not to make a moral statement, for example to the effect that the relative social acceptance of a variety of sexual expression is desirable, although from my own particular sociocultural perspective this might be the case. Nor is it relevant here to ask the question 'why now?', although this itself might be a fruitful line of investigation. The point here is that the manifestation of our 'desire for being sexually' is subject to an external as well as an internal dynamic, and that the configuration of such a totalisation has its own dynamic which may or may not result in conflict with the status quo. Those responsible for changes in social perceptions are forced to challenge the status quo, often at considerable risk to their social and economic wellbeing, as the following anecdote illustrates.

Mishra's pathway to self-discovery

Mishra was a visiting lecturer at an art college. She was in England for two years and came to therapy with me during the second of those years. She is from a non-Western culture, born into a relatively privileged family; in studying art she had rebelled against her family tradition. She has two elder siblings, one a lawyer and the other a medical doctor. She was married at the time of her therapy (her husband was also a lawyer); they would visit each other every three months.

She initially came to see me on account of what she described as 'cultural confusion': she found life in England intriguing and in many ways rewarding, but it posed challenges in terms of her sense of who she felt herself to be. Essentially, her self-construct was being questioned, as she increasingly challenged her perceptions of how, as a woman, she might live her life. During the therapy she began a sexual relationship with a colleague. Her sexual activity became a major theme of our discussions, which she described as part of her 'journey of self-discovery'.

Shortly after a visit from her husband she described her responses to sex:

> Sex with her husband: 'It felt like he was trying so hard to please me, I couldn't forget about myself, or him, I felt trapped in myself, I couldn't lose myself.'

> Sex with her lover: 'Feeling open, feeling passion and spontaneity, like there are no barriers, no walls between us, technique doesn't matter, I just go somewhere else.'

During the time of her therapy, Mishra broke off the relationship with her colleague. She confronted her husband with her experiences and they agreed on a trial period of reconciliation on her return, during which time she would attempt to discover how she might find an authentic expression of herself within the cultural constraints of her home. Mishra was already challenging the 'practico-inert', the status quo of her cultural context, through her decision to pursue a career in art, and to travel abroad. Her sense of the 'bad faith' of her lifestyle was apparent to her prior to her visit. In her search for authenticity she accepted the uncertainty of outcome. She openly used sex as a vehicle to lose herself, in order to rediscover herself. This was not a premeditated, reflective act; her body took her there. Through her sexual expression she began to know herself anew, to know the person who has always rebelled, who had felt uncomfortable with the perceived cultural constraints placed on her way of 'being-in-the-world'; she sought and found the intimacy of merger in order to discover the possibility of authenticity, but to do so she felt compelled to challenge the social context that she was born into, and its way of being sexually. Her sexual expression became a pathway for her for the potential for greater self-knowledge and more authentic ways of relating.

Conclusion: The singular universal and the paradox of bad faith

In this chapter I have tried to chart a course from the individual and her relationship with the 'other' to the wider context within which that individual exists, and show how the former interacts with the latter in a continual dialectic. In this I have followed the trajectory of Sartre's thinking, moving from the individualism of his early work, to the more socially aware and integrating approach of the later writings. The discussion of authenticity and awareness of the 'other' owes much to his labours in searching for an ethical basis for human behaviour, and the paradoxical result that we can never find one, but are condemned to search.

So too with sex; if we are embodied minds, if we think with our bodies as a whole and not just with our brains then, given our physiological nature, our sexual potential is a part of that search. Sex is one means through which we seek to find ourselves through others. But we are not entirely free agents in this pursuit: the quotation at the beginning of this chapter highlights our social nature; that we are creatures of our worlds, and respond to this in a constant dynamic. It is within this process that any freedom in sexual expression arises. We are never original, only sometimes brave.

But this rather pessimistic note should not detract from the main theme of this chapter: sexual potential is available to us as a conduit for self-discovery, as beings who are sexual and who can, if we choose, express our search to know ourselves through our sexual expression. But this search is paradoxical; we cannot know ourselves as an object with its sense of certainty, we can only have a sense of this construct, a sense that is defined through that which gives meaning to our lives. But this seldom seems enough, it is too uncertain; and so we seek for the unobtainable; our existential paradox.

Sexual potential and the way we express it becomes part of this 'pursuit of ourselves'; the expression varies with our physiology, our experiences, and our social and historical context, but it is always part of that pursuit of meaning. But it can be very hard to be active in that quest and not to fall into bad faith; not to 'look' at the 'other' as object, or feel and act as an object for the other; vehicles in the games of others. It is inappropriate, though, to speak of inauthentic or authentic sex, as though the act itself had an existence independent of our 'being'. That would imply a moral judgement, an escape from the paradox, as though there were moral rules governing sexual behaviour. We can say only that, in the act of sex, we act in good faith, or not. Furthermore, to be authentic in that act, as in any other act, I believe as an existential psychotherapist, creates the possibility of feeling more comfortable in the world.

What feels comfortable in sex is not just 'in our genes', or in our conditioning, or even in the result of past images and experiences, but in all of these, all combining in an unfinished dance of our sexual dialectic. The last word belongs to Sartre …

> For a man is never an individual; it would be more fitting to call him a universal singular. Summed up and for this reason universalized by his epoch, he in turn resumes it by reproducing himself in it as singularity.
>
> (Sartre, 1981, pp. ix)

References

Ally, M (2010) Sartre's integrative method: Description, dialectics and praxis. *Sartre Studies International, 16*(2), 48–74.

Anderson, T (1993) *Sartre's Two Ethics: From authenticity to integral humanity.* Chicago: Open Court Publishing.

Borchers, S (2005) Revamping Sartre's original project: Freedom's narcissistic wound. *Journal of Phenomenological Psychology, 36*(1), 1–19.

Catalano, J (1986) *A Commentary on Jean-Paul Sartre's Critique of Dialectical Reason.* Chicago: University of Chicago Press.

Catalano, J (2005) Sartre's ontology from *Being and Nothingness* to *The Family Idiot. Sartre Studies International, 11*(1&2), 17–30.

Johnson, M (2007) *The Meaning of the Body: Aesthetics of human understanding.* Chicago: University of Chicago Press.

Jopling, D (1992) Sartre's moral psychology. In C Howells (Ed) *The Cambridge Companion to Sartre* (pp. 103–39). Cambridge: Cambridge University Press.

Martinot, S (2005) The Sartrean account of the look as a theory of dialogue. In A van den Hoven & A Leak (Eds) *Sartre Today: A centenary celebration* (pp. 43-61). Oxford: Berghahn Books.

Merleau-Ponty, M (1962) *Phenomenology of Perception.* London: Routledge & Kegan Paul.

Mirvish, A (1984) Sartre, hodological space and others. *Research in Phenomenology, 14*(1), 149–73.

Mirvish, A (1992) Sartre, existential psychoanalysis and the nature of neurosis. *Bulletin de la Société Américaine de Philosophie de Langue Française, 4*(2&3), 112–130.

Mirvish, A (2002) Sartre on the ego, friendship and conflict. *Continental Philosophy Review, 35*(2), 185–205.

Mirvish, A & Rechtin, A (1999) Sartre and Kohut: Existential and self-psychological approaches to the phenomenon of conflict. *Journal of Phenomenological Psychology and Psychiatry, 30*(1), 48–65.

Morris, K (2008) *Sartre.* Oxford: Blackwell.

Rae, G (2009) Sartre and the Other: Conflict, conversion, language and the We. *Sartre Studies International, 15*(2), 54–77.

Sartre, J-P (1956) *Being and Nothingness: An essay on phenomenological ontology.* New York: Philosophy Library. (First published 1943)

Sartre, J-P (1968) *The Search for a Method.* New York: Vintage Books.

Sartre, J-P (1981) *The Family Idiot, Gustave Flaubert, 1821–1857: Volume 1.* London: University of Chicago Press.

Sartre, J-P (1984) *War Diaries.* New York: Verso. (First published 1940)

Sartre, J-P (1992) *Notebooks for an Ethics.* Chicago: University of Chicago Press.

Sartre, J-P (2004) *Critique of Dialectical Reason: Volume 1.* London: Verso. (First published 1960)

Sartre, J-P (2008) *Between Existentialism and Marxism.* London: Verso. (First published 1974)

Weber, J (2011) Bad faith and the Other. In J Weber (Ed) *Reading Sartre: On phenomenology and existentialism* (pp. 180–94). London: Routledge.

Wider, K (1997) *The Bodily Nature of Consciousness.* Ithaca, NY: Cornell University Press.

Part 3

A Gay Essence?

5

The Freedom to Be Fixed: Can I be a homosexual please?

– Dr Marc Medina –

> To be human is to be both free and unfree ... *because* real freedom is limited; *because* limited freedom is real.
> (Kurtz, 1982: 74)

> What is particularly important is that when we say that sexuality has an existential significance or that it expresses existence, this is not to be understood as meaning that the sexual drama is in the last analysis *only* a manifestation or a symptom of the existential drama.
> (Merleau-Ponty, 1962: 166)

> Same sex attraction feels eternal and lasts a lifetime. There is nothing momentary about the sense that being gay is something that has always been a part of us and will remain integral.
> (Tatchell, 1996: 35)

As existential psychotherapists we focus our attention on entering the client's world, to be there in the 'as-if' dimension whilst always retaining a mindfulness of being the other. Phenomenological inquiry, epoché and horizontalisation help us grasp the relevance a client attaches to their experience of Dasein. A key aspect of this approach to therapy is the joining with our clients as they embark upon a search for meaning and seek fundamental truths about themselves, whilst finding the courage and fortitude to think independently about their life and make changes that reflect their own worldview, and take account of the fundamental givens of their lives and of the world in which they live. The sanctity of the individual is fundamental and is at the heart of the work of Husserl, Kierkegaard and Nietzsche and indeed to a greater or lesser extent all subsequent existential philosophers, writers and practitioners. Prising psychotherapy away from the overarching dogmas of twentieth-century psychoanalytic and behaviourist thought has characterised the development of existential psychotherapy and seen its status and popularity grow. Van Deurzen-Smith warns against dogmas that 'monopolise claims to the truth' and points to the need for courage to stand against 'the domineering attitude of some psychoanalysts and other consecrated psychotherapists' (van Deurzen-Smith, 1997: 2). It is because of this heritage and to protect this heritage, that alternate perspectives and creative tensions within the existential tradition are both necessary and beneficial.

Whilst the body of literature that supports the practice of existential psychotherapy is constantly being added to, there is always the attendant risk, even for existentialists, that we become overly concerned with providing a too-concrete or a too-comprehensive theoretical model of how existential precepts relate to who we are and the way we live. This valiant attempt to 'cover all bases' could in certain circumstances lead us as practitioners to become abstracted from the client's deeply felt lived experience as has indeed been the case in other theoretical approaches. Our tentative formulations about aspects of our existence as human beings should therefore ultimately emanate from the experience we gain through being with our clients as they struggle to find meaning in the individual, relational and spiritual dimensions of their lives.

It is against this backdrop that this chapter will critically review some of the key contributions made towards an existential view of human sexuality and specifically same-sex sexuality, with particular reference to the link between theory and practice, abstracted thought and individual experience and self-derived and culturally imposed aspects of identity. Some new ways of conceptualising an existential approach to same-sex attraction that distinguishes between fixedness and stuckness, sedimentation and being securely situated, and real freedom and hypothesised potentiality will also be suggested. First, this new perspective will be shown to be fundamentally existential, in that it is primarily concerned with human freedom and second, phenomenological, in that it gives primacy to the embodied and lived experience of many lesbians and gay men who are now living, especially in this country, in a period of increasing acceptance. This 'post-liberationist' era requires us to revisit the relevance and usefulness of relying too heavily on deconstructionist theories and further, to dare to ask the question as to whether or not these theories of same-sex sexuality that seek to champion the individual, in practice, specifically psychotherapeutic practice, end up paradoxically marginalising and alienating the individual in a pious and ironic attempt to fit them into an alternative cultural edifice.

Theoretical dilemmas

It is arguably the case that there is no aspect of human behaviour that has provoked more thought, debate and literature than the sexual aspect of our existence. It is understandable therefore that many of the contributors to the modern existential-phenomenological psychotherapeutic tradition have made the observation that this area has been 'strangely neglected' (Cohn, 1997: 89), 'barely been explored' (Smith-Pickard & Swynnerton, 2005: 50) or has invoked 'some degree of hesitation' (Spinelli, 1997: 2).

This hesitation has likely emanated from the fact that at first glance sexuality, that is, the factors that affect our choices as sexual beings and why we may be attracted to same-sex, opposite-sex or partners of both sexes, could conceivably cause a problem for existential thinking. The idea that an individual may experience their sexual preference as a natural given and furthermore something that has always been and will always be fixed might seem problematic for the existential approach, as some would say that it challenges the Sartrean idea of existence preceding essence, the Heideggerian principle of Dasein and Merleau-Ponty's belief that sexuality never functions as an autonomous physiological mechanism. There are two important points to note here. First, it is by no means clear that these thinkers did not, and in the light of recent research would not, allow sexuality (in terms of same sex, opposite sex or attraction to both sexes) for many individuals to be afforded the status of an existential 'given' in a similar way to male and female body forms, that is, with respect to gender attraction, sexuality for these individuals is not experienced as elastic. Therefore whilst appetites may change, for example, saying, 'I fancied him one day but not the next', this does not in fact extend to saying 'and the following day I fancied her'.

Second, it seems that an existentialist view of same-sex sexuality does not appear to accept the self-identification of a client as always having been gay or straight; this is problematic as it is unphenomenological and ultimately a problem for existential thinking and teaching and not the individual.

Discussion of human sexuality within the existential paradigm also requires a clarification of the ontic and the ontological, and more specifically the connection between the two, when theorising about same-sex attraction, opposite-sex attraction and attraction to both sexes. When we talk about the possibilities and givens of being (ontological) we do so to both enhance and reflect the range of individual lived experience and human potentiality (ontic). It is therefore of central importance that ontological theorising does not 'speak from nowhere' in the area of human sexuality and thereby avoids hovering in an intellectual or theoretical vacuum. In other words, ideas about the structure and possibility of our being-in-the-world sexually must be informed by, connected to, and evidenced in, the individual's lived experience and in this case should definitely not ignore or preclude the idea of an individual's fixed sexual attraction to one or other or both genders.

It is of primary importance that we meet the human being that is actually 'there' and join with them as they explore the meaning that they attach to their deeply felt sexual preference both as an embodied self and as a fundamental experience of Dasein. How each individual relates to the concept of their own selfhood is ultimately significant and more specifically where they perceive the levers of control to be in coming to terms with who they are, who they have been and who they want to become. This meaning must always be the client's alone and we should therefore guard against the adoption of a theoretical frame, however loose, that encourages us to interpret or intertwine the purity of the client's experience with the notion of the plasticity of sexuality for all, which is in reality the possibility of bisexuality or asexuality for some.

It would be easy to be distracted by the reality that the personal struggle of many clients attempting to come to terms with their same-sex sexuality may on the surface appear to have marked similarities in emotional, physical and spiritual terms. The idea that to some extent there is a shared experience of being gay, especially when 'coming out', is just as plausible as the idea that there are aspects of being male or female that are shared, especially if we begin to view homosexuality as having the qualities of an existential given that may in the near future be proved to have some biological reality (Långström et al, 2010; Savic, Berglund & Lindström, 2005). This does not however constitute being swamped by the 'they' (Heidegger, 1927/1962) or sanctioning a determinism to being-in-the-world homosexually. As du Plock reminds us:

> Much of the value of being gay is the way in which it provides a space which each individual can invest with a different meaning. One of the joys and challenges of being gay is the opportunity such an identification provides for inventing oneself.
>
> (du Plock, 1997: 62–3)

It is certainly true that for many lesbians and gay men, the significance they attach to what they feel to be the innateness of their sexuality contributes to an enhanced sense of self and in turn offers the potential to contribute towards but not totally dominate their sense of personal and social identity. As Ellis puts it, 'our sexuality is both all pervading, deep rooted, permanent, and the last resort of our individuality and humanity' (Ellis, 1946: 3).

The self therefore is never complete but is and should be multifaceted, containing different surfaces and having different levels, and it is therefore in the capacity of self that we can speak of the real self or of there being a self. As such, the self is always moving between different contexts and the imperative of Being-in-the-world sexually becomes to engage authentically both inwardly and outwardly in daily living. It is a lack of authentic engagement with the world that is often the cause of distress for clients who seek help in coming to terms with same-sex attraction, which for many feels total and not in any way partial. Working existentially with these clients becomes about helping them establish an inner congruence and centredness, through acceptance of something that they have always felt, as they initially 'come out' to themselves and work out what their same-sex sexual attraction means to them uniquely. The challenge for these clients then often involves overcoming feelings of fear and shame by increasing their capacity to relate authentically with significant others in their lives and then others in general.

Van Deurzen asserts that clients engaging in existential therapy should be encouraged to manage the paradoxes of life in a creative and dynamic fashion and that 'freedom is only initiated once boundaries have been explored' (van Deurzen, 2002: 18). Kurtz (1982) views the concept of human finitude and essential limitation as the presence of the 'not' in the very being of any human individual and describes this as the first existential insight. Hence, by coming to terms with a sense of fixedness or givenness in the arena of sexual attraction the individual in turn paradoxically becomes unstuck and free to explore their sexual selves in more fruitful and meaningful ways. It is against this backdrop that we are able to review recent contributions to existential theorising on homosexuality and assess the implications of turning theory into practice – of using this thinking to teach existential psychotherapy students about working with clients who experience their sexuality as innate, fundamental, fixed or given.

Recent contributions

Prior to the publication of this book, in which some of his views may have been updated, the most comprehensive effort to summarise the existential perspective on same-sex sexuality has come from Ernesto Spinelli in his lecture and subsequent article 'Some hurried notes ... towards an existential phenomenological theory of human sexuality' (Spinelli, 1997: 4). He begins by rightly criticising the Victorian sexologists who took as their principle arena of investigation the 'medico-forensic study of abnormal sexuality' (Spinelli, 1997: 5), where the link between biology and sexuality was the fundamental assumption. It is certainly true that the sexological endeavour was fraught with prejudice, cultural assumption and biological guesswork, but it would be wrong to use such criticisms to ignore the possibility of a fixed form of sexuality. The example of same-sex sexuality is useful here as its exploration and categorisation was central to the sexological project. It is tempting to assume that this effort to categorise had the effect of creating the 'homosexual' and providing such individuals with a ready-made identity, an issue that will be addressed below, but the important point here is that the role of sexology may in fact have been to reflect rather create. The practice of sex between people of the same sex appears throughout history and there is much evidence to suggest that sexologists produced their definitions to 'understand a phenomenon which was appearing before their eyes' (Weeks, 1985: 93), in other words something that was already there. These were men and women who, despite the times and because of the times, were starting to outwardly express their deeply felt sexual desires.

Spinelli goes on to criticise Freud's view as expressed in his *Three Essays on the Theory of Sexuality* (1905/1958) but ultimately for the wrong reason. Freud's view of the abnormality of same-sex sexual acts was clearly wrong as Spinelli suggests, but the central thrust of Freud's developmental theory, that of a polymorphous sexuality and the idea that we are all born with an 'unmistakeably bisexual disposition' (Freud, 1930: 105–6) is tacitly accepted. Hans Cohn also admits that 'Freud is much nearer to a phenomenological view of sexual difference' (Cohn, 1997: 93). There is of course no substantive evidence for Freud's assumptions but plenty of evidence of individuals who experience their same-sex sexuality and heterosexuality as fixed as well as some who identify as bisexual.

In the end it is the individual's experience that is key and the phenomenological approach must deal solely with the phenomenon that our clients actually present, not an abstracted idea about the universality of bisexuality. Spinelli re-states Kierkegaard's injunction that as conscious beings we have outgrown the immediate domination of drives and instincts (Kierkegaard, 1969) and goes on to say that our desire to engage in sexual activities is not solely dictated by biology. It may well be true that we can master our desires and in the instance of same-sex sexuality many have had to do just that down the ages but this does not mean that those desires have not always been there. Furthermore, in the case of homosexuality, why would the individual want to 'master' these drives and instincts if he felt them to be an authentic expression of his true self? Whilst it would be wrong to exclusively equate biology and sexual destiny, it would be similarly misguided to rule out any biological formulation to same-sex sexuality, not least because such a formulation would only serve to confirm something many gay people have always deeply felt. An existential approach to homosexuality should therefore not stand or fall on the biological link that looks increasingly likely to be proven. Such a link does not mean that as lesbians and gay men we have lost control of our lived experience or that the individual has sidestepped the need to choose, create and face the fear of freedom that his or her very existence presents – it is the way we respond to the givens of our personal world that ultimately defines us as human beings.

Spinelli correctly makes the point that sexuality is not solely linked to the instinct to reproduce but then, without any further evidence, draws the conclusion that any connection to biological imperatives is therefore undermined, 'instead it places sexuality firmly in the arena of inter-relational being' (Spinelli, 1997: 8). He suggests, 'it is a sublime expression of each being's active desire to establish and engage with a relational presence between self and other' (Spinelli, 1997: 8). What Spinelli appears not to appreciate is that for many of us the relational dimension to sexual attraction is informed with a prior sense of attraction to same-sex, opposite-sex or partners of both sexes. It is still true nonetheless that it is precisely in the nuances of our experience of a specific other that attraction develops and the sexual dimension reveals itself.

Hans Cohn in his chapter 'Being-in-the-world sexually' in *Existential Thought and Therapeutic Practice* (1997, Chapter 2 this volume), agrees with Spinelli and largely eschews the idea that anything other than our specific experience of the other could inform our sexuality. He suggests that phenomenologically, 'the attempt to find a particular "cause" to explain an imprecisely defined area on the wide spectrum of sexuality is quite meaningless' (Cohn, 1997: 94, this volume: 67).

Meaningless for whom? It is certainly not meaningless for the client who despite an often oppressive social structure struggles to finds the courage to express himself as an integrated being by accepting a part of himself that he has always felt to be there and that will not be pushed down. So, whilst Cohn is correct to observe that the existential approach should not be tethered by the acceptance of narrow definitions, it is also true that as van Deurzen-Smith puts it, 'existential therapists are fundamentally concerned with what matters to the client and renounce any ambition to even implicitly push the client in any particular dimension' (van Deurzen-Smith, 1996: 192). Furthermore, as Denman suggests, in the context of psychotherapy it tends to be clients who are in the early stages of defining themselves as lesbian, gay or bisexual who 'need to talk quite a lot about cause' (Denman, 2004: 175). To advocate therefore as Cohn does, that same-sex sexuality is not a condition 'brought about by specific factors' (Cohn, 1997: 95, this volume: 67), that is, cannot be a given, severely limits the ability of the existential therapist to witness and accept the client's attempt to explain and explore what he or she feels to be the cause or origin of his or her sexual preference.

Spinelli takes this argument one step further by suggesting that the root to the acceptance of same-sex sexuality as a natural manifestation of intersubjective desire is to renounce any idea of a biological link, because he believes that any view that allows the individual to label themselves as lesbian or gay, to be a lesbian or gay man, in fact singles them out as 'different, unique, problematic and indeed perverse (Spinelli, 1997: 13). Unfortunately Spinelli continues to morph the language of the prejudice that he is clearly attempting to combat by saying that even if a biological basis for sexuality were found, it would be evidence of a 'biologically derived anomaly' and the 'admission of an inherent deficiency and abnormality in one's very being' (Spinelli, 1997: 14). There is no evidence to suggest that any biological or hormonal dimension to same-sex sexuality would constitute abnormal or flawed pathology, just different. It is also not the case, as Spinelli suggests, that such a biological discovery would lead to isolation or persecution of gay people.

Indeed research suggests (Haider-Markel & Joslyn, 2008; Quist & Wiegand, 2002; Sakalli, 2002) that those who believe that homosexuality results from uncontrollable factors are more likely to have positive attitudes towards LGBT people. It is also worth noting that some of the worst examples of persecution against LGBT people (e.g. present-day Iraq, Uganda, Nigeria) are a result of religiously based prejudice and focus on sexual behaviours and do not arise from any reasoning about the true nature of sexuality. Furthermore, whilst it is true to say that any biological link would necessitate democratic and enlightened societies guarding against forms of eugenics or attempts to eliminate perceived flaws, it would be very unwise in the long run to deny or hide possible biological links to avoid these challenges.

Spinelli seems to be proposing that the reason for prejudice against lesbians and gay men lies with the individual and collective actions of those who willingly define themselves and not amongst the sections of society that would seek to oppress and persecute LGBT people however they appear. To suggest that LGBT people seek a biological 'get-out-of-jail-free card in order that they can no longer be held 'accountable or responsible' (Spinelli, 1997: 14) for being the way they are sexually appears to be a dogmatic attempt to direct the argument.

Spinelli continues to follow Freud in asking the question 'why homosexuality ... [and] why exclusive heterosexuality?' (Spinelli, 1997: 14). The answer is in fact simple; because that is how a significant majority of people identify and feel themselves to *be*. Spinelli's argument is also employed by Peter Tatchell who uses the Kinsey research of the 1940s and 1950s to claim that 'most people are indeed born with a sexual desire that is, to varying degrees, capable of heterosexual and homosexual attraction' (1996: 37) and concludes that 'sexuality is a continuum of desires and behaviour' and 'a substantial proportion of the population is somewhere in the middle sharing an amalgam of same-sex and opposite-sex feelings' (Tatchell, 1996: 38). Not only is there no credible evidence for such a statement but what Spinelli, Cohn and Tatchell ignore here is that whilst this continuum or spectrum has been well documented (Kinsey, Pomeroy & Martin 1948/1998; Klein, 1993), the distribution along this continuum is not a uniform one, that is, there are many more heterosexuals than lesbians and gay men and, particularly for bisexuality, these surveys are most often not designed or not able to discern identities from behaviours and attractions. Tatchell's '1.5 million British people with bisexual histories' (Tatchell, 1996: 38) has to be seen in this light. It would be far more pertinent to ask what proportion of gay men or lesbians felt obliged to put themselves into that type of situation not out of innate desire but out of a sense of having to fit in. This is not bisexuality but a socially enforced behaviour. A spectrum of sexualities into which a population might fall does not equate to a spectrum of sexuality *within* us all and most definitely does not mean that someone cannot, and is not, able to be in a fixed location on the spectrum.

Spinelli addresses the issue of those who reinterpret their sexuality during their lifetimes by saying that he is certain he is not the only individual who has 'experienced the phenomenon' (Spinelli, 1997: 16). Whilst it is no doubt true that some of us will explore bisexual capacities that we may possess that develop and take shape as a result of our experience of being-in-the-world, this does not mean that all of us have these capacities or will want to explore them. To conclude therefore as Spinelli does, that the 'plasticity' of such re-definitions, whatever their direction, reveals that 'far from being fixed in biology, our sexual identities rely far more on constructionist variables' (Spinelli, 1997: 16–17), in fact distorts reality to serve theory.

Du Plock comments that upon reading Spinelli's paper he felt 'troubled and angry' (du Plock, 1997: 67), particularly with the idea that his sexuality had 'somehow been explained away and diminished' and that 'sexual orientation was being presented as a choice' (du Plock, 1997: 67). He reminds us of two key concepts. Firstly, the 'fundamental project' which Barnes expresses well when she says that:

> as a lack of being, the for-itself reaches out towards being. Consciousness is not a self and does not have a self; but as a self-making process, it pursues a self, as Sartre says it, it seeks to come to itself.
>
> (Barnes, 1993: 47)

The freedom to choose ourselves is therefore at the heart of self-acceptance of sexual orientation. Second, we have the existential concept of the self as pre-reflective consciousness – the awareness of consciousness as being aware of itself as being conscious. This is pure intentionality prior to awareness of the world and something that may not have been reflectively conceived but as Cannon puts it, is a clue to the 'fundamental project of being' (Cannon, 1991: 39). Whilst du Plock is right to move away from pathology in terms of an exploration of same-sex sexuality and towards an 'investigation of the ontological structures of the client's project of being' (du Plock, 1997: 69), on one level this could be seen as an attempt on his part to 'square the circle' in terms of existential theory as opposed to reformulate the debate.

In this instance, philosophical inquiry has downgraded the scientific perspective too far and has rather ironically, adopted a similarly hard-and-fast view of reality that in itself has entailed a high level of inhibition of perception. Some streams of recent scientific inquiry into the origins of same-sex sexuality has moved from the possibility of a biological link to the probability of one (Långström, et al, 2010; Savic, Berglund & Lindström, 2005). It should be possible for existential thinking to take such learning into account. Philosophical and phenomenological enquiry can build on this foundation without diverging from the existential project and can apply a neutrality and acceptance of the given aspects of a client's homosexuality as the basis for an exploration of their embodied and lived experience. Furthermore, if we are to continue to view sexuality as a purely existential choice then we have to examine our reasons for wanting everyone's sexuality to be plastic or fluid and flesh out what we are saying about those (probably a majority) who don't experience themselves in that way. Can they really change their sexuality because theory says they should be able to and if so, as du Plock asks, 'at what price?' (du Plock, 1997: 70). Surely we don't want to be associated with the dangerous and abusive so-called 'reparative' therapies enticing vulnerable and troubled gay men by the promise that they can change. As existential psychotherapists we should guard against becoming confused, as Medard Boss (1966) has done by stating that homosexuality was one of the 'perversions', that to be homosexual is anything but a natural aspect of the human condition, and we should always remain suspicious of anything that is being described as normal. Following the recent case of the British Association for Counselling and Psychotherapy (BACP) removing the accreditation of one of its psychotherapists because of aspects of her practice of reparative therapy, the organisation published 'Statement of Ethical Practice (1)'. The statement confirms that the 'BACP opposes any psychological treatment such as 'reparative' or 'conversion' therapy which is based upon the assumption that homosexuality is a mental disorder or based on the premise that the client/patient should change his or her sexuality' and concludes that such practices have 'no medical indication and represent a severe threat to the health and human rights of the affected persons' (BACP, 2012). This is also the position of the British Psychological Society (BPS, 2013).

This threat clearly includes any idea that a client may be able to 'switch on' or engender as yet unfelt feelings of opposite-sex sexual attraction as a result of focusing solely on their intersubjective engagement with others or indeed by conscious intention and guided behaviour change.

Identity and confusion

There has in my view been a great deal of confusion about homosexual identity; whether it exists, where it comes from and what its implications are for individual freedom of expression, collective activity, shared elements of consciousness and political and social equality. This confusion emanates largely from the work of Michel Foucault (1978) and other philosophers such as Derrida (1983) and Faderman (1975) and has latterly been built upon by those such as Tatchell (1996) and Spinelli (1997) to advance an argument that same-sex sexuality exists as a sexological categorisation because of historic and contemporary power relations in society and not because of the increasing visibility and relative confidence that people feeling desire for same-sex emotional and sexual attachment have found in different countries during different epochs. So, did homosexual identity emanate largely from LGBT people as individual and collective expressions of themselves or was it imposed upon us by wider society? Furthermore, has the advent of the homosexual allowed gay men to express themselves and find their own meaning in terms of their sexuality or has it imposed a ready-made and tight-fitting way of life into which we must all conform or face rejection and ridicule? In other words does *being* a lesbian or gay man limit our ability to be an autonomous self or does it in fact promote existential choice and freedom for the individual within the wider social context?

Weeks catalogues Ulrichs' 'third sex', Westphal's 'contrary sexual feeling' and Hirschfeld's 'intermediate sex' (Weeks, 1985: 93) to show why historians and commentators such as Foucault (1978) and Faderman (1975) appear to argue that sexologists 'made' the 'homosexual'. Whilst this analysis seems to fit with the rigours of deconstructionist theory, it is by no means as simple as has been suggested and in fact, in a fundamental sense, is the very opposite of what adherents of this theory claim. Foucault argues that 'the sodomite had been a temporary aberration: the homosexual was now a species' (Foucault, 1978: 43) whilst Tatchell believes that 'homosexuality was thus a categorisation invented by straights to marginalise and constrain queer love' (Tatchell, 1996: 44).

This is simply not a statement of historic fact. The term 'homosexual' was coined by an Austro-Hungarian, Karl-Maria Kertbeny, who was inspired to write on the subject by the suicide of a young friend who was homosexual (Tobin, 2005). Although Kertbeny did not declare himself a homosexual, he continued to write about it extensively. The German, Karl Heinrich Ulrichs (1825–1895), did declare himself to be a homosexual or an *Urning* in what we can now look back on as maybe the first 'coming out'. So the urge and need to self-identity as gay arose in a significant way from lesbians and gay men themselves as a key part of the process of their own personal liberation. Indeed gay men in the twentieth century have employed sexological descriptions for their own individual purposes and far from being ring-fenced or defined by them, have used them to advance a sense of self, without feeling unable to challenge and negate them as and when they wish. Tatchell cannot agree with this viewpoint and suggests that gay liberation will 'hasten the demise of homosexuality as a separate exclusive identity or behaviour' (Tatchell, 1996: 45) leaving the way clear to explore the 'plasticity' of sexual experience and change our place on the 'spectrum' of sexual behaviour.

Here we arrive at the nub of the constructionist argument often cited in existential literature, namely that through social and political liberation, human beings will become able to choose their sexual identity more consciously and thereby somehow change or extend their sexual orientation as opposed to more accurately reflect it.

Therefore liberation should not lead to, and in the case of certain countries where great strides towards gay equality have been made, has not led to, the creation of a new sexual desire or orientation within the individual, but most certainly has promoted the freer expression of all sexual desires and behaviours, particularly same-sex sexuality and bisexuality. Therefore, far from being a Foucauldian category of social oppression incapable of any 'social goods or common ends' (Sullivan, 1995: 90), same-sex sexuality has become more visible and integrated and LGBT people are more liberated and free to create themselves specifically because of this process of social and political liberation. Andrew Sullivan quotes Michael Walzer who has written of Foucault, 'he stands nowhere and finds no reasons. Angrily he rattles the bars of the iron cage but he has no plan or projects for turning the cage into something more like a human home' (Sullivan, 1995: 92). Whilst it is the case that the history of gay liberation does contain important incidences of more direct action, it is also true that a substantial degree of 'gay liberation' has in reality been achieved through reform of the system from within and not by efforts to destroy it.

During the last ten years in Britain laws of equality have been passed regarding civil partnership, same-sex marriage, employment, provision of goods and services, age of consent, adoption and service in the armed forces. This is not as Tatchell suggests 'equal rights on straight terms' (Tatchell, 1996: 42). It represents freedom for individuals to live their lives in the way that they choose. This will not and indeed has not led to the disintegration of same-sex sexuality and the elimination of difference; a gay man will still seek out another man for love and sex and a straight man will still seek a woman for the same, that is, the relevance attached to the choice will change and diminish but the individual's sexuality in terms of intention and desire will not.

For the vast majority of gay people the process of self-identification and self-discovery results in a 'whole being' but is not the whole of our being. The labels that are often attributed to us by others have traditionally seemed antithetic to the thrust of the existential psychotherapeutic tradition, which, for good reason in many instances, encourages clients to engage with and often overcome the limitations that certain labels can confer upon them. It is however important to understand that most LGBT people do not cling to a gay identity because it protects them from sexual ambiguities that exist within; instead, self-labelling, emanating from a feeling of fixedness, provides a platform upon which each individual, despite uncertainty and doubt, can meaningfully and authentically engage in the personal challenge of being-here. Many gay people value exclusive same-sex attraction as an integral part of self no more, no less. It is utterly abstract therefore to suggest that gay people set off on a new path towards a theoretical bisexuality, adrift again towards undesirable and unattainable goals. There is nothing more misery-making than trying to make something happen that cannot happen and there is no new set of anxieties in gay people arising from equality and liberation towards the possibility of having opposite-sex desire. It cannot be evoked or imposed without allowing theory to overlay existence and experience.

Towards a new perspective

Being-in-the-world homosexually is not about seeking the truth regarding same-sex sexuality per se. It is about working out how this sexual urge and emotional desire translates into intention and interrelation for each individual. This is the point at which biological presence and human existence intersect. We are, as Havelock Ellis reminds us, defined by it: 'sex penetrates the whole person; a man's sexual constitution is part of his general constitution. There is considerable truth in the dictum 'a man is what his sex is' (Ellis, 1946: 3). To a large degree the given aspect of our sexuality means everything and nothing to us at the same time: everything because when it upsurges it envelops all of the self and in fact is all of the self; and nothing because the way in which we respond to this sexual given is ultimately totally subjective and is only formed by 'being there' and experiencing the other through embodied engagement. With this in mind we can revisit the work of Merleau-Ponty who in *Phenomenology of Perception*, warns us against 'reducing' sexuality to existence' (Merleau-Ponty, 1962: 166) and says that existence is not just a set of physical facts but is more ambiguous in its setting and more accurately located where 'boundaries run into each other' (Merleau-Ponty, 1962: 166). This focus on consciousness and perception does not preclude the idea that there may be prior elements that inform this perception, which in turn translate into sexual response, and does not predetermine or downgrade our potentiality for being-in-the-world sexually, or indeed mean a de facto acceptance of biological determinism as the sole component in an individual's sexuality. The important point, as Merleau-Ponty suggests, in terms of an individual's freedom to 'choose' their sexuality and feel coherent as a sexual being is that their 'biological existence is synchronised with human existence' (Merleau-Ponty, 1962: 160). In the case of same-sex sexuality this is often the point at which the individual begins to recognise and respond to the given aspects of their sexuality in the intersubjective realm. Therefore Merleau-Ponty is correct to say that sexuality is indeed an intrinsic aspect of our existence and only has meaning as a result of our existence, but this does not negate the idea that other factors outside of our existence can form or contribute towards our sexual orientation. Whatever the imagined loss of freedom that others may observe therefore, there is a clear sense in which lesbians and gay men subsume their absolute freedom to forget their felt sense and in so doing exercise their right to self-define and self-actualise, challenge their status as outsiders and thereby open themselves to the possibility of attaining personal fulfilment.

Surrendering to what is there in terms of sexual attraction and coming to terms with what is felt, and what has been felt for some time can be very empowering and has a clear resonance with Heidegger's (1927/1962) concept of *Gelassenheit*. Heidegger used the term to distinguish meditative from calculative thinking and spoke of a 'releasement towards things' and an 'openness to mystery' that allows the individual to notice, to observe, to ponder and to awaken an awareness of what is actually taking place around them (Dalle Pezze, 2006). He suggests that in letting go of willing in this way we in fact let ourselves in, which is a different type of empowerment that allows the individual to inhabit the world in a totally different way (Heidegger, 1927/1962). Kemp (2011) also understands this point and comments that it is through this 'letting-be' that the human subject is transformed. The refusal to 'let be' in terms of sexual desire is at the heart of the self-repression that causes great pain to some lesbians and gay men who struggle to come to terms with their sexuality at different points in their lives. Tillich identifies the courage to participate 'with the whole of one's existence' (Tillich, 1952: 124) as being the key to the existential attitude and as existential psychotherapists it is therefore important that we are able to link personal courage with a client's ability to recognise and act upon something that they already know inwardly but have previously pushed away and ignored.

Kierkegaard (1844/1944) uses the term 'shut-upness' to describe this type of repression or living a lie and it is overcoming this state that should be a key aim of existential psychotherapy; to help the client to authentically re-engage in the 'with-world' (Heidegger, 1927/1962) and thereby start to grow. Nietzsche's (1990) use of the term *amor fati*, loosely translating to love one's fate, is also relevant here and is characterised by an acceptance of the events or situations that occur in one's life, with the resultant necessity for a person to review their entire attitude to life, the world and the self and accept their experience in order to gain their individual grip on life (van Deurzen-Smith, 1997). This type of fundamental reassessment of one's own being, aware of the past, open to the present, intuitively driven and imbued with a desire to overcome self-deception, is markedly existential and can form the basis of sound existential psychotherapeutic work with a client who has become blocked by blocking their sexual feelings.

Merleau-Ponty (1962) believed that sexuality is the basic way in which we project ourselves into the world and towards others, through our body. This extension or opening to the 'with-world' is fuelled by consciousness and intention and ultimately physical contact. Whilst it is true therefore that sexuality affects all aspects of the self in both the personal and interrelational realm, it would be wrong to downplay the significance of the sexual act itself and its potential for providing the primary meaning of a person's existence as a sexual being. Having sex is the embodiment of desire and envelops all of our body and to some degree reminds us of the mystery of our own sexual behaviour as lesbians, gay men, heterosexuals and bisexuals. Reclaiming the work of Merleau-Ponty in this respect can give us the confidence as existential therapists that in the area of same-sex sexuality we can stay true to our existential beliefs whilst remaining in constant contact with our clients – it requires us to change the meaning we attach to essential aspects of sexuality and thereby remain rigorously phenomenological with clients who experience their sexuality as fixed, but its manifestations as something they are free to shape if not to change. The belief in the uniqueness of this synthesis for each individual should surely be at the heart of an existential-phenomenological understanding of same-sex sexuality. Merleau-Ponty does not require us to embrace the idea of a fluid sexuality but simply to be aware that our sexuality comes alive and is only 'there' in the physical world when the synchronisation of our essence and our experience leads to a felt sense of incarnational completeness.

So from the point of view of the personal struggle that some lesbians and gay men feel in coming to terms with their exclusive feelings of same-sex attraction and the anxieties concerning the consequences of this state of being that can often occur, the challenge for the existential therapist emerges. The endeavour is about following the client carefully and if no sense of the client's opposite-sex attraction is revealed (which of course would be more easily discernable because of the relative ease with which these feelings are expressed and considered 'normal'), then helping the client to explore the real freedom and releasement that can come from accepting a fixedness is ultimately the therapeutically beneficent and indeed existentially congruent way of working.

Conclusion

Sexual identity, as opposed to simple sexual response, goes right to the heart of how we all think of ourselves – we feel it as an indivisible part of the 'self'. Consider a gay man who attempts to 'become straight' by having sex with a woman. The physical response may be there but the 'self' feels dislocated and lost. It feels 'unreal' just as having same-sex sex for the first time suddenly feels 'real'. Surely there is no other practical level on which we can deal better as psychotherapists in the area of sexuality than this. As existential psychotherapists we should be very careful not to be seduced by the idea of the universality of bisexuality because in practice this results in fitting our clients into predetermined and unsubstantiated theoretical models which marginalise their experience of 'being-in-the-world sexually' and ultimately alienates them from the therapeutic process.

For most people sexuality is not skin deep; it is not something fluid and polymorphous hovering just below our consciousness; it is profound and all-pervading and not ultimately at the mercy of the mores and cultures of passing centuries. In terms of human sexuality it is not about others telling us what 'we all are', it is a question of the individual saying who 'I am'. Our sexuality is born in the flesh, is our flesh, is experienced in the flesh and dies with the flesh. It is there just as we are there. As existential therapists it is important that we are able to transcend the theoretical debates regarding cause and identity and remain steadfastly open to the client's actual experience. What we hear is what we should work with, no more, no less. In the area of human sexuality this will often equate to the existential practitioner being able to honour the client's freedom to be fixed and thereby appreciate how fixing and anchoring in certain aspects of their being in fact opens the individual to the real freedom to become unstuck and create their own path. So the answer to the question 'can I *be* a homosexual please?' can only ever be yes, because that is what I am. The important question however still remains – what does *being* a homosexual mean to me?

References

Barnes, H (1993) Sartre's concept of the self. In K Hoeller (Ed) *Sartre and Psychology* (pp. 33–49). Atlantic Highlands, NJ: Humanities Press.

Boss, M (1966) *Sinn und Gehalt der Sexuellen Perversionen*. Bern: Huber.

British Association for Counselling and Psychotherapy (BACP) (2012) *Statement of Ethical Practice (1)*. Retrieved 10 October 2012 from http://www.bacp.co.uk/admin/structure/files/pdf/10302_sep_1_p2_web.pdf

British Psychological Society (2013) *Position Statement: Therapies attempting to change sexual orientation*. Leicester: BPS.

Cannon, B (1991) *Sartre and Psychoanalysis: An existential challenge to clinical metatheory*. Lawrence, KS: University Press of Kansas.

Cohn, HW (1997) *Existential Thought and Therapeutic Practice*. London: Sage Publications.

Cohn, HW (2014) Being-in-the-world sexually. In M Milton (Ed) *Being Sexual: Existential perspectives on sexuality* (pp. 62-75). Ross-on-Wye: PCCS Books.

Dalle Pezze, B (2006) Heidegger on Gelassenheit. *Minerva: An Internet Journal of Philosophy*, *10*, 94–122.

Denman, C (2004) *Sexuality: A Biopsychosocial Approach*. Basingstoke: Palgrave Macmillan.

Derrida, J (1983) Geschlecht: Sexual difference, ontological difference. *Research in Phenomenology*, *13*(1), 65–83.

Du Plock, S (1997) Sexual misconceptions: A critique of gay affirmative therapy and some thoughts on an existential-phenomenological theory of sexual orientation. *Journal of the Society for Existential Analysis*, *8*(2), 56–71.

Ellis, H (1946) *Psychology of Sex*. London: William Heinemann.

Faderman, L (1975) The female world of love and ritual. *Signs, 1*(1), 1–29.

Foucault, M (1978) *The History of Sexuality, Volume 1: An introduction*. Harmondsworth: Penguin.

Freud, S (1930) *Civilization and Its Discontents*. London: Hogarth Press.

Freud, S (1958) Three essays on the theory of sexuality. In J Strachey (Ed & Trans) *The Standard Edition of the Complete Psychological Works of Sigmund Freud*, 7 (pp. 123–243). London: Hogarth Press. (First published 1905)

Haider-Markel, DP & Joslyn, MR (2008) Beliefs about the origins of homosexuality and support for gay rights: An empirical test of attribution theory. *Public Opinion Quarterly, 72*(2), 291–310.

Heidegger, M (1962) *Being and Time* (J Macquarrie & ES Robinson, Trans). London: Harper & Row. (First published 1927)

Kemp, R (2011) The symbolic constitution of addiction: Language, alienation, ambivalence. *Health*. Retrieved 27 April 2012 from hea.sagepub.com/content/early/2011/11/12/1363459311425515

Kierkegaard, S (1944) *The Concept of Dread* (W Lowrie, Trans). Princeton, NJ: Princeton University Press. (First published 1844)

Kierkegaard, S (1969) *The Journals of Kierkegaard*. New York: Harper & Row.

Kinsey, A, Pomeroy, W & Martin, C (1998) *Sexual Behaviour in the Human Male*. Bloomington, IN: Indiana University Press. (First published 1948)

Klein, F (1993) *The Bisexual Option*. Binghamton, NY: The Haworth Press.

Kurtz, E (1982) Why AA works: The intellectual significance of Alcoholics Anonymous. *Journal of Studies on Alcohol, 43*(1), 38–80.

Långström, N, Rahman, Q, Carlström, E & Lichtenstein, P (2010) Genetic and environmental effects on same-sex sexual behaviour: A population study of twins in Sweden. *Archives of Sexual Behavior, 39*(1), 75–80.

Merleau-Ponty, M (1962) *Phenomenology of Perception*. London: Routledge & Kegan Paul.

Nietzsche, F (1990) *Ecce Homo* (W Kaufmann & RJ Hollingdale, Trans). New York: Vintage Books (First published 1908)

Quist, RM & Wiegand, DM (2002) Attributions of hate. *American Behavioral Scientist, 46*(1), 93–107.

Sakalli, N (2002) Application of the attribution-value model of prejudice to homosexuality. *Journal of Social Psychology, 142*, 264–71.

Savic, I, Berglund, H & Lindström, P (2005) Brain response to putative pheromones in homosexual men. *Proceedings of National Academy of Science USA, 102*(20), 7356–61.

Smith-Pickard, P & Swynnerton, R (2005) The body and sexuality. In E van Deurzen & C Arnold Baker (Eds) *Existential Perspectives on Human Issues* (pp. 48–57). Basingstoke: Palgrave Macmillan.

Spinelli, E (1997) Some hurried notes expressing outline ideas that someone might one day utilize as signposts towards a sketch of an existential-phenomenological theory of sexuality. *Journal of the Society for Existential Analysis, 8*(1), 2–20.

Sullivan, A (1995) *Virtually Normal*. New York: Vintage Books.

Tatchell, P (1996) It's just a phase: Why homosexuality is doomed. In M Simpson (Ed) *Anti-gay* (pp. 35–54). London/New York: Freedom Editions.

Tillich, P (1952) *The Courage to Be*. Glasgow: William Collins.

Tobin, RD (2005) Kertbeny's 'Homosexuality' and the language of nationalism. In MS Breen & F Peters (Eds) *Genealogies of Identity: Interdisciplinary readings on sex and sexuality* (pp. 3–17). Amsterdam: Rodopi.

Van Deurzen, E (2002) *Existential Counselling and Psychotherapy Practice*. London: Sage Publications.

Van Deurzen-Smith, E (1996) Existential therapy. In W Dryden (Ed) *Handbook of Individual Therapy* (pp. 179–208). London: Sage Publications.

Van Deurzen-Smith, E (1997) *Everyday Mysteries: Existential dimensions of psychotherapy*. London: Routledge.

Weeks, J (1985) *Sexuality and Its Discontents*. London: Routledge & Kegan Paul.

Part 4

Existential Perspectives on Affirmative Therapy

6

Gay Affirmative Therapy: A critique and some reflections on the value of an existential-phenomenological theory of sexual identity

– Prof. Simon du Plock –

Over the past two decades a number of authors in Britain and the US have written about the needs of gay-identified clients; these observations have led to important contributions to the literature on working with gay clients, contributions which significantly address and counterbalance the narrow view of homosexuality evident in psychoanalytic literature where, as Milton and Coyle note, it 'is defined as a perversion or as pathology' (Milton & Coyle, 1999: 45). Such writers have sought to identify ways of working with gay clients which place equal value on homosexuality and heterosexuality; in the process of this they provide a challenge to cognitive behaviourist and humanistic approaches which promote the efficacy of a universal methodology applicable to all clients and deny the relevance of 'difference'. Alderson makes this explicit when he says, 'To work with LGBTI [lesbian, gay, bisexual, transgender/transsexual and intersexed] individuals successfully, you need to become a LGBTI-affirmative therapist. LGBTI-affirmative therapists *view LGBTI status as equal to heterosexual status* and they emphasise a nonpathological view in their work with these clients' (Alderson, 2013: 53).

The ideas which inform this movement are, perhaps, most comprehensively expressed in the British literature by Davies and Neal (Eds) in *Pink Therapy: A guide for counsellors and therapists working with lesbian, gay and bisexual clients*, first published in 1996 and most recently reprinted in 2003. The tenets and guidelines for ethical practice with gay clients which contributors propose are specifically intended to place positive respect rather than therapeutic neutrality at the heart of the therapeutic alliance. As such, they offer a distinctive critique of existing ways of working and affirm gay identity, rather than an entirely new therapeutic model. Maylon states: 'Gay affirmative psychotherapy is not an independent system of psychotherapy. Rather it represents a special range of psychological knowledge which challenges the traditional view that homosexual desire and fixed homosexual orientations are pathological' (Maylon, 1982: 62). Davies agrees with Maylon, and sets out to indicate how this 'special range of psychological knowledge' might be expressed in 'a model of gay affirmative therapy that can span the psychodynamic and humanistic schools' (Davies, 2003: 25). In the course of setting out such a model in a chapter titled 'Towards a Model of Gay Affirmative Therapy', Davies expands on the 'Twelve Guidelines for Retraining' and the 'Ground Rules for Helping' proposed by Clark (1987). Clark's guidelines and ground rules are expressed in terms of consciousness-raising – for both therapist and client – and are explicitly urging the therapist to adopt an educative role. While other contributors to the text, and two subsequent texts in the 'Pink Therapy' series, (Davies & Neal, 2009; Neal & Davies, 2000), offer a range of ways of working affirmatively, these guidelines and ground rules occupy a prominent position in Davies' seminal chapter; as he concludes: 'This chapter presents a gay affirmative framework which is intended to augment the therapist's existing theoretical model. The guidelines given by Clark (1987) should take precedence over any theoretical constructs which run counter to them' (Davies, 2003: 39).

The genesis of gay affirmative therapy initially appears to provide something wholly admirable: a respectful way of working with a group which, historically, has been much abused in the name of 'treatment'. While this doubtless provides a very valuable corrective to the worst therapeutic abuses, from an existential-phenomenological perspective it raises as many questions as it answers. Reflection on such a gay affirmative therapy from an existential-phenomenological perspective should not be dismissed as merely an interesting intellectual exercise: the issues which are thrown up by doing so are, I suggest, relevant to our understanding of what it means to practise psychotherapy per se.

Perhaps the first characteristic of Clark's gay affirmative approach which strikes the reader is its prescriptiveness. In some respects this might seem entirely obvious, since if we wish to affirm something we must necessarily argue for this something and, equally important, argue against – or at least play down – whatever might be thought to stand in opposition to our favoured something. Clearly the existential-phenomenological therapist who wishes to be gay affirmative (or *anything* affirmative) is going to have a problem here, since the gay affirmative approach, at least in the strongly affirming form which Clark has devised, calls upon us to desist from bracketing. Perhaps this is not an insurmountable barrier – after all there is something exhortatory in existential work – the existential therapist, like Sartre, believes that men and women should reject bad faith responses to problems of living and should be as open as possible to what life brings. Van Deurzen, in her book *Everyday Mysteries* (2010), departs from a strikingly phenomenological approach in an impassioned attempt to show a client a number of crucial aspects of her situation which she believes the client has overlooked. Here the therapist is motivated to formulate what she thinks are the client's own doubts in order to avert a possible catastrophe.

We might argue that the therapist jumps ahead of the client and introduces her own fears and anxieties; we might equally well argue that the experienced therapist owes it to her client to bring her hard-won wisdom about the human condition to bear. Either way this intervention arises out of the therapeutic relationship and is not part of a pre-planned way of working; the therapist may hope for change but waits for the direction of change to unfold as the client explores how they live their life.

In contrast, Clark's (1987) 'Twelve Guidelines for Retraining' and 'Ground Rules for Helping', a structure which has education and consciousness-raising as its goals, are prescriptive in that they urge the therapist, for example, to encourage clients actively to appreciate their bodies and to trust physical contact. This agenda is normative and contains a great deal of scope for inauthentic communication. Davies claims that 'By being prepared to touch clients – even a hand on the shoulder when they leave – the therapist is saying that they trust and accept the client and their body' (Davies & Neal, 2003: 32–3). I would contend that whatever the therapist believes they are saying by their touch, the client will bring their own understanding to the gesture.

There is something odd about the way in which Davies believes that clients and therapists communicate. He states that 'It can be particularly healing for many gay men to be so *accepted* by a male therapist, when all physical contact with men has been sexualised in the past' (Davies & Neal: 33, my emphasis). Leaving aside whether there is any evidence to support this contention, I assume that the therapist has said something about why he is touching the client before he does so. Nevertheless, I wonder what those clients for whom physical contact has been equated with sex will make of their therapist's well-intentioned advances – assuming of course that they are indeed well-intentioned. They may find it seductive; they may more likely feel patronised by the 'accepting, healing' therapist. Either way, when the impulse to be with another, whether by talking or by touch, is recruited into the guidelines and ground rules, its potential for facilitating an 'I–Thou' relationship is seriously reduced. As a learned response to a 'type' of client I think this is misconceived. If we believe that gay clients live in a world which sends them powerful messages about their bodily impulses it may be more creative to meet this impulsively (within an ethical position), even playfully, showing how out of our therapeutic relationship numerous different ways of being can emerge. To attempt to counteract these powerful messages with alternative powerful messages rather than with the potentialities of the therapeutic relationship in the here and now is only to be further limited by implied limitations.

Milton (2007) is certainly correct in noting that while existential therapists are more concerned with the individual experience of sexuality than with the overtly political and interpersonal addressed by many contributors to lesbian and gay psychology (such as Bell, et al, 2002; Bennett & Coyle, 2001; Clarke, 2001). Milton says: 'this is not a rejection of a political focus, but an attempt to capitalise on the experience of the individual as they experience it' (Milton, 2007: 7).

The distance between existential-phenomenological therapy and Clark's gay affirmative therapy is obvious when we consider Clark's view of the client:

> Some therapists say all the right words of appreciation and never touch a client more than to shake hands. No matter how sophisticated your client or how profound the theoretical explanation of this stance, there is a primitive person inside the client who is recording a primitive message: 'If you really thought I was attractive, instead of just giving me some words to make me feel better you would find a way to touch me no matter what your ethics and training.'
>
> (Clark, 1987: 238)

The existential therapist does not attempt to say 'all the right words'. More importantly, the existential therapist (indeed any therapist) will not find all their clients physically attractive and to pretend to do so would be inauthentic and, in fact, to be lying in a relationship where authenticity and truth are vitally important. We might suggest that there is something primitive, or at least mechanical, about the therapist's attempt to make regular physical contact with the client. I have found that where I am able to maintain an open genuine attitude towards clients they will often initiate contact. It seems to me that my willingness to accept such contact *when it is initiated by the client* is likely to be more therapeutic than any contact I might decide to introduce into sessions.

The gay-affirming therapist seems to be doing rather a lot to (and perhaps for) the client: he or she is exhorted to help the client begin deprogramming, facilitate the identification and expression of anger, actively support appreciation of the 'body-self' and encourage them to establish a gay support system. Most problematic from an existential perspective is the twelfth guideline: 'Use the weight of your authority to affirm homosexual thoughts, behaviour and feelings when reported by your client' (Clark, in Davies & Neal, 2003: 34). Davies expands on this by stating:

> This is important to counteract experience of disapproval from authority figures ... by warmly encouraging them to share their homosexual thoughts and feelings with you, you afford the client an experience of 'good parenting' or positive regard which has often been missing in the process of 'coming out'.
>
> (Davies, 2003: 34)

Davies also feels that books have a place in therapy as they lend additional authority, and he talks of recommending certain books according to the client's needs. Rather than, even temporarily, adopting the position of a positive authority figure I would suggest that we might want to explore the client's experience of disapproval. In fact if the client introduces their experience of support and approval from an authority figure this is likely to be just as important to explore and clarify. To have more of an agenda than this is to abandon our naïve wonder when confronted with the being of another.

The feeling of familiarity which gay affirmative therapy has about it is explained by its roots: 'one of the roles of gay affirmative therapy is, as with any special population, to help facilitate and educate through raising awareness. Feminist therapy makes this explicit – the role of the therapist as teacher' (Davies, 2003: 35). Van Deurzen-Smith has written about existential therapy in terms of a tutorial in the art of living, but for her the aim is far more than to 'reassure the client that they are going through a normative experience' (van Deurzen-Smith, 1988: 22). She says:

> Existential counselling does not teach certain ways of being in every client. It does not condone skills training as a viable alternative for

people who are having difficulties in living meaningfully in their own way. Attempting to coach people who feel alienated in particular skills or ways of expressing themselves may be counter-productive and result in more rather than less alienation.

(van Deurzen-Smith, 1988: 22)

There is a danger here – in any sort of affirmative therapy – of the therapist becoming the very 'expert' we all agree we do not want to be. The underlying rationale seems to be that the affirming expert can and should counterbalance the damage done by negative authority figures in the past. I am not at all sure how this fits with an existential-phenomenological approach in which we expressly do not attribute causality for the present to past events. From our perspective, leaving aside whether it is actually possible to undo past damage in the present, the vital thing is to look at the way in which the client has chosen to construct a sense of self out of their past experience – how they have formulated a project with which to project themselves into the future.

Davies quotes Shernoff (1989), who argues that the unconditional respect and warmth of the therapeutic relationship makes it an ideal place to educate the client in safer sex behaviours (Davies, 2003: 36). Moreover, 'Shernoff maintains that we have an ethical duty to raise the issue of safer sex with all our clients regardless of their sexuality' (Davies, 2003: 36). On the contrary, my insertion of my own agenda regarding safer sex is likely to demonstrate to the client exactly how conditional my positive regard is. I believe clients will read the message as: if you want my respect you need to assure me your behaviour around condom use is what I expect it to be. This feels like a gross intrusion and anti-therapeutic.

Davies draws an interesting analogy between therapists introducing a question about suicidal ideation with a client who feels totally hopeless, and therapists introducing the subject of safer sex when a client is discussing relationships and sexuality. His purpose in this is to point out that therapists often introduce their own material and, in fact, might be considered to have acted unethically if they did not raise the question of self-harm in the case of a despairing client. All my clients wonder, at times and to varying degrees, what the point is in living. Trying to figure out their own particular point in living is pretty much the work of the therapy we undertake together. I can see, of course, that this is not the same as a client talking obliquely about killing themselves, but I do not believe that the following are analogous situations:

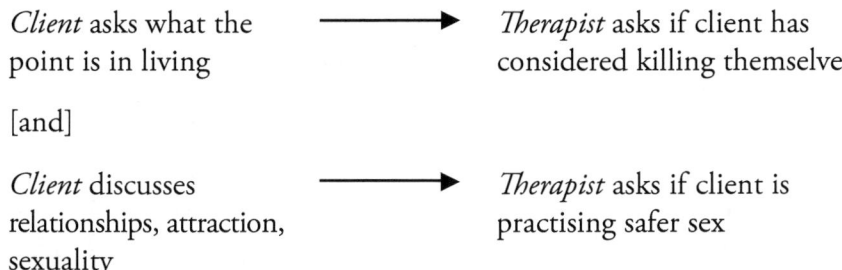

Of course it is disingenuous to deny that therapists are always giving information about their values, but in bracketing we minimise this. This reminds me of a situation I experienced in therapy where I was talking about feeling insecure in the flat I was renting. The therapist took this as a cue to pursue the advantages of owning over renting. I recall that I felt profoundly unheard: the real issue was what I was telling myself about myself when I ruled out the idea of becoming more secure.

It seems to me that the best safer sex education is probably afforded not by direct information-giving but by staying with the client's issues. To do otherwise places a burden on the therapist. Davies says 'Shernoff warns that therapists need to be familiar with HIV transmission and prevention issues and be aware of the variety of human sexual practices, as well as confident in speaking explicitly about sexual matters, which may require further training' (Davies, 2003: 37).

On the one hand this just sounds like common sense – what responsible therapist would not agree? Certainly a therapist who was unaware of the basic information about HIV transmission and who encouraged a client to engage in unsafe sex would be operating unethically. Where, though, do we draw the line? Statistically smoking-related disease, obesity, alcohol and substance use pose a greater threat than do HIV and AIDS. We are rapidly having to become paramedics just to keep up with the technical information in each of these areas. It is more important as therapists to establish the meaning of the behaviour for the client, and be knowledgeable enough to refer clients to agencies or specialists where appropriate.

Practical suggestions should probably be the exception rather than the rule in therapy. In gay affirmative therapy they seem to be an integral part of the work. Davies gives a case example in his discussion of working with people who are in the process of coming out:

> Dawn worked as a bank clerk and had for some time realized her attraction to other women. *At her counsellor's suggestion* she plucked up courage to telephone the local lesbian line ... Dawn presented at

her next counselling session feeling depressed and even more isolated. 'Those women were just like men. They were all so aggressive. If that's what being a lesbian means I'm certainly not a lesbian.'
(Davies, in Davies & Neal, 2003: 73, my emphasis)

It is not only gay-affirmative therapies who are given to assist in this way. I find a parallel here with my own experience at university of having a very experienced psychotherapist suggest contacting a gay group in the local town. In my case much of the following year was occupied with working on the results of this premature experience with the therapist, a therapist who had been an associate of Sartre and de Beauvoir in Paris. The conclusion of Davies' case example is particularly interesting, in that he reports:

> Dawn felt hurt and alienated by the other women, who had a greater awareness of the oppression of women and had found strength in their identities as women by not conforming to what heterosexual men would want of them (to be feminine, gentle and submissive). However, Dawn at that stage needed to find women who looked like her and who held similar views to hers. She was also angry at her counsellor for not helping her to make contact with lesbians like her.
> (Davies, in Davies & Neal, 2003: 73)

The implication is that first, we as the therapists can know about a socialising process in which people become more aware of oppression and can judge where in this process a client is, and second, the counsellor should help the client make contact with people like themselves. Both these observations seem to take us rather far from the existential approach. It might be argued that they are useful augmentations which enable the therapist to guide the client through a coming-out process. It might also be argued that they are a distraction from the existential work of assisting clients to clarify their meaning world; it is difficult to see how a therapist would be able, practically, to move between a naïve bracketing stance and 'therapist as resource'.

My own experience, and that of Dawn, suggests that the therapist can never know quite where in such a process a client is and that any consequent directing runs the risk of taking the client further from, not nearer to, an understanding of what it is they want or need. This is not to deny the existence of a coming-out process, simply to remind us that it is very varied and complex and not a discrete linear progression. Insofar as it is useful to bear in mind, we might want to think of it as a life-long experience as we enter new inter- and intra-personal/psychic relationships with ourselves and with others. Taken to extremes there may be a danger of becoming immersed in the 'They' (Heidegger, 1927/1962) if we end up viewing ourselves as a group going through some 'known' process; much of the value of the concept of being gay is the way in which it provides a space which each individual can invest with different meanings. One of the joys (and challenges) of being gay is the opportunity such an identification provides for inventing/reinventing oneself.

Davies and Neal's outline of a model of gay affirmative therapy is in the main humanistic-based, though it is intended to work with a psychodynamic approach too, and from the perspective of existential-phenomenological therapy it suffers from the many problems which Spinelli (1997) has identified. Moreover, gay affirmative therapy seems to have the potential to run counter to what Spinelli has identified as two of the characteristics typical of the humanistic model:

> [that] the therapist must be willing to set aside theoretically based assumptions, biases and generalizations about human experience so that the client can be viewed as a unique being who generates distinctive, singularly applicable meanings and world views, [and that] the humanistic model restrains therapists from assuming or presenting themselves as being more capable than clients of discerning or interpreting their experiences.
>
> (Spinelli, 1994: 257)

The logic of gay affirmative therapy adopting a broadly humanistic approach is clear: if the problems clients bring reveal an underlying experience of incongruence at the level of self-concept – incongruence between their current view of themselves and their ideal self, or between the self they believe they 'must' be, as opposed to the self that 'is' – the task of the therapist is integration, by providing the means for increased self-congruence. This is precisely the aim of the educational/guiding process which informs gay-affirmative therapy. Gay affirmative therapy conceptualises individuals as having innately positive natures and core unitary selves which are impeded by negative environmental influences.

The unconditional positive regard which humanistic therapists claim to be possible is problematic if they believe that their task is to assist the client through a normative process of, say, coming out. Spinelli's enquiries seem pertinent here:

> *How conditional on the assumption of innate positively directed growth is this 'unconditionality'?* In other words, if this assumption were to be removed or presented as doubtful, would humanistic therapists still offer these qualities? My own questioning of a number of humanistic therapists on this very point suggests that at the very least they would find it extremely difficult to maintain an accepting attitude towards their clients and, in some cases, would seriously question their basic rationale for providing therapy.
>
> (Spinelli, 1994: 265)

Like Spinelli, I end up recognising the wisdom of van Deurzen-Smith's position that 'people may evolve in any direction, good or bad, and that only reflection on what constitutes good and bad makes it possible to exercise one's choice in the matter' (van Deurzen-Smith, 1988: 56–7). The notion that people may evolve in any direction seems to be diluted in some forms of gay affirmative therapy by the idea that they progressively develop in one:

> Your primary objective should be to help the person to become more truly themselves, which means among other things, that you want to help the person to become more truly gay, developing conscious self-appreciation and integrity that includes the integration of gay thoughts and feelings. You will not encourage self-destructive behaviour and attitudes or encourage conformity, per se. You will instead seek to reinforce integrity by encouraging behaviour and attitudes that match inner feelings.
>
> (Clarke, 1987: 221, in Davies & Neal, 2003: 34)

This certainly does have the advantage of rejecting any obfuscation about the object of gay affirmative therapy. Presumably an unsuccessful therapy – and an unsuccessful client – would be one in which these goals were not realised.

There is an inner/outer split here: the therapist helps the client integrate the two, but in a particular way – by encouraging a greater expression of their inner world in the outer world. This does not – and I am sure it is not intended to – recognise one of the basic tenets of an existential approach, that self and world are co-constituted. It is not the case that the world imposes a way of living on a passive victim (the client) whom we may instil with strength and vision in the course of therapy.

I am indebted to a colleague for greater insight into this point. I recall explaining to my poor ignorant colleague that she could not possibly understand what it is like as a gay man to use public transport in some of the less salubrious areas of London. She countered that as a woman who used buses frequently she found my insistence on my special knowledge of threat and discrimination somewhat overdone. My reaction to this was to redouble my efforts to impress upon her that our two experiences were quite different and that the discrimination I experienced was the greater. At some point during this 'display of my suffering' (or perhaps a little later if I am strictly accurate) it dawned upon me that my laboured insistence on being the more sinned against, the more damaged by a 'vile macho society', said far more about the story of my identity I was telling myself than it did about the world in actuality. My anger was that my position 'you must agree that you can't understand me' was threatened. My feeling was that if this were not acknowledged my whole identity as helpless victim would be undermined. My story expressed who I was and any challenge to it was experienced as invalidating my sedimented self-concept. Transposing this into a therapy situation, I think that a therapist drawing on gay affirmative therapy would be very likely to validate my story and, further, affirm that my feelings correctly reflected a problem regularly encountered by gay people. I might even have received some advice about ways of reducing my risk when on public transport. While on one level such a response would be affirmative, it is likely to be affirming something which could more usefully be explored or even challenged. Worse, such a story would probably be received positively by a client because it provides an appropriate opportunity to 'afford the client an experience of "good parenting" or positive regard ... Sharing their lives with someone who is encouraging is experienced by clients as a very important facet of gay affirmative therapy' (Davies, 2003: 34–5).

So everyone wins: the therapist gets to affirm the client and in doing so feels affirmed as a gay-affirming therapist, the client gets affirmed and in all probability reacts to this in a pleased and therapist-affirming manner. What gets affirmed though is the client's sedimented self-concept. To cling tenaciously to the mantra 'I am this victim (or hero or genius) and you *must* recognise me as such' has about it the same degree of fixedness as attempting to be a stone or a chair – the person who does this makes themselves an object for the gaze of the other.

This is not to suggest that therapists should *never* affirm or advise, but to ask that when we do this we are careful to discern what our agenda is. The client's worldview is not the result of chance or accident. It has been constructed over time and is intended (or was intended in the past) to function as a defence against existential anxiety. Any attempt to demolish this would be anti-therapeutic and deeply disrespectful. At the same time we owe our clients an opportunity to see their lives from a new perspective, and colluding with their identity as victim (or anything else) may foreclose this. It may be that a gay-affirmative therapist is less likely, in their wish to introduce their own view of the 'healthy homosexual', to attend fully to the individual client than a sensitive therapist from another orientation.

Milton illustrates this argument, quoting an example in Hopcke (1989) in which a Jungian analyst is shown to work most effectively with a client's homosexuality when she works with his expression of it rather than the homosexuality per se. Milton deduces that,

> it is not an 'issue' that has intrinsic importance, but it is the client's experience of issues that leads the counsellor to the important context. If the counsellor should veer to the extreme of focusing exclusively upon the social issue at hand, which may be a temptation when faced with, say, urgent medical conditions or substance misuse, he or she may be experienced by clients as being more interested in the issue than other aspects of their experience. If this occurs, the counsellor may come to be seen as an 'expert' on the issue, and may have an end result of allowing the client to feel that they are not seen as a client, but as the bearer of a phenomenon, e.g. 'HIV patient' or 'drug addict'.
> (Milton, 1993: 24)

I would go further and say that this failure of bracketing fundamentally undermines the therapeutic alliance. In working some years ago with Tom (a pseudonym), a gay man aged thirty who presented with low self-esteem, I made the error of attributing this to his 'failure' to negotiate the coming-out process and develop a gay lifestyle. In my interventions I trod a bad faith path between my agenda and attempting to hear his. Eventually Tom began to throw in comments such as 'I don't know why I'm so depressed but I'm sure you could tell me if you wanted to – after all you are the expert here' whenever he felt a session was becoming difficult or challenging. I was suitably humbled at being treated as a *false* expert and paid greater attention to Tom's experience, but it was several months before he felt he could trust me again. Rather than affirm a client's account of how they come to be where they are in terms of their expression of their sexuality, it may be more helpful to consider the storytelling process itself. By this I do not mean merely that the existential-phenomenological approach provides a more useful way of conceptualising the function of this process than does gay affirmative therapy – I hope to suggest that it offers a more satisfactory perspective on sexuality itself. It is often worthwhile contemplating our emotional responses to events: I found myself intellectually convinced by Ernesto Spinelli's reading of his paper 'Some hurried notes expressing outline ideas that someone might one day utilise as signposts towards a sketch of an existential-phenomenological theory of sexuality' at the 1996 Society for Existential Analysis Annual Lecture from the Chair. But emotionally I felt troubled and rather angry. I was particularly struck by his assertion that:

> rather than express some form of pathology ... homosexual relations express the very same intersubjective desires to be with others as can be ascertained in all other sexual manifestations. That such may be the chosen means by which an individual both expresses and avoids intersubjective anxieties ... reveals nothing that is not similarly revealed in any other form of sexual relation, such that to distinguish this particular means of disclosure as inherently different, unique, problematic or perverse has no basis – other than at the level of an interpretative bias that must be challenged rather than condoned.
> (Spinelli, 1997: 17)

My gut-reaction then was that homosexuality – *my* homosexuality – had somehow been explained away, diminished. To express my reaction in the terms appropriate for an academic paper I would say that it seemed to me that sexual orientation was being presented as a choice. My sense, though, is that sexuality may not feel like a choice – may be not be available to consideration by us in the way that we are used to choices being available – for the simple reason that it is a choice of a different type, a part of the individual's fundamental project. Spinelli (2013) suggests that by this I mean that being gay is a foundational way of being rather than a choice one can make: this is not, in fact, my position; nor is it what I say. I do not argue that essence precedes existence, but rather, that sexual orientation may originate in a pre-reflexive manner as part of an individual's fundamental project, *and then* become expressed via a myriad of quotidian choices.

We need, at this point, to remind ourselves what the term 'fundamental project' refers to and what its function is. Barnes expresses it well when she says that 'as a lack of being, the for-itself reaches out towards being. Consciousness is not a self and does not have a self; but as a self-making process, it pursues a self or, as Sartre says, it seeks to come to itself' (Barnes, 1983: 47). This self-making process is revealed to us when we consider the way we attempt through ordinary introspection, or 'impure reflection', as

Sartre terms it, to review our past life and arrive at our essential core. In such a process of isolating and categorising our feelings about the past as though they were things themselves, we do not stray from the confines of the fundamental project.

Let us be clear about this. Human beings are thrown into the world and are what they make of themselves. We can never finally establish ourselves in the world as this or that kind of person but are free to choose ourselves within, and in relation to, the boundaries of existential givens. The fundamental project, like the Freudian complex, refers to the interpersonal world of childhood, and both existential and Freudian analysis seek to evince the crucial event of infancy and the psychic crystallisation around that event. While the complex is conceived as unconscious and subject to the laws of nature, the fundamental project is conscious and subject to continuing revision, even radical transformation. It is a 'pro-ject', or a throwing of oneself forward from the past towards the future in a particular way.

To understand this, I find it helpful to recall the nature of the self in existential philosophy, and, in particular, the self of pre-reflective consciousness. We will remember that consciousness, for the existentialist, is always aware of itself as consciousness. In being aware of an object, consciousness is aware of not being that object. To be conscious of a thing is to be aware that the awareness and the thing are not the same. Two components are inseparably bound in any act of consciousness: consciousness of the object, and consciousness's awareness of itself as being aware. This latter is individual, but it is void of individualising psychic qualities. While it may not be empty of emotion, it does not entail a sense of 'I' or 'me'. Barnes expresses this particularly clearly in her exposition of Sartre's implied theory of self-development:

> My consciousness at first is purely non-reflective-conscious: at this stage I am not aware of the world. I merely project myself out into the world, relating to it: I am pure intentionality. During this time my original project is shaped, the fundamental choice of my being is made: I choose myself through an attitude and action: I vote for my destiny with my feet and without making rational conscious choices. I become who I am by doing what I do.
>
> (Barnes, 1983: 42)

If it is this pure intentionality which accounts for the original 'choice of being' by which we regulate ourselves in the world we can see that, at least theoretically, this choice could have been other, and could, in consequence, have given rise to a quite different personality structure. What we perceive as our familiar personal self is, then, the product of consciousness. As Cannon puts it:

> These pre-reflexive choices, which include such things as my taste in food and clothing as well as *my way of relating to other people*, may never have been reflectively conceived ... Yet ... all of my concrete choices, all of my various ways of being, doing, and having are clues to my fundamental project of being – the meaning of my being in the world.
>
> (Cannon, 1991: 39, my emphasis)

This reminds me of a client who, in the course of a session, related that he had had an aversion to spinach as a child. On further exploration he explained that he had always associated it with growing up and becoming strong and independent – all possibilities which he wished to reject. The aversion was as strong as the message spinach symbolised: his mother (whom he feared losing) explicitly stated that if he ate spinach he would grow up and leave her. As an adult he invested spinach with a different meaning: although ambivalent to it he saw it as a link with childhood, and therefore something to be valued.

It might be objected that an aversion to particular foodstuffs is trivial in comparison with sexual orientation, yet it is worth remembering that such aversions are taken by many parents as major indicators of the emerging personalities of their offspring. Even as adults we recall such likes and dislikes with an emotional charge redolent of the power struggles which they symbolised. In this particular example the client did not object to spinach because he disliked its taste, he disliked its taste because he rejected what he believed it to mean – and this meaning was generated, was co-constituted, at what Cannon calls the 'point of conjunction' of the client's pre-reflective consciousness and the world.

A sexual orientation, I suggest, becomes just that, an orientation, a choice about being-in-the-world, just as sexual relationship is a choice about how to relate to the other. We pay too little attention to this 'orientation' of sexual orientation, falling into the trap (identified by Foucault) of foregrounding sex to the detriment of any analysis of the surrounding culture and the power relations in this culture. This reading directs our attention away from 'pathology', and towards an investigation of the ontological structures of the client's project of being. It also proposes

– because of its focus on motivation rather than causality – that a 'radical modification of our fundamental project' is always possible. We should not, though, assume such a modification is either necessarily desirable, nor should we underestimate the cost to the individual of such radical change. Sartre gives the example of a man who is hiking with friends and, on becoming exhausted after some hours, throws himself down at the side of the road, and refuses to go any further. Sartre, taking the role of the hiker, says that:

> Someone will reproach me for my act and will mean thereby that I was free – that is, not only was my act not determined by anything or person, but also I could have succeeded in resisting my fatigue longer – I shall defend myself by saying that I was too tired. Who is right? Or rather is the debate not based on incorrect premises? There is no doubt that I could have done otherwise, but that is not the problem. It ought to be formulated like this: could I have done otherwise without perceptibly modifying the organic totality of the projects which I am; or is the fact of resisting my fatigue such that instead of remaining a purely local and accidental modification of my behaviour, it could be effected only by means of a radical transformation of my being-in-the-world – a transformation, moreover, which is possible? In other words: I could have done otherwise. Agreed. But at what price?
>
> (Sartre, 1943/1956: 453–4)

The difference between an accidental modification and a radical transformation must surely be dependent on the meaning which the individual ascribes to fatigue, just as our attraction to certain foods, colours, shapes or physical attributes in another human being are dependent on the meaning which we give to them. Furthermore, it is the clarification of these meanings, of the client's meaning world, and bringing reflective awareness to bear on pre-reflective choices which constitutes the major part of existential psychotherapy.

Clearly much more could be said on this issue but even the reflections in this chapter should, I hope, indicate that the existential view of human beings as meaning-making, as Sartre's 'empty passion' is inimical to those ways of working which have identified themselves as affirmative therapy. Which is not to deny that this form of affirmative therapy may have its own internal logic and validity, but it is *not*, by definition, existential, and it is misleading and inaccurate to regard it as congruent with existential therapy. More important, this preliminary chapter provides a starting point for an understanding of sexuality which neither pathologises it, nor treats it as a thing in itself separate from the individual's project of being or their lived situation in their culture and society. In the final analysis, it is the experience of the client, and the experience offered to the client in therapy which is paramount. Milton and Coyle have stated:

> Lesbian and gay affirmative approaches are ... grounded in certain concepts, skills and qualities of being (most of which would characterise good practice with any client group), underpinned by a fundamental belief in the normality and value of lesbian and gay sexualities and a thorough understanding of the nature, dynamics and challenges of these sexualities. The extent to which such a stance can be easily incorporated within the various schools of therapeutic theory and practice will vary according to the core assumptions of these schools, with some requiring more significant amendment than others in order to accommodate the principles of affirmative practice.
> (Milton & Coyle, 1999: 53–4)

Should we conclude that the core assumptions of an existential-phenomenological orientation make it more amenable to the adoption of a lesbian and gay affirmative approach than are some other orientations? Or should we question the wisdom of such a grafting at all? After all, as Milton says:

> It is possible for the existential-phenomenological therapist to provide a non-pathologising, contextually aware, sensitive therapy which will be experienced as affirming of lesbians and gay men in their entirety. To recognise the other in their 'other-ness' includes but goes beyond particular social identities.
> (Milton, 2000: 96)

I would go further and argue the provision of such a relationship is not only possible but constitutes the bedrock of existential therapy; we would not identify the therapy as existential in its absence. The adoption of the methods of 'gay affirmative therapy' as it has been defined to date, rather than augmenting our practice, runs the risk of diluting the very existential-phenomenological attitude that clients find so valuable.

References

Alderson, K (2013) *Counselling LGBTI Clients*. London: Sage Publications.

Barnes, H (1983) Sartre's concept of the self. *Review of Existential Psychology and Psychiatry, 7,* 21–40.

Bell, S, Kitzinger, C, Hodges, I, Coyle, A & Rivers, I (2002) Reflections on 'science', 'objectivity' and personal investment in lesbian, gay and bisexual psychology. *Lesbian & Gay Psychology Review, 3*(3), 91–5.

Bennett, C & Coyle, A (2001) A minority within a minority: Identity and well-being among gay men with learning disabilities. *Lesbian & Gay Psychology Review, 2*(1), 9–15.

Cannon, B (1991) *Sartre and Psychoanalysis: An existentialist challenge to clinical metatheory*. Lawrence, KS: University Press of Kansas.

Clark, D (1987) *The New Loving Someone Gay*. Berkeley, CA: Celestial Arts.

Clarke, V (2001) Lesbian and gay parenting: Resistance and normalisation. *Lesbian & Gay Psychology Review, 2*(1), 3–8.

Davies, D (2003) Towards a model of gay affirmative therapy. In D Davies & C Neal (Eds) *Pink Therapy: A guide for counsellors and therapists working with lesbian, gay and bisexual clients* (pp. 24–40). Maidenhead: Open University Press.

Davies, D & Neal, C (Eds) (2003) *Pink Therapy: A guide for counsellors and therapists working with lesbian, gay and bisexual clients*. Maidenhead: Open University Press.

Davies, D & Neal, C (Eds) (2009) *Therapeutic Perspectives on Working with Lesbian, Gay and Bisexual Clients*. Maidenhead: Open University Press.

Heidegger, M (1962) *Being and Time*. (J Macquarrie & ES Robinson, Trans). London: Harper and Row. (First published 1927)

Hopcke, M (1989) *Jung, Jungians and Homosexuality*. Boston: Shambhala.

Maylon, A (1982) Psychotherapeutic implications of internalized homophobia in gay men. In J Gonsiorek (Ed) *Homosexuality and Psychotherapy* (pp. 59–69). New York: Haworth Press.

Milton, M (1993) Social issues in the counselling process. *Counselling Psychology Review, 8*(1), 20–6.

Milton, M (2000) Is existential psychotherapy lesbian and gay affirmative? *Existential Analysis, the Journal of the Society for Existential Analysis, 11*(1), 86–102.

Milton, M (2007) Being sexual: Existential contributions to psychotherapy with gay male clients. In E Peel, V Clarke & J Drescher (Eds) *British*

Lesbian, Gay and Bisexual Psychologies: Theory, research and practice (pp. 27–45). Binghampton, NY: The Haworth Medical Press.

Milton, M & Coyle, A (1999) Lesbian and gay affirmative psychotherapy: Issues in theory and practice. *Sex and Marital Therapy: The Journal of the British Association for Sexual and Relationship Therapy*, *14*(1), 43–60.

Neal, C & Davies, D (Eds) (2000) *Issues in Therapy with Lesbian, Gay, Bisexual and Transgender Clients*. Buckingham: Open University Press.

Sartre, J-P (1956) *Being and Nothingness: An essay on phenomenological ontology* (HE Barnes, Trans). New York: Philosophical Library. (First published 1943)

Shernoff, M (1989) AIDS prevention counseling in clinical practice. In JW Dilley, C Pies & M Helquist (Eds) *Face to Face: A guide to AIDS counseling* (pp. 76–83). University of California San Francisco: AIDS Health Project.

Spinelli, E (1994) *Demystifying Therapy*. London: Constable. (Republished 2006, PCCS Books)

Spinelli, E (1997) Some hurried notes expressing outline ideas that someone might one day utilize as signposts towards a sketch of an existential-phenomenological theory of sexuality. *Existential Analysis, the Journal of the Society for Existential Analysis*, *8*(1), 2–20.

Spinelli, E (2013) Being sexual: Human sexuality revisited. *Existential Analysis, the Journal of the Society for Existential Analysis*, *24*(2), 203–20.

Van Deurzen, E (2010) *Everyday Mysteries: Existential dimensions of psychotherapy* (2nd ed). London: Sage.

Van Deurzen-Smith, E (1988) *Existential Counselling in Practice*. London: Sage Publications.

7

Gay Affirmative Therapy: Recognising the power of the social world

– Prof. Darren Langdridge –

Gay affirmative therapy (GAT), which should more properly be known as LGBQ or queer affirmative therapy (QAT),[1] has been developed in an attempt to rectify previously discriminatory psychotherapeutic practice with lesbians, bisexuals and gay men (see McGeorge & Carlson, 2011; Rutter, 2012 for recent reviews). GAT aims to achieve this by providing a framework for practice that is affirmative of lesbian, gay and bisexual identities. This 'positive framework' is clearly challenging for psychotherapies which seek to avoid imposing specific expectations on their clients, invariably through some notion of therapeutic neutrality, and a number of existential psychotherapists have challenged the applicability of such a framework for their practice (see du Plock, 1997). This chapter seeks to build on my previous work (Langdridge, 2007a), which draws on Ricoeur's formulation of hermeneutic phenomenology to argue for the value of GAT (see also Lebolt, 1999 and Pixton, 2003, for empirical evidence in support of GAT). Here, I highlight the need to acknowledge the power of the social world into which we are thrown and the power of the therapist to work with their clients in countering the homo/bi-

---

1. I use the acronym GAT as a shorthand for LGBQ affirmative therapy as this has become commonplace within the field. My own preference would be for a more obviously inclusive term but – at present – none is in widespread usage. It is also worth noting the exclusion of Trans here. Affirmative therapy with Trans clients will undoubtedly raise some similar issues but is sufficiently distinct that it warrants proper consideration in its own right rather than being simply included here under some overriding framework that involves the denial of difference.

negativity and heterosexism that remains endemic in these late modern times, with practical case study illustrations of the value of a gay affirmative modification of existential practice when working with sexual minority clients.

The case for affirmative practice

In this section I briefly revisit the arguments first raised in my previous paper on GAT (Langdridge, 2007a), where I engaged with the then recent flurry of articles arguing against affirmative practice (Cross, 2001; du Plock, 1997; Goldenberg, 2000), on the basis of a theoretical stance in favour of therapeutic neutrality.

In my 2007a article on GAT I distinguish between two forms of affirmative therapy in common use amongst therapists: *ethically affirmative* and *LGB affirmative* therapies. Ethically affirmative therapy is – in my opinion – the minimum standard for anyone working with sexual minority clients and involves the therapist adopting a stance where LGB identities are equally valued to heterosexual identities, and the therapist sufficiently informed about those identities that they are sensitive to cultural diversity. Ethically affirmative therapy is often referred to as 'gay affirmative therapy' but I think this is a mistake, as any practitioner engaging with sexual minority clients needs to operate to this basic standard if their practice is ethical. It is unacceptable for a therapist to attempt to 'cure' their LGB clients or impose any other negative attribution upon them on the basis of their sexual orientation. It is also unacceptable to undertake psychotherapeutic work with people from an identifiable minority community without having sufficient awareness of that culture such that we are able to be suitably sensitive to the client's need: the therapist has a duty to educate him- or herself and should not rely on the client to do this for them. Milton (2000a, 2000b) has made a powerful case for such practice that I think is hard for any ethical existential therapist to counter.

LGB (and now I should like to add Q for queer or questioning) affirmative therapy, on the other hand, is a form of practice that involves much more active intervention on the part of the therapist, notably through the direct affirmation of the wide variety of LGBQ thoughts and feelings that a client might express. The key difference between this form of affirmative therapy and that which I term ethically affirmative is a move from (an apparent) therapeutic neutrality towards a stance in which the therapist might break cover and deploy their power to actively support the exploration of same-sex sexual thoughts and feelings by a client. This may include positive affirmation of even tentative expressions of same-sex desire, direct interventions to lessen the impact of guilt and shame, and also – where appropriate – adopting an educative role with a client, for instance around HIV (see Clark, 1987; Davies, 1996).

Very few existential therapists are likely to object to ethically affirmative therapy when working with sexual minority clients. Indeed, as I have mentioned previously, I think it is quite easy to formulate an argument that adopting a stance other than this is unethical practice. The position on LGBQ affirmative therapy is quite different, however, with a number of existential therapists voicing opposition, not on the grounds of homophobia or homonegativity but rather through a principled stance founded on their belief in the value of therapeutic neutrality, ostensibly achieved through the phenomenological attitude (see Cross, 2001; du Plock, 1997 and this volume; Goldenberg, 2000). I recognise the importance of the phenomenological attitude within existential counselling and psychotherapy for the way it supports the therapist in working towards an understanding of the client's lifeworld. But I do not believe that this is truly achievable in any simple sense; or that it is the only method available to the existential therapist wanting to work through the challenges of same-sex thoughts and feelings within the context of a wider homonegative and heterosexist social world.

The notion of therapeutic neutrality, whether achieved through the phenomenological attitude or some other method, warrants critical interrogation or we risk the emergence of what might be termed a *naïve phenomenology*, where the therapist contents him- or herself that they truly know the other and their world in its entirety. Striving to understand the world of a client in their own terms is undoubtedly central to much counselling and psychotherapy practice, my own included. But any such attempt, including that derived through the phenomenological attitude is, and always must be, merely an approximation. We can never bracket off our entire natural attitude, no matter how hard we try. Similarly, no amount of empathy enables us to live the life of another, to feel their love, pain or loss. It is also the case that from moment to moment within the therapeutic encounter we repeatedly disclose ourselves to our clients, whether intended or not. Who we are, what we think and feel will inevitably leak out no matter what stance we choose to adopt in relation to our clients. There is nothing wrong with this, as long as we don't pretend that it is otherwise and risk the loss of a critical awareness of our own thoughts and feelings – our own ideology – through a naïve phenomenological attitude.

In order to deepen this argument and theoretically locate my own position with regard to affirmative therapy and the existential therapies, in my 2007a article I laid down a foundation for practice that drew directly on the philosophy of the hermeneutic phenomenologist Paul Ricoeur (see also Langdridge, 2007b, 2013). Ricoeur has done much of the work for us here with his critical intervention into phenomenological philosophy through the development of his hermeneutic and narrative theories. His work offers a theoretical justification for the break with the classic Husserlian phenomenological reduction and the incorporation of social theoretical hermeneutics into the (psycho) analytic process of counselling and psychotherapy.

My use of Ricoeur's philosophy for justifying affirmative therapy essentially revolved around his distinction between *demythologising* (empathic) and *demystifying* (suspicious) hermeneutics, along with the notion of the *critique of the illusions of the subject* (Langdridge, 2007a). Ricoeur (1970) provides an elaborate justification of the need for a multi-layered appropriation of meaning in which both empathy and suspicion are needed for a full understanding. An empathic hermeneutic is the stuff of Husserlian phenomenology (and therefore also most existential therapeutic practice) where we seek to understand the meaning of whatever is the subject of our analysis in its own terms. There is no place for external theoretical frameworks but simply the phenomenological attitude. In contrast, a hermeneutic of suspicion entails the use of an external theoretical framework to uncover further layers of meaning, as one might see in psychoanalysis. I argue that instead of psychoanalysis, which serves to undermine the phenomenology of the client, we should draw on hermeneutics of suspicion from critical social theory and turn them primarily on the social world into which client and therapist are both inevitably thrown. This includes a critique of the illusions of the subject – that is, a critical analysis of the position of the therapist – as much as a critical interrogation of the material provided by the client. In these terms, therapist and client work together, initially through the phenomenological attitude and then as co-critics through the appropriation of hermeneutics of suspicion from social theory, to open up new ways of understanding the experience of the client. This allows the therapist to move beyond a naïve phenomenology, recognise their own ideological position and most importantly work together with the client struggling with same-sex thoughts and feelings to find new ways of understanding their experience in a broader social context.

Power, politics and affirmative practice

When thinking through the position I have labelled 'naïve phenomenology', the risk, in political terms, is a denial of difference. The feminist political philosopher Iris Marion Young (1990) has convincingly shown how such a denial of difference stems from the moral ideal of impartiality (similar in practice to the notion of therapeutic neutrality), which inevitably results in relations of domination and repression. Young argues that the moral ideal of impartiality is a search for an abstract universal position detached from the particularity of existence, from our history, culture and personal perspective: in other words, a traditionally masculine notion of the political sphere where the personal must be relegated to the private. She argues that the 'view from nowhere' denies difference in three ways: first, denial of the particularity of situations through the adoption of a universal position; second, abstraction from our particular, personal and embodied desires to take the perspective of a rational agent and third, reduction of the plurality of life into a singular universal.

The moral ideal of impartiality is not only an impossible fiction but also ideologically pervasive for the way it justifies the notion of the impartial or neutral decision-maker, whether this is within the public sphere of politics or the private arena of counselling and psychotherapy. There are consequently many dangers with the notion of a moral ideal of impartiality, not least the silencing of individuals and groups whose needs do not conform to the universal as constructed. It is here where we see the loss of the particularity of the lesbian, gay, bisexual or queer subject, and the silencing of their specific needs. Through the gaze of therapeutic neutrality we lose sight of the particularity of sexual minorities and their specific therapeutic needs, needs that result from our immersion in a world in which oppression is still rife and identities are forged, at least in part, through particular group membership. Disadvantage accrues with difference and privilege with the identity of the mainstream, which is unfortunately still the Anglo-white-heterosexual-able-bodied-male subject within the West. The failure to take group differences seriously is an inevitable consequence of the ideal of (individual liberal) impartiality.

A politics of difference can be distinguished from the crude individualism of an ostensibly impartial liberalism by its focus on group oppression. In these terms, identities emerge from – rather than pre-date – the shared experiences and common histories of groups of people. We are therefore all variously 'inside' and 'outside' the variety of social groups we encounter, and experience privilege and disadvantage accordingly. This is no crude essentialism in which sexual identities are simply fixed a priori, not at all, but rather a position in which sexual identities, like any other aspect of selfhood, are the product of individual experience inextricably linked to a particular social context. That is, whilst a person's sexual identity might be legitimately experienced as pre-given, there is no assumption of necessary fixity to this aspect of selfhood and instead the meaning of any person's sexual identity is recognised within their unique personal-social-political situation. For some, this might mean an understanding of their sexual desire as fixed and unchangeable whilst for others it might entail a more free-floating notion of sexual desire and sexual practice. Key here is the need to recognise how such positions are differently implicated in/affected by oppression and the unequal distribution of power, and the implications of this for a person's capacity to construct a positive sense of selfhood. Young (1990) is particularly concerned with countering the 'five faces of oppression' – exploitation, marginalisation, powerlessness, cultural imperialism and violence – something she argues is only achievable within a politics of difference. Neutrality/impartiality are dangerously associated with assimilation and the perpetuation of the five faces of oppression, whilst active political engagement with difference and the promotion of justice and emancipation offers hope of differentiated inclusion, expansion of the normative and notably the possibility of an expanded range of possibilities in living for our clients.

This move involves us bridging the private (clinical) and public (political) domains; something that Samuels (1993) argues enriches both. We cannot escape the political in our work as therapists; it is present in every moment of our work. Client and therapist are inevitably situated within a broader political world and unable to escape the power of ideology. A refusal to engage with the political, whether knowingly or not, leads only one way, towards the conservative and the preservation of the status quo. As existentialists know only too well, we cannot choose not to choose. That is, we cannot ignore our decisions when working with a client, well not unless we inhabit the position of 'mauvais foi' (bad faith) (Sartre, 1943/2003). Such an undesirable position involves us in the abdication of our responsibility and the denial of our power to effect change, and is surely not something one would advocate for the socially responsible existential therapist. Most importantly, it would also lead us leaving our clients to battle on alone against the heterosexism and homo- and bi-negativity into which they have been thrown, something that I cannot countenance when I am so familiar with this struggle myself.

If we are to move beyond a 'naïve phenomenology' within counselling and psychotherapy that is not engaged with the wider social-political context – and therefore does not engage adequately with difference – then we must bring hermeneutics into existential practice to supplement the phenomenological method and bridge the private and public. A hermeneutic stance provides space for difference, for critique as well as tradition but – whilst commonplace within the phenomenological research tradition – has yet to be fully realised within the traditions of counselling and psychotherapy that draw on phenomenology. Without the critical stance afforded by hermeneutics there will be a continual denial of difference as a consequence of the liberal individualism that results from the (apparent) neutrality of the (existential) therapist.

Within the context of needing to deploy hermeneutics of suspicion I think it is important to distinguish between classic 'depth hermeneutics', such as those of Freud, Marx and Nietzsche that were discussed by Ricoeur (1970) in *Freud and Philosophy* and my own development of 'imaginative hermeneutics'. Depth hermeneutics requires us to dig beneath the surface to uncover the hidden meaning that lies beneath, as we see within psychoanalysis. This form of hermeneutics is fundamentally at odds with the phenomenological method, as it inevitably leads to the privileging of the therapist's meaning over that of the client. Imaginative hermeneutics on the other hand involves an exercise in imaginative play, drawing on ideas from critical social theory (such as feminism, queer theory, post-colonial theory) to work together with a client as co-critic of the limitations placed upon us by the social worlds we inhabit. The aim in deploying such imaginative hermeneutics is a perspectival shift in understanding such that new possibilities are opened up for the client in their ability to make sense of their experience.

Affirmative therapy in practice

The preceding theoretical discussion provides a framework for affirmative practice but it is still necessary to elaborate what this means in practice. In this section I outline five key principles that I think are necessary for effective LGBQ affirmative practice. These principles are derived from the theoretical discussion above and then shown in application in the case study that follows. These principles are for me the bedrock of a 'strong' LGBQ affirmative therapy and augment the fundamentals of practice that I have previously referred to as 'ethically affirmative' therapy (Langdridge, 2007a), which I argue must be the standard for all therapists (regardless of orientation) when working with sexual minority clients.

1. Client and therapist as co-critic: this is the best relational stance within which to think through affirmative therapy in practice. The collaborative nature of practice is perhaps not surprising given that an appreciation of the impact of power differentials is central to affirmative therapeutic theory. That is, anything but a truly collaborative therapeutic relationship would be anathema to affirmative practice. What is also vital is space for open and honest critical discussion, a space for critique and not just tradition and the status quo.

2. A critical stance concerning the place of sex and sexuality in the social world: honest and open exploratory discussion of power and politics as they relate to the client and the social world they inhabit is essential. Here one needs to be sensitive to the particular context of the client and their experience to determine what might be most relevant. But one might think of the following, for instance:

    a. An affirmative therapist might usefully work with a client to provide a challenge to heterosexism, the assumption of heterosexuality that underpins so much culture and has a demonstrable negative impact on the mental health of LGBQ people; or

    b. Explore the sexual feelings of a client with them within a broader queer perspective, in which fixity of orientation is no longer so central.

3. Positive affirmation of same-sex thoughts and feelings and constructive challenge to negative self-attributions: here, the stance is unapologetically in favour of positive affirmation should a client express same-sex thoughts or feelings. The counterpoint is that the affirmative therapist, whilst allowing space for negative attributions on the grounds of same-sex desires, might also take the opportunity where appropriate to challenge such self-attributions.

4. Working within a position focused on opening up new possibilities for a client's narrative identity: affirmative therapy is always about opening up possibilities rather than restricting options available to a client. That is, in order to avoid the charge levelled against affirmative therapy that it risks the premature closure of possible sexual identities, a central principle is that the therapist works with

the client to increase their awareness of possible ways of living that might have not been readily apparent. This is within the context of the ongoing process of (narrative) identity construction that we all engage in as we move through life and encounter challenges to the way we configure the episodes of our lives into a meaningful whole.

5. Acknowledging the educative role of the therapist: an affirmative therapist will take the opportunity to provide information for a client when appropriate and also enquire about sexual fantasies, practices and both physical and mental health. Affirmative therapists are unafraid to offer practical advice and encourage the development of appropriate support networks. Breaking a conservative view of the therapeutic frame is – in this context – entirely appropriate given that the therapist may well have valuable information about local organisations/networks that may be beneficial for a client. Beyond this, it is also important that affirmative therapists seek to explore the impact of a possible queer identity on the physical and mental health of a client. There is sufficient evidence for us to know that growing up within a heterosexist context has a profound effect on self-esteem and the capacity to care for oneself (see Ritter and Terndrup, 2002, for a summary). It is therefore appropriate that the affirmative therapist asks about self-harm and behaviours that might pose a risk for a client, not with the aim of judging such activities but rather their active exploration to ensure the client is fully cognisant of the psychological context of their actions and any possible implications for their physical and mental health and wellbeing.

Duncan's struggle to 'be normal': Affirmative therapy in practice[2]

Duncan came to see me because of difficulties he was having with his sense of satisfaction with life. He was in his early thirties and had been in a relationship with Colin for five years. He adored Colin and the life they had together but found himself increasingly unhappy, feeling bored and

---

2. Please note that in the following case study all identifying details have been changed. Whilst this should ensure that it is not possible for any individual to be identified the essence of the case has been preserved.

unfulfilled. Duncan and Colin had recently moved from their house, which was close to the city centre and most of their friends, out to the surrounding countryside. They had plenty of visitors, mostly family, but keeping in touch with people now required much more effort and planning. When asked what prompted the move Duncan replied that Colin wanted a house to renovate and Duncan just wanted him to be happy. It appeared that Duncan had remarkably little input into the choice of house, its location, or indeed about their chosen lifestyle in general. When Duncan described their lifestyle it appeared quite traditional: two people living together in a monogamous relationship within a small community where everyone knows each other, family visits and holidays overseas with family, shopping on Saturday and quiet visits to the local pub on Sundays. During the week evenings were mostly occupied with various hobbies from flower arranging to playing video games. Duncan worked as an occupational therapist, whilst Colin stayed at home earning money occasionally by arranging the flowers for friend and family events.

Duncan repeatedly compared his own relationship with that of friends who had more sexually open arrangements, notably threesomes and occasionally sex outside the couple. He said he wanted to be with Colin but wanted the sexual life of his friends, with the possibility of having sex with others separate from Colin. I asked Duncan what prevented them from having a more sexually open relationship and he replied that 'Colin would not want it'. When I asked about the possibility of a threesome, as it did not involve them being separate, he recoiled in horror at the thought. Threesomes were seemingly a great idea, as long as it did not involve Colin. With further exploration it became clear that Duncan had quite a convoluted view of sex, one that was simultaneously very experimental and traditional. That is, with Colin his view of sex was very traditional, something only to be conducted at night in the dark and never to be discussed with anyone else. Whilst in his fantasies and – as it turned out also in reality – he enjoyed random anonymous and quite risky sexual encounters. Duncan was initially reluctant to disclose his sexual infidelity, wanting instead to focus on the more traditional sex life with Colin, but did eventually feel able to talk this through with me. He was psychologically split with him strongly identifying monogamy with his 'loving relationship' with Colin but feeling irresistibly drawn to what he felt was his 'dark side', illicit sexual encounters with younger men, many of which did not involve safer sex. Duncan thought these sexual urges were a 'disgusting' part of himself, something he wanted rid of but something he also found enormously exciting.

Through the course of our work it became clear that Duncan was struggling with his 'desire to be normal'. He wanted to be like his brother and sister, who were both married with children, but – even with him coming close to this in his life as it was now with Colin – he still felt deeply depressed and unfulfilled. He was 'torn between a happy life with Colin and my dark side'. Duncan and I established a good rapport with me listening carefully within the phenomenological stance, exploring his lifeworld and actively recognising his struggle. In order to work through his struggle I sought to bring in discussion of the broader meanings of some of the material he was raising, notably that which involved negative self-attributions derived from normative understandings of sex and relationships. I gently challenged the meaning of his 'dark side' and whether it was really 'disgusting' to engage in anonymous sex. We also explored his lifestyle and what he found satisfying and what was not. This included discussion of decision-making in the relationship and whether he was recognising his own desires or being driven by Colin, his desire to be part of his family like his brother and sister and broader social forces and expectations. Duncan's struggle was centred on the construction of his identity as someone 'normal', leading him to split his fantasy life off into masturbation, secret liaisons and his friend's sex lives. I challenged the notion of 'normal' and we explored new possibilities in how he might seek to live his life, both in relation to Colin and separate from him. I also actively intervened to ask about his risky sexual practices and the implications of this for both his own health and that of Colin.

Duncan's mood brightened considerably through the course of our work as we worked together through a critical hermeneutic stance on the sexual world in which we both live. The disclosure of my own sexual orientation as a gay man further reinforced our collaborative relationship and understanding of the challenges he had faced growing up within a heterosexist world. He was clear that he wanted to stay with Colin and recognised that much of his life was truly good for him. He did however wish to change some aspects of his life and start to explore how he might have more say in the lifestyle that they were leading. This included the possibility of discussing their sex life but he was not determined to open up their relationship. He felt guilty about his secret sex life and wanted to find a way to 'make this more honest' but did not feel ready to discuss this with Colin at this stage. He was however determined to ensure that he would not put himself or Colin at risk by only practising safer sex in these encounters. My own feeling was that Duncan had gained considerable awareness of his sexual life in context and with this demonstrated greater mastery of his life. This could not be a simple 'happy ever after' story as there could not be a resolution in which everyone was immediately happy but this was a story of the value of affirmative therapy. Without my active intervention and our experience as co-critics of the social world into which we have both been thrown I doubt there would have been quite so much progress in Duncan recognising the limits placed on the construction of his narrative identity and what alternative possibilities there were for him. I could have opted to stand quietly by as he struggled alone to be 'normal' and through this reinforce the status quo and inadvertently support negative aspects of Duncan's developmental experience. Instead, my focus was on opening up new possibilities so Duncan himself could choose what made most sense in how he might understand himself as a gay man now and in the future.

Conclusion

In this chapter I have sought to both extend existing theory on the use of LGBQ affirmative therapy in existential counselling and psychotherapy and also develop and demonstrate its utility in practice. For me, recognition of the power of the social world to both allow and limit our understandings of self is central to all therapeutic practice, regardless of our theoretical perspective. Whilst I identify and work with a fairly classic 'British School' of existential therapeutic perspective (see Langdridge, 2013) that does not mean I think it is enough to rely solely on the phenomenological method. For me, contemporary existential practice must build on the phenomenological and existential foundation through the critical application of hermeneutics, much as we have seen within the world of phenomenological research (see, for instance, Dahlberg, Dahlberg & Nyström, 2008; Langdridge, 2007b; Finlay, 2011; Finlay & Evans, 2009; Smith, Flowers & Larkin, 2009). It is no longer good enough for therapists to pay lip service to structural inequalities and power differentials. Instead we must recognise the way that the social world structures our being-in-the-world, with the unequal distribution of power and – as a consequence – privilege and opportunity. As therapists we have a unique opportunity to offer our clients more than neutrality, not that this is ever truly possible anyway. Where we know of deep structural inequalities, where we see continuing oppression, and where we understand the impact that this has on the lives of people growing up within such inequality and oppression, we must surely have more to offer than simply passive acceptance within a phenomenological attitude. For me, it is my duty to offer more, to use the weight of my authority and privilege to not only listen and understand but also act as co-critic of the heterosexist and homonegative world we still inhabit so that my clients receive as much from me as I can possibly give. This is in the hope that – as a result – I may better enable my clients to realise a sense of self that best equips them to make sense of their present experience and also see new possibilities for living, as they journey into the future as lesbian, gay, bisexual or queer men and women.

References

Clark, D (1987) *The New Loving Someone Gay*. Berkeley, CA: Celestial Arts.

Cross, MC (2001) The appropriation and reification of deviance: Personal construct psychology and affirmative therapy. A response to Harrison. *British Journal of Guidance and Counselling, 29*(3), 337–43.

Dahlberg, K, Dahlberg, H & Nyström, M (2008) *Reflective Lifeworld Research*. Lund: Studentlitteratur.

Davies, D (1996) Towards a model of gay affirmative therapy. In D Davies & C Neal (Eds) *Pink Therapy: A guide for counsellors and therapists working with lesbian, gay and bisexual clients* (pp. 24–40). Buckingham: Open University Press.

Du Plock, S (1997) Sexual misconceptions: A critique of gay affirmative therapy and some thoughts on an existential-phenomenological theory of sexual orientation. *Journal of the Society for Existential Analysis, 8*(2), 56–71.

Finlay, L (2011) *Phenomenology for Therapists: Researching the lived world*. Chichester: Wiley-Blackwell.

Finlay, L & Evans, K (2009) *Relational-centred Research for Psychotherapists: Exploring meanings and experience*. Chichester: Wiley-Blackwell.

Goldenberg, H (2000) A response to Martin Milton. *Journal for the Society of Existential Analysis, 11*(1), 56–71.

Langdridge, D (2007a) Gay affirmative therapy: A theoretical framework and defense. *Journal of Gay & Lesbian Psychotherapy, 11*(1–2), 27–43.

Langdridge, D (2007b) *Phenomenological Psychology: Theory, research and method*. Harlow: Pearson Education.

Langdridge, D (2013) *Existential Counselling and Psychotherapy*. London: Sage Publications.

Lebolt, J (1999) Gay affirmative psychotherapy: A phenomenological study. *Clinical Social Work Journal, 27*(4), 355–70.

McGeorge, C & Carlson, TS (2011) Deconstructing heterosexism: Becoming an LGB affirmative heterosexual couple and family therapist. *Journal of Marital and Family Therapy, 37*(1), 14–26.

Milton, M (2000a) Is existential psychotherapy a lesbian and gay affirmative therapy? *Journal of the Society of Existential Analysis, 11*(1), 86–102.

Milton, M (2000b) Existential-phenomenological therapy. In D Davies & C Neal (Eds) *Pink Therapy 2: Therapeutic perspectives on working with lesbian, gay and bisexual clients* (pp. 39–53). Buckingham: Open University Press.

Pixton, S (2003) Experiencing gay affirmative therapy: An exploration of clients' views of what is helpful. *Counselling and Psychotherapy Research, 3*(3), 211–15.

Ricoeur, P (1970) *Freud and Philosophy: An essay on interpretation* (D Savage, Trans). New Haven, CT: Yale University Press.

Ritter, KY & Terndrup, AI (2002) *Handbook of Affirmative Psychotherapy with Lesbians and Gay Men*. New York: Guildford Press.

Rutter, PA (2012) Sex therapy with gay male couples using affirmative therapy. *Sexual and Relationship Therapy, 27*(1), 35–45.

Samuels, A (1993) *The Political Psyche*. London: Routledge.

Sartre, J-P (2003) *Being and Nothingness*. (HE Barnes, Trans). London: Routledge. (First published 1943)

Smith, JA, Flowers, P & Larkin, M (2009) *Interpretative Phenomenological Analysis: Theory, method and research*. London: Sage Publications.

Young, IM (1990) *Justice and the Politics of Difference*. Princeton, NJ: Princeton University Press.

Part 5

Contemporary Concerns

8

Being Sexual: Childhood and sexuality

– Prof. Ernesto Spinelli –

At the same time as I am writing this chapter, the UK Office of the Children's Commissioner has published a major study stating that during a period of 14 months to October 2011, there have been 2,409 verified child and adolescent victims of sexual exploitation in the UK (Berelowitz et al, 2012). The report has further identified 16,500 children who were at 'high risk' of sexual exploitation in 2010–11. Deputy Children's Commissioner, Sue Berelowitz, has stated: 'The reality is that each year thousands of children in England are raped and abused by people seeking to humiliate, violate and control them' (Butler, 2012). As if this were not sufficiently disturbing, just weeks before the publication of this report, British society was caught in the grips of a major scandal and its subsequent furore over revelations of the sexual abuse of some 300 children and adolescents over a 40-year period by a radio and television celebrity beloved by many for his dedication to charities and good works (Cree, 2012).

Rape and abuse justifiably provoke dismay and disgust. When such acts are carried out upon children, these responses are substantially augmented. Why this might be so was considered by Professor Stevi Jackson in her text *Childhood and Sexuality* (Jackson, 1982). She writes:

> In modern Western societies children are set apart from the rest of the population, regarded as a special category of people with their own needs. We have particular obligations toward them: we are expected to protect and take care of them, to put their interests before our own. Any event or circumstance that affects them, especially if it is seen as placing them 'at risk', easily becomes a public issue. In a sense, children are ideal victims, creatures particularly deserving of our sympathy, so

that any real or imaginary threat to them can be used to manipulate public opinion.

(Jackson, 1982: 1)

The present chapter, which re-views and extends a number of ideas I have proposed elsewhere (Spinelli, 2001, 2002), attempts to explore the relation between our culture's current views on childhood and sexuality. It argues that the interplay between the terms childhood and sexuality is a problematic one and it explores what might make it so, or perhaps more accurately, appear to be so. As the above quote suggests, at least for many in contemporary Western society, children differ from adults in a great many ways – physically, mentally, emotionally, and relationally. As an extension of this argument, childhood is commonly perceived to be not only different, but 'special' and 'innocent' such that the introduction of sexuality would somehow threaten the maintenance of these qualities. If this view must, nonetheless, concede that children are sexual beings then it argues that their way of being sexual must be of a different 'kind' to that of adults. For it must also retain qualities of 'specialness' and 'innocence'.

Existential thought, in common with several other relationally attuned theoretical systems, argues that childhood cannot be seen to be primarily a 'given' or 'natural' condition of being. Of course, all human beings undergo dramatic physical changes from infancy to the point of their death, but what we call 'childhood' refers to much more than that. Far more significantly, childhood is a social institution.

> The form childhood takes is shaped by many other aspects of social life … Our feelings about children and sex are not a natural response to people of a particular age but result from the way childhood is defined within our society.
>
> (Jackson, 1982: 22)

Within Western society, the assumptions surrounding childhood and its relation to the experience of being sexual have undergone, and continue to undergo, dramatic conceptual and behavioural changes. In my own lifetime, I have been witness to several of these shifts. For example, during the 1970s, when my friends and I were at an age when the possibilities of parenthood were becoming foremost in our thoughts, the dominant discourse, largely influenced by the writings of Wilhelm Reich and Jean-Paul Sartre among others, took it as a 'given' that children would enact sexual behaviours from infancy, that it was their right to be sexual, and what should we, as parents and adults, countenance, if not actively support, of its expression? Should our children, for instance, be permitted, perhaps even encouraged, to be present during moments of sexual intimacy and pleasure between their parents? Should parental rearing include teaching children how best to masturbate so that their lives might be 'fully orgasmic'? Today, such views seem inconceivable for anyone to treat seriously much less promote. Almost certainly, they would be seen by many to be arguments in defence of paedophilia and any parent claiming to have assisted in their expression would be subject to criminal investigation.

It is, I believe, indicative of how much our views have changed and how dangerously perverse ideas from less than 40 years ago now seem to be that I find it necessary to clarify that I am in no way suggesting a return to these older views nor promoting them as desirable options for parents or families to consider undertaking. While the discussion that follows raises what I imagine to be some relevant concerns regarding children's experiences of being sexual, I want to make it absolutely clear to all readers that none of my comments should be understood to be either overt or covert defences of child pornography or paedophilia. I remain as aware as any of my psychotherapeutic colleagues of the long-term physical and psychological injuries that can be inflicted upon those people who, as young children, suffered the unwanted and undeserved attentions of sexual predators – be they strangers or, far more commonly, family members. Like my colleagues, I have no hesitation in expressing my revulsion at the behaviour of those who, for whatever reasons, construct the means with which to permit themselves the enactment and enjoyment of sexual violence toward children – no matter how seemingly affectionate, tender or focused upon the 'pleasuring' of the child they claim these acts to be. If my arguments succeed in provoking a sense of unease, I would hope that it would remain apparent that this felt discomfort is not one that is intended to exculpate moral responsibilities.

That it is incumbent upon me to make these clarifications may well say something about the way our society today both expresses its fears and seeks to resolve them. Be that as it may, what seems far more significant is the more general conclusion that the prevalence of any current set of assumptions adopted by a society at any given time makes the consideration of possible alternatives to the accepted view appear to be, at best, odd and at worst, so alien and threatening that just to give voice to them raises alarms. Moreover, alternatives have existed in the historical development of our current notions of childhood and, in conjunction with these, so too has our unease regarding the sexual being of children come to the fore.

Existential thought has had little to say about such concerns not, I believe, out of disinterest, but because much of the existing discourse has been so rigidly demarcated by psychoanalytic perspectives that theoretical and therapeutically focused alternatives are not easy to put forward nor are they likely to be willingly embraced. Some initial evidence of change, at least insofar as more broad-based discussions on child development (Adams, 2013; Briod, 1989; Kirby, 2005; Langdridge, 2005) and therapy with children (Scalzo, 2010) are concerned, exists and more, I am fairly certain, will be forthcoming. In the interim, this chapter attempts to clarify some of the primary concerns that might subsequently be more fully developed from an existential-phenomenological perspective. I will begin with an overview of the development of modern-day notions of childhood.

Childhood

Child development

Recent years have seen major developments in the understanding of children from birth to the first few years of life. Much of this has emerged through advances in cognitive science which have refuted long-held beliefs regarding early childhood. For example, although the idea that the difficulty of remembering early events in our lives is due to mechanisms of repression has been a key assumption of a great many models of child development, contemporary psychological research has provided strong evidence to suggest that, rather than repression, this difficulty is due to major differences between children from birth to around the age of five and older children and adults in the ways that they both process and reflect on their experience and subsequently retain memories of it (Gopnik, 2009). Similarly, recent studies by Alison Gopnik and her team have suggested that 'it is possible that babies literally don't see the difference between their own pain and the pain of others ... [and] that children's conception of a continuous separate self develops slowly in the first five years' (Greenberg, 2010: 27).

Perhaps the most significant debates regarding the understanding of child development have been those that have challenged models that promote a generalised stage-like process of development. Stage models have dominated child psychology and continue to hold significant appeal not only to researchers but also to educators, legislators and parents. However, their limitations have become increasingly apparent.

Whatever the specific stage focus adopted, be it intellectual, moral, social or even sexual for example, stage models impose a somewhat simplistic linear perspective of development. More significantly, in their emphasis on any one particular focus, stage models maintain compartmentalised modes of understanding development and cannot easily adopt systemic or interrelational perspectives wherein the various foci influence and are influenced by one another. Among researchers who have pursued this critique, Esther Thelen has proposed a developmental model derived from dynamic systems theory (the study of how complex phenomena both stabilise and change over time) (Thelen, 2005). Thelen's approach attempts to encompass all the possible factors that may be in operation for an individual at any given developmental moment. From this perspective, human development emerges as a constantly fluid, causally non-linear and multiply determined interaction between any particular person and the world. In addition, Thelen's model combines previously opposing notions of stability and instability into an ever-shifting continuum whose constancy lies not in stasis but in the very motion between temporary states of stability and instability. Novel circumstances provoke novel 'self-assemblies' that are not solely the result of a combination of genetics and culture but are, just as importantly, also influenced by the 'interweaving of events at a given moment' (Thelen, 2005: 271). In this way, issues of human development reveal unique patterns arising from the interaction of time, body and experience that cannot be truly generalised nor open to rigid patterns of prediction. By placing its emphasis upon unique interactions of conditions, dynamic systems theory challenges the power and appeal of stage-based theories of human development.

Existentially focused approaches to child development also 'shift away from stage or age-specific tasks toward more global consideration of the existential challenges facing the individual throughout the course of his/her life. An existential perspective ... questions the implicit determinism found in stage theories' (Kirby, 2005: 41) and reminds us that the preferred notion of universal stages of human development is a hypothetical abstraction rather than an unquestionable 'given'. Inspired by the philosophical writings of Martin Heidegger (Heidegger, 1962, 2001), the existential psychiatrist and psychotherapist Medard Boss questioned basic underlying assumptions regarding the very idea of development as a linear, uni-directional growth process (Boss, 1963, 1979). Instead, Boss pointed out that, existentially, human beings are always 'all present beings' such that, rather than develop it is more accurate to say that we *reveal and are revealed* through experience (Boss, 1979). Our interactions with the world provoke novel ways of disclosing who and how we are being within the actual conditions of being. This revealing or disclosing undoubtedly highlights shared, or universal, aspects of being human. But, equally, it cannot truly be generalised from the standpoint of some general and predictable series of stages or patterns. Nor is it seen to be the case that even when the process of disclosure is explored from the standpoint of the uniqueness of any particular being's experience, it does not follow any straightforward sequential 'building-block' fashion. For existential theory, what we term as development expresses itself in a far more complex, multi-directional and multi-dimensional manner. In adopting such perspectives, existential theory can be seen to converge closely with approaches inspired by dynamical systems theory.

At the heart of all existential views on questions of development lies the assumption of relatedness. In this way, developmental concerns are no longer located within, or expressive of, some hypothesised internal mechanism which is accessible only to any one particular being. Rather, what development expresses is the dynamic of ongoing, ever-shifting interactions between beings or between any particular being and the world context he or she inhabits. This relational perspective regarding child development in particular was elaborated by the existential philosopher and psychologist, Maurice Merleau-Ponty (Merleau-Ponty, 1964). In his overview of Merleau-Ponty's analysis of the development of children's relations with others, Darren Langdridge argues that the recurring dilemma encountered 'by classical, and indeed, contemporary psychological theories is that ... a person's psyche is that which is given only to themselves' (Langdridge, 2005: 91). Merleau-Ponty takes this to be the critical limitation of dominant dualist approaches and proposes an intersubjective alternative wherein the awareness of self and other is a simultaneous phenomenon rather than a sequential one of awareness of self leading to the awareness of others, or vice versa. This intersubjective 'turn' raises various pivotal issues concerning child development that are beyond the remit of this chapter. For our purposes, it can be seen that in promoting a relational context it is not only our views on development that are brought into question; it forces us to reconsider how we construe childhood itself.

The construction of childhood

As has been established by various authors, childhood as we understand the term to mean today, is a relatively recent invention whose origins lie in the social and religious upheavals of the seventeenth century. For several centuries prior to these events, children were most often perceived as being 'miniature adults' who shared similar duties, responsibilities, interests and passions to their 'full-sized' counterparts. These 'miniature adults' worked long hours, dressed in the same (if smaller-sized) clothes, ate the same food and participated in the same gatherings and festivities as did the other members of their community. To have segregated them from such would likely have been viewed as being cruel and unjust. During the Medieval period, for example, most children by the age of seven were considered legally responsible for their own actions and although denied the legal status of adults, they were still held to be legally responsible for their behaviour and 'subject to the same penalties as adults if they broke the law' (Jackson, 1982: 32). Although their social position was subordinate to that of adults, the idea that children's psychology or developmental status required special attention in matters of daily life seemed absurd. Equally, it would not have been unusual for these 'miniature adults' to have witnessed, if not participated in, various forms of sexual activity that, today, would be viewed as being entirely unacceptable (Jackson, 1982; Lescariges & Hinitz, 2000).

Significant social and ideological changes that expressed a dramatic ideological shift which would radically alter the nature and meaning of childhood became apparent towards the end of the sixteenth century. Through them, childhood would come to be seen and treated as a distinct and special category of being. These radical changes emerged full blown during the seventeenth century largely as a result of the Reformation and Counter-Reformation movements. Both Puritans and Catholics (mainly from the Jesuit Order) began to focus on educational reform through which they could maintain 'the spiritual well-being of children as part of a wider campaign against moral laxity' (Jackson, 1982: 42). As much as they were at odds with one another, both camps shared the view that the child was corrupt, tainted by original sin, an uncivilised being whose demoniac nature had to be tamed (Jackson, 1982; Lescariges & Hinitz, 2000). Through such views, notable shifts in social attitude and behaviour towards children and family life in general took hold, first amongst wealthier citizens and subsequently among all but the lowest classes: children began to be dressed in ways that distinguished them from adults; childhood illnesses and inappropriate behaviours were distinguished from those of adults and, as well, were treated in distinctive ways either via the new specialisation of paediatrics which provided child-specific medical interventions or through the spiritual intercessions and 'treatments' of the clergy; and through the restructuring of schools so that they now incorporated differing levels of grading, each with its own appropriate textbooks and focused educational topics whose ultimate aim was 'to break the spirit of [children's] naturally evil natures' (Jackson, 1982: 42).

This initial 'demoniac' view of childhood was modified during the late eighteenth and early nineteenth centuries. Rather than children, who began to be romanticised as 'noble savages', it was now argued that it was society itself that was corrupt and the continuing basis for sin and evil in the world. This Romantic view argued that children's souls were purer, expressive of a more innocent state of being, if only by merit of their being younger, children had had far fewer experiences of 'the baser instincts' directed toward violence and sexuality. Now, more than anything, children required protection from exposure to impure thoughts and deeds (Jackson, 1982; Lescariges & Hinitz, 2000). The segregation of children from the world of the adult was one obvious safeguarding manoeuvre. The attempt to educate at least some children so that the influence of both religious faith and an appreciation of 'higher' intellectual qualities could counteract their more 'animalistic' tendencies and urges was another. The wearing of specially designed clothing, distinct to that of the adult, and intended to hold in check the temptation of 'impure thoughts' was emphasised even more strongly than before. Also, in similar fashion, any evidence of the young child's curiosity surrounding the body and its functions – and particularly its sexual and reproductive functions – or, worse, of the child's indulging in 'base and sinful' activities such as solitary or mutual masturbation, required swift and unequivocal controls (usually physical punishment combined with fear, shame and guilt-inducing injunctions) for the sake of protecting the child's soul and mind from premature and irreparable spiritual and mental degeneration (Jackson, 1982; Lescariges & Hinitz, 2000).

Prior to these dramatic and socially pervasive shifts it had made little sense to conceal instances of sexual behaviour from children. More to the point, the way that society was structured before the seventeenth century made the avoidance of sexual awareness impossible to maintain regardless of the child's class or background. Family life was organised in ways that could not shield children from becoming aware not only of sexual behaviour but also that its 'charge' permeated so much of everyday life. Sexual references were plentiful in discussion, banter, songs, jokes and narratives. Fairy tales, for example, were more for the enjoyment of adults than of children and in their unexpurgated form contained a substantial amount of explicit references to sexual behaviour. In the original version of the Brothers Grimm's *Sleeping Beauty*, it is an act of rape rather than a chaste kiss that finally awakens her (Jackson, 1982). Now, however, it became the task of society to segregate children from all evidence of sexual being. Children began to be excluded from adult gatherings and festivities and, instead, were provided with their own mealtimes and social events. Texts, songs and rhymes were expurgated of all sexual references and innuendo. Everything regarding the relationship between childhood and sexuality changed. In brief, children's innocence became equated with sexual ignorance.

Theorising childhood sexuality

It was through the rise of rationalism that modern psychology was established as a distinct discipline. Through it, the earliest scientific theories of child development emerged. At first, and particularly with regard to matters of sexual experiences during childhood, these closely resembled earlier views that had romanticised children and imbued them with an innocence which both denied sexual expression and sought to prevent its occurrence (Sulloway, 1980). The emphasis on sin may have been replaced by a focus on mental health, but the underlying concerns remained much the same.

With this in mind, we can better comprehend just how disturbing and radical were the ideas about infantile sexuality proposed by Freud and his contemporaries and why they generated so much heated debate and condemnation (Sulloway, 1980). Although many of these 'new' perspectives had been advanced by earlier theorists, it was the critical link made by Freud between them and his overall model of psychology that made them so revolutionary (Gay, 1989; Sulloway, 1980). Freud posited early childhood sexuality to be different from that of the adult in that early expressions of sexuality had no permanently focused object. This 'polymorphous perversity' permitted any part of the infant's body, as well as any perceived external object, to become 'libidinally charged' toward auto-erotic sexual gratification. It was only when a fixed and stable object-choice (typically, the child's mother) became identified as the external satisfier of the child's sexual aim that the child began to approach an experience of being sexual that shared common characteristics with that of adult expressions (Freud, 1905/2001). Rather than be viewed as a sexual innocent, the child stood revealed as being sexually omnivorous and was now to be seen as the source to the adult's relative sexual normality or lack of it. This basic hypothesis underwent numerous revisions by Freud himself. Even so, he continued to accept its fundamental accuracy. Others, especially those psychoanalysts who never entered Freud's 'inner circle', posited even more radical elaborations. Melanie Klein, for example, took Freud's ideas to the extreme by arguing that, among other notions, the psychic world of the young infant is best understood as seething with sexual desires that are often expressed through the child's play activity. This activity, when properly interpreted, disclosed the child's preoccupation with attempts at both incorporating and destroying the play-object. Through such observations, Klein hypothesised the existence of an innate infantile phantasy of male and female genitalia bound together in permanent intercourse. As such, unlike Freud's vision of a childhood sexuality that must undergo various phases before it reaches its genital focus, Klein considered this focus to be all-too apparent from birth – if the adult dared witness it (Klein, 1975).

In contrast to these views, Freud's once 'Crown Prince' and subsequently one of his major detractors, Carl Gustav Jung, dismissed the very notion of pre-adolescent sexuality. Instead, he argued that the language of psychoanalysis imposes itself upon, or 'sexualises', childhood behaviours. Adults, including adult psychoanalysts, interpret some of the child's behaviour as being sexual not because the child experiences these as such but rather because the adult has decreed them to be so (Jung, 1975). Jung's argument is, I think, a valid one and is certainly deserving of much greater consideration. In many ways, it foreshadows various contemporary cultural critiques focusing upon the premature sexualisation of children via portrayals of childhood in the media, advertising and product marketing (including clothing) (Kaeser, 2001). Nonetheless, it could still be argued that even if Jung's argument is substantially correct, it might still be the case that the adult's 'sexualising' interpretations of the child's actions might conceivably still accurately reflect the child's own lived experience of being sexual. In other words, that the child cannot name or label the experience as sexual need not imply that it is not felt or experienced sexually. In this way, Jung's hypothesis shares intriguing similarities with Freud's own early, and subsequently abandoned, 'seduction hypothesis' wherein he argued that those repressed pre-adolescent experiences of sexual abuse become 'un-repressed' at adolescence because, by then, a language has been found to express and bring meaning to the earlier experience (Sulloway, 1980).

Variations on these competing viewpoints regarding the relationship between childhood and sexuality still prevail. We can begin to see how these contrasting influences have endured, at least in part, such that they continue to inform and dominate contemporary views of childhood and, in turn, how they infuse and identify our society's deepest recurring fears for and about children. But is it not possible that these competing ideas may, at the very least, exacerbate our concerns, if not actually *be* their source-point?

Children being sexual

What seems indisputable is that from an early age, children become aware of, and curious about bodies: their own, other children's, their caregivers', other people's in general. This interest reveals to them that bodies are both similar and different in all kinds of ways. Because some parts of bodies are usually covered by clothes or provoke strong, often confusing, reactions from others, children's curiosity about these parts of their own, and others', bodies is likely to be intensified. They may 'peek' at these hidden parts when the opportunity arises. They may seek out ways of naming them and often receive replies that further swell their curiosity. They may play games by themselves or with other children involving the exposure of those parts of their bodies that have been designated as 'secret', or perhaps even 'naughty'. They may, privately or in public, touch or rub their genitals.

While acknowledging the unreliability of memory in that we review our remembrances of the past from the biased perspective of the present (Spinelli, 1994/2006), I suspect that most of us could single out events from our childhood that would encompass our version of some or all of the above. But ... are any or all of these activities necessarily childhood expressions of being sexual?

It is precisely because the meanings we give to memories are so linked to current context that we need to remain cautious. Might it not be the case, as Jung's views would suggest, that adults interpret their own childhood activities as being primarily, if not solely, sexual not because they were directly experienced as such during their childhood but because sexual meanings are being imposed upon them by the adult's biased conclusions as to what they expressed? While, as children, we might well have invoked or carried out some or all of the above behaviours, were they for us, at the time, clear-cut expressions of being sexual or might they have been far more mysterious and unfocused experiences? Could their enactment have had at least as much, if not everything, to do with provoking awe and laughter from ourselves and our companions? Or have served as expressions of secrecy which, in turn, permitted a sense of personal empowerment as well as a retort to the power of adults? 'You think that you know me and what I do?' we might well goad in private, 'Well, guess what? You don't!' And even when the delight and physical excitation experienced by our fondling and being fondled was genitally focused, were we interpreting such feelings as specifically 'sexual' as might an adult, or were they localised focal-points contained within a much more diffuse lived experience that included elements of curiosity, private and shared secrecy, intimacy, humour, comparison and ritual and which, together, provoked the general experience of pleasure?

> The ways in which we express our sexuality depend on how we interpret our feelings and desires and what we decide to do about them. We should not assume, when children do apparently sexual things, that they are motivated by the same wants and needs that [adults] feel. Children may experience sensations similar to an adult's, but they are not usually able to make sense of them in the same way … [Masturbation in childhood may provoke similar or the same physical sensations as in adulthood], but it is doubtful if the act meant the same in childhood. As adults we can relate masturbation to other aspects of sexuality … But this ability to make sense of masturbation in sexual terms is likely to be beyond the reach of the child.
>
> (Jackson, 1982: 69–70)

At the conclusion of a major research project focused on children's sexual thinking, Ronald and Juliette Goldman stated: 'what in our view is the greatest need is a conceptual structure for children's sexual thinking' (Goldman & Goldman, 1982: 393). Alas, nothing of the sort has, as yet, been produced.

Arousing and erotic experiences

In *The Mirror and the Hammer: Existential challenges to therapeutic orthodoxy* (Spinelli, 2001), I suggested that it might be worthwhile to distinguish physically pleasurable experiences as being either *arousing* or *erotic*.

Arousing experiences refer to those physical sensations that may be felt diffusely throughout the whole of one's body or that are localised upon particular parts of the body (such as the genitals) or both and whose aim and focus lies in their maintenance of a persistent state of pleasurable body-alertness and excitation that lasts until such time as the participant/s cease/s the activities that are required to provoke them.

Erotic experiences may share similar features to arousing experiences but are distinguishable from them in that their intent is the release of physical tension through orgasm. As such, from a felt standpoint, erotic experiences must be in part, or may be entirely, genitally focused.

Pleasurable experiences may be both *arousing* and *erotic* or may shift from one to the other. When these are enacted between one or more partners, it is possible that while one participant experiences arousal, the other(s) may be experiencing erotic excitation and vice versa or that both (or all) experience either only arousal or erotic excitation. In addition, this distinction clarifies that although one or both or all partners might not experience any specifically erotic excitement in their physical encounters this need not suggest that no arousal is being experienced or that the arousal being experienced is necessarily less adequate, or less fulfilling, than its erotic counterpart.

I remain aware of the tendency in Western culture to interweave these terms, and it is also the case that arousal can suggest more general states of 'being alert' whereas, in contrast, the term erotic is more commonly employed to designate non-pornographic depictions of nudity and sexual activity. Nonetheless, it remains my view that this limited distinction provides an initial means with which to address and clarify a possibly critical divergence between child and adult experiences of being sexual. What I am suggesting is that childhood experiences of looking at or fondling the whole or parts of one's own or another's body, or having parts or the whole of one's body fondled by another, are most typically pleasurable instances of arousal and far less commonly, if ever, expressions of erotic pleasure.

What value might this distinction have? For one thing, it acknowledges that children may seek out arousing experiences while still remaining unaware of their erotic counterpart. Further, it clarifies that while interactions between children and adults may provoke arousal for either or both participants, such experiences need not be erotic for either or both parties. Given our culture's fears regarding the sexual abuse of children, this latter point may help to both clarify and assuage the increasingly dreaded confusion felt by many adults (parents in particular) with regard to their experience of physical pleasure when holding, fondling, bathing, or engaging in other forms of physical contact with a child. For instance, one of my clients confessed to me her delight in kissing the whole of her three-month old son's body, including his genitals, as part of their evening post-bathing ritual. She added that her own experience of these activities provoked a sense of bonding and near-spiritual closeness with her son such that, in her words, 'it made the whole of her body tingle'. Was she, she wanted to know, a sexual predator and pervert? Might she be inadvertently sexually abusing her child? While it can provide no easy or straightforward resolution to such questions, nonetheless, the proposed distinction between arousal and erotic excitation could well assist their exploration and clarification. Finally, it may also be the case that the cultural concerns and alarms raised by child pornography and paedophilia alert us to this distinction. Experiences of arousal may be condoned or even encouraged between children and adults, while erotic demands upon a being who might neither understand their meaning nor consent to their imposition clearly remain identified as examples of an abusive assertion of power.

In general, the proposed distinction between arousing and erotic experiences may help to clarify at least some of the recurring concerns regarding the conjunction of childhood and sexuality, not least with regard to legitimate fears surrounding the sexual abuse of children by adults. Nevertheless, a further, related, set of concerns remains to be addressed.

The 'adultification' of children and the 'infantilisation' of adults

In spite of current Western society's desire to maintain their special status, children are more and more likely to be expected (and to expect themselves) to develop and maintain viewpoints, responsibilities and attitudes that, increasingly, liken them to the adult. From their own accounts, and by the reckoning of their parents and educators, today's children have taken on adult-like lifestyles, concerns and anxieties that even in their parents' or grandparents' generations would have been inconceivable. However, this shift in perspective is not uni-directional. For, just as children have begun to adopt more adult-like stances, interests and behaviours, so, too, have adults become increasingly 'infantilised' in terms of their relationship toward themselves, others and the world in general such that the demarcations between childhood and adulthood have, and continue to, become increasingly 'fuzzy' and indistinct from one another.

From *Star Wars* to *Harry Potter*, from super-hero comic books to PlayStation 3, from favourite music to most desired holiday destination, what was once the domain of the child and young adolescent has become infiltrated by the adult. This shift can be seen in the lack of distinction in the choice of (mainly simple, 'fast') food – as well as the way that it is eaten. It can be heard and read in the increasingly strident and tantrum-like rants that pass as critical argument by television and radio commentators as well as by Internet bloggers and social networkers. Perhaps, most obviously, it presents itself in clothing – be they caps and t-shirts emblazoned with the names or distinctive features of a favourite sports team or celebrity, or casual footwear or designer wear 'for those special occasions'. While we might well applaud the possible equalisation of status that perhaps is being expressed, we must also consider the possible, if unintended, consequences.

While it is true that children of previous generations engaged in fantasy games that centred around their playing at 'grown-ups' by dressing in their parents' clothes or focusing upon adult roles and activities, what is different today is that such games are being played out more and more frequently in the presence and with the encouragement of their parents and other adults. One undesirable outcome of this is that it has become commonplace to be confronted with media accounts of parental purchases of 'sexy' clothes and undergarments for their pre-adolescent offspring or with television programmes that parade young children dressed up and gyrating suggestively in imitation of adult actors and singers. Of course, in many instances, shared activities cement feelings of bonding and affection that are not only of psychosocial importance but which are also the source of enjoyment by children and adults alike with no sense of obvious harm and danger. However, it has become increasingly evident that children's concerns over matters such as their appearance, their weight or height, the colour of their hair, the 'brand' of their possessions and their social standing among peers increasingly provoke levels of distress and anxiety that are far more akin to the vexations of adults than they are to the tribulations of childhood.

If this blurring of the previously constructed 'line' between childhood and adulthood has become more confused in general, why should it be surprising to find that this confusion extends to how our society interprets what is and is not appropriate in the ways that children experience and express being sexual? Might it not already be the case that this evolving conjunction of boundaries has begun, however inadvertently, to impose a much more obviously adult worldview concerning being sexual upon children's own curiosity, attitudes and experiences? And, in parallel, might it not also alter adults' assumptions of how children are to be understood and treated as sexual beings?

These questions generate a disturbing level of unease in that they go right to the heart of our greatest fears regarding childhood and sexuality. On the one hand, paedophilia as far as contemporary Western culture views it, expresses desires and activities considered by the vast majority of us (this author included) to be deeply repugnant and a betrayal of our most deeply held values and aspirations regarding the relations between adults and children. But, with some growing concern, let us also recognise our culture's ever-increasing interest in, and appreciation of, a sexual terrain that, at the very least, approaches the boundaries of paedophilic inclinations. For example, consider the adult obsession with the retention (however artificial) of an ever-more youthful 'look' such that, year by year, the epitome of sexual aesthetics emphasises a body contour and facial appearance that approximates early adolescence. Consider as well the current adult fixation with the removal of all body hair, and not least pubic hair, not only to further expose and highlight one's genitals but, as well, so as to bring forth an imitation of an acceptably sexualised pre-pubescence. Might not these contemporary developments, among any number of others, serve to indicate 'normal' society's uneasy flirtation with that which it also deems to be the most primal of current taboos?

This is not to suggest that we should therefore seek to reconsider, condone or reduce our censuring of paedophilia nor to minimise or deny its many disturbing and destructive consequences. Rather, what is being asked is that we be more honest in considering the role that those of us who are 'sufficiently normal' may be playing, however unthinkingly and unwillingly, in providing the means to an exculpatory rationale for those who seek the means to enact abusive behaviour towards children. Presented with a general cultural tendency to make more opaque what distinctions may exist between child and adult 'ways of being' (whether in general or specifically sexual), adult abusers of children might well convince themselves that their wants and needs (be they of companionship, or sex, or both) are of an equivalent kind and, therefore, are shared by the very children whose ever-more precariously maintained hold on a childhood will be brought to a sudden and infelicitous end by their oppressive acts.

In brief, just as children increasingly are adopting a 'miniature adult' worldview, so, too, are adults exhibiting with ever-growing rapidity, the characteristics of 'overgrown children'.

Once again, our explorations highlight undesirable and troubling confusions with respect to our views of children as sexual beings. Perhaps, this dilemma has always been with us. But even so, the way in which we experience and struggle with that dilemma today is novel and reflects divided stances all too similar to those presented by psychotherapy clients.

Sedimentation and dissociation: An existential perspective

Elsewhere (Spinelli, 1994/2006, 2007), I have proposed that each of us develops and maintains a worldview. The worldview comprises the sum total of all the dispositional stances (which is to say, the sum total of all the beliefs, values, views, attitudes, meanings, assumptions and conclusions, together with their associated behaviours, feelings and emotions) regarding the reflective constructs labelled 'self', 'others' and 'the world'. In response to experiential challenges to any dispositional stance, the worldview may either be open and flexible to its reconstitution or may resist redefinition of that dispositional stance and reject any threat to its continued maintenance. In the latter case, these inflexible dispositional stances can be said to be sedimented.

Dispositional stances such as: 'I can't tolerate making mistakes', 'You can't trust others', 'Full moons generate temporary madness' can all be examples of sedimentation if the worldview they express is being maintained as fixed, certain and secure. In order to achieve this, sedimentations must override any experientially derived challenge that is construed as threatening or destabilising of their certainty, security and fixedness. On reflection, without sedimentation the primary sub-structures that make up the worldview – the self-, other- and world-constructs – could not be construed or defined as (relatively) fixed and permanent essences. *How* sedimentation occurs currently remains an open question, whether considered from the perspective of philosophical, psychological or neurobiological investigation. *That* sedimentation occurs, on the other hand, is both obvious and evident.

Sedimentations in the worldview, or any of its sub-constructs, can only be maintained via the strategy of dissociating the challenging experience either from the whole of the worldview or from that sub-structure whose sedimented dispositional stance is under threat. Dissociation, in this sense, refers to the worldview's maintenance of a sedimentation by its distancing from, denial or dis-ownership of the impact and consequences of experientially derived challenges upon it.

For example, in order to continue to hold his sedimented worldview claim that he had never experienced any form of sexual feelings during his childhood, it could be argued that my client, Ted, was forced to dissociate any contradictory challenges to this claim. In order to do so, he might, for example, have to suppress any counter-examples either by claiming to have no memory of them or by denying their existence. Equally, he might explain such challenges as expressing something other than sexual feelings. Not uncommonly, he might resort to statements of temporary 'possession' that acknowledge the challenge ('Yes, they were sexual feelings') but which disown it and exculpate Ted of any responsibility for their appearance ('When those feelings manifested themselves, I wasn't being "me" in some way – forces of some kind, be they chemical, environmental, circumstantial or supernatural temporarily took me over and it was due to them that this false/possessed version of "me" experienced sexual feelings').

The value of sedimentation and dissociation is that, together, they maintain the relative certainty and security of the dispositional stances that, in turn, maintain the stability of the worldview. De-sedimentation of fixed stances and re-ownership of dissociated experiences might logically appear to be attractive and sensible options. But what is being missed is that the consequence of such strategies is the destabilisation of the worldview as well as the unpredictability of the extent and duration of that destabilisation. A more flexible worldview receptive to the challenges of life experiences is also a worldview riddled with ever-increasing levels of uncertainty, instability and complexity. Sedimentations and dissociations allow the worldview to appear to be unified and coherent; their removal confronts us with a worldview that is all too clearly chaotic and contradictory.

It seems to me that our current Western concerns surrounding childhood sexuality reveal a socially derived worldview that seeks to maintain competing and contradictory sedimentations and must, in turn, generate contrasting dissociations. For, when we consider our society's current attitudes and expectations regarding children's experiences of being sexual, what becomes apparent is that while it has accepted many of the assumptions and hypotheses provoked by the Freudian revolution, it also still clings to notions that are more aligned with a pre-Freudian perspective. On the one hand, we tend to concede that children are sexual to some degree while at the same time we wish to imbue them with some sort of state of sexual innocence.

Unlike previous historical shifts in the history of childhood sexuality, our current worldview does not take an either/or position insofar as its sedimented stance argues neither solely in favour of children being perceived as 'miniature adults' nor solely champions a view of them as distinct and 'special' beings characterised by their innocence as expressed through their ignorance of sexual being. Rather, what is novel about contemporary Western culture's stance on childhood and sexuality is that it attempts to hold *simultaneously* both competing and contradictory sedimentations. As a consequence, it confounds and is confounded by its dissociations which in part must reject all instances of children's and adult's differing relations to being sexual while at the same time must also disown all instances of their shared existence. The following passage from Stevi Jackson's *Childhood and Sexuality* encapsulates this dilemma:

> The image of children as sexual innocents is still with us, implying that children lack sexual interests and desires and cannot cope with sexual knowledge. Yet the steps we take in order to preserve this innocence suggest there is some uncertainty, that we fear children are not as innocent as we might wish. The conflicting images of the innocent and demoniac child continue to pull us both ways. Hence the paradox that even when underestimating children's sexual potential we overestimate it; even when we insist that children must be 'protected' from sex we treat anything they do or say that seems sexual as if it were motivated by fully formed sexual interests. Thus, while preventing children from becoming sexually aware, adults often respond to them as if they already were.
>
> (Jackson, 1982: 78)

Alas, as far as the interface between childhood and sexuality is concerned, the most truthful conclusion we can arrive at is that confusion reigns. For now at least, perhaps the only step we are able to take towards its diminution is to accept that this is so.

References

Adams, M (2013) Human development from an existential phenomenological perspective: Some thoughts and considerations. *Existential Analysis, 24*(1), 48–56.

Berelowitz, S, Firmin, C, Edwards, G & Gulyurtlu, S (2012) *I Thought I Was the Only One in the World: The Office of Children's Commissioner's Inquiry into Child Sexual Exploitation in Gangs and Groups. Interim report, November 2012.* London: NSPCC Publications.

Boss, M (1963) *Psychoanalysis and Daseinsanalysis.* New York: Basic Books.

Boss, M (1979) *Existential Foundations of Medicine and Psychology*. Northvale, NJ: Jason Aronson.

Briod, M (1989) A phenomenological approach to child development. In RS Vale & S Halling (Eds) *Existential-Phenomenological Perspectives in Psychology: Exploring the breadth of human experience* (pp. 115–26). London: Plenum.

Butler, P (2012) Thousands of children sexually exploited each year, inquiry says. *The Guardian,* Wednesday 21 November 2012. Retrieved 23 December 2013 from http://www.guardian.co.uk/society/2012/nov/21/thousands-children-sexually-exploited-inquiry

Cree, V (2012) The Jimmy Savile revelations are causing a classic moral panic. *The Guardian,* Friday 23 November 2012. Retrieved 23 December 2013 from http://www.guardian.co.uk/social-care-network/2012/nov/23/jimmy-savile-moral-panic

Freud, S (2001) Three essays on the theory of sexuality. In *Standard Edition, Vol 7*. London: Vintage Classics. (First published 1905)

Gay, P (1989) *Freud: A life for our time*. London: Anchor Books.

Goldman, R & Goldman, J (1982) *Children's Sexual Thinking*. London: Routledge & Kegan Paul.

Gopnik, A (2009) *The Philosophical Baby: What children's minds tell us about truth, love, and the meaning of life*. London: Bodley Head.

Greenberg, M (2010) What babies know and we don't. *NYRB, 57*(4), 26–7.

Heidegger, M (1962) *Being and Time* (J Macquarrie & E Robinson, Trans). New York: Harper and Row.

Heidegger, M (2001) *Zollikon Seminars: Protocols–conversations–letters* (F Mayr & R Askay, Trans). Evanston, IL: Northwestern University Press.

Jackson, S (1982) *Childhood and Sexuality*. Oxford: Basil Blackwell.

Jung, CG (1975) *Critique of Psychoanalysis* (RFC Hull, Trans). Princeton, NJ: Bollinger Series/Princeton University Press.

Kaeser, F (2001) *Towards a Better Understanding of Children's Sexual Behavior*. NYU Child Study Center. Retrieved February 2013 from http://www.aboutourkids.org/articles/towards_better_understanding_children039s_sexual_behavior

Kirby, S (2005) Human development. Existential perspectives. In E van Deurzen & C Arnold-Baker (Eds) *Existential Perspectives on Human Issues* (pp. 39–47). Basingstoke: Palgrave Macmillan.

Klein, M (1975) *The Psycho-analysis of Children*. New York: Delta.

Langdridge, D (2005) The child's relations with others: Merleau-Ponty, embodiment and psychotherapy. *Existential Analysis*, *16*(1), 87–99.

Lescariges, C & Hinitz, BF (2000) *History of Early Childhood Education.* New York: Falmer Press.

Merleau-Ponty, M (1964) The child's relations with others. In JM Edie (Ed) *The Primacy of Perception* (pp. 96–158) (W Cobb, Trans). Evanston, NB: Northwestern University Press.

Scalzo, C (2010) *Therapy with Children: An existentialist perspective.* London: Karnac Books.

Spinelli, E (1994) *Demystifying Therapy.* London: Constable. (Republished 2006, PCCS Books)

Spinelli, E (2001) *The Mirror and the Hammer: Existential challenges to therapeutic orthodoxy.* London: Continuum.

Spinelli, E (2002) Paradise lost? *CPJ, 13*(8), 15–9.

Spinelli, E (2007) *Practising Existential Psychotherapy: The relational world.* London: Sage Publications.

Sulloway, FJ (1980) *Freud, Biologist of the Mind: Beyond the psychoanalytic legend.* London: HarperCollins.

Thelen, E (2005) Dynamic systems theory and the complexity of change. *Psychoanalytic Dialogues, 15*, 255–83.

9

Open Non-monogamies: Drawing on de Beauvoir and Sartre to inform existential work with romantic relationships

– Dr Meg-John Barker –

The last decade has seen an explosion of interest in openly non-monogamous relationships (Barker & Langdridge, 2010a) such that it is now likely that at some point during their practice most therapists will come across clients who have such arrangements. In addition to this, the kinds of relational and existential challenges and tensions that lead people to develop consensually non-monogamous relationships are present in *all* relationships, and thus the material in this chapter will also be relevant to the high numbers of people who conduct non-consensual non-monogamies (or infidelities), as well as to those who commit to a monogamous relationship (Barker, 2011), especially given that the dividing line between monogamy and non-monogamy is becoming less well-defined (Barker, 2010).

When considering the appropriate existential therapeutic theories and practices to draw upon when working with openly non-monogamous clients the obvious place to look is to the writings and lives of Simone de Beauvoir and Jean-Paul Sartre. They were pioneers in their own non-monogamous relationships, especially given that such arrangements were far more rare then than they are today. It is surprising that they are rarely covered in the popular literature on open non-monogamy (e.g. Easton & Hardy, 2009; Taormino, 2008) given that we have such a wealth of material about non-monogamous experiences from their accounts. In addition to this, it is clear that Sartre's and de Beauvoir's philosophies of human relations were intrinsically linked to their own ways of relating: their theories informed the ways in which they conducted their relationships and were also profoundly influenced by their experiences within these relationships. We can see this when we track the themes that flow from their letters and autobiographical accounts, through their works of fiction, to their more explicitly philosophical works (Fullbrook & Fullbrook, 2008). Existential thinkers since Sartre and de Beauvoir have not engaged with questions of open non-monogamy until very recently, with writers such as Richards, Barker and Langdridge whose existential work is featured in this book and who also all contributed to the collection *Understanding Non-monogamies* (Barker & Langdridge, 2010b).

In this chapter I begin by reviewing the forms of open non-monogamy which have emerged in recent years, focusing on the most common ways in which these are structured and managed. I then outline the relationship structures in de Beauvoir's and Sartre's own lives, drawing some links between the non-monogamies that they practised and the versions that are popular today. I briefly cover Sartre's and de Beauvoir's theories of freedom and relating in relation to non-monogamous relationships, and then turn to existential therapy, considering the key ways in which, in drawing upon these approaches, we might work with people in non-monogamous (and other) relationships.

Open non-monogamies

Barker and Langdridge (2010a) argue that openly non-monogamous relationships have recently reached a critical point in terms of public awareness, with regular newspaper and magazine articles and documentary programmes on the topic, as well as celebrities discussing their non-monogamous arrangements. The Internet has been crucial in enabling people to find others who share their relationship preferences or orientations and in developing communities of like-minded people who have then become the focus of research and/or media reports, leading to more people becoming aware of these possibilities. Certainly, the public reception that my own work in this area has received has shifted markedly over the past decade, from a response of scepticism, salacious interest, and ridicule (see; Ritchie, 2010; Ritchie & Barker, 2005), to a portrayal of open non-monogamy as a more reasonable alternative to the common dishonest modes of having more than one romantic or sexual relationship (see Barker, 2013).

Given that the majority of societies globally are non-monogamous rather than monogamous (usually taking the form of polygamy, Rubin,

2001), personal histories and current experiences of non-monogamous relating are highly likely to be present in any multicultural country such as the United Kingdom or United States, despite not being legally recognised. However, this chapter focuses on the non-monogamies which have emerged specifically within these minority world ('Western') contexts (see Rambukkana, forthcoming, for more on diverse global non-monogamies). The most common current forms of these are swinging, open relationships, and polyamory.

In swinging and open relationships, the norm is to have one main romantic partner, as in monogamy, but the relationship is open in some way to sexual encounters outside of this main partnership. Swinging generally occurs between heterosexual people, often within a party or nightclub context, although there are also the linked activities of dogging (where people meet to watch each other having sex in public spaces like car parks), and couples seeking singles (and vice versa) online for sex. Open relationships are particularly common amongst gay men, with this form of non-monogamy being the norm in some gay men's communities. Gay couples might cruise together for threesomes at nightclubs, or individually meet people online for casual sexual hook-ups, for example.

Polyamory involves being open to multiple love relationships and occurs across sexualities although there is particular crossover between polyamorous and bisexual communities. There are many different ways of conducting polyamory: Primary/secondary arrangements retain the hierarchy between the main couple and other relationships but accept that other relationships can be emotionally close as well as sexual. Triads, quads, and families are based upon multiple, equally important, relationships, and those involved may all be romantically attached to each other. Also there are arrangements where one individual has two partners (in a 'V' with that person at the apex of the V) or more. Polyamorous relationships can be polyfidelitous or open such that people can also engage in additional relationships or sexual encounters outside a main unit (see Barker & Langdridge, 2010b; Labriola, 2010; Taormino, 2008 for details on various forms of open non-monogamy).

Polyamory also differs from swinging and open relationships in that many polyamorous people see it as something that they *are* (an identity) rather than something they *do* (a behaviour or practice), akin to a sexual identity like being lesbian, bisexual, heterosexual, or gay (Barker, 2005). There are also more explicit communities of polyamorous people than there are for other open non-monogamies.

In addition to these main forms of non-monogamy, further relationship styles have reached popular awareness in recent years which blur the boundaries between monogamy and non-monogamy. For example, the 'new monogamy' or 'monogamish' relationship is somewhat open to sexual or emotional closeness outside a main couple (being close to one's ex-partner, or engaging in online sex, for example). In 'hook-up culture' individuals have multiple sexual liaisons rather than forming close romantic relationships. 'Friends-with-benefits' or 'fuckbuddy' arrangements mix friendship and sex without some of the expectations and commitments which frequently go with a romantic partnership. Research suggests that people in monogamous and non-monogamous relationships alike are having to negotiate the rules of their relationships due to shifts in gender equality, greater acceptance of same-sex relationships, altered job prospects, and changing technologies, which all bring new possibilities and challenges (Barker, 2012).

In terms of how non-monogamous relationships are arranged, three main aspects are key: (1) distinguishing different types of relationship; (2) transparency and disclosure; and (3) contracts or agreements.

First, as we have seen, virtually all non-monogamous and monogamous relationships draw clear distinctions between sexual and love (or emotionally close) relationships and have explicit or implicit rules about who it is acceptable to be physical and emotionally close to and how.

Second, in terms of transparency and disclosure, non-monogamous people also have different arrangements on a spectrum from the 'don't ask, don't tell' position of not wanting to know any details about their partners' other relationships, to arrangements where all information is shared, where it is important that different partners know each other or form a close bond, or even where any additional sexual or romantic relationships are engaged in together (Adam, 2004).

Finally, there is a continuum from those who prefer a clear contract or agreement about how their relationship will be managed, to those who prefer the flexibility of being trusted to make their own choices or who want to engage in ongoing processes of negotiation (Finn, 2010, refers to these different positions as 'freedom-of-contract' and 'freedom-from-contract'). The aim of contracts and agreements is generally to attempt to ensure the safety and security of people in the relationship by agreeing what freedoms are present, and what the limits on these are. For example, people often have agreements around what activities are acceptable with other parties, ways of keeping their relationship special, or whether they have any rights of veto over their partner's additional lovers/partners (sometimes called 'metamours'). Words like 'relationship anarchy' and 'polytical' have emerged for less contractual forms of non-monogamy which are often more explicitly politically or philosophically driven. These also sometimes challenge the ways in which romantic love is privileged over other kinds of relationships in most monogamous and non-monogamous arrangements (see Barker, Heckert & Wilkinson, 2013).

Sartre's and de Beauvoir's relationships

Reading the autobiographical and biographical accounts of de Beauvoir's and Sartre's lives it is clear that there is no one, easily accessible, truth as to why they embarked upon an openly non-monogamous relationship, just as there are no easy answers to the popular questions of which of them was the bigger philosophical influence upon the other, or whether their additional relationships were nurturing or damaging to those who engaged in them (I suspect, as with most relationships, that the answer is 'both').

I am inclined to believe that, like their shared philosophies, Sartre's and de Beauvoir's' relationship decisions were co-constructed. As Fullbrook and Fullbrook (2008) point out, the gender assumptions and norms of the time meant that even the author of *The Second Sex* (de Beauvoir, 1949/1997) was under pressure to present Sartre as the driving force in both their relationship and their work, just as she struggled to acknowledge any of her same-sex sexual relationships (Rowley, 2006). Sexual stereotypes have led many to read de Beauvoir as reluctantly agreeing to Sartre's non-monogamy. However, it seems more likely that de Beauvoir's aspiration, from childhood, for an equal mutually supportive partnership, and for individual independence, gave her a strong personal motivation to explore alternatives to the standard script of marriage and motherhood. It is de Beauvoir, in *The Prime of Life* (1960/1965), who tells the story of her and Sartre seeing a cat who had become stuck behind some railings due to going there for affection and food and becoming too big to escape (clearly a metaphor for the kind of monogamy that she and Sartre wanted to avoid). Also de Beauvoir had a sexual relationship with René Maheu prior to, and during, her early relationship with Sartre, and seems to have been at least as proactive as Sartre in pursuing additional relationships, and in challenging aspects of their original agreement as their relationships developed.

Looking back on de Beauvoir's and Sartre's relationships with the understandings that we now have about non-monogamous arrangements we can see that they began with something like a 'primary/secondary' agreement, or an open relationship, agreeing that they had an 'essential love' and that all other relationships that they engaged with would only be 'contingent'. De Beauvoir also reported that they agreed not to even have contingent affairs for the first two years following their initial contract, whilst Sartre was in military service, although it seems that they did have sexual relationships during this period, so this may have been a construction for her readers (Fullbrook & Fullbrook, 2008).

Before the war de Beauvoir and Sartre transformed their relationship into a 'trio' to incorporate Olga Kosakievicz: one of de Beauvoir's students who she grew close to and who also forged an influential relationship with Sartre (although it seems most likely that she was only sexually involved with de Beauvoir). This relationship seems akin to a modern polyamorous triad where there are close links between all of the people involved and the threesome is regarded as a relationship in its own right. It also set the theme of Sartre and de Beauvoir becoming involved with much younger people who they attempted to mentor and took some financial responsibility for.

Following the trio, the relationship developed into more of a 'family' as first Olga, and then de Beauvoir, became involved with another student, Jacques-Laurent Bost, and Sartre seduced Olga's younger sister Wanda. Now there was a kind of 'W' arrangement with de Beauvoir involved with both Sartre and Bost (the middle 'V'), Sartre involved with Wanda, and Bost involved with Olga (Olga and Wanda being at the start and end points of the 'W'). The bonds between them all involved friendship, intellectual companionship or tutelage, and sexual contact to differing degrees which also shifted over the course of the rest of their lives. However not all of the sexual bonds or other commitments were known about by all concerned, and much was hidden particularly from the Kosakievicz sisters who, it was felt, would not agree to Bost and Sartre's' sexual relationships with de Beauvoir.

In 1939 de Beauvoir reports that she and Sartre replaced their initial renewable contract with a more permanent one which promised that they would always be together because nobody else could understand them in the same way that they understood each other. However, during the war when de Beauvoir became involved with Bost, she challenged some elements of this by announcing, in letters to Sartre, that Bost was now a second 'essential' relationship in her life. Sartre would also go on to propose marriage to some of his other female partners, so both of them disrupted the primary/secondary hierarchies in their relationships at various points.

Following the war, relationships with the Kosakievicz sisters and Bost waned somewhat, whilst remaining a feature of their lives, and first Sartre, then de Beauvoir, developed intense and important relationships on their individual trips to America: Sartre with Dolores Vanetti, and de Beauvoir with Nelson Algren. At this stage they were in a kind of 'Z' arrangement, with the vital (but by this stage probably not sexual) relationship with each other, and each of them having another primary, and sexual, relationship (the two ends of the 'Z'). Over the years the people in the Z changed: Algren was replaced by Claude Lanzmann, and Vanetti by a series of women including Michelle Vian, and Arlette Elkäim (who Sartre subsequently adopted). Sartre continued to support many of the women he had been involved with, and several of them looked after him during his illness towards the end of his life. However he often kept them in the dark about each other, assuming that none of them would be happy with his ongoing sexual relationships with other women.

Finally, there was a brief return to the 'trio' arrangement in de Beauvoir's and Sartre's later years, as both became close to the much younger Sylvie le Bon, who de Beauvoir eventually adopted as her daughter having come to regard their relationship as thoroughly 'interwoven' and seeing her, in many ways, as a younger version of herself.

So we can see that Sartre and de Beauvoir engaged in most of the possible non-monogamous structures (which we reviewed above) during their relationship, including primary/secondary agreements, group relationships, separate equally important relationships, and an ongoing shifting family network.

In terms of how they managed their relationships, the three key aspects outlined previously were all present:

1. distinctions were made between different kinds of relationships (on the basis of sex and emotional closeness)
2. there were differing degrees of transparency and disclosure
3. the emphasis was sometimes upon clear contracts to maintain a sense of security and sometimes on being free from contractual agreements (often when agreements were stretched or broken).

However, we can also see that initial understandings of each of these aspects were gradually challenged. The essential/contingent distinction (1) did not stick. Whilst it is clear that some of those involved did distinguish between non-sexual (acceptable) and sexual (unacceptable) relationships, a lot of the key relationships in both de Beauvoir's and Sartre's lives were not the sexual ones, including their relationship with each other for much of their life. In addition to their romantic/sexual relationships, both had key relationships with family members (de Beauvoir's sister and Sartre's mother) as well as friends and colleagues such as Zaza (Elisabeth Le Coin), Albert Camus, and Pierre Victor.

Although they committed to radical transparency (2) in their initial arrangement, were extremely frank about their other relationships in letters to each other, and were open about the fact of their non-monogamy to others in general, it is clear that Sartre and de Beauvoir both lied to their other partners, and perhaps to each other, about what was going on, perhaps deciding – on others' behalves – that 'don't ask, don't tell' was a necessary policy to sustain the relationship.

Finally, the contractual agreement (3) shifted over time as both de Beauvoir and Sartre challenged elements of it. Perhaps the commitment to an ongoing intellectual and close personal relationship was the only element that remained throughout. In terms of relationships with others, although it seems that they aspired to a freedom-from-contract, de Beauvoir – and particularly Sartre – felt a keen sense of responsibility and duty to the people in their lives. This was reflected in a rigorous division of time and financial support between them, as well as implicit agreements about who knew what about which relationships.

De Beauvoir's and Sartre's philosophies of relating

As previously mentioned, it is clear that Sartre's and de Beauvoir's relationship experiences were intrinsically linked with their philosophies. We can see this, for example, in the ways in which themes of freedom and intersubjectivity are discussed in their letters, phenomenologically explored in the rich descriptions in *She Came to Stay* (de Beauvoir, 1943/1954, which was clearly based upon relationships with the Kosakievicz sisters), and then philosophically presented – often with the same examples – in *Being and Nothingness* (Sartre, 1943/2005; see Fullbrook & Fullbrook, 2008, for a detailed working through of these links). Here I will outline key themes in de Beauvoir's and Sartre's work on freedom and relationships and draw out implications for open non-monogamies.

In *Being and Nothingness* (1943/2005) Sartre examines the conflict inherent in our being free to make meaning for ourselves whilst also finding ourselves engaged in 'an *already meaningful* world which reflects to me meanings which I have not put into it' (Sartre, 1943/2005: 531, italics in original). It is here that we see the tension between our own freedom and the perceptions that others have of us. As Sartre puts it, 'the true limit of my freedom lies purely and simply in the very fact that an Other apprehends me as the Other-as-object' (Sartre, 1943: 546). We can see Sartre's own struggles with this in the ways in which he capitulated to what he assumes his partners – and the wider world – expect of relationships, particularly sexual exclusivity, despite his own ideals.

Sartre argues that it is because of the Other that we perceive ourselves, for example, as handsome or ugly, Jewish or Aryan, or as a certain personality or job role (as vulgar or as a waiter). We are thrown into a world where meanings already exist about what it is to belong to these categories (and, presumably, also about where lines are drawn between categories and which are seen as relevant). When we experience ourselves being looked at by the Other we find ourselves viewed in these ways and may well feel constrained to act as the Other expects an ugly person, or a Jewish person to act, for example. This relates back to Sartre and de Beauvoir's theme of being-for-others and the threat that the Look of the Other can annihilate us and limit our possibilities. We are in constant competition with others, encountering them as rival consciousnesses. We experience ourselves as objects for others (which robs us of our freedom and status of being-for-ourselves), and we also objectify others (which robs them of the same).

> While I attempt to free myself from the hold of the Other, the Other is trying to free himself from mine: While I attempt to enslave the Other, the Other seeks to enslave me ... Conflict is the original meaning of Being-for-Others.
>
> (Sartre, 1943: 386)

Of course, according to de Beauvoir and Sartre, being robbed of our freedom is not necessarily experienced negatively. In fact the anxiety of freedom and the responsibility of being called upon to choose and choose again are existential givens that we may be very happy to deny. We might consequently choose to observe how we are viewed by others in the world and to conform to this entirely, allowing them to objectify us and becoming that object for them. We can become utterly the stereotype of a gay man, a women in love, or a waiter, for example, mineralising this version of ourselves into something fixed and inflexible. But if we do this we are in 'bad faith' because we fail to acknowledge that we are still *choosing* to be this way. In *The Ethics of Ambiguity* (1948/1976) de Beauvoir considers many ways in which people avoid moments of 'original choice': by rejecting the terror of freedom and passion entirely and becoming a 'sub-man', by dedicating themselves seriously to some pursuit disingenuously acting as if it is their duty and they could not do otherwise, or by falling into nihilism.

In Sartre's early, rather pessimistic, view of human relations our only real options are to accept the freedom of the other and objectify ourselves, or to objectify the other and experience ourselves as free. However, even these strategies eventually fail because we cannot ever fully escape the, often uncomfortable, existential given of our own, and others', freedom. We can speculate about the ways in which de Beauvoir and Sartre sometimes objectified themselves for others in their own relationships: Sartre the seducer or rescuer responsible for so many women; de Beauvoir the mentor, the independent sexual woman, or the old woman no longer able to freely engage in relationships. We can also see objectification of others in their attempts to set up their protégées in lives that they thought they should live (as artists, philosophers, or actors), and the struggles for freedom that their partners sometimes put up, and sometimes did not, in the face of this. The American partners, Algren and Vanetti, particularly, demonstrate a shift from acceptance of the roles in which de Beauvoir and Sartre cast them, to rejection of these roles.

It was de Beauvoir who put forward a way out of the trap of human relationships which she and Sartre both illuminated in their work. She makes a philosophical argument (1948/1976) for an ethics of reciprocity, whereby it is in all of our interests to recognise the freedom and subjecthood of others, not only because this is the reality of the situation, but also because we need others to be free in order to trust their validations of us and to aid us in our own goals. She argues that 'no existence can be validly fulfilled if it is limited to itself. It appeals to the existence of others' (de Beauvoir, 1948/1976: 67) and that 'to will oneself free is also to will others free' (de Beauvior, 1948/1976: 73). This seems similar to the I–Thou relating which Buber (1937/2004) viewed as a constant potential, despite our tendency to return to the I–It mode of fixing the other, or being fixed by them. De Beauvoir (1949/1997) presents a detailed analysis of the ways in which the objectification of others is gendered (with women societally objectified, putting them in a different position in relation to grasping their freedom to men). She argues that, as well as being deeply problematic for women, this denies heterosexual men the possibility of an equal partner who will protect, support and stimulate them in a reciprocal way: 'he would be liberated himself in their liberation' (de Beauvoir, 1948/1976, cited in Fullbrook & Fullbrook, 2008: 196).

The potentials of mutual reciprocity and an ethics of maximising each other's freedom through relationships is something that both Sartre and de Beauvoir explored on a social level in their later work (e.g. Sartre, 1960/2004). However, it clearly has implications for interpersonal relationships as well. A key goal of existential therapy could be regarded as encouraging people to affirm both themselves and others in their lives as free subjects.

Existential therapy with people in openly non-monogamous relationships

Phenomenological stance

As with Sartre's and de Beauvoir's philosophies, all existential therapy begins with the phenomenological method: bracketing our own assumptions as much as possible; horizontalising such that we pay attention to all aspects of the client's life and worldview; and verifying our understandings with them in order to build up a rich description of their experience, meanings and values (Adams, 2001). From what we have covered in this chapter regarding open non-monogamies, there are specific aspects for the therapist to be mindful of in relation to each of these aspects of phenomenology.

When it comes to bracketing it is important to be aware that we live in a mononormative society (Barker & Langdridge, 2010a, 2010b). Just as de Beauvoir (1949/1997) highlighted that the situation is not the same for women and men in patriarchal society, it is similarly not the same for heterosexual and lesbian, gay, bisexual, trans and queer people under heteronormativity (see the chapters by Langdridge and Richards in this volume), and it is not the same for monogamous and non-monogamous people under mononormativity. In all cases we find ourselves in an already meaningful world where the commonly taken-for-granted meanings do not fit our experiences of ourselves. As therapists we need to both reflexively interrogate and bracket any assumptions we hold about the normality, naturalness, or rightness of monogamy. More than this, given the intense mononormativity of wider society, it may be necessary to actively affirm the acceptability of openly non-monogamous forms of relating to bring them onto more of an equal footing with monogamy (see Langdridge, this volume, for a detailed consideration of affirmative practice).

In relation to horizontalising it is vital that therapists do not fix upon their client's non-monogamy as a more important aspect of their lives than any other. Bracketing any assumptions of mononormativity should help with this. For the majority of openly non-monogamous people seeking therapy (as with any other non-normative group), their relationship structure will be no more pertinent to their presenting issues than it is for monogamous people. So, whilst it is useful to be aware of all aspects of the client's lived experience (including their relationship set-up and their experience of difference if it is outside mononormativity), therapists should be careful not to focus overwhelmingly on this, especially since the client is likely to have had other people – including therapists – pathologising and stigmatising this aspect of their lives (see Richards & Barker, 2013).

Turning to verification, it is important that the therapist educates themselves regarding the different forms of open non-monogamy that exist such that they will be able to work with non-monogamous clients in an informed way rather than unethically requiring clients to educate them on all aspects of non-monogamy. However, it is also vital to verify how things are for this client, rather than making generalisations about all non-monogamous people/relationships based on a limited degree of knowledge or experience. This could involve asking clients to create genograms, sculpts, or other diagrams of the people in their lives and how they are related, for example, and should also involve checking out what the meanings of non-monogamy are for each particular client (see below).

Phenomenologically it is also valuable to experiment with different ways of gaining rich descriptions of everyday relational experiences. I have found creative methods such as making collages or plasticine/lego sculptures (Barker, Richards & Bowes-Catton, 2012), or memory work (Langdridge, Barker, Stenner & Reavey, 2012) to be valuable resources for getting beyond the story that people feel they need to tell due to mononormativity (for example, that they don't get jealous or that they are completely free with no sense of obligation or guilt) to their lived experience. It is vital that such exploration is undertaken in the context of a shared assumption between client and therapist that open non-monogamy is not problematic per se. The following quote is a wonderful example from de Beauvoir of a rich phenomenological description of the complexities of jealousy within non-monogamy.

> They are in their pajamas; they are drinking coffee, smiling at one another ... There is an image that hurts me. When you hit against a stone at first you only feel the impact – the pain comes after. Now, with a week's delay, I am beginning to suffer. Before, I was more bewildered – amazed. I rationalized, I thrust aside the pain that is pouring over

me this morning – these images. I pace up and down the flat, up and down, and at each step another strikes me. I opened his cupboard. I looked at his pajamas, shirts, drawers, vests; and I began to weep. Another woman was stroking his cheek, as soft as this silk, as warm and gentle as this pull-over – that I cannot bear ... Between them there is an intimacy that used to belong only to me. When they wake up does he snuggle her against his shoulder calling her his doe, his honeymouth? Or has he invented other names that he says in the same voice? Or has he found himself another voice? He is shaving, smiling at her, with his eyes darker and more brilliant, his mouth more naked under the mask of white foam. He appeared in the doorway holding a great bunch of red roses in his arms, wrapped in cellophane: does he take her flowers? My heart is being sawn in two with a very fine-toothed saw.

(de Beauvoir, 1967/2006: 122–3)

Multiple meanings and freedom

If clients do wish to explore their relationships, or decisions about non-monogamy, as part of therapy, then it is useful for the therapist to be aware of the various meanings that non-monogamy can have, as well as being open to potential further meanings for their particular client. For example Barker (2005) found that some people view open non-monogamy as a preferable alternative to infidelity; others engage in it for hedonistic reasons; some regard it as a political (feminist and/or anti-capitalist) move away from monogamous marriage; and for others it is part of communal and sustainable living; or a spiritual practice.

Importantly, whilst it is often assumed that open non-monogamy is about wanting more freedom from monogamous constraints, it can equally be engaged in for reasons of safety. For example, some openly non-monogamous people hope that having several partners will provide greater security for themselves (if they were to lose one of the relationships) or their family (in terms of greater financial income or more caregivers for children, see Barker & Langdridge, 2010b). We can see such themes of non-monogamy bringing more freedom and/or safety when we compare de Beauvoir's and Sartre's accounts of their time in America (freedom) to those of periods of illness when they were surrounded by supportive partners (safety).

One useful way which I have found of exploring non-monogamy with clients is to construct continua with them to investigate where they, and the various people in their lives, are at on different dimensions of relationships. For example, going back to the ways of distinguishing relationships outlined previously (1), it can be useful to ask clients for their preferred place on continua of sexual contact and of emotional closeness (from having one person to many on each of these continua, see Barker, 2011). We could do the same for continua of transparency (2) (from 'don't ask, don't tell' to complete transparency) and contracts (3) (from an explicit contract covering everything to no contract). People might be at different places on such continua at different times and in different relationships, and further continua can be constructed for aspects which are particularly relevant to the client (such as living arrangements or time spent with different people, see Barker, 2012).

Perhaps a fundamental continua from an existential perspective is the one from freedom to belonging, and it can be useful to conceptualise the tension in this way to explore where different partners' values are in relation to it. Such continua can be used as a jumping-off point for many valuable conversations. For some, freedom may be associated with healthy independence, for others selfishness or flightiness. Belonging may be felt to be about mutual support, or security, or dependence, or obligation.

The continua model can increase awareness that often choosing more freedom means moving away from belonging and vice versa. This is a helpful reminder for those who have utopian views of being able to do whatever they like and retaining very close bonds with their partners, for example people who expect partners to be comfortable with them making absolutely no commitments day to day. Similarly it can help to confront those who prefer the belonging end of the continuum with the fact that they would not want to constrain their, or others', freedom completely or that life does involve uncertainty. It can be useful to consider what the potentials and pitfalls are of different positions on the continuum. However, at the same time, the continuum model is limited because it is possible to experience greater freedom as enabling a greater sense of safety and vice versa. For example, a sense of groundedness in a supportive relationship can make one feel more free, and a sense of being more self-sufficient and being respected and trusted by partners to follow one's own path can make one feel safer in relationships and more committed to them. This relates to the kind of mutuality and reciprocity that de Beauvoir spoke of: each person trying to maximise the other's freedom through their sense of commitment and responsibility to them.

It is also worth being aware that living outside societal norms often involves facing one's freedom and the inevitable uncertainty of life in profound ways. Mononormativity can offer a comforting script or set of check boxes for life (falling in love, marriage, home, kids, retirement, etc.) which can provide a way of avoiding the anxiety of freedom (until the script is called into question by experiences that fail to fit it). This can mean that openly non-monogamous people are more used to confronting uncertainty and freedom and embracing their independence, as de Beauvoir imagined.

However, in many cases there is a huge temptation to find and cling to other scripts in 'bad faith' in order to avoid this anxiety. This happens, for example, when people regard a certain form of non-monogamy as the only 'true way' or when they treat it as something one naturally is rather than any kind of choice, and foreground this aspect of their identity before all others. There can also be problems when people objectify others by insisting that they fit their model of non-monogamy, when they want different rules for themselves and others, or when they fail to appreciate that others will have different needs and values to those that they hold. It can also be problematic when people fail to face up to the realities and complexities of relationships, for example by thinking that they can have infinite numbers of partners despite having limited time, or by constantly searching for 'new relationship energy' (Barker, 2010). Interestingly, Sartre and de Beauvoir recognised this latter issue, noticing how new relationships with younger people left them feeling freer and younger as different sides of themselves were drawn out in those relationships (Rowley, 2006). It is a challenge in monogamy, non-monogamy, and all human relationships, to maintain ongoing relationships without losing our sense of freedom or the ability to be different sides of ourselves and to see different sides of our partners. The temptation to objectify both ourselves and others over time is strong. It is worth challenging any naïve hopes that a perfect relationship structure will be found which resolves the inevitable tensions of human relating.

Relationship ethics

Such conversations can lead us into useful considerations about clients' relationship ethics and how various practices do, or do not, fit with these. Such matters are rarely considered explicitly and can therefore be very useful to explore: How would clients like to be treated in relationships? How would they like to treat others? These explorations may involve looking in depth at both explicit and implicit agreements, as well as exploring the ways in which people care for themselves, as well as others, in an everyday context (given that the objectification of the self and of others is often linked, see Barker, 2010).

Considerations of relationship ethics often fail to extend beyond the particular dyad in question. This may be a particular risk in couple work or in individual therapy which focuses on one particular dyad in a client's life. On deviations from normative monogamy de Beauvoir wrote:

> If the two allies allow themselves only passing sexual liaisons then there is no difficulty, but it also means that the freedom they allow themselves is not worthy of the name. Sartre and I have been more ambitious; it has been our wish to experience 'contingent loves': but there is one question we have deliberately avoided: How would the third person feel about the arrangement?
> (de Beauvoir, cited in Rowley, 2006: 299–300)

So it is important to encourage clients to consider relationship ethics beyond the dyad (or triad or quad). Similarly, both clients and therapists can find themselves focusing on romantic relationships to the exclusion of other relationships due to their primacy in popular culture (Barker, 2012). It can be useful to challenge this through horizontalisation by opening up to the whole constellation of people in their lives and how they treat them: something that de Beauvoir and Sartre seemed to come to through their own experiences of relationships shifting over time. We may even usefully widen the net beyond people. In many ways work was the primary partner in both Sartre's and de Beauvoir's lives, and we could also consider their relationships to Paris, to America, to the war, to communism, or to existentialism itself. Barker, Heckert and Wilkinson (2013) point to the potentials for wider social mutuality and reciprocity that can open up when people consider the multiple loves of polyamory as potentially involving all kinds of human relationships, as well as relationships with non-human creatures, oneself, various projects and values, or the planet.

Conclusions

Whilst this chapter has focused on people in openly non-monogamous relationships, hopefully it is clear that such explorations are valuable across clients in all relationship arrangements. Bracketing our assumptions about monogamy/non-monogamy can mean that we engage in useful discussions about relationships and different possible agreements with *all* clients rather than only seeing this as relevant to those who are outside mononormativity. For example, the question of why monogamous clients choose not to be non-monogamous should be just as present to us as the question of why non-monogamous clients choose not to be monogamous.

From our explorations of open non-monogamies, good existential practice with all clients would involve: reflexively engaging with our own assumptions about relationships; educating ourselves on the current range of relationship styles and structures that are available to clients; and not assuming that open non-monogamy is relevant simply because it is part of a particular client's life. If a client brings up issues of open non-monogamy specifically, we might helpfully consider taking an affirmative stance (given wider cultural mononormativity) as well as possible practices for enabling an in-depth rich description of everyday experience (such as the use of continua, visual methods, or memory work). It is worth being alert to themes of freedom and safety, as well as to issues around how relationships are defined and distinguished, levels of transparency, explicit or implicit contracts and agreements, and relationship ethics.

References

Adam, BD (2004) Care, intimacy and same-sex partnership in the 21st century. *Current Sociology, 52*(2), 265–79.

Adams, M (2001) Practising phenomenology: Some reflections and considerations. *Existential Analysis, 12*(1), 65–84.

Barker, M (2005) This is my partner, and this is my … partner's partner: Constructing a polyamorous identity in a monogamous world. *Journal of Constructivist Psychology, 18*(1), 75–88.

Barker, M (2010) Self-care and relationship conflict. *Sexual and Relationship Therapy, 25*(1), 37–47.

Barker, M (2011) Monogamies and non-monogamies: A response to: 'The challenge of monogamy: Bringing it out of the closet and into the treatment room' by Marianne Brandon. *Sexual and Relationship Therapy, 26*(3), 281–7.

Barker, M (2012) *Rewriting the Rules: An integrative guide to love, sex and relationships.* London: Routledge.

Barker, M (2013) *Reviews.* Retrieved 1 August 2013 from http://rewritingtherules.wordpress.com/reviewsreports

Barker, M & Langdridge, D (2010a) Whatever happened to non-monogamies? Critical reflections on recent research and theory. *Sexualities, 13*(6), 748–72.

Barker, M & Langdridge, D (Eds) (2010b) *Understanding Non-monogamies*. New York: Routledge.

Barker, M, Heckert, J & Wilkinson, E (2013) Queering polyamory: From one love, to many, and back again. In T Sanger & Y Taylor (Eds) *Intimacies: Relations, exchanges, affects* (pp. 190–208). London: Routledge.

Barker, M, Richards, C & Bowes-Catton, H (2012) Visualising experience: Using creative research methods with members of sexual communities. In C Phellas (Ed) *Researching Non-heterosexual Sexualities* (pp. 57–80). Farnham: Ashgate.

Beauvoir, S de (1954) *She Came to Stay* (Y Moyse & R Senhouse, Trans). New York: Norton. (First published 1943)

Beauvoir, S de (1976) *The Ethics of Ambiguity* (B Frechtman, Trans). New York: Citadel Press. (First published 1948)

Beauvoir, S de (1997) *The Second Sex*. London: Vintage. (First published 1949)

Beauvoir, S de (1965) *The Prime of Life* (P Green, Trans). Harmondsworth: Penguin. (First published 1960)

Beauvoir, S de (2006) *The Woman Destroyed* (P O'Brian, Trans). New York: Harper Perennial. (First published 1967)

Buber, M (2004) *I and Thou* (R Gregor-Smith, Trans). London: Routledge. (First published 1937)

Easton, D & Hardy, J (2009) *The Ethical Slut*. Oakland, CA: Greenery Press.

Finn, M (2010) Conditions of freedom in practices of non-monogamous commitment. In M Barker & D Langdridge (Eds) *Understanding Non-monogamies* (pp. 225–36). New York: Routledge.

Fullbrook, E & Fullbrook, K (2008) *Sex and Philosophy: Rethinking de Beauvoir and Sartre*. London: Continuum.

Labriola, K (2010) *Love in Abundance: A counselor's advice on open relationships*. Oakland, CA: Greenery Press.

Langdridge, D, Barker, M, Stenner, P & Reavey, P (2012) Becoming a subject: A memory work study of the experience of romantic jealousy. *Forum: Qualitative Social Research, 13*(2). Retrieved 1 August 2013 from http://www.qualitative-research.net/index.php/fqs/article/view/1712

Rambukkana, N (forthcoming) *Non-monogamies in the Public Sphere: Intimacy, privilege and the space of discourse*. Vancouver, BC: University of British Columbia Press.

Richards, C & Barker, M (2013) *Sexuality and Gender for Counsellors, Psychologists and Health Professionals: A practical guide*. London: Sage Publications.

Ritchie, A (2010) Discursive constructions of polyamory in mono-normative media culture. In M Barker & D Langdridge (Eds) *Understanding Non-monogamies*. (pp. 46–54). New York: Routledge.

Ritchie, A & Barker, M (2005) There aren't words for what we do or how we feel so we have to make them up: Constructing polyamorous languages in a culture of compulsory monogamy. *Sexualities*, 9(5), 584–601.

Rowley, H (2006) *Tête-à-tête: The lives and loves of Simone de Beauvoir and Jean-Paul Sartre*. London: Chatto & Windus.

Rubin, R (2001) Alternative family lifestyles revisited, or whatever happened to swingers, group marriages and communes? *Journal of Family Issues* 7(6), 7–11.

Sartre, J-P (2004) *Critique of Dialectical Reason Volume 1* (A Sheridan-Smith, Trans). London: Verso. (First published 1960)

Sartre, J-P (2005) *Being and Nothingness: An essay on phenomenological ontology* (HE Barnes, Trans). London: Verso. (First published 1943)

Taormino, T (2008) *Opening Up: A guide to creating and sustaining open relationships*. Berkeley, CA: Cleis Press.

10

Trans and Existential-Phenomenological Practice

– Christina Richards –

> Always be a first-rate version of yourself instead of a second-rate version of someone else.
> (Judy Garland)

Existentialism is concerned with freedom and authenticity (Cox, 2009) – philosophies which permeate the process of transitioning gender. Indeed the recognition of freedom (painful as it may be), the eschewing of the comfortable social norms of not transitioning gender, and the attainment of a more personally congruent and authentic gender as well as (in some cases) embodiment, are often the sine qua non of the process of transitioning gender – and consequently any psychological interventions which a trans person may seek as part of this process. Trans then, and the existential project, are fundamentally intertwined.

But what do we mean by the term 'trans'? First, it should be made clear that it is not to do with sexuality; as with cisgender people, trans people may be of any sexuality or none.[1] It may therefore seem strange to include trans within a book on sexuality, but as the fields are so often linked it makes sense to include them rather than being slaves to taxonomies. Similarly, trans should not be erroneously conflated with some form of genital configuration or surgery, as this is quite aside from the point – many trans people do not have any form of genital surgery (Barrett, 2007). Trans people then, are simply those who move from the gender which they were assigned at birth. If the person was assigned female at birth

---

1. A cisgender person is a person who is content to remain the gender they were assigned at birth – thus if you identify as the gender on your birth certificate then you are cisgender.

and identifies as male they will be a trans man or trans boy. Similarly, if the person is assigned male at birth and identifies as female they will be a trans woman or trans girl. Those who come to identify as a gender outside of the dichotomy of male and female are also often included under the umbrella term trans, however, for reasons of space this chapter will concern itself with people who transition across the dichotomy. For more information on people situated outside of the gender dichotomy see the relevant chapter in Richards and Barker (2013).

It is also important to note that people are only trans men, women, boys or girls in instances when the fact that they are trans is pertinent, for example when discussing trans identity matters or visiting an endocrinologist – otherwise they are simply a man and a women respectively. Unfortunately the key error many practitioners make when seeing trans people is to assume that the fact that they are trans is pertinent – most often it is not. Similarly, many practitioners ask trans people about genitalia when they would not similarly ask a cisgender person such questions. This focusing on trans issues and/or genitalia unnecessarily both destroys rapport and is inimical to existential-phenomenological practice which cautions strongly against the imposition of the practitioner on the information presented by the client (van Deurzen & Adams, 2011). Similarly, in general trans people will be seeking assistance with the usual issues of psychotherapy, unrelated to being trans, such as bereavement, separation, job changes, etc., and this should be respected, with their trans status generally being ignored and practice proceeding as with any other client. It is important also to respect trans clients' gender of presentation and not to take a neutral, or open stance towards it unless it is the matter under discussion. Taking a neutral stance to the gender of a trans person who has transitioned will cause offence – just as with a cisgender person – and will similarly damage rapport.

Keeping this vital caveat in mind, the remainder of this chapter concerns itself specifically with the matters relating to being trans, which trans people may bring to an existential-phenomenological practitioner (particularly one working from the scientist-practitioner stance such as a psychologist). These issues generally fall roughly into one of three interrelated groups: issues pertaining to whether to transition from one gender to another, issues pertaining to transphobia, whether internalised or from others, and issues pertaining to matters which may impact trans people in particular ways, such as reproduction, ageing, sexuality and such. Of course the latter two categories may not pertain directly to people being trans. For example, cisgender people may be discriminated against as well and therefore discrimination is not de facto a trans matter, even if the content pertains to the person being trans. The person shouting 'tranny' may just as ignorantly be shouting 'nigger' – the characteristics of the person being shouted at are not necessarily pertinent to the prejudice (although the client may believe them to be so). Similarly, challenges to reproduction faced by some trans people may be similar to those faced by, for example, people in same-sex relationships and those with fertility problems. One issue which is necessarily trans specific is that of transition (although again much is to be learned from consideration of other forms of transition), so it is to this which we turn first.

Choosing not to choose is still a choice: Transition

Some trans people will seek assistance with the decision as to whether to transition from their birth-assigned gender. The decision may be relatively simple for a young person in an urban area, a person of financial means, a person whose friends and/or partner are supportive etc., or it may be complicated by people's concerns about how others may react and whether the decision is a good one for them. A simple, open phenomenological exploration of the client's lifeworld may well be enough to assist in such cases. Indeed for many trans people exploration with the help of a psychotherapist will not be necessary.

For some people though, the notion of transition seems to be more complex with various obstacles appearing to intrude. For such people it is not uncommon for them to say that they would transition if only they were able, for example if only their wife would 'let' them. It can be useful to explore that 'letting' in some detail. This is because trans is not necessarily harmful (being shot is necessarily harmful – it always hurts; being trans is not, as it does not and is experienced differently by different people). If it is taken as axiomatic that transitioning is entirely reasonable for some people (and it should be), then a phenomenological exploration of the perceived constraints the person faces, *and their own part and responsibility in acceding to them*, can be undertaken. This is because some people are unwilling to recognise their own part in not transitioning, while maintaining the bad faith position of saying that they would transition if not for the opprobrium of others. The exact nature of what others have actually said (as opposed to what people might say) can be usefully explored, as can the nature of the client's wish not to upset others. Not infrequently trans people in such situations are quite willing to undertake a 'will to power' regarding other matters, but not transitioning, as they have a degree of internalised transphobia. Thus they will fight for the right to move house, or job, or to have children, as these are seen as acceptable – but not for the right to transition, as it is thought not to be.

This wish to be accepted by society is what hamstrings many older trans people who have always 'played by the [heteronormative] rules',[2] not uncommonly rather successfully. The fear engendered by moving into a personally authentic way of being which is necessarily outside these rules – transitioning – means that some trans people will not transition as they do not wish to be subject to any [unfamiliar] social opprobrium. For those who do transition there may be a strongly retained sense of guilt as a form of penance. The trans person is in effect saying that they are still within the heteronormative social system, they are still 'normal' because, while they are trans they are (naturally) guilty about it. Not to be guilty would be to accept being trans as OK and would therefore mean that they were outside heteronormativity and so a 'freak'. This may be particularly the case if the person has children as there may also be a similar guilt to prove that the person is still a good parent, despite the fact that the literature shows that being trans in no way adversely affects children (e.g. Green, 1978, 1987).[3] Similarly, some trans parents may give children undue say in whether, and how, they transition in a way in which they would not accept for a decision about a house move, for example. In both cases it is appropriate for children to be listened to, to have age-appropriate explanations, and for the adults to make the adult decisions involved.

In the situations described above we can see how some trans people may eschew their acceptance of their freedom for the comforts of conformity, and how this is paradoxical as they will nonetheless be free to transition, or to choose otherwise, as they will (Sartre, 1943/2003). We can also see how being trans is fundamentally inextricable from being authentic as it is about a process of becoming more oneself. Indeed when trans people do claim their freedom, whether to transition full time, part time, or otherwise, they are acting in good faith through acting in accord with their considered authentic nature (Sartre, 1943/2003), in a way in which a cisgender

---

2. Heteronormativity is the view that heterosexuality, and the cultural accoutrements of this, are an unimpeachable norm. The cultural accoutrements might include marriage, children, job roles, gendered division of labour, etc.

3. Although, as with other forms of change, acrimony does affect people. It follows therefore that a well-handled transition, whether there is a separation or not, is important. A contentious separation, or acrimonious continuance of any relationship between carers, will be damaging.

person who has not considered and claimed their gender status (but who has rather unthinkingly accepted the gender they were thrown into) is not. Thus the key with both trans and cisgender clients is to allow, when necessary, an open exploration of gender as a means towards authenticity.

Of course gender is a slippery concept. It is sometimes considered to be biological in nature as the essentialists would have it, often regarding it as synonymous with biological sex. Others consider gender to be constructed (as the social constructionists assert), suggesting that one is not born, but rather becomes, a woman [or a man] after de Beauvoir (1949/1977). Many trans clients would prefer a biological explanation for their being trans in order to obviate blame. However, caution should be exercised if discussing this because, given that trans is fundamentally reasonable, there is nothing to be blamed for. Indeed we seldom spend much time considering why people are cisgender. Notwithstanding this, there is a good deal of evidence for a biological aetiology, at least for those people who transition while still fairly young (e.g. Bao & Swaab, 2011; Cheung, De Vries & Swaab, 2002; Garcia-Falgueras & Swaab, 2008; Kruijver, 2004; Kruijver et al, 2000; Swaab & Garcia-Fulgeuras, 2008; Zhou et al, 1995). However, just as de Beauvoir was arguing with regards to womanhood, the issue is more complex than most biological or constructionist writing and research on gender captures. While one may be biologically trans, how one is trans, and when one transitions, are different matters entirely – and matters which are constrained by the vagaries of the social world which the trans person is thrown into. If the person is thrown into the pre-Bronze Age Czech Republic they may be buried as a female; if they are thrown into nineteenth-century America as native American they may be welcomed as a shaman (Herdt, 1996) and if they are thrown into twenty-first-century Western cultures they may engage medical technologies to allow them to physically transition (Barrett, 2007).

Transition then may have many different aspects which require consideration and acceptance, preferably from others but certainly from the trans person themselves. Issues such as their work/career will need to be considered, as will relationships, friendships, family, etc. Some trans people opt to move away from previous jobs/workplaces, etc., and start anew, and this can be relatively successful, but seems a shame given the effort required to build a life. It is important that trans people in these instances are not simply moving from one position of bad faith (of living in an uncomfortable gender) to another (of living alone as a trans person through following a trope that this is what must happen in these instances). Many trans people, for example, live very successfully with their old partners, friends and work after a period of sometimes stressful renegotiation. It is important that in eschewing the rules of the trans person's old life, about body, mind and relationships, that a new set of restricting rules are not unthinkingly taken up in bad faith from the media, trans Internet sites and such like (see Barker, 2012). Above all transition should be a search for a personally authentic way of being-in-the-world which is available to the client.

Thus the style of a person's being-in-the-world – their worlding if you will (Spinelli, 2007) – will be a biopsychosocial combination which may also be affected by hormones, surgeries, etc. (see 'further reading' for the effects of these). It is important for existential-phenomenological practitioners to be familiar with both the freedoms afforded in engaging with a personally authentic gender, as well as the constraints of biology, technology and the society which trans people are thrown into.

Asking the transitioning client what sort of man or woman (depending on whether they are transitioning to male or female respectively) they would like to be can be useful as they may have a notion of an archetype without having considered who they wish to be – again an inauthentic mode of expression. A note of caution, however, is that many older trans people will need to go through a sort of second adolescence during transition which will necessarily involve trying out different persona, much as a cisgender teenager will during their adolescence. There is a subtle line between noting inauthenticity, exploring identity, and questioning a nascent identity, which practitioners should be cognisant of. While the client may appear to be an adult and therefore have a stable form of identity, they may still be in the process of becoming the type of woman or man they want to be (which is not to say that their inherent sense of *being* a woman or man need be unstable) and psychotherapy may destabilise a reasonable, if nascent, identity. For this reason caution is needed in these areas and mandatory psychotherapy should never be practised with this population as it is harmful (Lawrence, 2003; Loewenberg & Krege, 2007).

On some occasions then, a phenomenological exploration of the circumstances a trans person finds themselves in prior to transition, and the potential circumstances after transition, are useful interventions. It is important, however, for practitioners not to allow the decision-making process to act as a proxy for action. Some trans people will continue to consider for a long time, always with a reasonable reason not to transition, but without choosing not to – at least for the time being. It may be that they wish to wait for the children to start school, to settle in, to pass exams, to move up a school, pass exams, get to university, graduate, marry, have their first child (the client's grandchild), for that child to start school ... All of these are reasonable, but all allow the transition to be safely put off until some time in the future. While the temporality of the decision to transition is not only in the present (see Merleau-Ponty, 1945/2002), the act of 'choosing' becomes the de facto choice – it is not only 'choosing not to choose' (in the sense of ignoring the issue) which is the choice (Sartre, 1943/2003) – but also that 'continuously being in the process of choosing' which is the choice. After sufficient phenomenological exploration considering if, or when, to transition then a *leap to faith* (Kierkegaard, 1844/1980) may need to be made into trying an identity and can profitably be explored with those clients who are adamant that they will transition. It is important that clients do not look for certainties about where to jump to and from here. It can be useful to ask clients for specifics as to when it would be possible to transition, with times and dates, and if something will occur to stop this. If you engage with the client over a sufficient period of time it can be useful to revisit this retrospectively if the transition has not occurred at that time. The decision as to whether to transition, (as with Kierkegaard's notion of faith) is a difficult and paradoxical one as it is often of such magnitude that it needs to be from a position of certainty, while at the same time being too encompassing to allow for this.

Such leaps to faith sometimes occur after a major life event destabilises a client's life, or apparently removes an obstacle which was thought to be insuperable – not uncommonly the death of a parent. Death, as ever the great existential satori, can give clients a sense of their own finitude, with the determination to live some part of their life authentically in terms of their gender. Indeed for some clients it is dying, not living, in a personally authentic gender role which is the motivating factor, as they realise that age will afford them little time. Whether for life or death the finitude – inextricably bound with the client's fundamental project of personal authenticity of gender – acts as a great motivator.

Transphobia, etc.

Transphobia is unfortunately all too common in both public and private discourses. In its crudest sense it refers to a person being shouted at on the street, attacked, or discriminated against for work, or the provision of goods or services. Within the UK there are now legal protections under the Single Equality Act 2010, and the provision for trans people to be legally recognised as their gender for all purposes, including marriage, prisons, etc., under the Gender Recognition Act 2004;[4] however this does not stop discrimination entirely (see Lombardi et al, 2001). In addition to these crude discriminations trans people may be discriminated against by friends and relatives through misunderstanding or personal concerns (although of course, friends and relatives may also be very supportive, or rather neutral) due to a misunderstanding and/or a fear about the person not being 'normal' through disregarding the heteronormative contract. Clinicians can usefully explore this with clients while maintaining a generally positive stance towards trans to offset the heteronormative cisgender bias of much mainstream media.

It can be useful for existential-phenomenological practitioners to reflexively engage with their own assumptions (Etherington, 2004; Finlay & Gough, 2003) in order to effect such epoché as is possible before undertaking the phenomenological exploration of the trans person's current, and aspirant, worlding, as recommended above. For this reason it is important for clinicians to be educated about trans to the extent that they are about cisgender matters in order to effect an adequate epoché and so not bias any responses or directions in the therapy. It is not possible to undertake a phenomenological enquiry of a client's lived experience if a therapist has no knowledge of the world of that experience beyond tabloids and worthy documentaries. Therefore activist and professional literatures should also be engaged with (see further reading list). Similarly 'being with' the client is for friends, not paid professionals (whether through charity, taxation or directly). Professionals should not expect clients in distress to teach them the basics of the field as that is properly the place of CPD (Continuous Professional Development) – again for which the professional pays, rather than being paid by the client. Practitioners who don't do this and who assume that they can 'have a go' without basic knowledge will damage rapport, perhaps irreparably, both towards themselves and often towards other professionals (Richards & Barker, 2013).

Relating to trans people through their trans identity is, of course, bad faith (see Sartre, 1943/2003). This false primacy of one aspect of the

---

4. It is worth UK clinicians being familiar with this Act as it also makes it a criminal offence to disclose a trans person's trans status without their explicit approval (implicit approval is insufficient). This means that it is a police matter with a criminal record, not a civil suit (although this may follow). It is an 'absolute offence' – which means 'reasonableness criteria' do not apply. This includes disclosing to supervisors, secretaries, etc., even if it is 'usual policy'. If the clinician does not gain consent the criminal record (and fine, etc.) is the clinician's. I therefore recommend gaining explicit written consent as part of your usual consenting and confidentiality procedures.

person's identity stymies any form of horizontalisation in the therapy and is a form of I–It relating (Buber, 1958) in which the person is seen as 'a transsexual', rather than as a professor, a mother, a cook, an academic, etc. It is consequently important for clinicians not to 'other' their trans clients through identifying them solely through that lens, even when it is a trans issue which is being brought to the therapy. Similarly trans people may have split the trans aspect off from themselves or their past selves and so be I–Me relating (see Cooper, 2003) through disowning those aspects, rather than seeing themselves as coherent selves and so be I–I relating (Cooper, 2003). To some extent this will be a necessary part of any transition during which social norms for a gender become introjected until they are 'natural' – as with cisgender people being taught norms in adolescence.

The acceptance of a trans self, or of a past in a certain gendered form, is not as simple as suggesting that one comes to terms with having been one gender and moving towards another. First this will simply not have been the case for many trans people who transitioned when young – they will not have actually been their birth-assigned gender in any meaningful sense, although they may have gone through a few of the motions for a while as a means of avoiding violence or obtaining their basic needs. Even those people who transitioned later and who inhered more of the social norms of their birth-assigned gender will not have totally been of that gender. In both these cases it can be useful to consider being trans as simply another (not lesser) mode of being a gender. This is why I have used a gap between trans and woman, or trans and man in this text rather than transwoman or transman (we might also say women [or man] with a transgender history). The trans is not inextricably bound up in their gender. Just as there are many women who have had a hysterectomy and remain women despite not having the 'vitally important' capacity of bearing children: and men who do not have a penis through cancer, yet remain men despite not having the 'vitally important' capacity of having a penis, trans people are another sort of man or woman who remain men and women respectively despite not having 'vitally important' parts of that gender.

In realising that being trans is not inimical to being a 'real' man or woman (and the word 'real' should always be questioned in therapy) a trans person may be able to become more at ease with themselves, and their past, and so to I–I relate (Cooper, 2003). This fairly long philosophical consideration of trans is important, and may be important in client work, as the false logical positivism of the biological essentialist discourse – that one *is* a rough reading of one's biology at birth – cuts down a human sciences approach and limits the freedom to create a self with a social world – an axiomatic tenet of existentialism.

General issues

I haven't really considered the importance of a personally authentic embodiment for trans people as it should be self-evident in this client group. Needless to say, surgery and hormonal manipulation of carefully selected clients who request it unequivocally improves quality of life (Gijs & Brewaeys, 2007). Similarly I haven't touched upon comorbidity in trans people as, if in a stable situation and if able to obtain any assistance needed physiologically, there are no higher rates of psychopathology in this group (Hill et al, 2005; Hoshiai et al, 2010). Trans people may, however, be subject to *minority stress,* that is distress at being discriminated against or being part of a minority group as touched upon above (see Bouman et al, 2010).

Other than issues relating to general stress and anxiety about the physical trials of transition (and bear in mind that these may be entirely physical, before searching for meaning) and the day-to-day trials of transphobia (although these are often less than many people assume, but see Lombardi, et al, 2001) trans people may approach a therapist about issues such as relationships, work, family, etc. Sometimes these will be incidental to the fact that a person is trans, and, as above, a phenomenological exploration that is not overly concerned with the trans status can be useful. It may be helpful to think of it like a tentative whisper of a question by a clinician's shoulder, rather than a neon sign over the client's head. If a client is considering reproductive issues, is it to do with their being trans at all? It may be that they are grieving because they chose not to store gametes when transitioning at 18, and are now taking a different view at 30; or it may not be as they are quite happy to adopt, or they did indeed store some gametes against the possibility of a change of mind. In these instances a cautious consideration, rather than an assumption that it must be about trans, or that it isn't about trans, is likely to pay dividends.

Conclusion

In general trans people go about their daily business without the need for interventions from helping professionals of any kind. Trans people may, however, approach psychologists and psychotherapists for assistance with the usual work of bereavement, life changes, relationships, etc., during which professionals should be cautiously aware of people's trans status without giving it undue prominence, and indeed be prepared to ignore it. In those rare instances where a trans person's status is pertinent, professionals can be well served through having adequate knowledge of the field and then applying a generally affirmative phenomenological approach within a human sciences model of a wider understanding of gender than that offered by biological essentialist discourses – towards whatever end a client can authentically claim. This should help as, to paraphrase Søren Kierkegaard (1849/2004); 'The most common form of despair is [indeed] not being who you are.'

Further reading

As readers may be aware, there is a dearth of literature pertaining to existential work with sexuality and gender, indeed the very purpose of this book was, in part, to address that lacuna. The following volumes and papers should succinctly cover many clinical eventualities and also contain signposts to further sources of information.

Barrett, J (Ed) (2007) *Transsexual and Other Disorders of Gender Identity*. Oxford: Radcliffe.

Bornstein, K & Bergman, SB (Eds) (2010) *Gender Outlaws: The next generation*. New York: Avalon Publishing Group.

Lev, AI (2004) *Transgender Emergence*. London: Haworth Clinical Practice Press.

Richards, C (2011) Transsexualism and existentialism. *Existential Analysis, 22*(2), 272–79.

Richards, C & Barker, M (2013) *Sexuality and Gender for Counsellors, Psychologists and Health Professionals: A practical guide*. London: Sage Publications.

Serano, J (2007) *Whipping Girl*. Emeryville, CA: Seal Press.

References

Bao, AM & Swaab, DF (2011) Sexual differentiation of the human brain: Relation to gender identity, sexual orientation and neuropsychiatric disorders. *Frontiers in Neuroendocrinology, 32,* 214–26.

Barker, M (2012) *Rewriting the Rules: An integrative guide to love, sex and relationships.* London: Routledge.

Barrett, J (Ed) (2007) *Transsexual and Other Disorders of Gender Identity.* Oxford: Radcliffe.

Beauvoir, S de (1997) *The Second Sex* (HM Parshley, Trans). New York: Vintage. (First published 1949)

Bouman, WP, Bauer, GR, Richards, C & Coleman, E (2010) World Professional Association for Transgender Health consensus statement on considerations of the role of distress (Criterion D) in the *DSM* diagnosis of Gender Identity Disorder. *International Journal of Transgenderism, 12*(2), 100–6.

Buber, M (1958) *I and Thou* (2nd ed; R Gregor-Smith, Trans). London: Continuum.

Cheung, WCJ, De Vries, GJ & Swaab, DF (2002) Sexual differentiation of the bed nucleus of the stria terminalis in humans may extend into adulthood. *The Journal of Neuroscience, 22*(3), 1027–33.

Cooper, M (2003) 'I–I' and 'I–Me': Transposing Buber's interpersonal attitudes to the intrapersonal plane. *Journal of Constructivist Psychology, 16*(2), 131–53.

Cox, G (2009) *How to Be an Existentialist: Or how to get real, get a grip and stop making excuses.* London: Continuum.

Etherington, K (2004) *Becoming a Reflexive Researcher: Using our selves in research.* London: Okica Lingsley.

Finlay, L & Gough, B (2003) *Reflexivity: A practical guide for researchers in health and social sciences.* Oxford: Blackwell.

Garcia-Falgueras, A & Swaab, DF (2008) A sex difference in the hypothalamic uncinate nucleus: Relationship to gender identity. *Brain, 131,* 3132–46.

Gijs, L & Brewaeys, A (2007) Surgical treatment of gender dysphoria in adults and adolescents: Recent developments, effectiveness, and challenges. *Annual Review of Sex Research, 18,* 178–224.

Green, R (1978) Sexual identity of 37 children raised by homosexual or transsexual parents. *American Journal of Psychiatry, 135,* 692–97.

Green, R (1987) *The 'Sissy Boy Syndrome' and the Development of Homosexuality.* London: Yale University Press.

Herdt, G (1996) *Third Sex, Third Gender.* New York: Zone Books.

Hill, DB, Rozanski, C, Carfagnini, J & Willoughby, B (2005) Gender identity disorders in childhood and adolescence: A critical inquiry. In D Karasic & J Drescher (Eds) *Sexual and Gender Diagnoses of the Diagnostic and Statistical Manual (DSM)* (pp. 7–34). New York: Haworth Press.

Hoshiai, M, Matsumoto, Y, Sato, T, Ohnishi, M, Okabe, N, Kishimoto, Y, Terada, S & Kuroda, S (2010) Psychiatric comorbidity among clients with gender identity disorder. *Psychiatry and Clinical Neurosciences, 64,* 514–19.

Kierkegaard, S (1980) *The Concept of Anxiety* (R Thomte & AB Anderson, Trans). Princeton, NJ: Princeton University Press. (First published 1844)

Kierkegaard, S (2004) *The Sickness unto Death.* (A Hannay, Trans). New York: Penguin Books. (First published 1849)

Kruijver, FPM (2004) *Sex in the Brain.* Amsterdam: Netherlands Institute of Brain Research.

Kruijver, FPM, Jiang-Ning, Z, Pool, CW, Hofman, MA, Gooren, LJG & Swaab, DF (2000) Male-to-female transsexuals have female neuron numbers in a limbic nucleus. *The Journal of Clinical Endocrinology & Metabolism, 85*(5), 2034–41.

Lawrence, AA (2003) Factors associated with satisfaction or regret following male-to-female sex reassignment surgery. *Archives of Sexual Behavior, 32*(4), 299–315.

Loewenberg, H & Krege, S (2007) Follow-up of 107 male-to-female transsexuals after sex-reassignment surgery. Presentation at the World Professional Association for Transgender Health Biennial Symposium. September, Chicago, IL.

Lombardi, EL, Wilchins, RA, Priesing, D, & Malouf, D (2001) Gender violence: Transgender experiences with violence and discrimination. *Journal of Homosexuality, 42*(1), 89–101.

Merleau-Ponty, M (2002) *Phenomenology of Perception.* London: Routledge. (First published 1945)

Richards, C & Barker, M (2013) *Sexuality and Gender for Counsellors, Psychologists and Health Professionals: A practical guide.* London: Sage Publications.

Sartre, J-P (2003) *Being and Nothingness* (HE Barnes, Trans). London: Routledge. (First published 1943)

Spinelli, E (2007) *Practising Existential Psychotherapy: The relational world.* London: Sage Publications.

Swaab, DF & Garcia-Falgueras, A (2008) Sexual differentiation of the human brain in relation to gender identity and sexual orientation. *Functional Neurology, 24,* 17–28.

Van Deurzen, E & Adams, M (2011) *Skills in Existential Counselling and Psychotherapy*. London: Sage Publications.

Zhou, JN, Hofman, MA, Gooren, LJ & Swaab, DF (1995) A sex difference in the human brain and its relation to transsexuality. *Nature, 378,* 68–70.

Part 6

Sexuality and the Consulting Room

11

A Dangerous Methodlessness: Sexuality in the therapeutic relationship

– Marcia Gamsu –

In 'Beyond the Core Conditions' (Thorne, 1987) Brian Thorne describes his unorthodox work with Sally whose presenting issue was terror about sex. This fear had persisted during 16 years of marriage and previous therapy had not provided any lasting help. The work began as couple counselling and continued as individual therapy. Thorne quickly felt that verbal communication did not touch Sally's fears and became convinced that physicality had a significant role to play in his work with her. Despite his uncertainty and fears of professional censure, this physical exploration involved removing Sally's clothes, sensual massage and eventually a naked embrace. Thorne states that he was mindful of his physical attraction to his client and rather than putting this to one side, used this to help Sally work through her paralysing fear of sex, without stepping into a full sexual relationship. He also suggests that love and mutuality provided the basis of the work and that the physical intimacy was at Sally's instigation/with her consent. According to Thorne's account Sally was able to overcome her sense of overwhelming fear and guilt about sex as a result of the work. She had the following to say about the therapy: 'we accomplished a revolution – we accomplished a complete cycle in the way forward, and we accomplished a coup d'état' (Thorne, 1987: 64).

Reflecting on his work, Thorne suggests that we should be less fearful of engaging in an exploration of sexuality with our clients if this is based on love, mutuality and respect. Nevertheless Thorne equates full sexual intercourse with abuse and warns against falling in love with one's client because this involves a loss of the boundaries which are necessary for therapy to take place.

So how is this brief account of the work of a person-centred pioneer relevant to the readers of this book? Regardless of approach, sexual behaviour within therapy is now clearly prohibited by a number of ethical codes (British Association for Counselling and Psychotherapy, 2010; British Psychological Society, 2009; Council for Healthcare Regulatory Excellence (now the Health and Care Professions Council), 2008; UK Council for Psychotherapy, 2009) and while this chapter will not look at these codes in detail, it is acknowledged that existential practitioners are also bound by them. This chapter moves on from these codes to consider an existential perspective on sexuality and the implications this might have for existential therapy.

The Thorne case study appears to provoke a salacious interest and/or outrage on the part of a significant percentage of people who become acquainted with it (Newman, 2010). Presenting the case study to groups of students training to become existential psychotherapists and counselling psychologists, the author has met with responses ranging from 'it's not normal' to concerns about whether Sally genuinely consented to the physical relationship with Thorne. Literature on the subject reflects this prohibitive stance, expressing a near universal consensus that sexual relationships between client and therapist are invariably abusive (Jehu, 1994; Pope & Vasquez, 2011; Russell, 1993; Rutter, 1990).

This chapter looks at the rationale underpinning this consensus, attempting to bracket an assumption that because there is near universal agreement on the taboo surrounding client–therapist sexual intimacy, there must be obvious and compelling reasons for this. It considers what an existential/phenomenological stance towards sexuality within the therapeutic relationship might be, particularly focusing on the relative importance of client autonomy/intersubjective relationship between client and therapist and the implications of focusing on one or other of these phenomena in responding to sexual attraction in the therapy room. It then goes on to consider what the consequences might be if we give love pride of place within therapy. For example, how might the risk and uncertainty that is arguably part and parcel of love find a place in a profession which places a high value on transparency and safety? What might the implications be if this love is expressed in a sexual manner?

The evidence

Evidence suggests that clients are very likely to fare badly from sexual relationships with their therapists. Surveys report clients being left with guilt (especially if the client has disclosed information about the relationship to a third party) self-hatred, impaired ability to trust, confusion about roles and boundaries, feelings of isolation, helplessness and anger (Pope, 1988; Russell, 1993). In other words, the kind of feelings one would expect from a victim of abuse. Whilst a number of those questioned in the surveys were also reluctant to conclude that the issue was as simple as the therapist being the abuser and them being abused, it is possible to consider that this is 'false' consciousness. Perhaps the victim of the abuse is still in the thrall of their seductive therapist or is simply not yet aware of their powerlessness and the harm that they have suffered as a result. Furthermore, even when a relationship happens after termination of therapy, the relationship seems likely to harm the client. A 1991 survey by Pope and Vetter found that out of 958 questioned, 866 thought it had been damaging for them and 134 attempted suicide (Gabriel, 2005).

Despite the danger that such surveys point to, the significance of their figures may not be exactly as it appears at first glance. People make sense of their experiences in terms of the prevailing current discourse on the matter. A discourse, in which a sexual relationship between a therapist and client is by definition both illicit and abusive, is going to affect the way the parties to such relationships conduct the relationship and make sense of it. Such a relationship will need to be carried out in an atmosphere of secrecy and being involved in it is likely to create feelings of guilt and betrayal (Denman, 2004). The parties may well interpret their roles in line with commonly held views on such relationships; for example, the client may well come to see themselves as a victim and may experience guilt at the thought that they have been complicit in their own abuse. Were the prevailing discourse different, it is arguable that the client might not experience herself as having been harmed by the relationship. Imagine, for example, a time and place where there is a belief that wisdom and strength is transmitted through sexual contact with an older, more experienced man or woman. Although such a scenario may provoke discomfort and is at odds with our current values, a young patient having sex with an older therapist in this context may well consider the relationship to be beneficial rather than damaging to him or her.

As an aside, the forbidden nature of the relationship can also have an effect in a more subtle way. As Bataille (2006) points out, the existence of a taboo makes us both wary of stepping over a boundary and attracts us towards it. It shapes and intensifies the experience of what lies in the forbidden zone (Denman, 2004).

The changing discourse

Although the current prevailing discourse is that sexual behaviour between client and therapist is an abuse of power, this was not always the case. There were numerous sexual relationships/encounters between early analysts and their patients including those of Carl Jung, Sandor Ferenczi, Otto Gross, Ernest Jones, Karen Horney and Erich Fromm which were often framed by those involved as passionate love affairs (Baur, 1997). There were also a number of instances of behaviour which whilst not involving sexual intimacy would probably be seen as highly inappropriate today, such as Klein's analysis of her patient on her bed (Baur, 1997). Freud was hardly encouraging of such relationships, but his protégées nevertheless informed him at least to a degree of their attraction to and involvement with their patients. When Ferenczi told Freud of his proposed engagement to his (Fernenczi's) patient who was the daughter of his ex-lover, Freud wrote that he would send congratulations when they were due. Freud also wrote to the girl's mother expressing his concerns, but these were focused on the mother–daughter dynamic rather than the analyst–patient issue (Brabant, Falzader & Giampieri-Deutsch, 1993). Freud also admitted that he himself had come 'very close to [an indiscretion] a number of times and had a narrow escape' (Baur, 1997: 20).

Articles written in the 1970s, when the subject began to be discussed, considered that whilst therapy itself failed if feelings of attraction were acted on, nevertheless the relationships that developed *in themselves* could be either good or bad. For example, a 1974 article reviewing 34 cases of sex between therapists and clients estimated that in 7 cases the relationship was positive, for 11 it was mixed and for 16 couples it was a very negative experience. The authors suggest that these relationships fell into various categories from power disguised as attraction to what they described as the 'genuine human relationship' that sometimes develops between therapist and client. They ask their colleagues not to engage in knee-jerk reactions. They urge therapists not to take the risk in engaging in sexual relationships with clients, but also include guidelines for transferring the patient to another therapist and for creating greater parity in the relationship should therapist and (former) client be determined to enter into a relationship (Baur, 1997).

However, this pragmatic and nuanced narrative seemed to change by the late 1970s into a discourse that is recognisable today, in which all client–therapist sexual intimacies are considered abuse and in which genuine consent does not exist (Baur, 1997; Jehu, 1994; Russell, 1993;

Rutter, 1990). This is the case regardless of the power differential between the parties and regardless of the circumstances.

The following sections of this chapter examine what it is about our current stance towards therapy that makes us view sex between therapist and client as invariably abusive. It argues that such a view arises from the importance which we now place on client autonomy (within therapy and in other professional relationships). This marks a shift from paternalism with its assumption that the expert professional would use his power in a benign manner for the benefit of the patient. The current emphasis on autonomy in professional relationships is itself reflective of a broader worldview which places the individual at the heart of what it is to be human. Within therapy, such thinking obviously protects the client from unwanted exploitation, including sexual exploitation. But more ambiguously it also calls into question a dynamic in which the therapist appears to be too involved with the client. Connection and interdependence as goals of therapy may be viewed with some suspicion (Heywood, 1999). A therapist who steps over boundaries with the client (for example, allowing the client to contact him or her between sessions) may then be seen as creating dependency and entrenching a sense of helplessness on the client's part. This is particularly the case if sexual attraction is a part of the dynamic, creating the suspicion of neediness on the therapist's part and fear of the development of an enmeshed, co-dependent relationship. Such a relationship may be regarded as abusive because it is a threat to the client's autonomy.

A technical approach to therapy: Sex as a loss of detachment

Despite the welcome protection from sexual exploitation that comes with respecting the client's autonomy, an over-emphasis could potentially lead to a conclusion that the therapeutic relationship has limited importance. A common view of therapy might be that a therapist who is reasonably detached from his client uses his or her professional skills to help the client change. Despite the easy appeal of such thinking, it is worth considering some of its implications. Depending on how far we take the emphasis on autonomy we can be left with a technological, dehumanised enterprise. The appropriately professional therapist can become the detached uncaring therapist using the tricks of his or her trade to effect changes in the client. If the client is an individual who is separate from and disconnected from the therapist, it makes sense for the therapist to believe that she can gain an objective view of what is wrong with them, diagnose them and apply techniques to transform them, whilst all the time remaining detached from them. Although the therapist may well feel warmth for and care about the client, this is extraneous to what actually creates change. The therapist then, rather than being someone who thinks for him- or herself, becomes a kind of production line worker or functionary.

Furthermore, since what happens to the client in this scenario is not affected by his or her interpersonal relationship to the therapist, it is not very far from this to believe that their issues more generally originate primarily from their internal processes, rather than arising in an interpersonal world. Hence it makes sense for the therapist to treat the client as a bundle of symptoms caused by some kind of cognitive dysfunction, rather than a person trying to make sense of his ambiguous and fluctuating relationships with others. At its most extreme then, an insistence on the autonomy of the client in isolation from relationships with both therapist and others can make both the person of therapist and client seem irrelevant, leaving a collection of symptoms to be treated by a technician, and perhaps a computer program. Whilst such an approach to therapy might sound alarming it also appears to make the process transparent and predicable. The efficacy of different forms of therapy can be evaluated using randomised controlled clinical trials, which attempt to avoid the 'distortions' of the actual person of client and therapist. Furthermore, because standards can be set for psychotherapy work, it is believed that it can be effectively regulated. This is arguably empowering for clients, enabling them to make informed decisions about what therapy to choose and providing a framework for responding to therapeutic malpractice.

Sexual expression between therapist and client is arguably highly inappropriate if we adopt this technical and depersonalised stance towards therapy. From such a perspective, acting on sexual attraction would make it difficult or impossible for the therapist to maintain the requisite degree of detachment in order to act in a professional manner with the client. It is likely to be seen as an unwanted intrusion into the client's private space. But this protection may come at a price: an over-emphasis on symptoms and a downplaying of the humanity of the client.

From an existential perspective, such a therapeutic approach is open to challenge. Existential therapists point to qualitative research demonstrating that far from being irrelevant, the characteristics of the therapist and client and their particular relationship are important, if not the most important, predictors of the efficacy of a particular piece of therapy (Cooper, 2003; Spinelli, 1994/2006). Arguably however, this does not necessarily imply that what the therapist does is irrelevant, just that the significance of what he or she does and its effect are inextricably bound up with the relationship in which he or she does them.

> Hans Strupp, one of our first research mentors, offered an analogy to illustrate the inseparability of these constituent elements. Suppose you want your teenager to clean his or her room. Two methods for achieving this are to establish clear standards and to impose consequences. A reasonable approach, but the effectiveness of these two evidence based methods will vary on whether the relationship between you and the teenager is characterized by warmth and mutual respect or by anger and mistrust. This is not to say that the methods are useless, merely that how well they work depends on the context in which they are used.
> (Norcross & Lambert, 2011: 5)

Furthermore, what the therapist does is central in shaping the therapeutic relationship, so that even attempting to distinguish between 'doing' and 'being' is problematic or 'put differently, treatment methods are relational acts' (Norcross & Lambert, 2011: 4).

If warmth and mutual respect can be seen to be inextricably bound up with successful therapy, can this ever be given sexual expression? Could sexuality within therapy ever be a therapeutic method? In order to explore this question further, the following sections consider what type of therapeutic relationship is in line with existential philosophy. They begin by asking what existential thinkers have to say about autonomy, connectedness and love.

An existential perspective on relationship

According to Spinelli, 'the principle of relatedness or inter-relation is so pivotal to the whole rationale of existential phenomenology that its presence resonates through every argument presented by the approach' (Spinelli, 2007: 12).

Rather than the individual experience being primordial and relationship being a secondary process, Spinelli argues that the experience of subjectivity can only be seen against a background of relatedness, which is a fundamental and irreducible facet of existence. In therapy speak, the commonly held view is that the client first needs to find themselves and only when they have done so and built up sufficient strength as an individual can they focus on developing their relationships. But for existential psychotherapists, there is no separate self that is there to be found and there is no self which exists in isolation from a network of relationships. As a result:

> it can be argued that existential psychotherapy's focus is not even primarily on the client per se, but rather on the particular ways through which relatedness expresses itself: first, through the narratives of the experience of being that are provided by the client and secondly and no less importantly, *through the psychotherapist's and client's current lived experiences of relatedness as it unfolds and enfolds them both during the therapeutic encounter.*
>
> (Spinelli, 2007: 12, emphasis added)

However, it can be argued that not all existential philosophers and practitioners do in fact give such a central place to the notion of interpersonal relatedness, choosing to place greater focus on existential issues such as isolation and authenticity (Yalom, 1980). There can be a tension between relatedness and authenticity and I explore this in the following section, focusing on Heidegger's discussion in *Being and Time* (Heidegger, 1996).

Martin Heidegger: Authentic non-relationship?

The influence of Heidegger looms large in the discourse of British existential psychotherapy and appears to support a view that it is impossible to conceive of a person without his considering his relationships with others. Heidegger's notion of Dasein does indeed make being-in-the-world part of its ontological structure (an inherent, irreducible characteristic of our being). One implication of our always existing in the world means that we also always exist in a world of relationships with others. This is the case even if we are alone or feel alienated from others; these are just different ways of experiencing our essentially relational existence.

But if being alienated from others is just another way of being-in-the-world with others (even if it characterised by of the 'modes of deficiency and indifference', Heidegger, 1996: 114), then what difference might our being-in-the-world with others make to how we respond to sexual attraction in therapy? Heidegger spends little time describing relationships with others (devoting more space, for example, to describing our relationship with tools). Arguably he is less interested in the specifics of people's lives than in providing a description of the general characteristics of existence. Heidegger was critical of interpretations, such as those of Binswanger, which confused the unchanging characteristics of being (ontology) with people's concrete specific experiences (the ontic) (Heidegger, 2001). But given the fact that existential therapists are dealing with their clients' (and indeed their own) specific experiences, including that of sexual attraction, it nevertheless seems important to consider what Heidegger's view might be on the forms of our relationships with others.

Roger Frie, drawing on Binswanger, points out that for the most part Heidegger views others as a threat to authentic existence (Frie, 1997). Others cause us to be drawn into what Heidegger calls the everyday modes of living. This is characterised by a life which is lacking in passion, commitment and engagement but is rather guided by a lazy curiosity, a readiness to be guided by common opinion and futile but frenzied activity. Living like this makes us feel safe because it enables us to turn away from the anxiety we experience in connection with the ultimate groundlessness of our existence and an anticipation of the possibility of our death. Conversely engaging with this anxiety and the possibility of our own death can free us from our muddled inauthentic way of being (Heidegger, 1996). Given that we will all ultimately have to experience the moment of death ourselves without the safety of our reliance on others, anticipation of the instance of death makes us aware of the fragility of our dependency on others and frees us from being dominated by them. This enables us to return to our own existence and to our own genuine possibilities (Heidegger, 1996). In other words, freeing ourselves from others enables authentic living (Frie, 1997).

Heidegger does very briefly describe an authentic mode of relating to others which he terms leaping ahead. Such a relationship involves enabling the other to live authentically by engaging fully with his or her own existence (his or her possibilities). Heidegger contrasts this with another way of being which involves taking care of someone's projects for them, which exonerates them of responsibility and can cause the other to become 'dependent and dominated' (Heidegger, 1996: 114). He calls this leaping in. Not surprisingly, existential psychotherapists are encouraged to practice a form of therapy akin to leaping ahead rather than one based on leaping forward. In other the words the therapeutic relationship is one in which the client is enabled to live his or her life authentically as opposed to a relationship which creates dependency on or even domination by the therapist (van Deurzen, 2010). Yet, it is interesting to think a little further and consider what kind of relationship Heidegger is pointing to here. Leaping ahead leaves the other free and this seems to mean free from the other person. Phrased differently, this is arguably a relationship which involves disconnecting from the other.

> Whilst this attitude does not denote indifference towards the other, neither does it allow for the mutuality of the I–Thou, or reciprocal love relationship. Leaping ahead is starkly opposed to the notion of intersubjective reciprocity. Emancipatory solicitude does not engage with other directly. Dasein's solicitude emancipated the selfhood of others only by liberating them from itself. As Michael Theunissen puts it 'Dasein's help must be as indirect as the 'Socratic midwife service' … which in turn means that it can only consist in this, that I free the Other from me.
>
> (Frie, 1997: 80–1)

Warmth, care (in ordinary rather than Heideggerian terminology) and love do not have an obvious place in this model of an authentic relationship. Sexuality seems alien to it and Sartre points out Heidegger's Dasein appears asexual (Sartre, 1998). From a Heideggerian perspective sexual expression in therapy would arguably be seen as fostering confusion; at best as an impediment to the client to becoming strong and independent and at worst an expression of domination on the part of therapist.

An alternative model: Ludwig Binswanger

In *Basic Forms and Knowledge of Human Dasein* Binswanger (1964) argues that Heidegger seems to ultimately overlook the possibility of a genuine relationship with others (his authentic relationship is non-relationship), leaving us with a choice between inauthentic being with others and authentic selfhood (Frie, 1997). A consequence of this is that as Binswanger put it, 'Heidegger left love to freeze outside the doors of his projection of being' (Heidegger, 2001: 304, translators' afterward).

For Binswanger, love discloses something fundamental about existence, which is our relationships with others or we-hood. Binswanger suggests that the human self can never be fully understood without focusing on its inter-human relationships. He coins the word we-hood to describe our essential relational existence and argues that our sense of being separate individuals emerges from this primary connectedness (Frie, 1997). In other words, for Binswanger, relational existence precedes individual experience. As Spinelli describes above, this relational existence is not about two individuals coming together, which would make the individual the primary phenomena, but is the ground from which individual experience arises. As Binswanger puts it, we-hood is not 'a bridge between two existential depths, but an independent original mode of human existence out of which I and Thou are first born' (Frie, 1997: 93).

If individual experience is routed in interpersonal relationships, tearing ourselves away from the influence of others, as per Heidegger, is a denial of what defines us as being human. It is not a route to authenticity, quite the opposite. For Binswanger, authenticity or self-realisation can only be achieved through relationship. This relationship is one that involves reciprocal love; Binswanger seems to use the words we-hood and love interchangeably: we-hood ('we of love' as 'being of loving encounter') (Heidegger, 2001). This we-hood transforms our experience of space and time (Frie, 1997). For example, whilst in everyday encounters we make room for each other and allow the other his or her own physical space, when there is this loving encounter space doesn't need to be apportioned between people and can seem limitless. This transformation is at its most marked in intimate sexual encounters so that each partner's sense of having their own separate space changes to a space encompassing both partners, even though each also maintains his or her individuality. A similar shift can happen with our sense of time; intensely engaging with the other can lead to a sense of time standing still (Frie, 1997).

What implications might this have for the therapeutic relationship in general and for sexuality in therapy specifically? Firstly, loving relationships are the route to self-realisation. Love, rather than professional detachment, is arguably then the most therapeutic attitude to have towards the client. But what kind of love is this? Binswanger, like Buber, says that when we are loved in this way, we're loved as someone unique, rather than as someone bound by any role (Frie, 1997). A therapist influenced by Binswanger would presumably then allow themselves to connect in a spontaneous way to the needs of the human being in front of them, rather than being constrained by his or her own role as therapist in a professional relationship with a person who is in the role of client. Does this mean a therapist can have sex with his or her client? Binswanger's descriptions of the transformations of space and time when there is we-hood sound both romantic and erotic. How much could this be a part of therapy?

A possible answer to this lies in the importance that Binswanger gives to mutuality and reciprocity in relationship. This can breakdown when one person starts to see the other as an object to be possessed and this can happen not just by straightforward domination but also in adoration (the other as a valuable and desirable object, but an object nevertheless) (Frie, 1997). Arguably, whilst this is a possibility in all sexual relationships, it is a particular danger when sexuality is expressed in the therapeutic relationship.

It is easy to see how attraction between therapist and client could be tinged with mutual objectification, with the therapist dominating the client and the client projecting all manner of desirable qualities onto the therapist.

A further answer may lie in the weight that Binswanger gives not just to relationship, but also to the individuality of the people who comprise this. For Binswanger whilst both people exist together as part of a web both also maintain their distinct individuality (Frie, 1997). Whilst both need to recognise the other's similarities with him or herself, they also need to recognise the other is not a carbon copy of him or her, but a unique human being. A failure to recognise the other's difference can create a danger that the other will be dominated and dependent (Frie, 1997). This is a particular danger in therapy. Whilst it can be argued that sexual relationships are often poised on the boundary between merger and individuality and that there is always a possibility of losing a sense of the distinctiveness of self/other, the particular dynamics of the therapy relationship create a much greater likelihood of a total blurring of boundaries should the relationship become sexual. This can then lead to dependency and domination. But whilst the distinctiveness of each person needs to be honoured, Binswanger would argue that too much insistence on the other's individual status is also problematic, because it is only through entering a genuine relationship with the other that one can become genuinely autonomous. Relationship and autonomy are in a dialectical relationship with each other; engaging with one pole takes you to the other one and neither can be ignored. Binswanger's emphasis however seems to be on relationship.

Sex, mutuality and uncertainty

Binswanger's writing suggests that we might have a less fearful response to connectedness and love in therapy because this is simply the other side of the coin to separateness and individuality. We might also allow a sexual dynamic to have some place in therapy. Although Binswanger warns against relationships that are likely to foster dependency, a certain degree of need, dependency and attachment are often a feature of love (as is sexual attraction). Putting the argument more strongly, a refusal to allow love and perhaps even dependency to arise may, with certain clients and in certain circumstances, actually impede the client's ability to become stronger and more autonomous. For Carter Heywood, a therapist who rigidly holds onto boundaries may be abusing the client as much as a therapist who rides roughshod over them:

> For 'abuse' is not just a matter of touching people wrongly. It is, basically, a failure to make right-relation, a refusal to touch people rightly. We as professionals – indeed, we as people on this planet – are as likely to destroy one another and ourselves by holding tightly to prescribed role definitions as we are by active intrusion and violation.
> (Heywood, 1999: 10)

Heywood, whose thinking on therapy is in line with Binswanger's description of the mutual love relation, argues that for psychotherapy to be 'healing' it needs to be a genuinely mutual relationship, in which both therapist and client are 'touched, moved and changed, in the moment – and both know it' (Heywood, 1999: 32). Heywood herself fell in love with her therapist and sought the possibility of a friendship on termination of therapy, which her therapist refused (in a manner which seems somewhat unskilled and punitive). She suggests that the mutuality which is a prerequisite of good therapy involves openness to uncertainty and vulnerability on the part of both client and therapist and this includes allowing the possibility of the relationship changing into friendship. This openness to the relationship morphing into something new is of particular importance to Heywood, demonstrating a commitment to the openness and transformations inherent in a mutual relationship. In fact she goes so far as to suggest that flatly ruling out this possibility is unethical! Although Heywood does not suggest that the therapist must also be open to the possibility of the relationship becoming sexual (on the termination of therapy), her argument could support this.

However, whilst it may be the case that what Heywood describes points to a gold standard in therapy, most therapists would arguably be unwilling and unable to give to every client what Heywood holds to be the basis for ethical practice. What if the therapist does not like the client or is not in a position in his or her own life to open up to a relationship involving so much uncertainty? It seems a little unfair to describe the boundaries that such a therapist needs to protect him or herself as unethical. However, Heywood's argument does point to one of the questions raised by this discussion: how much uncertainty are we willing to tolerate as therapists and how much uncertainty is therapeutic for the client. Is there a point at which a lack of boundaries is destructive of the therapeutic enterprise? At the very least, Binswanger's we-relationship with its movement away from roles and its transformation of space and time stands in opposition to the predictability of evidence-based practice, techniques and professional codes. If eroticism/romantic love enters the picture this unpredictability is compounded. Part of the reason for this is that such experiences stand in stark opposition to a sensible, rational and purposive approach to the other. Irving Singer suggests that when we love someone, the worth with which we imbue him or her goes beyond anything that is evoked by the person's objective qualities or how much he or she satisfies our own personal values or goals (Singer, 2009). This means that there is something creative about love. It can't be determined in advance and it's not reducible to any pre-existing component parts. Nor does it necessarily fit with our prior projects. We might not know how important something is to our happiness until we meet someone who seems to embody it. As a result love is highly unpredictable:

> Purposive attitudes are safe, secure, like money in the bank; the loving attitude is speculative and always dangerous. Love is not practical, and sometimes borders on madness. No wonder then, that the fear of love is one of the great facts of human nature. In all men and women there lurks an atavistic dread of insolvency whenever we generate more emotion than something has the right to demand of us.
> (Singer, 2009: 14–5)

This notion of wastefulness is also something that George Bataille points to in his compelling and controversial book *Eroticism* (Bataille, 2006). For Bataille the exuberant extravagant nature of (full, unrestrained) sexuality brings about the ultimate destruction of order and boundaries. Interestingly, given the subject under discussion in this chapter, Bataille argues that work is completely impossible in these circumstances because work always involves some kind of rational calculation of what is efficient and productive. In other words, the amount of effort that is invested in labour is to some extent in proportion to what is produced at the end. Even in the most enlightened therapy there is likely to be some implicit aim that therapeutic work is directed towards and a certain investment of effort to achieve this but in Bataille's thinking, eroticism is the enemy of this. Eroticism is the expression of a blind force of nature that cannot be entirely contained within boundaries and cannot be explained through reason. Disorderliness (for example, the dishevelled, half-clothed person) is part of eroticism and sexual activity seems to involve the expenditure of a lot of energy for reasons that defy explanations based on rationality (Bataille, 2006). As result, work and eroticism are antithetical to one another. Therapy as a professional enterprise simply cannot happen if eroticism enters the picture (Denman, 2004).

It is further arguable that eroticism within therapy not only threatens the boundaries which define therapy as a professional enterprise, but also those which in some way define the very person of therapist and client. As Binswanger describes, it is necessary for each party in a relationship to acknowledge the independent existence of the other in order to avoid love becoming domination (Frie, 1997). If the client loses a sense of their own individuality, such as their own values, fears, strengths, preferences, then the relationship has arguably become a dangerous and potentially abusive one. According to Bataille, any genuine eroticism is destructive of the individual self. Immersion in sexual activity involves us forgetting what might, from another perspective, be termed our self-construct. It means losing ourselves in an impersonal force of nature. In more theoretic terms, eroticism is destructive of the individual personality: 'In fact the individual splits up and his unity is shattered from the first instant of the sexual crisis' (Bataille, 2006: 105).

If both client and therapist lose their sense of individuality in this way, as they well might in the intense relationship that may unfold, how can therapy happen? Therapy is arguably predicated to some degree on some boundaries which maintain client's and therapist's sense of their own discreet lives and worlds. This notion of the destruction of the individual also raises the further issue of what we mean by abuse. It could be argued that abuse is something that is damaging to the client, but this sounds similar to what Bataille says, that eroticism is destructive of the individual personality. But if this is abuse, so is existential therapy! Existential therapy involves a challenge to a client's sedimented self-constructs with the hope that he or she is then able to live in way which more accurately reflects existence as he or she experiences it (Spinelli, 2007). At the same time existential therapy implicitly recognises that too violent an attack on a person's self-concept is going to be antithetical to this enterprise. To some degree, we need some sedimentation in our view of ourselves (Spinelli, 2007). A certain caution is necessary and sexual relationships in therapy arguably mark a failure to honour this.

Conclusion

From a Binswangerian perspective, connectedness and love, rather than being a threat to the client's development, form a part of the most enriching and dynamic therapeutic encounters. Romance, sexual attraction and sexual relationships are on a continuum with this. How far are we able to allow for this in therapy if we are concerned to protect the client from being dominated by a more powerful therapist? Whilst a cold and detached therapist can be seen to dehumanise the therapeutic relationship, an interfering and overbearing therapist can wreak considerable damage. Existential therapy is about human existence and a therapist who has a highly technical objective approach to therapy, perhaps conveying the sense that sexuality is inappropriate in the therapy room, could be seen to be disregarding this and harming the client. The ideal relationship from a Binswangerian perspective is one in which there is mutual warmth or love, but the unequal knowledge and differing roles of therapist and client are likely to make this difficult. The relationship can without due care slip into one in which the therapist dominates the client and the risk of this is very high if the relationship develops into a more intense and complex intimate connection.

The question of sexual attraction also calls into question how much uncertainty we consider tolerable or desirable within existential psychotherapy. If we are to call ourselves professionals, we need to comply with ethical codes, with their clear prohibitions on sexual activity within therapy. Work, rationality and eroticism do not sit well together. Some degree of objectivity and distance seems to be required to be able to help a client to live in a way which feels more satisfactory to him or her and sexual relationships with clients are likely to make this difficult. On the other hand, uncertainty is one of the pillars of existential thinking (Spinelli, 2007). If we believe that uncertainty is unavoidable, we need to find a way of working with sexuality within therapy that honours this.

References

Bataille, G (2006) *Eroticism* (M Dalwood, Trans). London: Marion Boyars Publishers.

Baur, S (1997) *The Intimate Hour: Love and sex in psychotherapy*. New York: Houghton Mifflin.

Binswanger, L (1964) *Grunformen und Erkenntnis Menschlichen Daseins* [Basic Forms and Knowledge of Human Dasein]. Munich: Reinhardt.

Brabant, E, Falzeder, E & Giampieri-Deutsch, P (Eds) (1993) *The Correspondence of Sigmund Freud and Sandor: Vol 1* (T Hoffer, Trans). Cambridge, MA and London: Belknap Press of Harvard University Press.

British Association for Counselling and Psychotherapy (2010) *The Ethical Framework for Good Practice in Counselling and Psychotherapy.* Retrieved 29 November 2012 from http://www.bacp.co.uk/admin/structure/files/pdf/9479_ethical%20framework%20word%20feb2010%20%28revised%29.pdf

British Psychological Society (2009) *Code of Ethics and Conduct.* Retrieved 29 November 2012 from http://www.bps.org.uk/sites/default/files/documents/code_of_ethics_and_conduct.pdf

Cooper, M (2003) *Existential Therapies.* London: Sage Publications.

Council for Healthcare Regulatory Excellence (2008) *Clear Sexual Boundaries between Healthcare Professionals and Patients.* Retrieved 29 November 2012 from http://www.professionalstandards.org.uk/docs/psa-library/responsibilities-of-healthcare-professionals---clear-sexual-boundaries.pdf?sfvrsn=0

Denman, C (2004) *Sexuality: A biopsychosocial approach.* Basingstoke and New York: Palgrave MacMillan.

Frie, R (1997) *Subjectivity and Intersubjectivity in Modern Philosophy and Psychoanalysis.* Lanham, MD: Rowman and Littlefield Publishers.

Gabriel, L (2005) *Speaking the Unspeakable: The ethics of dual relationships in counselling and psychotherapy.* Hove: Routledge.

Heidegger, M (1996) *Being and Time* (J Stambaugh, Trans). Albany, NY: State University of New York Press.

Heidegger, M (2001) *Zollikon Seminars: Protocols–conversations–letters* (F Mayr & R Askay, Trans). Evanston, IL: Northwestern University Press.

Heywood, C (1999) *When Boundaries Betray Us.* Cleveland, OH: The Pilgrim Press.

Jehu, D (1994) *Patients as Victims: Sexual abuse in psychotherapy and counselling.* Chichester: John Wiley & Son.

Newman, M (2010) Stark facts exposed about anti-regulation therapist and readers comments. *The Times Higher Education.* Retrieved 8 April 2013 from http://jobs.timeshighereducation.co.uk/story.asp?storycode=410179

Norcross, J & Lambert, M (2011) Evidence-based therapy relationships. In J Norcross (Ed) *Psychotherapy Relationships That Work: Evidence-based responsiveness* (pp. 3–24). New York and Oxford: Oxford University Press.

Pope, K (1988) How clients are harmed by sexual contact with mental health professionals: The syndrome and its relevance. *Journal of Counselling and Development, 67*(4), 222–6.

Pope, K & Vasquez, M (2011) *Ethics in Psychotherapy and Counselling: A practical guide.* Hoboken, NJ: John Wiley & Son.

Russell, J (1993) *Out of Bounds: Sexual exploitation in counselling and therapy.* London: Sage Publications.

Rutter, P (1990) *Sex in the Forbidden Zone.* London: Unwin Hyman.

Sartre, J-P (1998) *Being and Nothingness* (H Barnes, Trans). London: Routledge.

Singer, I (2009) *The Nature of Love: 1: Plato to Luther.* Cambridge, MA and London: The MIT Press.

Spinelli, E (1994) *Demystifying Therapy.* London: Constable. (Republished 2006, PCCS Books)

Spinelli, E (2007) *Practicing Existential Psychotherapy: The relational world.* London: Sage Publications.

Thorne, BJ (1987) Beyond the core conditions. In W Dryden (Ed) *Key Cases in Psychotherapy* (pp. 48–77). London: Croom Helm.

UK Council for Psychotherapy (2009) *Ethical Principles and Code of Professional Conduct.* Retrieved 29 November 2012 from http://www.psychotherapy.org.uk/index.php?id=45

Van Deurzen, E (2010) *Everyday Mysteries: Existential dimensions of psychotherapy.* Hove: Routledge.

Yalom, I (1980) *Existential Psychotherapy.* New York: Basic Books.

12

Individual Therapy and Foucault's Dark Shimmer of Sex

– Dr Paul Smith-Pickard –

For some obvious, and not so obvious, reasons, sex and psychotherapy may be seen as an uncomfortable pairing. Nevertheless it is still tempting to see the paradox of the therapeutic encounter as that of a loving encounter albeit one without sex. An encounter where therapist and client are unconsummated lovers bound to each other by the desire to make a difference to each other.

With this in mind the chapter explores the ways in which existential sexuality, as described in my earlier chapter, is articulated and focuses on the world of lovers and how lovers relate in order to rethink the nature of relating in individual therapy. The metaphor of lovers in this paradox is provocative but also a potent one as it is a metaphor that has the potential and sometimes the possibility of becoming an actuality. Of course there is no suggestion here that sex or sexual activity could ever be part of a therapeutic encounter. However existential sexuality will inevitably be present in the consulting room linking the client and the therapist together, body to body, regardless of gender, age, or class.

The ever-present phenomenon of existential sexuality is a cornerstone of interaction between people and as a fundamental aspect of primary relatedness it cannot be considered as an optional extra that one can choose to include or exclude from therapy. Taking this position (that of existential sexuality always being present), I would suggest there are two basic options available to us with regard to therapeutic practice. We either find ways to usefully and ethically engage with this primary relatedness or attempt to deny its presence. In denying it we can either ignore it completely or attempt to de-eroticise it by reframing it in terms such as erotic transference.

If we are to find ways of working with existential sexuality it will require us to take a closer examination of the issues involved. These include the recognition of ways in which the 'other' provides us with existential validation, an experiential awareness rather than cognitive understanding of embodiment, exploring the unclear relationship between sex and sexuality, and observing how the structures and dynamics of existential sexuality are articulated. This may not provide us with any definitive answers but will hopefully illuminate the questions we need to address. Of course, in facing this challenge we cannot assume that we all have the same goals in therapy or that we all work in the same way. In order to place the content of this chapter in a context I feel it would be helpful to be transparent about some of the goals in my own practice.

I see you

I regard myself as an existential psychotherapist and would describe my way of working as dialogic and relationally interactive. My goal is to create a climate of encounter where clients feel that they are seen and have a voice. Where they are able to both meet and hear themselves, hopefully in new and unexpected ways. What they do with that experience is largely up to them as it is ultimately their choice and responsibility whilst my responsibility is to support and challenge them in that process. If I can facilitate a process where a client comes face to face with him- or herself in hitherto unknown ways and meet him- or herself afresh, thereby breaking the familiarity and assumptions within their lives to become informed authors of their lives, I feel I am doing my job. In other words I become a complementary 'other' in a client's existential search for the possibilities of selfhood.

Our lives are full of complementary relationships and as RD Laing once said, in order to be a lover there has to be a beloved, otherwise we are only a would-be lover. It is through other people that we know who we are, and it is also through us that they too find a sense of identity; 'One recognises oneself' says Laing, 'in that old smile of recognition from that old friend' (Laing, 1990: 87).

I was interested to find that in the Zulu language there is a traditional greeting *Sawubona* which means literally 'I see you' to which the response *Ngikhona* means 'I am here'. In other words, by recognising me, you bring me into existence. The Zulu culture also has a saying; 'A person is a person because of other people', and that can be seen in two ways. The first is the relational context we find ourselves in, where we are always contextually placed in a shared world where we are acting upon others and them upon us. The second concerns the ways in which we both existentially validate another and elicit validation for our selves through acknowledging the other person and being acknowledged by the other person in return.

In the therapeutic encounter client and therapist become the necessary other for each other in creating an identity that complements and distinguishes their respective roles in the encounter. They have the potential to bring each other into existence in the therapy and it is how that potential is realised that creates genuine engagement or not. It also leaves us with some interesting questions and dilemmas.

For example, how does a therapist tell a client 'I see you' and what allows us to hear the 'I am here' of a client, and does the inevitable presence of sexuality in the room turn us all into would-be lovers in a quest for mutual existential validation?

Embodied inter-experience

Despite having been marginally involved in the world of academia, I have always seen myself primarily as a practitioner and am more inclined to operate from the perspective of what Bourdieu (2000) describes as the world in which I live rather the world in which I think. Which is to say that any theoretical constructions that I may place on therapy are hugely mediated by the experience of working with clients. Far from being a Cartesian division of mind and body, Bourdieu's two worlds point to the fact that there is a world of ideas that is extracted as a second order language from the world of living our everyday lives and which mediates our immediate experience of living and changes our perspectives and expectations. Both worlds live in relation to each other and support as well as subvert each other in the creation of meaning. There are some similarities perhaps to a formal written language and the spontaneity of speech. Sometimes I am given an opportunity, such as writing this chapter, to put some framework of ideas together that reflects the philosophical basis for what takes place in individual therapy. In doing so a dialogue is created between what I think and what I live, and hopefully something new emerges. It is a form of phenomenological enquiry as it gives me an opportunity to step back, reflect, and playfully disrupt common-sense assumptions. A process of reflection that is in line with Merleau-Ponty's phenomenological method that 'slackens the intentional threads which attach us to the world and thus brings them to our notice; it alone is consciousness of the world because it reveals that world as strange and paradoxical' (Merleau-Ponty, 1945/1996: xiii).

Because these reflections and theoretical constructions appear on the page as language they can only be abstractions from an experience where speech forms but one aspect of the encounter. Not everything that takes place in therapy can be verbally articulated. Much, if not most, of what takes place in that therapeutic space belongs to a dimension of human existence that is a pre-linguistic experience that according to Frie, 'cannot be adequately represented in, or expressed through language [where] the nonverbal affective dimension specifically resists being drawn into discourse' (Frie, 2003: 148).

I have called this level of engagement that functions without words, embodied inter-experience (Smith-Pickard, 2009: 75–6). This phrase is a description of human interaction that focuses on the embodied consciousness of mutual reciprocal experiences. That is experiences that are shared and 'known' by the body. The therapeutic encounter is saturated through and through with embodied inter-experience and this silent narrative is the primary way in which I see sexuality articulated. In order to work with this dimension we need an adequate sense and awareness of our own embodiment in order to develop a whole-body perceptual awareness in line with Merleau-Ponty's 'magical relation' with things, '… this pact between them and me according to which I lend them my body in order that they inscribe upon it and give me their resemblance' (Merleau-Ponty, 1997: 146).

Daniel Stern also describes inter-experience and uses the language of neuroscience to do so:

> Our nervous systems are constructed to be captured by the nervous systems of others, so that we can experience others as if from within their skin, as well as from within our own. A sort of direct feeling route into the other person is potentially open and we resonate with and participate in their experiences, and they in ours.
>
> (Stern, 2004: 76)

Clearly there is more going on in the therapeutic encounter than a talking cure and a large part of my own therapeutic presence with a client is intentionally designed to bring about bodily awareness and a level of self-consciousness in both my client and myself. I do this in the awareness that we are linked through existential sexuality and that my bodily awareness is part of the deployment of existential sexuality in the room. However before we explore what this means let me first of all turn to the ambiguity of the body and what it means to 'feel' embodied.

Embodiment and ambiguity

The dual aspect of having a body and being a body brings us into the relational space of other people's lives where we are exposed to the gaze of others in this closely woven texture of existence we call the world. However having and being a body does not necessarily mean that we have a strong sense of embodiment. When I was first introduced to the concept of embodiment I approached it as an abstract idea. My body was a thing that I possessed and used when I wanted to but never really thought about it all that much. It carried me around and performed functions like walking and carrying and lifting and had limitations. In other words my body was an organic object for me, albeit a unique and personal one. But this object was also an unknown universe. I covered it with clothing and forgot about it.

I knew that I found it impossible to remain still when I listened to certain types of music and that my body had an involuntary desire to dance. I had also experienced levels of excitement and nervousness when I was visited by sexual attraction and desire towards another. How could I not realise that the site of these feelings and emotions was deep within my body? Perhaps it was because I felt that these experiences belonged to my innermost self and that although they had a reference to others they still felt intensely private and there was always a risk of exposure and judgement. It was here that I found a clue to the experience of embodiment in the form of shame and desire. Not the experience of shame or desire but an understanding of what the experiences of shame and desire felt like, not as ideas but as bodily felt senses.

Shame and desire

Shame and desire both bring about an incarnation of consciousness with strong physical affects. They reveal themselves in our bodies. To feel shame is to feel exposed, inadequate and insufficient as a person. It is the self, judging the self to be fundamentally flawed, defective, unworthy and existentially discounted. We experience it as an implosion of intense feeling where we disappear inside ourselves, destroying the interpersonal bridge between other people and ourselves. It is the affect of inferiority says Kaufman, 'a wound made from the inside, dividing us both from ourselves and others' (Kaufman, 1996: 17). However, the self judging the self is only a part of the story because this judging is done in the full, if only tacit, awareness of the existence of the other. This awareness, that another can perceive us, this self-consciousness, is the constant horizon of our existence.

> To have a body is to be looked at (it is not only that), it is to be visible. To be sure if a woman of good faith who closes her coat (or the contrary), were questioned, she would not know what she has just done. She would not know it in the language of conventional thought, but she would know it as one knows the repressed, that is, not as figure on a ground but as ground.
>
> (Merleau-Ponty, 1997: 189–90)

So what Merleau-Ponty is saying here is that our self-consciousness of ourselves is always mediated by the presence of the other and therefore subjectivity is always intersubjectivity and that intersubjectivity is the ground of our being. When he uses the phrase 'the language of conventional thought', it is his way of indicating an accompanying pre-linguistic non-verbal experience that I would call the 'narrative of embodied inter-experience'. The 'ground' he mentions is the constant presence of existential sexuality where the other has the potential to see me and to be seen by me. Both shame and desire rise up from this ground.

Desire is also experienced as a bodily disturbance where what we desire is not simply another's body but a body alive with consciousness that can desire us back in turn. The self-consciousness of desire also helps us to recognise the ambiguous dimensions of the body that we simultaneously experience as being both a subject and an object. Unlike shame, desire projects us out into the world towards another person and the self-consciousness of their body. We attempt to capture their consciousness as a bodily awareness through a form of enchantment. This desire for the other's attention, the other's reciprocal desire for us, has an erotic dimension that is potentially sexual when the possibility of sex emerges as figure from the ground of existential sexuality.

So does what happens here have any relation to what takes place in therapy and does it perhaps provide some explanation as to why many therapists are cautious about allowing erotic elements into the consulting room?

Clearly embodiment is more than recognising that one has a body. It is our way of existing with others and goes beyond the confines of our skin. It is both how we project ourselves out into the world to be shared by the world, and how we allow the world to encroach and impact upon us. It is not a choice to be in relation with the world we find ourselves in. There is no separation of mind and body, or body and world. They are part of the same system of mutual reciprocity. I am in the world and the world is in me so that we experience our bodies ambiguously as both substance and idea; it is our way of existing in a world of other bodies. It is experienced as both actuality and as possibility in a dynamic ebb and flow of mutual connection with the world. It is both the site of my experience and a field of infinite possibilities.

The dark shimmer of sex

Much of my writing in the past has avoided writing about sex for two main reasons; one was in order to focus on aspects of sexuality that are not genitally oriented, and second because I find it difficult to imagine how sex could ever be a legitimate aspect of psychotherapy. In avoiding the issue of sex I have perpetuated the artificial splitting of sex from sexuality in my attempt to prevent the two terms being conflated into the same meaning. They are not the same but they belong to each other as they both refer to sexual aspects of our existence.

Both Sartre and Foucault ask whether sexuality is supported and anchored by sex or if sex is simply a complex idea formed within sexuality. For them sex is simply an aspect of sexuality and Foucault sees sex as an initiatory experience on the journey towards oneself, 'It is through sex – in fact, an imaginary point determined by the deployment of sexuality that each individual has to pass in order to have access to his own intelligibility, to the whole of his body, to his identity' (Foucault, 1976/1990: 155).

According to Foucault in the cultural deployment of sexuality, sex functions as a unique signifier that evades the relations of power within sexuality and turns them upside down. This has been done by inquiring into sexual behaviour and the normalisation of sex thereby reducing power in relation to sex to law and taboo. This stance towards sex is one that we have become accustomed to in our profession where it is enshrined in various codes of ethics. In other words sex has either been separated out from sexuality or conflated with it and we have focused on sex to such an extent that Foucault suggests it has become more important than our souls. 'Sex', he says prophetically, 'is worth dying for' (Foucault, 1976/1990: 156).

In Foucault's account of the history of sexuality the desire for sex becomes one of the essential elements in the deployment of sexuality. But is it a desire to face and meet oneself through the other and have access to our own intelligibility through that reciprocal encounter?

> It is this desirability that makes us think we are affirming the rights of our sex against all power, when in fact we are fastened to the deployment of sexuality that has lifted up from deep within us a sort of mirage in which we think we see ourselves reflected – the dark shimmer of sex.
> (Foucault, 1976/1990: 157)

This mirage has some similarities to therapy in that they both require the presence of the other, another unique existent, in the journey towards our own intelligibility and we might ask how much of the therapeutic encounter is 'fastened to the deployment of sexuality' (Foucault, 1976/1990: 157) and from the perspective of existential sexuality is it more accurate to say therapy is rooted in the deployment of sexuality? Can we talk about the dark shimmer of therapy alongside the dark shimmer of sex and can we learn something that will provide new perspectives on how we might practise psychotherapy by exploring the world of lovers?

The world of lovers

When we turn to existential narratives describing sex and sexuality there is a lack of clarity in the ontic or ontological status of sexuality and it is difficult to escape from normative images of heterosexuality. This is clearly evidenced in the work of Sartre, Merleau-Ponty and de Beauvoir as well as later in the work of RD Laing. From where we stand today the perspective of sex and sexuality in the works of the post-war existentialists seems entrenched in heterosexist and phallocentric images of sexual behaviour that run alongside their ontological perspectives.

I have found it helpful to turn to more contemporary feminist writers such as Judith Butler, Iris Marion Young and more recently Adriana Cavarero to shine a light on the hegemony of normative heterosexuality and dominant male perspectives.

The same-sex feminist view of lovers as 'narratable selves' that we find in the work of Adriana Cavarero releases us momentarily from the power image of the phallus. In *Relating Narratives*, Cavarero (1977/2006) offers us the image of the 'narratable self', which offers a new perspective on existential sexuality and in her image of lovers she offers us a link between the narratable life story and the sexual.

Her work is indebted to, and pays homage to, the ideas of Hannah Arendt and the work of both writers is grounded in the existential fact that we are unique existents who live together and are exposed to each other through our bodily senses. Cavarero recognises that each of us has a sense of self that is founded in our unique history and life story. The significant contribution that she makes is to recognise that we are all narrate-able and that furthermore we are dependent on the other for the narration of many aspects of our own life story. This narrate-able self is one of fluid potential that grows out of our unique life stories. It is about 'who' we are as unique existents rather than 'what' we are in our social identity.

When we meet another person for the first time the only thing that we know about this stranger with any certainty is that they, like ourselves, have a unique life story that can be told. They, like us, are narrate-able and being narrate-able we both have a desire to hear our own story narrated by another as well as a desire to hear it from our own mouths.

Cavarero enables us to relocate sex within sexuality by examining the vulnerable naked space in which we might invite our lover to see 'who' rather than 'what' we are in an act of reciprocal storytelling and caresses where we both tell our life story and hear it told to us from our own mouths.

Within this mirage of sex the fragments of our unique life stories are told in a consummate reciprocity with our lover, as we attempt to reveal the intangible sense of 'who' we are in our unique existence. The stories lovers tell in this intimate and vulnerable space are not rehearsed information but the involuntary acts of memory. This reciprocal act of caresses and storytelling links us through our bodies, both sexually and in an embodied non-verbal narrative of existential sexuality, interwoven with a spoken narrative that emerges from the involuntary recall of the intangible 'who'. These are often stories told in free fall and a reverie where we meet and witness ourselves in a new light, and in the lover's acceptance of who we are in our bare humanity there is a tender redemption.

It is like a dance of possibilities where we become something or someone we never could have become by ourselves. Who we meet in this dance may not be who we thought we were or who we could be or even who we wanted to be.

Bearing in mind that a caress does not necessarily require physical touch we might be left with the question of how much of this intimate exchange of caresses and life story sounds similar to therapy?

Can psychotherapists be open to the possibility that sex, existential sexuality and the narrate-able self can give us clues as to how we can work with our clients in new ways or with a fresh awareness?

When someone tells us their life story does our listening simply solicit information or are we able to listen with a whole-body attention to 'who' they are both overtly and covertly inviting us to see? How much are we simply gatherers and processors of information from 'out there'? How much bare humanity is there? How much tender redemption?

So we must ask ourselves how can we listen to the intimate 'who' of a client's 'narrate-able self' and not cling for safety to the social signifiers telling us 'what' they are? Often the narrate-able self is hidden behind a well-rehearsed account of the past that presents us with a seemingly impenetrable shield of selected information. Narratives are often 'out there' beyond the confines of the room and the immediacy of interpersonal connection. It is like someone flying a kite and saying to me, 'look up there at my beautiful kite' when I want to reach out to the hand that holds the string. How then can we make meaningful connection?

One way in which we may be able to have some effect here is in the way we listen. Wilberg (1997) inverts the notion of speech preceding listening with the idea of 'maieutic listening' referring to the Socratic mode of inquiry. This style of listening aims to bring a person's latent ideas into clear consciousness. He proposes that what clients say to us is the result of the way we listened to them. Our listening gave birth to their speaking – listening was the midwife of speaking hence the Socratic title.

So how can we listen to the narrate-able self and how does it reveal itself to us? Can we induce it through some form of maieutic attention?

The lover's gaze

It is obviously far too simplistic to suggest that a life story is linguistic and sexuality is only embodied, or that we can even talk of such a separation.

What we have in the therapy room is an interwoven matrix of embodied possibilities, ambiguous stanzas of speech, contradictions and taboos.

I say ambiguous stanzas rather than speech or language because nobody actually talks in prose. Concrete language occurs as diverse spurts of speech resembling stanzas that carry several focuses of awareness where, as in poetry, there is meaning even in the spaces and the juxtaposition of diverse thoughts. It takes a particular style of listening to hear the matrix of meaning in the stanzas of concrete language because we are required to follow and hold several incomplete trains of thought simultaneously. It goes without saying that this style of listening is a valuable asset as a psychotherapist and is one that many of us have become very familiar with over the years. However a matrix of meaning is not the same as the intangible sense of self, hidden in a life story and in order to 'hear' this sense of self we need to learn to listen with our whole body and to offer our body into that space in a sort of embodied maieutic listening where we are able to sense the intangible 'who' and allow them to impress themselves upon us. I realise that for some of us it may not be possible or even acceptable to listen like a lover to the free fall of our client's life story in order see the person within the story. To listen like a lover is to hold our client in a lover's gaze.

This lover's gaze is not an objective view but one that seeks the immeasurable 'who', the uniqueness of the other person.

Reflections

With all that has gone before, it may seem as if I am inviting you to explore the controversial territory between taboo and professional conduct but that would be a misperception. I am not inviting you to challenge external authority and prohibitions; it is important to recognise that there are lines that cannot be crossed and to find an internal authority to be able to work ethically and respectfully. We need to develop an internal compass to guide us into knowing where we feel safe to go and what is just too dangerous. Part of my own internal compass for working in this relational free fall is that if I can't take it to supervision I am definitely outside the boundary of therapy.

Existential sexuality is a fluid dynamic tension of proximity and distance between therapist and client. It moves around, shifts, ebbs and flows, we embrace it and then we shut it out, we might want it but it might also frighten us, we gain contact and then we lose it, we welcome it and then reject it. It can sometimes feel as if we are wandering dangerously close to the edge between sex and existential sexuality, seduction and engagement, where we might want to hide behind the skirts of our professionalism for fear of what we might find at the edge. We may wish to deny the presence of existential sexuality altogether but it is, in Merleau-Ponty's words, 'always present like an atmosphere' that 'spreads forth like an odour or a sound' (Merleau-Ponty, 1945/1996: 168).

This is not about bringing the sexual into therapy but about realising that in the sexual world of lovers there are structural elements that can be usefully and purposefully mirrored in therapy. It is also about acknowledging the ever-present and unavoidable background of existential sexuality. We can't ignore it because it is always there and traversing this edge of sexual ambiguity in the consulting room we may become metaphorically naked and vulnerable like lovers and at this edge in the dark shimmer of therapy, however dangerous this mirage may seem, we might just find real therapeutic gold.

Traversing the edge we may also see ourselves reflected in the dark shimmer of sex and be surprised at who we meet there.

References

Bourdieu, P (2000) *Pascalian Meditations* (R Nice, Trans). Cambridge: Polity Press. (First published 1997)

Cavarero, A (2006) *Relating Narratives: Storytelling and selfhood* (P Kottman, Trans). Abingdon: Routledge. (First published 1997)

Foucault, M (1990) *The History of Sexuality: Vol.1: An introduction* (R Hurley, Trans). London: Penguin. (First published 1976)

Frie, R (2003) Language and subjectivity: From Binswanger through Lacan. In R Frie (Ed) *Understanding Experience: Psychotherapy and postmodernism* (pp. 137–60). London: Routledge.

Kaufman, G (1996) *The Psychology of Shame: Theory and treatment of shame-based syndromes*. New York: Springer Publishing.

Laing, RD (1990) *The Self and Others*. London: Penguin.

Merleau-Ponty, M (1996) *Phenomenology of Perception* (C Smith, Trans). London: Routledge & Kegan Paul. (First published 1945)

Merleau-Ponty, M (1997) *The Visible and the Invisible* (A Lingis, Trans). Evanston, IL: Northwestern University Press. (First published 1948)

Smith-Pickard, P (2009) Existential sexuality and the body in supervision. In E van Deurzen & S Young (Eds) *Existential Perspectives on Supervision* (pp. 68–78). Basingstoke: Palgrave.

Stern, DN (2004) *The Present Moment in Psychotherapy and Everyday Life*. New York: Norton.

Wilberg, P (1997) Heidegger and Hara: An introduction to maieutic listening. *Journal of the Society for Existential Analysis, 8*(1).

Part 7

Existential Contributions to Specific Modalities

13

Existential Group Therapy: Hell is other people?

– Christina Richards –

> Mick Jagger can't even make a successful solo album, and the Stones are the biggest rock group that ever was.
> (Don Henley)

Sexuality and gender are, usually, intersubjective in nature. Even those sexualities which would at first blush appear not to be so – such as asexuality and solo sex – and those genders which appear to be unconstructed – such as cisgender[1] – are nonetheless part of a social world in which sexuality and gender *of some sort* are expected and may therefore be regarded as intersubjective. The existential-phenomenological approach is therefore perhaps especially well-suited to address issues relating to these rich and complex facets of human nature; and within this approach the intersubjectivity of group psychotherapy would seem especially well-suited to the task.

But why *group* existential psychotherapy? After all individual psychotherapy too is intersubjective. The answer to this question lies in the numbers of interconnections and identities possible, as well as in the pull of the group itself towards some aim – what Spinelli (2007) calls the 'group-construct' and Foulkes (1964/1984) calls the 'matrix'. An example may help illustrate this. Some years ago I facilitated a group in which I asked trans women what they wished to change about their bodies. In this I was seeking a descriptive phenomenology after Spinelli (2007), rather than a didactic 'imparting information' or a 'corrective recapitulation of the primary family group', etc. after Yalom and Leszcz (2005) – see 'The

---

1. See Chapter 4 in Richards & Barker (2013) for the construction of this gender form.

task of the group' section below in the main text. One member said that *of course* she wished to change her genitals as they were such a great signifier of maleness; another suggested that genitals were unimportant – after all who sees them on a day-to-day basis? – it was naturally her face which she wished to change; yet another group member said that faces were rather variable, with male and female faces having a great deal of overlap, for her, facial hair was of the utmost importance to address. Each person looked at the next, both troubled by what they saw and also changed in the seeing – they saw each person there as both different and *at the same time* as the same as themselves. The healing of the group came about in the recognition of an individual interrelatedness in which a mirror was held up by each member to the other group members through their own self-revelation. Sedimented ideas were thus challenged by the group in a way which individual therapy would have struggled to manage; while members recognised that they were not alone in struggling with the very human notions of communicating their selves in a personally authentic manner. No explicit interpretation was needed, by me or by other group members.

Group psychotherapy can be especially useful therefore, in expanding the 'everybody knows' aspects of members' understandings, especially those which are seldom spoken about publicly (such as sexuality) where what 'everybody knows' is often flat-out wrong. People who generally gain information from mass media sources can be relieved to learn that they are not alone in struggling to adhere to those messages because very often they are designed to make the viewer feel inadequate (see Barker, 2011). One of the primary aims of group therapy in relation to sexuality is therefore breaking through the façade of presented bad faith 'normality' and creating sufficient trust for people to express their actual desires – a search for the authentic through phenomenology in other words.

But what is the existential-phenomenological practitioner who wishes to run a group actually to do? First, I'll endeavour to ground this chapter in a little of the pragmatics of the contemporary clinical approach within the NHS, returning to the 'how to' of actually running the group under 'Group administration' later on. I will explore what little existential-phenomenological literature there is on running groups, before turning to the issues of sexuality within existential-phenomenological groups.

The (multidisciplinary) existential-phenomenological approach

Unfortunately, there is a dearth of existential-phenomenological literature pertaining specifically to group psychotherapy, with what little there is generally integrating it in with other modalities such as cognitive techniques for breast cancer (Kissane et al, 1997; Kissane et al, 2003); psychoeducational techniques for people with a bipolar diagnosis (Goldner-Vukov, Moore & Cupina, 2007); or holistic group therapy (Ventegodt et al, 2004). There appears to be no literature pertaining specifically to existential group psychotherapy and sexuality.

More generally, Yalom and Leszcz's (2005) *The Theory and Practice of Group Psychotherapy* is an excellent place to start, but draws upon 'existential themes' rather than being explicitly existential. Similarly, Cohn suggests that Foulkes' critique of group psychoanalysis was 'essentially phenomenological informed' (Cohn, 1997: 55) bringing it only somewhat within the existential-phenomenological tradition. Indeed, Foulkes himself suggests that 'every good psychotherapist is, or should be, an existentialist in his actual contact with his patient' (Foulkes, 1964/1984: 145), but cautions against existentialists throwing the 'baby [of biological science] out with the bathwater' (Foulkes, 1964/1984: 145). This is true in much of modern practice where an amalgam of styles and methods will most likely be necessary – with 'pure' existential-phenomenological group therapy rarely funded.

This means that clinicians working within the United Kingdom's National Health Service (NHS) and other organisations (especially those within multidisciplinary teams which may include clinicians from other backgrounds, as is common in sex therapy) will need to ensure that their practice is phenomenological in its mode of enquiry, and philosophically informed in its mode of practice, without clinging too much to the anchor of historical celebrity which all too often renders existential practice moribund in the (post)modern world; and (if you'll excuse the extended metaphor) threatens to sink the ship of existential-phenomenological practice altogether amid the storms of contemporary literature and current commissioning shortages.

Therefore the recommendations for practice within this chapter are based upon what extant literature there is as well as upon my clinical experience working as a group psychologist within the NHS while practising alongside a consultant psychiatrist and on other occasions a consultant psychologist. If you have more time and patients with more money than NHS commissioning allows, then some adaptation may be undertaken, but it is important to be aware of the cautions throughout this chapter about the laxity that greater latitude can allow. Towards the end of the chapter I will present an outline of my preferred 'dynamic administration' (how many members, where to put the chairs, etc.), although again this is flexible as existential-phenomenological practice allows for a good degree of latitude where more psychodynamically orientated practices, for example, would not. As always though, there must be a reason for any interventions, and they must be in the patient's interest (over whatever timescale). The latitude afforded by the existential-phenomenological approach should never be taken for carte blanche, or as an excuse to do nothing.

The primary purpose of the existential-phenomenological approach to group therapy relating to sexuality is to allow patients to (verbally) investigate their sexual worlds with others. This is paradoxical and requires careful handling by the group facilitators. The paradox arises because the group can both allow and deny expression, usually according to whether or not an understanding has been reached among the group members that free expression is to be supported and encouraged. If facilitators do not handle the group well, members may endeavour to quash free expression as each member strives to cover their uncertainties about themselves by leaping upon anything not socially normative said by another in an 'I may be odd, but look at him – he's *really* weird' manner. This was why Foulkes suggested that the socialising benefit of groups is useful in treating '… perversions, e.g. homosexual [sic], fetishists, transvestites …' (Foulkes, 1964/1984: 282). Of course, Foulkes' was a moral stance inimical to existential (and most contemporary) thought. But what, to him, was a treatment modality that should be engaged with only cautiously – the push to be part of a group norm can be a strong one and may lead to a place of inauthenticity for group members. For this reason the group facilitators have to walk a fine line between addressing problematic group norms as they develop (everyone must be like the loudest or most popular members or do what the papers/movies say) while not quashing real understandings and emerging norms which are part of the work and may assist people (for example, a norm such as 'it's OK to be gay').

I–Thou relating

One of the key tensions of group psychotherapy then, is to allow the process of being in a group to change people, while at the same time 'allowing' individuality; indeed it is not uncommon for members to hold themselves as being 'outside' the group for some time, especially at first. In some cases this can have a protective benefit which should be addressed only slowly (provided the patient is engaging properly – coming on time, allowing others time to talk and talking themselves, etc). While Cohn (1997), Foulkes (1964/1984), Szasz (1974) and other existential thinkers and practitioners have posited a social component to much psychological distress, contemporary thought suggests that the particular reasons for a person's actions and identities are both individual *and* within a social context; in what we might imagine to be a feedback loop from biology to person to society and back again with no one thing being discrete (e.g. Clark, 1997; Richards 2010). Regarding sexuality (and other aspects of people's lives), this understanding allows for the recognition that social opprobrium doesn't necessarily equate with individual pathology (e.g. Flowers & Langdridge, 2007; Richards, 2011a) and that any extant psychopathology may be as a result of the stress of being a part of a group under social opprobrium (sometimes called 'minority stress' – Bouman et al, 2010). In these cases membership of a group can be a positive influence in which a patient's personal identity can be reinforced by the group if the group is positive towards it. Thus the person is an individual within a group, within several larger groups of friends, family, community, country, etc. Clinicians should avoid the temptation to consider the group to be overly important in the client's world. It is to be hoped that they have much else going on. If group members find themselves struggling to leave to a marked degree it is possible that an unhealthy degree of dependence has developed. After all, patients will need to live in the world as well as (and hopefully instead of) the therapy room.

This notion of 'being-an-individual-within-groups' follows the existential conceptualisations of Heidegger who suggests that we are thrown into the world with others and that 'being' (Dasein) is necessarily a being-with-others (Heidegger, 1962/2008), meaning that any 'self' is necessarily a relational self. This paradox of being an individual, but inextricably bound in the world with others, is a primary cause of the paradox regarding the nature of groups as normalising and *at the same time* able to alleviate individual problems with living, which may not apparently be social. For example, Buber (1958) suggests that one may I–It relate to an other, perceiving them as an object, or I–Thou relate, perceiving them as a person quite as 'personish' as oneself. As seen above, this recognition and acceptance of the other as a person may be achieved in a therapeutic group, in which a person's idiosyncrasies are allowed to come forth: one can see that others are in a similar boat to oneself, and that their differences are not so terrifying after all but are part of a human struggle to make meaning and engage with the process of living.

Additionally, this opening to another's humanness may also allow the development of what Cooper (2003) calls I–I rather than I–Me relating my oneself to oneself. Thus an individual relates to themselves as a person rather than an object as well as having the possibility of relating to another person in this manner. Consequently, Cohn's assertion that existential group therapy is to address 'disturbances in relatedness' (Cohn, 1997: 55) may be widened to include disturbances in relatedness to self as well as others. We may consider then, that Sartre's (1989/1944) statement: 'Hell is other people' doesn't contain enough explicit consideration of the relational nature of the self. It would, perhaps, be better to say: 'Hell is my relation to other people (and also to myself)'.

The task of the group

It is worth bearing in mind that while, in general, the group will sway individual group members (for good or for ill) it is possible for individual members to sway the group, especially if there are other dynamics pertaining to status, age, gender, etc., occurring. In some cases a minority of people in a group can influence individual decisions of the majority on a topic (e.g. Asch, 1951; Maass & Clark, 1988; Moscovici, Lage & Naffrenchoux, 1969). This means that it is particularly important to ensure that the group stays on task and is not co-opted by one group member. While some groups with limitless time may be able to follow each thread as it emerges, the reality of most time-limited practice is that there will be a task to be undertaken for which money has been paid (either by the patients themselves or through taxation or charitable donations). Clinicians should, of course, horizontalise as necessary and pay attention to the full range of the patient's experiences, perhaps drawing upon van Deurzen-Smith's (1997) four life-worlds of the personal, spiritual, social and physical. In work around sexuality the temptation can be to pay too much attention to one of these at the exclusion of the others. It is worth being mindful therefore that if one, the physical say, is taking up a great deal of time, other areas of Being may be being missed.

This horizontalisation does not, however, give complete latitude. The difficulty with many psychotherapeutic groups is that many patients' previous experience of groups is at social gatherings and that script may be carried over to the therapy room. Conversation may therefore meander in a light and untroubling way (after all one doesn't talk about sex with strangers) if the facilitator does not intervene. Similarly, the task of most therapy groups is not usually to simply 'be with' one another (an overused phrase in counselling and psychotherapy which hides a multitude of inadequacies). Instead, the tasks will often be made explicit through the referral process; perhaps the group is for erectile dysfunction, or rape survivors, for example. While simply being with others in a similar position can be important, as stated above, that is the role of a support (rather than psychotherapeutic) group. The task outlined by the referral is often diagnosis orientated and it can be a useful place for group members to start exploring the meaning of this, perhaps with the facilitator suggesting that it is acceptable to question a diagnosis, or at least to explore its meaning and pragmatic effect.

Within the explicit task of the referral, the group may have many other tasks also. The more phenomenological of these include descriptive investigation of a number of factors including: group members' interactions; material brought in from outside; dispositional tensions between group-construct and each group member's self-construct and other-construct (how people get along); challenges to the group-construct of each member's worldview; challenges to each member's worldview by the group-construct (Spinelli, 2007: 203).

Effectively Spinelli is calling for a phenomenological inquiry into both the material brought into the group (perhaps a diagnosis) and an inquiry into the group itself (the interrelational factors). In shorter time-limited groups the former may be most useful, and in longer groups the latter. Of course if the task of referral is a matter pertaining specifically to a relational aspect of sexuality (as most are), sufficient time will need to be available for the group to form adequate relational bonds to be subject to phenomenological investigation.

Yalom and Leszcz (2005: 2–3) also suggest that therapeutic groups are characterised by several overarching themes which they call *therapeutic factors*, namely:

- instillation of hope
- universality (the recognition of common factors)
- imparting information

- altruism
- the corrective recapitulation of the primary family group
- development of socialising techniques
- imitative behaviour
- interpersonal learning
- group cohesiveness
- catharsis
- existential factors (detailed below).

As always, caution is needed with the interpretation of these, as existential-phenomenological groups for sexuality often render a greater tension between individualism and the group. 'Corrective recapitulation of the primary family group', for example, may mean individuating from the group successfully (and peacefully), rather than becoming subsumed within it. But, in order to individuate, the member must first become a part – which may be difficult if people are not accepting of certain sexualities and practices.

Similarly, Cohn sets out Foulkes' tasks for groups as:

- socialisation
- mirroring (participants literally or verbally reflecting the utterances, behaviours, etc. of group members such that members can see themselves – at least somewhat)
- 'chain' phenomena in which group members all contribute freely to a theme
- theorising in which group members consider the causes of their condition
- support
- silences with many different meanings to be understood
- the 'condenser' phenomena in which deep material is suddenly discharged into the group
- resonance in which a group member responds to a phenomena at the level of development to which they have reached
- scapegoating in which the group's need to punish and a member's need to be punished is met (Cohn, 1997: 53–4).

To which we might add:

- deification in which the group members' wish for the facilitator to lead the group to its solution and become angry at their unwillingness to do so before finding their own way to the solution (see Richards, 2011b for more on the therapeutic alliance).

Foulkes' tasks are drawn from psychodynamic practice, but shorn of the 'expert' interpretation of meaning, they are still of much use to the existential-phenomenological practitioner. This is because instead of expert interpretation of silence for example, the group itself may construct meanings in an intersubjective manner, or the individual patient may be assisted to determine their own meaning. Work with sexuality can often drive facilitators to impose meaning, as professionals usually have strong beliefs of their own, whether professionally, socially or otherwise derived, and this should be avoided as it is inimical to phenomenological practice.

Similarly to Cohn above, Yalom and Leszcz (2005: 2–3) suggest existential themes that relate to the task of the group including:

- recognising that life is unfair
- that there is no escape from some pain and (all) death
- that one must still face life alone, even if close to other people
- living life honestly and not getting caught in trivialities
- taking responsibility – which should be recognisable as being based in the existential 'givens'.

We will return to these themes specifically in relation to sexuality below.

A last general point relating to the task of group therapy which may be of use is that relating to the 'Johari Window' of Luft and Ingham (1955):[2]

---

2. This is from their Johari Window model. The 1955 reference outside of Luft's 1969 book appears to be apocryphal, with the 'journal' widely quoted as the original reference being apparently unobtainable. I suspect it was a training aid with no actual academic reference. Consequently the Luft book reference is given.

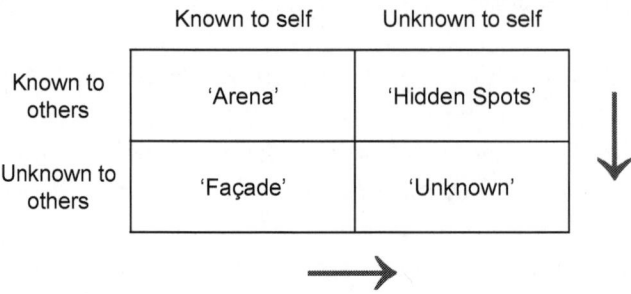

Figure 1. The Johari Window with arrows of therapeutic change

In this model, group members have an 'arena' of what is known to themselves and others, and give more information to the group through achieving a smaller 'façade' (that which is known to self and not known to others – the participant's particular wish for change). This may open up understanding in the individual of their 'hidden spots' which were not known to them but were known to others (the sedimentation and universalisation of their particular wish to change); and in turn this may reduce the patient's 'unknown' areas which were opaque to both themselves and others.

I find this model useful when considering sexuality. So often people have internal worlds in this area which are quite at odds with their external façade, as well as sedimented ideas about normality which preclude examination of desires and so lead to a (closely guarded) 'unknown' which may be blown open by the end of a relationship or an outing on a social networking website, for example. The managing of the therapeutic change though elucidation in a gentle and matter-of-fact manner can often be the primary business of group psychotherapy for sexuality – whether it is coming out for the first time, or coming to terms with a life-changing event.

Administration

Therapeutic change needs to be carried out within a well-managed and boundaried space, the facilitation of which is sometimes called dynamic administration or 'structural conditions' (Spinelli, 2007: 203). Within therapy for sexual matters these are particularly important because, if patients are to be forthcoming, they need to trust that confidentiality will be kept for example, and to have the limitations of this explained to them.

It can be useful to also explain to administrative staff the need for discretion so that there are no untoward conversations. It is also important to impress upon group members the need to keep confidentiality and not to discuss the group (either matters arising or its composition) with people outside of the group. Ideally this holds true even with other group members as useful material may not be brought to the session and cliques within the group can form.

My own practice, which I outline now, is time limited, publicly funded and deemed a specialist service in the British NHS. This, as much as the existential-phenomenological perspective, influences the work. Of necessity I tend to co-facilitate an 'open' group in which members can join once the group has started. Both the reason for referral to the group as well as the personality of the aspirant member need to be evaluated to ensure a good fit with the extant group. It would be inefficient to have a group with only two people in it if the others had left and it was a 'closed' group which could admit no new members. It does mean however, that each new member must be introduced into the group, and familiarised with the way the group does things. Group members are often quite accommodating, but it can be useful to allow some time for the new member to settle in, and to make specific reference in the preceding two sessions to the fact that a member will be leaving.

The group I co-facilitate consists of up to eight members, with never less than five. We use two facilitators because running a group with only one facilitator can be very tiring; and it is useful to have someone present who is not concerned with the immediate needs of the group and so is able to be more aware of the processes. Each member has twenty sessions and may miss two before being discharged. Each session is one and a half hours long and they are one month apart. We have found it useful to have more than an hour as otherwise not everyone may get a chance to speak. Monthly sessions are perhaps a little too far apart to effect ideal interpersonal relations between the group members, but they allow for people to travel from further afield, and also allow people to come who would otherwise not be able to attend due to time constraints. Of course, as stated above, this means that we are often working more with the material that is brought rather than with the relationships between the people who bring it. It is useful, however, for people to hear how others deal with similar situations without feeling directly defensive about their own issues.

I find it important to acknowledge my power as the facilitator – I have the key to the door and can cancel the group in extremis, for example. I will also occasionally leverage power if a group member is being scapegoated (see above) or, rarely, to mitigate against common social opprobrium of a transgressive, but not coercive sexuality (see below). Of course this does not follow the pure phenomenology of the group, but in time-limited therapy other ways of looking at issues must sometimes be brought in by the facilitator if things are to be considered in a timely manner. People may be unfamiliar with some sexual practices, for example, and so be propagating myths found in popular culture, which does not always discriminate between those identities and practices which are transgressive but not harmful – such as cross-dressing – and those which are necessarily coercive – such as rape (Denman, 2004). Investigation of members' attitudes towards these myths, followed by some cautious education, can be beneficial. Of course it is important to respect group members' views and to aim towards group members accepting responsibility for their parts of the group, and the freedom which is attendant to their group membership.

Regarding the other issues of group administration: I generally do not concern myself too much about the exact positioning of the chairs except to ensure that they are of the same type (for both facilitators and patients) and in a rough circle. The room should be uncluttered, well lit and ventilated, and easily accessible. We generally send out an invitation letter with the first appointment explaining about the group and how it works, and the referring clinician will also have explained the nature of the group and the work and something of the sexual matters which the patient is being referred for. It is important that all clinicians at this stage and beyond are familiar with sexual language and themes as patients will soon pick up if clinicians are uncomfortable and this may be very damaging if patients are in the process of an exploration of their emerging identity. Clinicians should engage in reflexive practice with a supervisor knowledgeable about sexuality and should educate themselves appropriately (see Richards & Barker, 2013).

Talking about sex and sexuality

If you have set everything up as well as possible, group members should hopefully come ready to talk. The type and amount of talk by each group member is one of the most difficult aspects of group psychotherapy for sexuality because people deal with breaking the social taboo about talking about sex differently: some prefer to monopolise whereas some prefer to be silent and listen. Similarly to stopping scapegoating, it is important for facilitators to ensure that everyone has a chance to speak and that no one situates themselves as 'above' the others or speaks too much. This can be done through facilitating I–Thou relating between the group members and modelling it as a facilitator as far as is possible. For this reason both Spinelli (2007) and Cohn (1997) suggest that the facilitator should be on a level with the group members – not 'outside' and 'above' (Cohn, 1997: 55). This also allows a hermeneutic of description (this is a description of the interaction which does not concern itself with 'why' but only 'what', see Langdridge, 2007) of the various interrelations between facilitator and others, and facilitator and group and also gives the group members the opportunity to try out new ways of relating which may be unfamiliar to them. However, it perhaps doesn't allow for a hermeneutic of suspicion (a critical investigation) of some aspects of the group not directly related to the facilitator (Langdridge, 2007; Ricoeur, 1970), when the facilitator is situated solely within the group. The hermeneutic of suspicion is a second pass of the material presented which is a critical investigation grounded only in the material, but made with reference to additional knowledge sources such as the academic, mainstream and community literatures (Langdridge, 2007; Ricoeur, 1970). One might suggest that it allows for phenomenology, but not existential practice, at least until group members are familiar with this double hermeneutic and so are able to perform it themselves. The facilitator as group member model doesn't, of course, recognise the power relations (or their use) detailed above.

One common issue of facilitator power relations is that of the group wishing the facilitator to provide answers, to punish, and/or to legitimise, as we saw regarding Foulkes' group tasks above. As stated above, judicious *factual* education about sexual matters can sometimes be useful, as can some basic aspects of psychoeducation. However, facilitators will need to actively resist the wish of the group for them to give answers to more emotive issues. There is a difference between the statements; 'condoms reduce the risk of transmission of STIs' (factual) and; 'you should use a condom as it reduces the risk of STIs' (value). The former might be useful in a shorter term group if a long discussion has taken place over whether condoms work at all, such that values and feelings have the space to be discussed, whereas the latter is never useful as self-direction is a basic tenet of existential-phenomenological practice. Similar to the wish to be provided with answers, some group members may wish for the facilitator to punish them for what they perceive as an aberrant sexual practice or to legitimise such a practice. Facilitators should resist both and only undertake the latter after much thought and if it is in the patient's best interest.

One of the main benefits of the phenomenological approach is that it allows a rather freer exploration of the matter in hand than some other more theory-driven modalities. As this approach does not take heteronormativity as an a priori basis it is therefore a useful mode of enquiry for more marginalised sexual practices and identities (see British Psychological Society, 2012; Richards & Barker, 2013). Facilitators in existential-phenomenological groups may have to strive to keep the phenomenological mode of enquiry, however, as most patients work from an implicitly logical-positivist stance, while at the same time holding sedimented beliefs about 'proper' behaviour (whether proper for heteronormativity or for another community norm, see Plummer, 1995; Schrock & Reid, 2006). Horizontalisation of enquiry as part of phenomenology can be especially useful as aspects of practice and identity may have been closed off in a bid for normativity. Facilitators may need to consider utterances carefully for meaning, and encourage group members to act similarly, such that not only the surface, or most 'obvious' meanings are attended to. Descriptive analysis following Spinelli (2007) can be useful as through describing phenomena in detail a nomatic understanding of experience can be gained (the 'what'), which further expands understating of the noetic experience (the 'how').

One methodology of particular use in the phenomenological exploration of sexualities is that of 'visual' methods. This involves the group members making a model of their sexuality or relationship (or some aspect of it) out of Plasticine, Lego or through collage, etc. The group participant then explains their model to the group who ask them about it and their explanation. It differs from historical projective techniques in that, crucially, there is no interpretation of the model by anyone other than the modeller. This method is of particular use in sexualities as it steps around common tropes from written and spoken language which can conceal, rather than illuminate, the phenomenology of a person's experience (see Barker, Richards & Bowes-Catton, 2012; Gauntlett, 2007).

Descriptive exploration, with or without the utilisation of visual methodologies, can assist people to break beyond the bounds of an assumed identity and to assume an identity which is personally authentic, or at least to select which extant rules fit best for them. For example, Foucault (1976/1998) shows how sexuality as an identity, rather than a practice, has been constructed historically; and Butler (1999) does similarly with gender through decoupling meaning from flesh (e.g. considering if long hair must always be feminine, or the meaning of transplanted organs).

These troublings of fixed identities as boxes into which people have to fit are an exact match with the existential notions of freedom, particularly freedom to choose, which suggests that unthinking adherence to a norm, because it is a norm, is in bad faith (and that people must face the uncertainty provided by establishing their own identity(s). Thus the phenomenological method leads us to a point of uncertainty from which existential notions spring. The critical role of the facilitator of a group considering sexuality is therefore to keep options open and to be wary of received understandings being uncritically accepted. Similarly, the existential notions of the *Übermensch* – overcoming the herd (Nietzsche, 1895/1968) – may be useful for more marginalised groups, as well as the notion of the leap to faith (Kierkegaard, 1844/1981) for those people seeking to come out about their gender or sexuality, but who feel stymied by the lack of assurity that they will be safe if they do so.

The group setting is the ideal forum to try out these new ways of being and relating in a comparatively safe environment (or at least an environment where people will be called upon to explain their criticisms in turn). Similarly to being thrown into the world with others (Heidegger, 1962/2008) the patient will have been thrown into the group and so the group can act as a microcosm of the wider world. In this microcosm the group can act as an external 'Panopticon', a term used by Foucault (1977/1991) which refers to a type of circular prison in which the inmates are constantly watched for aberrant behaviour. The idea is that the watching becomes internalised such that the prisoners take on the watcher's values. Foucault's idea was that society can act as a sort of Panopticon. The group acts to interrogate each member's actions and offer support as necessary – and so replace each patient's internalised Panopticon until such time as a new self-model can be established. It is here too that the group acts in a different manner from the individual therapist, as while the individual therapist may claim, or be given, 'expert' status and may so represent society, they cannot, on their own, form a society – whereas a group can act as a small society in its own right.

One aspect of this trying out and establishing of a new 'self' within a small society may be that of sexual relating. Of course this is similar to that found within individual therapy, but with the added complexity of a variety of different people being present and the possibility of sexual attraction moving between them. Group members who do establish sexual and/or romantic relationships may need to be asked to leave the group (see Yalom, 1991), unless there is a great deal of time available for the discussion of the matter, and they are willing to undertake this. This is due to the fact that their emotional involvement (or defences against the social opprobrium often made against having no emotional involvement, while still being physically sexual) may stymie the flow of the group to a very marked extent as they eschew their freedom for the safety of love or sex. Yalom (1991) argues that this is inimical to therapy – I take the softer view that, if between patients, it makes therapy especially difficult. Of course sexual relationships between facilitators and patients are grossly inappropriate. Dealing with patients becoming attracted to facilitators is beyond the scope of this article, but should, briefly, not be reciprocated and should be dealt with in supervision and in line with the governing bodies' recommendations. A Binswangerian unpacking of this complex issue can be seen in Gamsu (this volume). Here again, the depth of feeling about sex and relationships, both between group members and pertaining to wider social discourses, makes good group management for sexual matters particularly vital.

Some group members may endeavour to use the group (as with any therapy) as a substitute for life itself. It can be useful to consider the ending of the group for members as a small death and what meaning that may have, both individually and together. Themes of death and meaning come up quite regularly as many people join groups because they are 'stuck' in some way, often as a means of avoiding loss. It is important for this to be recognised and, crucially, for learning acquired in the group to be tested in the world outside of it. Otherwise group members may find themselves only talking about their desires, or exhibiting their identities, within the safety of the group. The safe experimental space becomes a container, a cage even, in which the identity or behaviour can be 'safely' contained. If this is the case the facilitator and group members may need to make this apparent, as lives should not be lived in, and for, therapeutic groups. One extreme example of this is sexualised behaviour within the group – either through clothing or behaviour. Again, while it runs counter to pure existential-phenomenological practice in which patients would take full responsibility for their actions, the facilitator may need to step in to stop the behaviour before it can be explored within the group if it would be damaging to the patient, other patients or the group itself. This might include overtly sexualised behaviour such as stripping to nakedness or near nakedness for example. Drives and emotions can run high in groups relating to sexuality and so, as with groups of people with some forms of acquired brain injury, psychosis, etc., more egalitarian power relations may have to be sacrificed to more effective group administration in extreme cases.

Conclusion

Sexuality is a particularly emotive topic which both individuals and social systems often have strict views upon. Group psychotherapy is a useful place to challenge and perhaps loosen those views simply through having differing viewpoints available for discussion. It can similarly be a useful place to try out new identities and discuss practices and desires away from the opprobrium such talk would usually invite, but also (somewhat) away from expert discourses which can constrain individual exploration. Facilitators should be mindful that good group administration will need to be maintained if the heart of the matter is to be attended to, rather than accepted social platitudes being perpetuated or patients becoming unable to talk due to the Hell of others seeing them as they are, or might be. However, facilitators should also be mindful that space will be needed for useful, supportive conversation to grow. Good existential-phenomenological group facilitation involves managing the tension between the freedom needed for phenomenological enquiry on the one hand; and the need for safety, and the facticity of the group on the other. In this way it is very similar to managing our own Being-in-the-world-with-others and is similarly simple ...

Further reading

As readers may be aware, there is a dearth of literature pertaining to existential group work and also pertaining to both common and less common forms of sexuality. The two following volumes should succinctly cover many clinical eventualities and also contain signposts to further sources of information.

Richards, C & Barker, M (2013) *Sexuality and Gender for Counsellors, Psychologists and Health Professionals: A practical guide*. London: Sage Publications.

Yalom, ID & Leszcz, M (2005) *The Theory and Practice of Group Psychotherapy* (5th ed). New York: Basic Books.

References

Asch, SE (1951) Effects of group pressure upon the modification and distortion of judgment. In H Guetzkow (Ed) *Groups, Leadership and Men* (pp. 177–90). Pittsburgh, PA: Carnegie University Press.

Barker, M (2011) De Beauvoir, Bridget Jones' pants and vaginismus. *Existential Analysis, 22*(2), 203–16.

Barker, M, Richards, C & Bowes-Catton, H (2012) Visualising experience: Using creative research methods with members of sexual communities. In C Phellas (Ed) *Researching Non-heterosexual Sexualities* (pp. 57–79). Farnham: Ashgate.

Bouman, WP, Bauer, GR, Richards, C & Coleman, E (2010) World Professional Association for Transgender Health consensus statement on considerations of the role of distress (Criterion D) in the *DSM* diagnosis of Gender Identity Disorder. *International Journal of Transgenderism, 12*(2), 100–6.

British Psychological Society (2012) *Guidelines and Literature Review for Psychologists Working Therapeutically with Sexual and Gender Minority Clients*. Leicester: British Psychological Society.

Buber, M (1958) *I and Thou* (2nd ed; R Gregor-Smith, Trans). London: Continuum.

Butler, J (1999) *Gender Trouble*. New York: Routledge.

Clark, A (1997) *Being There*. London: The MIT Press.

Cohn, HW (1997) *Existential Thought and Therapeutic Practice: An introduction to existential psychotherapy*. London: Sage Publications.

Cooper, M (2003) 'I–I' and 'I–Me': Transposing Buber's interpersonal attitudes to the intrapersonal plane. *Journal of Constructivist Psychology, 16*(2), 131–53.

Denman, C (2004) *Sexuality*. Basingstoke: Palgrave Macmillan.

Flowers, P & Langdridge, D (2007) Offending the other: Deconstructing narratives of deviance and pathology. *British Journal of Social Psychology, 46*(3), 679–90.

Foucault, M (1991) *Discipline and Punish: The birth of the prison* (2nd ed; A Sheridan, Trans). New York: Vintage Books. (First published 1977)

Foucault, M (1998) *The History of Sexuality Vol 1: The will to knowledge* (R Hurley, Trans). London: Penguin Books (First published 1976)

Foulkes, SH (1984) *Therapeutic Group Analysis*. London: Karnac. (First published 1964)

Gauntlett, D (2007) *Creative Explorations*. London: Routledge.

Goldner-Vukov, M, Moore, LJ & Cupina, D (2007) Bipolar disorder: From psychoeducational to existential group therapy. *Australasian Psychiatry, 15*(1), 30–4.

Heidegger, M (2008) *Being and Time* (7th ed; J Macquarrie & E Robinson, Trans). New York: HarperCollins. (First published 1962)

Kierkegaard, S (1981) *The Concept of Anxiety: A simple psychologically orienting deliberation on the dogmatic issue of hereditary sin* (New ed; R. Thomte, Trans). Princeton, NJ: Princeton University Press. (First published 1844)

Kissane, DW, Bloch, S, Miach, P, Smith, GC, Seddon, A & Keks, N (1997) Cognitive-existential group therapy for patients with primary breast cancer: Techniques and themes. *Psycho-Oncology, 6*(1), 25–33.

Kissane, DW, Bloch, S, Smith, GC, Miach, P, Clarke, DM, Ikin, J, Love, A, Ranieri, N & McKenzie, D (2003) Cognitive-existential group psychotherapy for women with primary breast cancer: A randomised controlled trial. *Psycho-Oncology, 12*(6), 532–46.

Langdridge, D (2007) *Phenomenological Psychology.* Harlow: Pearson.

Luft, J & Ingham, H (1955) The Johari Window: A graphic model of interpersonal awareness. In J Luft (1969) *Of Human Interaction* (p. 177). Paolo Alto, CA: National Press.

Maass, A & Clark, RD (1988) Social categorization in minority influence: The case of homosexuality. *European Journal of Social Psychology, 18*(4), 347–67.

Moscovici, S, Lage, E & Naffrenchoux, M (1969) Influences of a consistent minority on the responses of a majority in a colour perception task. *Sociometry, 32*(4), 365–80.

Nietzsche, F (1968) *The Will to Power* (W Kaufmann & RJ Hollingdale, Trans). New York: Vintage Books. (First published 1895)

Plummer, K (1995) *Telling Sexual Stories: Power, change and social worlds.* New York: Routledge.

Richards, C (2010) Trans and non-monogamies. In D Langdridge & M Barker (Eds) *Understanding Non-monogamies* (pp. 121–33). London: Routledge.

Richards, C (2011a) Transsexualism and existentialism. *Existential Analysis, 22*(2), 272–9.

Richards, C (2011b) Alliance ruptures: Etiology and resolution. *Counselling Psychology Review, 26*(3), 56–62.

Richards, C & Barker, M (2013) *Sexuality and Gender for Counsellors, Psychologists and Health Professionals: A practical guide.* London: Sage Publications.

Ricoeur, P (1970) *Freud and Philosophy: An essay on interpretation* (D Savage, Trans). New Haven, CT: Yale University Press.

Sartre, J-P (1989) *No Exit and Three Other Plays*. New York: Vintage Books. (First published 1944)

Schrock, DP & Reid, LL (2006) Transsexuals' sexual stories. *Archives of Sexual Behavior, 35*(1), 75–86.

Spinelli, E (2007) *Practising Existential Psychotherapy: The relational world*. London: Sage Publications.

Szasz, TS (1974) *The Myth of Mental Illness* (2nd ed). London: Harper Perennial.

Van Deurzen-Smith, E (1997) *Everyday Mysteries: Existential dimensions of psychotherapy*. London: Routledge.

Ventegodt, S, Clausen, B, Langhorn, M, Kromann, M, Andersen, NJ & Merrick, J (2004) Quality of life as medicine III: A qualitative analysis of the effect of a five-day intervention with existential holistic group therapy or a quality of life course as a modern rite of passage. *The Scientific World, 4*, 124–33.

Yalom, ID (1991) *Love's Executioner and Other Tales of Psychotherapy*. London: Penguin Psychology.

Yalom, ID & Leszcz, M (2005) *The Theory and Practice of Group Psychotherapy* (5th ed). New York: Basic Books.

14

Existential Sex Therapy

– Dr Meg-John Barker –

We live in a sex-saturated culture. Sexual iconography has increased dramatically in advertising during the last decade, and images of entwined couples, arched backs and orgasmic expressions bombard us from billboards, cinema screens and newspapers (Gill, 2007). Women's magazines and 'lads' mags' tell us the kinds of sex we should (and should not) be having (Attwood, 2005). TV stations attract viewers with endless documentaries on sexual practices. Porn is ever-more freely available on the Internet providing another mythologised version of sex. The overwhelming message is that 'everyone is always ready, willing and able to have sex' (Miracle, Miracle & Baumeister, 2003: 101).

Alongside this hyper-sexualisation there is an ever-increasing anxiety about sex and a concern with being unable to have 'functional' sex. Every morning my email spam-filter is full of advertisements for the latest sex-aid drug. I recently tried to explain the common sex therapy technique of 'sensate-focus' to a client. He responded that he was familiar with it having read about it in *The Sun*. Another client was reluctant to believe that the clinic could offer her partner and herself anything more than the myriad of sexual self-help books that they had already purchased. The prevalence of sexual 'dysfunctions', as defined by the American Psychiatric Association's *Diagnostic and Statistical Manual* (*DSM-IV-TR*) (APA, 1994), is so high as to question whether it even makes sense to judge it a 'disorder' under the common normality/abnormality model: the 2000 UK national survey of sexual attitudes and lifestyles (NATSAL) found that 35 per cent of men and 54 per cent of women reported some kind of sexual 'dysfunction' (Mercer, 2006). Reviewing their US study with similar findings, Laumann, Paik and Rosen (1999) report that such people are four to five times more likely than others to be unhappy and dissatisfied with their lives.

Popular culture and psychiatric understandings also perpetuate anxiety about sex by defining what kinds of sex are and are not acceptable (both in definitions of 'dysfunctional sex' and 'paraphilias'). The popular TV programme (and then movie) *Sex and the City* specialised in 'freak of the week' episodes[1] which defined the kinds of hot, adventurous sex people should be having as well as policing the boundaries against bad sex as the thing that was wrong with the boyfriend du jour (e.g. 'erectile dysfunction', wanting to be urinated on, or using baby talk). Sex shops like Ann Summers have a similar role in encouraging spicy sex and policing the boundaries against dangerous sex (fluffy handcuffs – yes, ball-gags – no, Storr, 2003). It is small wonder that the omnipresent call from clients at sex therapy clinics is 'I just want to be normal'.

It is within this conflictual culture of sex that we operate as psychosexual therapists. Conventional sex therapy could be seen, to some extent, as reinforcing the assumption that it is good, natural and important to have a certain frequency of a certain kind of sex, whilst those who do not are 'sexually dysfunctional'. One therapeutic approach which has rarely been applied to sex therapy, but which offers quite a different perspective, is existential therapy.

This chapter considers what we could gain from taking an existential approach to sex therapy. First it outlines the implications of the critical stance that existential therapy takes towards diagnosis. Following this, it introduces what existential therapy itself involves, particularly exploring the focus on the lived experience of the client, and the importance placed on multiple meanings and dimensions of experience. As well as reviewing the small amount of theory and research on existential sex therapy (e.g. Adams et al, 2006; Kleinplatz, 1998, 2004), I reflect on my own thoughts having spent the last three years studying existential therapy and working in a sex and relationship problems clinic.

A critical existential approach to diagnosis

The existential therapist Yalom (2001) states that therapists should 'avoid diagnosis' and suggests that diagnoses are often counterproductive because they diminish the ability of the therapist to relate to the other as a person.

---

1. Following the popular 'monster of the week' format from sci-fi and horror shows like *The X Files* and *Buffy the Vampire Slayer*.

This resonates with my own experience. It is very easy when faced with a client file or GP letter diagnosing 'premature ejaculation' or 'vaginismus' to form all kinds of assumptions about the kind of person you are about to meet, how easy they will be to work with, and so on. Yalom warns that diagnosis can mean that we attend too much to features that fit an initial diagnosis and not enough to those that do not but may also be important. He reminds us that sometimes diagnoses can become a self-fulfilling prophecy as people come to see themselves as 'sexually aversive' for example.

More fundamentally than this, existential psychotherapy follows the anti-psychiatry approach of Laing (1962) and Szasz (1974) in suggesting that diagnosis and treatment on the basis of symptoms miss the *meaning* of these symptoms and behaviours and thus dehumanise the individual. Spinelli (2005) argues that symptoms are expressions of attempts to defend against existential anxieties, so medical interventions and behavioural treatments can only offer a temporary amelioration. Kleinplatz (2003) concurs, saying that the goal of sex therapy is generally to eliminate barriers to sexual functioning so that 'normal' sex can resume, and that this focus on relieving symptoms neglects the vital intrapsychic, interpersonal, systemic and sociocultural meanings surrounding client experiences and behaviours. I will return to this consideration of meaning in more depth shortly.

Many sex therapists writing today agree with the existential distrust of medical and behavioural diagnosis and treatment. Leonore Tiefer writes that 'it is never the wrong place to recommend ignoring the *DSM*' (Tiefer, 1995: 54). There are several edited collections of sex therapy approaches which shun the conventional pathologising language of 'dysfunction' (e.g. Green & Flemons, 2004; Kaschak & Tiefer, 2001; Kleinplatz, 2001; Ussher & Baker, 1993). On the face of it, it may seem strange to critique an approach that has been so effective. As Kleinplatz (1998, 2004) herself points out, the PDE5 inhibitors have been very successful in providing men with erections and systematic desensitisation with dilators enables most women to engage in penile-vaginal intercourse,[2] so why question these approaches? The answer is that these categorisations and treatments construct a problematic distinction between functional and dysfunctional sex which is, at best, limiting and constraining and, at worst, dehumanising and risks exacerbating rather than alleviating suffering.

---

2. Kleinplatz does point out that, despite this, compliance levels with pharmacological and physical treatments for 'erectile dysfunction' are low and many women are reluctant to follow the 'vaginismus' techniques, so there seem to be some limitations to these approaches even under their own definitions.

Denman (2004) states that the *DSM* categories and conventional sex therapy treatments *construct* what 'normal sex' is as part of a dominant discourse which is also reflected and perpetuated in mainstream media, self-help literature and everyday conversation. The psychiatric/psychological construction is particularly problematic because it has a veneer of value-free scientific objectivity obscuring the 'intensely political and value-laden content of the discourse' (Denman, 2004: 275). As Fishman (2004) points out, the medical and psychological industries are idealised and have huge 'expert' power, which means that their way of seeing things is often accepted as taken-for-granted fact rather than one, deeply problematic in this case, way of viewing the world. The *DSM* categories and medical treatments can be seen as part of a regulative discourse (Foucault, 1976) which is bound up in economic concerns (Viagra™ and co are big business) and conservative politics; for example, Boyle (1993) and others suggest that the recognition and treatment of 'female sexual dysfunctions' emerged when women's sexual dissatisfaction became a threat to heterosexual marriage and the nuclear family.

We can see how *DSM* categories and medical opinion are historically and culturally constructed when we consider times in the past when masturbation was discouraged or homosexuality was 'treated' (Kutchins & Kirk, 1997), or when we reflect that Masters and Johnson (1970) stated that 90 per cent of sexual dysfunction was psychogenic in etiology and 10 per cent organic, whilst post-Viagra™ statistics now put it at 80 per cent organic and 20 per cent psychogenic (Kleinplatz, 2004).

Kleinplatz (1998, 2004) also critiques the medical and behavioural psychology approaches for being goal- rather than pleasure-oriented. Despite attempts of more mainstream authors like Wincze and Carey (2001) to redefine the goal of sex therapy as mutual pleasure and to highlight the 'myth' that sex equals intercourse, the *DSM* categories and sexual response cycles they are based on (Kaplan, 1979) clearly construct the goal of treatment as enabling erections and orgasms, rather than exploring broader possibilities for enhancing sexual pleasure. The possibility that someone who is unable to have erections or to be penetrated may not be in need of treatment is seldom considered. As Denman (2004) argues, the promotion of sexual 'disorders' creates a limited notion of 'good', 'normal', 'natural' sex (Rubin, 1992), which people are expected to conform to, dampening their own 'erotic imagination'.

Several authors have argued that the model of 'good', 'normal', 'natural' sex promoted by the *DSM* and sex therapy is heterosexual, penile-vagina penetrative sex resulting in orgasm,[3] where the man takes an active role and the woman a passive one. Ogden describes it as the 'doing it' theory of sexual normality and the 'didja come?' theory of sexual satisfaction' (Ogden, 2001: 18). Despite Kaplan's (1979) recognition that the sexual response stages may not be sequential, the implication of her model – and the *DSM* criteria that draw on it – are that there should be a linear progression from desire, through arousal/excitation to orgasm via penetrative intercourse. Adams (2006) points out that the existence of the categories of 'vaginismus' and 'premature ejaculation' reveal the prioritising of penetrative penile-vaginal sex. As Boyle asks, 'premature for what?' (Boyle, 1993: 79). This prioritisation is also revealed in the lack of categories relating to anal/oral sex (e.g. being unable to overcome the 'gag reflex') or a female version of premature ejaculation. Hite (1981) reports that some women do experience problems in orgasming too quickly, but of course this does not interfere with penile-vaginal penetration so there is not a diagnostic category for it. The category of 'erectile dysfunction', which is the most common presenting problem at many psychosexual clinics, gains its significance from the fact that sex is seen as complete when the man ejaculates (Denman, 2004).

This construction of a certain kind of 'normal' or 'functional' sex has been criticised for excluding same-sex sexual experience, or for assuming that this is equivalent to heterosexual experience (Boyle, 1993) and for implying that other forms of sexual contact are inferior (Adams, 2006). AIDS activists have questioned the focus on penetration as the only sex (Jackson, 2006). Sensate focus (Masters & Johnson, 1970) constructs certain kinds of touching as desirable whilst others, such as those involved in sado-masochistic activities, are still rendered pathological under the *DSM* (Langdridge & Barker, 2005). Although the *DSM* states that lack of sexual desire/arousal has to cause 'marked distress or interpersonal difficulty' in order to be diagnosed, there is still an implication that sexual contact is a necessary human activity, which excludes those who are celibate or self-defined as asexual (Scherrer, 2008). In the medical and psychological professions there is also a tendency to assume that sex only occurs between able-bodied people (Denman, 2004, Shakespeare, 2003). I saw a couple where one had multiple sclerosis. They came to the clinic

---

3. This privileging of penile-vaginal penetration is also seen in the treatment of people who are born ambiguously sexed and are traditionally assigned as male or female by doctors based on whether they are physically able to penetrate a vagina or to be penetrated. 'Corrective' surgery carried out often deadens sexual sensation (Fausto-Sterling, 2000; Kessler, 1998).

as their last port of call having been told by all the other doctors and counsellors that they approached that they should not expect to continue a sexual relationship.

Conventional approaches to sexual 'dysfunction' have also been critiqued for perpetuating the construction of the naturally sexually active and initiating man, and the sexually passive and penetrated woman which is also present in the everyday language of sex (penetrating rather than enveloping, euphemisms like 'nail', 'fuck' and 'screw', and the lack of positive words for female genitalia, Weatherall, 2002). The multi-million-selling self-help text, *Mars and Venus in the Bedroom*, explicitly states that women should sometimes lay there 'like a block of wood', that sex is a natural male need, which ends with the man's orgasm (Potts, 2002). Jackson (2006) argues that such polarised views of men and women prevent us from seeing similarities between, and variations within, each gender category. It completely excludes much trans experience (Kessler & McKenna, 2000) and is also constraining, limiting and pressurising for both women and men: disempowering women (Jackson, 2006) and pressuring men to act as unemotional machines, focused purely on their 'performance' (Croissant, 2006; Grace et al, 2006; Marshall, 2002; Potts, 2000; Tiefer, 2006; Vares & Braun, 2006).

Under this model, women are not supposed to be sexually active, and their need for clitoral stimulation to reach orgasm is viewed as something 'additional' because the clitoris is not as easily stimulated by penetration as the penis (Boyle, 1993). Ussher and Baker critique the categorisation of 'vaginismus' saying: 'that this is a description of a woman who cannot (or does not want to) have sexual intercourse could easily be overlooked in the discussion of peri-vaginal muscles and reflexes of the thighs' (Ussher & Baker, 1993: 27). Bass (2000) and Potts (2002) point out the potential negative impact of a 'performance perfection' approach to male sexuality on men's identities and wellbeing. Zilbergeld (1999) states that the image of 'natural' masculinity in our culture is of men who are always ready for sex, hard, and able to go all night long. The construction of soft penises as 'dysfunctional' reinforces such stereotypes (Kleinplatz, 2004). Many men attending the clinic where I work are terribly anxious about whether their penis size and performance is adequate, and locate much of their distress and relationship problems in this area.

There is, however, a problem when we come to work with clients from a more critical, or existential, perspective, and that is that diagnostic terms and ideas of 'sexual dysfunction' are dominant understandings which many of them may, themselves, draw on. I would be very wary of overtly deconstructing such categories which may be a vital part of the client's way of viewing their issues. However, clients often express some reservations themselves and I have found open engagement with these to be useful, particularly in relation to the losses and gains which come with embracing a diagnosis. For example, the following client, Steve, brought the possible label of 'sexual addiction' into the room (as yet not categorised under the *DSM*, but no less problematic for that, see Irvine, 2005; Keane, 2002).

> Steve: My partner was looking online and she came across some stuff about sex addiction, you know?
>
> Me: Mmhm
>
> Steve: So I ordered a book on it, here [gets a book out of his bag]
>
> Me: And how did you find it?
>
> Steve: Like phew. It was pretty intense. I mean there's a lot I recognise in there. About the kind of background I have, and how it feels so out of control once you get online.
>
> Me: Sounds like it was useful to see that this might be an experience you share with others?
>
> Steve: Yes ... it was a relief in a way [sounds doubtful]
>
> Me: You don't sound completely sure.
>
> Steve: Well there was also stuff in there that didn't fit me so well. But ... maybe I should just accept it.
>
> Me: I think it can be useful with any new word, or idea, like this to think about both what you gain from it, but also what might be lost.
>
> Steve: It does feel like I might lose something. I mean, thinking about what I was doing online in therapy was really useful to me. It helped me to realise that I wanted to be more creative, have more of an impact, in my life. The stories in the book are kind of simplistic. They don't get into that kind of thing.
>
> Me: Any other gains or losses?
>
> Steve: (pauses) Well a major gain is the fact it gives me a story: something you can say to other people and they are like 'oh

well, that's not really your fault'. But on the other hand that feels a bit out of control. And it has changed over time. It's not something I do so much now. I don't like to think it's something I'll always be.

An existential approach to sex therapy

As well as working critically and openly with diagnosis, what else might an existential approach have to offer and what kind of framework for sex therapy would such an approach involve?

Existential therapy is hard to pin down because there are many different branches which emphasise different elements (Cooper, 2003). Broadly speaking it sees people as meaning-constructors who are actively involved in making sense of their worlds. Existential therapists aim to engage phenomenologically with clients, bracketing off their own ways of seeing the world as much as possible in order to gain a full picture of the client's unique lived experience and the worldviews which shape this (Spinelli, 2005). Clients are encouraged to explore the assumptions underlying these worldviews to see how they may have become rigid and fixed and to consider what alternative ways of understanding may be possible (and potentially more useful). Obviously this creates the opportunity for working more openly with cultural assumptions around sex and how clients engage with these, as in the example above.

Clients are particularly encouraged to see how the existential 'givens' of human being may be involved in their difficulties, and to face up to these. The givens include the fact that we will all die (and do not know when), the fact that we are free to make choices in life, the fact that we are alone despite our being thrown into a world where we are inevitably connected to others, and the fact that life has no inherent meaning: we create it for ourselves (Yalom, 1991). In the remainder of this chapter I illustrate how many such themes emerge within existential therapy for sexual difficulties.

I will consider what existential therapy has to offer sex therapy under three main headings: exploring how existential therapy prioritises the lived experience of the client (Spinelli, 2005); how the focus is on the meaning of the experience for the client (Kleinplatz, 1998, 2004); and how it may be useful to explore the different existential dimensions with clients (Adams, et al, 2006; van Deurzen-Smith, 1997; van Deurzen, 2002).

The lived experience of the client

Kleinplatz (1998, 2004) is one of the very few sex therapists to explicitly address existential themes, drawing on Frankl (1978), Laing (1967), May (1969) and others in her existential-experiential approach to sex therapy.[4] Kleinplatz emphasises the need to listen to the client's lived experience and to use this as a way in to exploring their worldview and what is meaningful and important to them.

In her (1998) paper Kleinplatz describes her work with Ms Smith who was terrified of vaginal penetration. Ms Smith had a background where sex-talk was taboo and had had an 'awful' relationship with a man who pressured her to let him penetrate her, before she embarked on a much more positive relationship with her now-fiancé. Rather than attempting the standard desensitisation treatment, Kleinplatz encouraged Ms Smith to describe her lived experience of being orally assaulted by her previous partner. This resulted in her confronting her feelings of powerlessness in many relationships and exploring feelings of anger and ways in which she could take control. Over six sessions her feelings of shame around her body disappeared and she reported a new-found sense of freedom. In follow-up she reported that her 'vaginismus' had disappeared.

In her (2004) paper Kleinplatz reports on a man who came to see her because of his 'erectile dysfunction' and his feelings of being flawed because he was taking a PDE5 inhibitor. Rather than treating the 'erectile dysfunction', Kleinplatz chose to work with the 'whole person'. Instead of focusing on his erections, she asked him to talk about whatever scene was compelling his attention at the present time. He described being in bed with his partner the previous night and her saying 'I want you inside me right now'. He reported his tense, desperate response and his focus on his penis. Kleinplatz suggested that he listen to the message his penis was giving him: a common idea in existential therapy that difficult feelings or sensations may have valuable messages. He realised that, in contrast to his own desire to be accommodating, the penis was angry at being expected to perform and wanted prior attention. He gave voice to these desires with his partner and she was very happy to caress and stroke his penis, as well as exploring other desires with him which he had previously tried to ignore.

Yalom describes one case when he worked with someone presenting with sexual problems. Like Kleinplatz, Yalom started with the lived

---

4. Although the related form of 'experiential psychotherapy' referred to by both Kleinplatz and Mahrer (Mahrer, 1996; Mahrer & Boulet, 2001) should also be considered in relation to existential issues.

experience of the client, but also attempted to bracket both his own and his client's assumptions about what was going on. The client, Marvin, initially suggested that he was a therapist's dream because his problems were so clearly sexual: he had problems gaining and sustaining an erection. He commented that 'sex is at the root of everything. Isn't that what you fellows always say?' (Yalom, 1991: 230). However, by exploring Marvin's dreams with him, Yalom discovered that Marvin's problems were much more about dread of impending death than they were about sex per se. Marvin was nearing retirement age and part of him was very aware of all that he had not done with his life (e.g. having children or a meaningful career). Sex was a way in which he tried to soothe himself but it did not always work and then the anxieties crept in. Yalom writes:

> I believed that Marvin was entirely wrong when he said that sex was at the root of his problems; far from it, sex was just an ineffective means of trying to drain off surges of anxiety springing from more fundamental sources. Sometimes, as Freud first showed us, sexually inspired anxiety is expressed through other devious means. Perhaps just as often the opposite is true: *other anxiety masquerades as sexual anxiety.*
>
> (Yalom, 1991: 240)

Client meanings

One strong message that I have taken from my existential training is that anything can be a way in to exploring how a person makes sense of their world and what is valuable and meaningful to them (e.g. dreams, fantasies, the way daily life is structured, how people engage with food). Sexual issues are no exception to this, although I have found, even within existential circles, that people often see sex therapy as something very specific rather than another way of gaining entry into client understandings, ways of being, and existential issues. As we can see in Yalom's example above and my own example with Steve, sex is often a handy existential barometer, and explorations of it within the context of the client's whole lived experience can be very revealing about what they regard as meaningful, and how they relate to others, themselves, and their own mortality.

Psychological and medical models of human experience often search for one universal cause–effect explanation for human experiences and behaviours in a reductionist fashion. Existential therapists would instead see any experience or behaviour as having many possible meanings for different individuals (and even within the same individual on different occasions). For example, I have worked with two men who were unable to orgasm during penetrative sex. One linked this very much to his inability to express himself in other aspects of his life, whilst the other was fearful of letting go of control and being made fun of.

It is important to be aware of the multiple possible meanings of having/losing an erection, being penetrated, having an orgasm, and all other aspects of sex which may vary between people and even within the same person on different occasions. An orgasm, for example, can be experienced as: a mechanical release, a demonstration of one's masculine or feminine sexuality, a relief of stress, a loss of control, allowing someone to see you at your most vulnerable, a display of intimacy, the height of physical pleasure, a transcendent spiritual experience, a performance demonstrating prowess, a giving of power to another, an exerting of power over another, a form of creative self-expression, a humorous display of our rather-ridiculous humanity, an unleashing of something wild and animalistic, a deeply embodied experience, an escape from bodily sensations and pain, and/or a moment of complete aliveness or freedom.

Mitchell (2006) interviewed heterosexual women and their partners about how they saw their ability to orgasm. Women regarded it as: 'important but not essential', as signifying their partner's commitment, being about *mutual* enjoyment, and being important for their partner's sexual confidence. Their partners saw women's orgasms as: very important, vulnerable to relationship difficulties, a complicated skill they had to learn ('it's like the Bermuda triangle down there', one said), and an unlevel playing field, since it was perceived as being more difficult to get a woman to orgasm than a man.

Given the multiplicity of possible meanings, Kleinplatz (1998, 2004) warns against focusing on 'dysfunctional' penises or vaginas rather than exploring client's own meanings. She suggests that PDE5 inhibitors might restore performance to a man whose wife has died, or who is sensing a rift between his own desires and those of his partner, or who does not feel comfortable with his new girlfriend, leaving him feeling alone and empty because his loss, tension or anxiety has not been addressed. She suggests instead that we ask what the meaning of a non-penetrable vagina or soft penis is for the individual, and what they might gain from it. For example, she points out that it can be 'against the rules' for men to say that they do not want sex (because they are expected to be always 'up for it' and to prove their partner's desirability through it, Zilbergeld, 1999). Being unable to 'perform' may be the only way to get out of sex. Similarly 'vaginismus' may be a way of saying 'no' to unwanted sex.

Within this consideration of meaning it is important to take account of the wider subcultural and cultural meanings surrounding sexual practices. Milton (2000) particularly emphasises the need for existential therapy to be 'lesbian and gay affirmative', and indeed lesbian, gay, bisexual and transgender (LGBT) clients I have worked with so far have had both similar and different meanings to heterosexual clients (for example, many gay men have open relationships where trust and sexual fidelity are not tied together, and there may be various meanings surrounding different practices such as oral sex, anal sex and mutual masturbation and the positions taken within these). Hall, a lesbian sex therapist, argues that 'the meanings attributed to sexual encounters are ... fluid' (Hall, 2001: 161) and suggests that clients 'map' their sexual territory, giving them permission to move between different 'zones' at different times (e.g. zones for 'earthmoving sex, silly sex, mood-elevating sex or sorrowful sex ... sex for intimacy and sex for distance ... sex-free zones ... mechanical sex ... once-a-month-if-we-feel-like-it-or-not sex ... only-if-I-don't-have-to-lift-a-finger sex ... and ... maybe I'll feel like it after we start sex', (Hall, 2001: 174–6).

In relation to cultural differences there can be assumptions amongst therapists that people with certain cultural/religious backgrounds will be resistant to some of the standard 'treatments'. At conferences I have heard therapists and psychiatrists stating that women *must* be prepared to touch themselves, to insert objects into their vaginas, to mutually masturbate and so forth, otherwise there is no point them coming to therapy. Butler and Byrne (2007) argue that cultural differences should be celebrated rather than pathologised. Butler describes working with a Muslim couple who wanted to have penile-vaginal sex to become pregnant despite the female partner's difficulties being penetrated, and who were concerned that sexual self-touching was forbidden in their religion. In her explorations with them from a 'non-expert' stance, Butler found that sexual touching was permitted within a marriage if performed within the couple and not as masturbation, and that some laws of the Koran could be put aside if there was a medical justification. This created opportunities for the couple to explore different types of touching, and the female partner eventually became pregnant through the use of a syringe rather than penile-vaginal intercourse.

Embodiment and the existential dimensions

As stated earlier, psychological and medical models of sexual 'dysfunction' distinguish between psychogenic and organic aetiologies displaying the Cartesian mind/body split inherent in much medical discourse and current Western thinking. Many clients come with similar notions of their problems as being *either* psychological *or* physical, generally wanting to be told that it is one or the other (e.g. physical because it can be quickly 'fixed' or psychological because it means they are not 'sick'). I often work with clients around a possible alternative to this mind/body split based on Merleau-Ponty's (1962) notion of embodiment. Psychological and physical processes cannot really be teased apart in any meaningful sense.[5] Kleinplatz (1998) warns that medical/behavioural techniques based on such a Cartesian split and focusing on physical performance can alienate individuals from their own bodies. The subjective experience of the individual as an embodied self is lost and the body fragmented into different physical parts to be treated. Treatments do not engage with the lived experience of what it means to have a penis or vagina and often train people to ignore their own images, feelings and sensations in favour of more 'erotic' ones.

Kleinplatz's (1998, 2004) existential-experiential psychotherapy and Aanstoos' (2001) phenomenology of sexuality are both predicated on the integration of mind and body with no primacy of one over the other. In a similar way to the way van Deurzen-Smith (1997) regards emotions as reflective of what we value in life (jealousy as attempts to hold on to what is valued, guilt as a reaction to its loss, etc.), Kleinplatz sees embodied experiences as ways of expressing underlying experiences (e.g. the soft penis saying 'no' to sexual contact discussed above).

Linked to the concept of embodiment are the existential dimensions emphasised by van Deurzen (2002). In their recommendation of an existential framework for sex therapy, Adams et al (2006) draw on these dimensions suggesting that counsellors of new mothers who present with sexual problems consider the physical changes associated with pregnancy and childbirth and the need for the mother to come to terms with her new physical self (*Umwelt* – physical), the transition into new roles and

---

5. Mental processes like emotions and memories occur on a physical level in the neural connections of our brains and relate to other aspects of our bodies (genitalia, etc.) through our central nervous system. Similarly, physical processes require certain psychological states in order to take place (e.g. comfort, desire, arousal, etc. for orgasm).

identities accompanying motherhood (*Eigenwelt* – personal identity), the interpersonal relations between the mother and her partner, the mother and child and the mother in her wider social world (*Mitwelt* – social) and the way in which motherhood and sexual relations relate to the woman's wider meanings and values (*Überwelt* – spiritual). Adams et al (2006) emphasise the importance of this latter dimension suggesting that therapists facilitate the new mother's exploration of her, often changing, values; Ogden (2003) highlights the spiritual aspect that many women feel is part of sexual experience at its best, which underlines the need to take account of this dimension in sex therapy.

For someone who is experiencing problems attaining an orgasm, at the level of *Umwelt* we might ask whether the body is expressing something that is otherwise impossible (e.g. lack of trust in the partner, fear at loss of control or that degree of intimacy). At the *Eigenwelt* we can ask what orgasm means for the person's sense of self (e.g. does it signify being too enmeshed in someone else and losing oneself? Does it remind them of their physicality and the fact that this will end?) At the *Mitwelt* we can ask how orgasm is (or is not) involved in relating with others (e.g. is it something to share, to give to someone else or to take from them?) At the *Überwelt* we can consider orgasm as a spiritually meaningful experience, the meanings given to it by the person, and whether sex is being made the ultimate source of meaning to avoid considering other possibilities.

Doan (2004) and Kleinplatz (2004) both warn that *DSM* diagnoses and conventional therapies often neglect the interpersonal dimension (*Mitwelt*). Doan reminds us that 'sex occurs *between* people' (Doan, 2004: 152) but the *DSM* forces therapists to diagnose *one* of the people involved. Kleinplatz (2004) suggests that it is important to work within the relationship context and to be aware of the meanings that sex and sexual 'dysfunction' may have for everyone involved.[6] For example, she suggests that 'erectile dysfunction' is often read as proof of undesirability by the sexual partner.

In my therapy with Helen, a young nurse who presented with 'vaginismus', our work focused very much around the *Mitwelt*, and the way in which her approach to sex related to her approach to people in general. Although sex was painful she would try to engage with it because she feared losing her boyfriend if she did not. After the first few sessions

---

6. I say 'everyone' because it is important to remember that sex can occur between more than two people, for example in some forms of open non-monogamy (Barker & Langdridge, 2009).

she shifted focus from her body and relationship to her relations with others much more broadly.

> Helen: Is it OK to have a rant? [laughs quite joyfully at the thought of it]
>
> Me: Absolutely. This is your space to be wherever you are today. And I'm keen to hear what's got you so stirred up.
>
> Helen: It's this doctor at work. He's always leaving extra work for us and yesterday, right at the end of my shift, he dumped down a load of files for me to go through. [Her voice is slightly raised and fists clenched, although still seemingly amused with herself for giving voice to the anger]
>
> Me: You're fuming about this aren't you? [smiles]
>
> Helen: Yes I am. Because I just went ahead and did it. Again. It's just like everywhere.
>
> Me: Everywhere?
>
> Helen: At home as well.
>
> Me: At home?
>
> Helen: Yes because it's always 'don't upset your mum' [we've explored her childhood somewhat previously]
>
> Me: So everywhere you have to do things for other people?
>
> Helen: And I'm sick of it. I always have to be the good friend, the good nurse, the good daughter, the good girlfriend [she counts these off on her fingers as she enunciates each one]
>
> Me: And what's that like?
>
> Helen: [looks up at me and sighs] Knackering.

Over the course of therapy Helen challenged her previous assumptions that she had to make herself into what other people wanted her to be (a theme explored in depth by existential authors such as Sartre, 1943/2005 and de Beauvoir, 1949). Letting go of the desire for other people to see her in certain ways, although by no means easy, meant that she was able to find a clearer idea of who she wanted to be. By the end of therapy she was able to be clearer about when she wanted sex and when she didn't, which resulted in it being much more enjoyable. Her fear of losing her boyfriend decreased as she realised that whilst she loved him, she was also OK on her own.

Conclusions

I began this chapter with a rather negative view of the hyper-sexualisation of culture and concern with having 'good' sex. In their book Wincze and Carey (2001) present a more optimistic picture, arguing that there is increased openness about sex and access to information and understanding since Viagra™, meaning that people are more likely to engage with sex therapy and to understand what it can involve. Anxieties around sex mean that men, in particular, are far more likely to engage with therapy than they were in the past. Being able to perform sexually is so intertwined with idealised masculinity that men are willing to engage with emotional and psychological explorations to address this (even though these are in opposition to ideals of 'rational masculinity', Connel, 2002). Psychosexual clinics, in the UK at least, are places where many people who would not normally have access to psychotherapy can come (those with little money, or from cultures where psychotherapy is unfamiliar, for example, because it is free and in a medical context). I would encourage sex therapists to critically and creatively engage with diagnostic categories, and to take up the opportunity to work with the lived experiences of clients, exploring multiple meanings surrounding sex at the various dimensional levels, and considering the relationship between sexual experiences and wider existential themes.

References

Aanstoos, CM (2001) Phenomenology of sexuality. In PJ Kleinplatz (Ed) *New Directions in Sex Therapy: Innovations and alternatives* (pp. 69–90). Philadelphia: Brunner-Routledge.

Adams, LG, Harper, AL, Johnson, EP & Cobia, DC (2006) New mothers and sexual intimacy: An existential framework for counselling. *The Family Journal: Counselling and Therapy for Couples and Families, 14*(4), 424–9.

Adams, N (2006) Kiss me Kate: A new view of women and sex. *Lesbian & Gay Psychology Review, 7*(3), 276–81.

American Psychiatric Association (APA) (1994) *Diagnostic and Statistical Manual of Mental Disorders* (4th ed). Washington, DC: American Psychiatric Association. Retrieved 20 December 2006 from http://www.behavenet.com/capsules/disorders

Attwood, F (2005) Fashion and passion: Marketing sex to women. *Sexualities, 8*(4), 392–406.

Barker, M & Langdridge, D (Eds) (2009) *Understanding Non-monogamies*. London: Routledge.

Bass, BA (2000) Two positions for sexual intercourse useful in the treatment of male sexual dysfunction. *The Family Journal: Counselling and Therapy for Couples and Families, 8*(4), 416–8.

Beauvoir, S de (1949) *The Second Sex* (HM Parshley, Trans). New York: Vintage.

Boyle, M (1993) Sexual dysfunction or heterosexual dysfunction? *Feminism & Psychology, 3*(1), 73–88.

Butler, C & Byrne, A (2007) Queer in practice: Therapy and queer theory. In L Moon (Ed) *Feeling Queer or Queer Feelings: Counselling and sexual cultures* (pp. 89–105). London: Routledge.

Connel, RW (2002) *Gender*. Cambridge: Polity Press.

Cooper, M (2003) *Existential Therapies*. London: Sage Publications.

Croissant, JL (2006) The new sexual technobody: Viagra in the hyperreal world. *Sexualities, 9*(3), 333–44.

Denman, C (2004) *Sexuality: A biopsychosocial approach*. London: Palgrave Macmillan.

Doan, RE (2004) Who really wants to sleep with the medical model? An eclectic/narrative approach to sex therapy. In S Green & D Flemons (Eds) *Quickies: The handbook of brief sex therapy* (pp. 151–70). New York: WW Norton and Co.

Fausto-Sterling, A (2000) *Sexing the Body: Gender politics and the construction of sexuality*. New York: Basic Books.

Fishman, JR (2004) Manufacturing desire: The commodification of female sexual dysfunction. *Social Studies of Science, 34*(2), 187–218.

Foucault, M (1976) *The History of Sexuality, Vol. 1*. New York: Pantheon.

Frankl, V (1978) *The Unheard Cry for Meaning: Psychotherapy and humanism*. New York: Simon & Schuster.

Gill, R (2007) Supersexualize me: Advertising and the 'midriffs'. In F Attwood, R Brunt & R Cere (Eds) *Mainstreaming Sex: The sexualization of culture* (pp. 93–110) London: IB Tauris.

Grace, V, Potts, A, Gavey, N & Vares, T (2006) The discursive condition of Viagra. *Sexualities, 9*(3), 295–314.

Green, S & Flemons, D (Eds) (2004) *Quickies: The handbook of brief sex therapy.* New York: WW Norton and Co.

Hall, M (2001) Not tonight dear, I'm deconstructing a headache: Confessions of a lesbian sex therapist. In E Kaschak & L Tiefer (Eds) *A New View of Women's Sexual Problems* (pp. 161–78). New York: Haworth Press.

Hite, S (1981) *The Hite Report: A nationwide study of female sexuality.* New York: Dell.

Irvine, JM (2005) *Disorders of Desire.* Philadelphia, PA: Temple University Press.

Jackson, S (2006) Feminist perspectives on female sexuality. Presentation at the 2nd European Female Sexual Dysfunction Conference *The Picture in 2006.* September, London.

Kaplan, HS (1979) *Disorders of Sexual Desire.* New York: Brunner/Mazel.

Kaschak, E & Tiefer, L (2001) *A New View of Women's Sexual Problems.* New York: Haworth Press.

Keane, H (2002) *What's Wrong with Addiction?* Melbourne: Melbourne University Press.

Kessler, SJ (1998) *Lessons from the Intersexed.* New Brunswick, NJ: Rutgers University Press.

Kessler, SJ & McKenna, W (2000) Gender construction in everyday life: Transsexualism. *Feminism & Psychology, 10*(1), 11–29.

Kleinplatz, PJ (1998) Sex therapy for vaginismus: A review, critique and humanistic alternative. *Journal of Humanistic Psychology, 38*(2), 51–81.

Kleinplatz, PJ (Ed) (2001) *New Directions in Sex Therapy: Innovations and alternatives.* Philadelphia, PA: Brunner-Routledge.

Kleinplatz, PJ (2003) What's new in sex therapy: From stagnation to fragmentation. *Sex and Relationship Therapy, 18,* 95–106.

Kleinplatz, PJ (2004) Beyond sexual mechanics and hydraulics: Humanising the discourse surrounding erectile dysfunction. *Journal of Humanistic Psychology, 44*(2), 215–42.

Kutchins, H & Kirk, SA (1997) *Making Us Crazy: DSM: The psychiatric bible and the creation of mental disorders.* London: Constable.

Laing, RD (1962) *The Divided Self.* London: Penguin.

Laing, RD (1967) *The Politics of Experience and the Bird of Paradise.* New York: Penguin.

Langdridge, D & Barker, M (Eds) (2005) Contemporary perspectives on sadomasochism (S/M). Special Issue of *Lesbian & Gay Psychology Review, 6*(3), 143–287.

Laumann, EO, Paik, A & Rosen, RC (1999) Sexual dysfunction in the United States. *Journal of the American Medical Association, 281,* 537–44.

Mahrer, AR (1996) *The Complete Guide to Experiential Psychotherapy.* New York: Wiley.

Mahrer, AR & Boulet, DB (2001) How can experiential psychotherapy help transform the field of sex therapy? In PJ Kleinplatz (Ed) *New Directions in Sex Therapy: Innovations and alternatives* (pp. 234–57). Philadelphia, PA: Brunner-Routledge.

Marshall, BL (2002) Hard science: Gendered constructions of sexual dysfunction in the 'Viagra' age. *Sexualities, 5*(2), 131–58.

Masters, WH & Johnson, VE (1970) *Human Sexual Inadequacy.* Boston: Little Brown.

May, R (1969) *Love and Will.* New York: WW Norton and Co.

Mercer, C (2006) Understanding the epidemiology of FSD. Presentation at the 2nd European Female Sexual Dysfunction Conference *The Picture in 2006.* September, London.

Merleau-Ponty, M (1962) *Phenomenology of Perception.* London: Routledge.

Milton, M (2000) Is existential psychotherapy a lesbian and gay affirmative psychotherapy? *Journal of the Society for Existential Analysis, 11*(1), 86–102.

Miracle, TS, Miracle, AW & Baumeister, RF (2003) *Human Sexuality: Meeting your basic needs.* Upper Saddle River, NJ: Prentice Hall.

Mitchell, K (2006) Medicalising female sexual experience: The case of female orgasmic disorder. Presentation at the 2nd European Female Sexual Dysfunction Conference *The Picture in 2006.* September, London.

Ogden, G (2001) The taming of the screw: Reflections on 'a new view of women's sexual problems'. In E Kaschak & L Tiefer (Eds) *A New View of Women's Sexual Problems* (pp. 17–22). New York: Haworth Press.

Ogden, G (2003) Spiritual dimension of sex therapy: An integrative approach for women. *Contemporary Sexuality, 37,* 13–20.

Potts, A (2000) The essence of the hard on: Hegemonic masculinity and the cultural construction of 'erectile dysfunction'. *Men and Masculinities, 3*(1), 85–103.

Potts, A (2002) *The Science/fiction of Sex: Feminist deconstruction and the vocabularies of heterosex*. London: Routledge.

Rubin, G (1992) Thinking sex: Notes for a radical theory of the politics of sexuality. In CS Vance (Ed) *Pleasure and Danger: Exploring female sexuality*. (pp. 267–319) London: HarperCollins.

Sartre, J-P (2005) *Being and Nothingness: An essay on phenomenological ontology* (HE Barnes, Trans). London: Verso. (First published 1943)

Scherrer, KS (2008) Coming to an asexual identity: Negotiating identity, negotiating desire. *Sexualities, 11*(5), 621–41.

Shakespeare, T (2003) I haven't seen that in the Kama Sutra: The sexual stories of disabled people. In J Weeks, J Holland, & M Waites (Eds) *Sexualities and Society: A reader* (pp. 143–52). Cambridge: Polity Press.

Spinelli, E (2005) *The Interpreted World: An introduction to phenomenological psychology*. London: Sage Publications.

Storr, M (2003) *Latex and Lingerie: Shopping for pleasure at Ann Summers*. Oxford: Berg.

Szasz, T (1974) *The Myth of Mental Illness*. New York: Harper & Row.

Tiefer, L (1995) *Sex Is Not a Natural Act*. Boulder, CO: Westview Press.

Tiefer, L (2006) The Viagra phenomenon. *Sexualities, 9*(3), 273–94.

Ussher, JM & Baker, CD (1993) *Psychological Perspectives on Sexual Problems: New directions in theory and practice*. New York: Routledge.

Van Deurzen, E (2002) *Existential Counselling and Psychotherapy in Practice*. London: Sage Publications.

Van Deurzen-Smith, E (1997) *Everyday Mysteries: Existential dimensions of psychotherapy*. London: Routledge.

Vares, T & Braun, V (2006) Spreading the word, but what word is that? Viagra and male sexuality in popular culture. *Sexualities, 9*(3), 315–32.

Weatherall, A (2002) *Gender, Language and Discourse*. London: Routledge.

Wincze, JP & Carey, MP (2001) *Sexual Dysfunction: A guide for assessment and treatment*. London: Guildford Press.

Yalom, ID (1991) *Love's Executioner and Other Tales of Psychotherapy*. London: Penguin.

Yalom, ID (2001) *The Gift of Therapy*. London: Piatkus.

Zilbergeld, B (1999) *The New Male Sexuality*. New York: Bantam Books.

15

Three's Company, Two's a Crowd: Existential Couple Therapy

– Prof. Simon du Plock –

It is surprising how little has been written by existential therapists with regard to couple therapy; as Spinelli remarks,

> This seems somewhat startling to me not only because quite a few existential-phenomenological therapists offer couple therapy, but also since it is apparent that this approach provides a unique and novel perspective ... I have found the experience of working with a couple to be both stimulating and illustrative of the importance given by existential-phenomenological theory to the idea of *being-with-others*.
> (Spinelli, 1997: 101/2006: 77)

I intend, in this chapter, to outline my way of working with a couple. As will become evident, my method owes much to what Spinelli calls his 'tentative and idiosyncratic' approach (1997: 101/2006: 77). I am indebted to Luke and Mike, (not their real names), a couple with whom I have worked, who agreed to be recorded and who gave me permission to draw on this material in the course of this chapter. While I have taken care to ensure that I have disguised any potentially identifying material, Luke and Mike, on reading a draft of the chapter, agreed that my account preserves the essence of our sessions. Reflecting on couple therapy and addiction helps illuminate the nature of sexuality since it draws our attention to the challenges inherent in intimate relationship. Existential practitioners will be familiar with Sartre's formulation of this in *Being and Nothingness* (1943), when he reflects on the power dynamics of relationships and concludes that we are constantly locked into an interplay of dominance and submission, in which we either attempt to capture the freedom of the other (the sadistic strategy) or give ourselves up to the domination of the other (the masochistic strategy). A third option exists, according to Sartre, but it is a bleak one, and that is to withdraw from intimate relationship altogether. Couple therapy provides an arena in which clients can become more fully aware of the nature of the strategies they have adopted in response to the challenge of being in intimate relationship.

My approach to working with couples is distinct from my work with individuals. When I meet with an individual client, my focus is primarily on the relational field which the client and I inhabit, and how we co-create this. My objective is always to attempt to meet my client with what May (May et al, 1958: 37) has termed 'Here-is-a-new-person' in mind. My intention in doing this is to create the optimal conditions for authentic encounter with the other. Such an authentic encounter, one in which my personal preconceptions and biases are minimised, enables me to meet the client with genuine curiosity and naïvety about their way of being-in-the-world. This creates the optimum conditions for the client to notice that another approaches their being with care and encourages them, in turn, to take their being seriously – May's (1983: 99) 'I am' experience. I believe that my approach reflects Nietzsche's attitude of encouraging people to become objective towards themselves, rather than becoming lost in subjectivity. Greater objectivity may help clients to take renewed responsibility for making active choices to author their own lives.

Human being is inevitably being in relation; as Cohn expresses it, we never meet *only* the client, we are 'always and inevitably in a context with others' (Cohn, 1997: 33). It follows that couple therapy provides increased opportunity to work, since the relational world presented in the consulting room is far more richly textured, not least because in individual therapy the therapist assists the client to reflect on the ways in which they create meaning in their world, while in couple therapy the therapist has the opportunity to observe how two people attempt to create meaning, both as individuals and in common. Clients' ways of being in relationship are not just reported and reflected in their way of relating to the therapist; they are present in the room in the real-time interactions of the two members of the couple to each other and to the therapist.

One approach to working with couples

I have found the most facilitative way I can explore issues with clients in couple therapy is via the concept Spinelli (2007: 198) has termed 'the couple-construct'. This concept has grown out of his earlier notion of the 'self-structure' (Spinelli, 1994: 348/2006: 227), which directs our attention to how each of us assembles, over time, a set of beliefs, values and assumptions about who we believe ourselves to be. An exploration of the individual's self-structure will clarify the role of the presenting problems (whether that be depression, anxiety, eating concerns or addictions) in providing them with a sense of structure in their life which they might not otherwise have. A key element of existential couple therapy is the clarification of the extent to which these beliefs, values and assumptions about the difficulties are shared, or not, by both partners (van Deurzen & Iacovou, 2013).

Much of my work with couples focuses on the particular ways in which their unique couple-construct functions to both open up and limit their way of being-in-the-world as a couple. I engage in this process of clarification with them not with the intention of helping them 'move on' in some way, but to enable them to engage as fully as possible with me so that we can all 'see what is there'. This is especially important where denial of a wide spectrum of ways to live is a key feature. When both clients can genuinely see the way they have constructed their 'way-of-being-in-the-world' as a couple, they may elect to modify it. This is not, though, to underestimate how difficult this is likely to be, nor the degree of support they may require from the therapeutic alliance; as Spinelli makes clear, the couple may decide to separate if they discover that their individual understandings of being a couple are too divergent.

I generally utilise the following template for exploring the couple-construct. Sessions are 75 minutes, rather than the 50-minute 'therapeutic hour' of one-to-one work, as I have found this necessary given the complexity of the dynamics in the room:

> *Session one*: I meet with the couple and we explore what brings them into therapy, and the nature of the emerging couple-construct. It is important, I feel, to provide a safe enough container for the couple to feel a connection with me and begin to tell their story. While I tend to begin the initial session by welcoming them and asking them to tell me something about what has brought them to see me, much as I begin an individual therapy, I also ensure that there is time towards the end of the session for me to describe how I work, and how, typically, sessions will be structured, and the rationale for this particular structure. I also take this opportunity to check whether, on the basis of our work so far, they wish to commit to further sessions. If they are able to confirm this, I explain that I will meet with them individually for the following two sessions.

Session two: I meet one member of the couple without the other being present with the objective of focusing on their experience of being with their partner in the couple-construct that they have created. This also provides an opportunity for us to reflect on the values and beliefs they hold with regard to being in a couple, and the extent to which these are realised in their current couple-construct.

Session three: I repeat this process with the other member of the couple.

Session four: I meet with the couple together and we reflect on the experience of the previous two sessions, and relate what was explored in each session to their couple-construct.

Session five: I meet with the couple to clarify the extent to which their individual constructs and couple-construct remain the same or have changed, and to consider whether they wish to continue to work with me or leave therapy at this point.

During Session five I offer clients the opportunity to continue to work for a further cycle of five sessions. In this second cycle we use the first session to review their objectives for continuing in therapy. The next four sessions generally follow the pattern of the first cycle of therapy. We may repeat these cycles until the couple feel that they have addressed the issues which brought them to therapy to the extent they wish. In practice I have found that most couples are able to complete this work in two or three cycles, but sometimes one is adequate.

In my meetings with each individual, I typically invite them to reflect on:

1. Their individual sense of who they are, what is important to them, what they hold to be fundamental to their identity, and as it was the case with Luke and Mike, where addiction is a concern, the extent to which it impacts on identity, and the degree to which this includes being an 'addict'.
2. The same, but as they imagine their partner might respond to the question.
3. How their couple-construct supports and/or destabilises their sense of self and what they hold to be important for themselves.

4. The same, but as they imagine their partner might answer the question.
5. As a result of this reflection, how do they feel about their partnership? What is their 'felt-sense'? Are they clearer about aspects that feel satisfying, and aspects where they might want to work towards making a change? If addiction is a feature of the partnership, in what ways is it shaped by this phenomenon?
6. If there are areas where they might like to make changes, how do they feel this might impact upon the couple-construct? How do they feel this might change the quality of their partnership?

Working with Luke and Mike

I resonate with Spinelli's view when meeting couples in conflict that:

> ... our first task together will be that of clarifying the underlying assumptions, biases, values and beliefs of the currently existing couple-construct. Via such descriptive clarification, the couple's inter-relational sedimentations and dissociations can be highlighted ... descriptive classification can reveal not only poorly perceived defining aspects of the existing couple-construct, but also those poorly perceived defining aspects that each member of the couple maintains with regard to his or her own self-construct or to the 'other-construct' of his or her partner.
> (Spinelli, 1997: 104–5/2006: 79–80)

He goes on to assert that each member of the couple makes sense of the conflict which besets them by viewing it through the lens of their own worldview. They are likely to assume that this perspective is shared by their partner and, given this assumption, they are likely to hold it without checking that it is, indeed, the case.

Luke and Mike sent me a joint email requesting an appointment, as they both felt that their relationship had run into difficulties. It seemed from their brief email that they shared the view that they were drifting apart after being together for five years, having met when they were both in their mid-thirties. They said they had got my contact details via a colleague of Mike's (he was a nursing manager in a London hospital) who was a past student of mine. They asked for an early meeting as they felt they had 'hit a wall', were no longer communicating with each other, and constantly argued. I was struck that it appeared they were in agreement about the state of their relationship, even if they were not able to agree about much else, and I wondered if this would provide some foundation for our work together, should they wish to work with me. I also noted the apparent urgency of their request for a meeting, and wondered if this would motivate them to explore their couple-concept with me, or whether it would lead them to look to me for ready-made 'solutions' to their problems. I offered them an appointment later the same week and received an acceptance almost immediately.

Session one

They arrived together, though I noticed they seemed awkward with each other and made little eye contact. They took the chairs I indicated and looked expectantly at me. As I routinely do when meeting with couples, I welcomed them both and invited them to tell me what brought them to see me. The atmosphere seemed to become more relaxed as they launched into a description of how they had met 'on the gay scene', and how what both thought would be a one-night stand developed into an ongoing relationship, even though they both continued to have sex with other men they met on the scene. When I asked them what they thought had led them to identify each other as potential ongoing partners, they both said that they had recognised something in the other that was important for them: Luke felt that Mike was a real 'buddy', while Mike referred to their relationship as one of 'soul mates'. I wondered what these two terms, at first sounding so different, might mean for each of them. I was also struck that neither gave any indication of noticing that the other had used such a different term in referring to them, but at this early stage in the meeting decided to sit back and listen to more of their story.

They went on to describe how they had, over a period of time, found a way to create a relationship which was 'open and flexible enough' to enable them to share a flat while also 'playing away' – having regular sex with others they met on the gay scene, but not bringing them back home to their flat. I reflected to them that the creation of this 'open' relationship seemed to be important to them, and they agreed that it was as they both felt monogamy was a trap; neither wanted to feel 'dictated to' by the other or by social norms.

They told me that they had found themselves drifting apart over the last 18 months, and that this sense of drifting had accelerated over the past few months, to the point that they were no longer emotionally or sexually intimate; instead all their energy was fed into quarrelling – it seemed they could identify little, if any, common ground at this point. When I asked them if anything in particular had happened 18 months ago, Luke immediately said Mike had started a mental health degree. He added that six months later he had been promoted to a nurse manager grade, and he had recently received a further promotion. Mike agreed that the more successful he became, the more their relationship suffered. He felt this was a real puzzle, since Luke was very successful – he was a company executive with a high income who frequently travelled abroad on business. So far as Mike was concerned, Luke had no reason to feel envious or threatened by his recent professional recognition. When I asked them to tell me more about themselves, Luke described how what he experienced as a very happy childhood had abruptly come to a halt when he was 12 and his parents divorced acrimoniously. He and his sister were 'packed off' to separate boarding schools and he quickly had to learn to fend for himself. Being good at sports, he became popular, but he was aware of avoiding close friendships throughout his school years and later at university, a wariness he attributed to a fear of being hurt again as he had been when his parents split up. As he expressed it, he was good at team games, but 'inside' he never felt a desire to be part of the team. Mike also seemed something of a loner; having grown up in a blue-collar family in the Midlands, he was always aware of feeling 'different' and not fitting in. On leaving school he had little sense of direction and had trained as a nurse because a careers tutor had said he would be 'good with people'. Once qualified he took the first opportunity he could to transfer 'down south' and had only become career-minded quite recently, after successfully completing some internal training and realising he had a flair for managing a drug addiction unit.

Luke broke in at this point to say that he had initially been very pleased when Mike began to take his job more seriously; they were living together and their income disparity was starting to feel like an issue. But he thought Mike's addiction studies had led him to change his social habits and this, in turn, impacted on Luke. Now Mike avoided drugs, drank less, and rarely wanted to go clubbing at weekends. Mike retorted that Luke needed to look at his own drug use, and that if he could change his behaviour in a more healthy direction, then so could Luke. Luke shifted uneasily in his seat on hearing this and, looking directly at me, said 'You see? *This* is the problem – Mike's changed and now he's trying to change me. But I don't need to change. I'm comfortable with who I am and if that involves recreational drugs that's up to me.' Mike came back saying 'If we really are a couple then it isn't just up to you. You should be glad I have your interests at heart, and the more I work with addicts the more I worry about you.' Luke looked exasperated at this point and, throwing up his hands, said: 'I don't need anyone worrying about me, I'm just fine. Maybe you need to think about how sanctimonious you're getting with all your academic wisdom!'

I was aware at this point that we were drawing towards the end of our time, so I reflected back to them what I thought I was hearing, and asked them to correct me if this was not their sense of the situation. It seemed to me that they had originally felt drawn together on the basis that they had a lot in common. I was not too sure at this point what this had involved, and it would be interesting to explore this further if they decided to work with me. Part of this, though, seemed to be a shared perspective on the value of having an 'open relationship', something which perhaps previous potential partners had not favoured. I had not heard much about what this 'open relationship' involved, but it did seem to include regular drug and alcohol use. This relationship had worked well for several years, but when Mike began to be more enthusiastic about his own career and started to change his drug and alcohol use, it seemed that this threatened the continuation of the relationship. Similarly, Luke's wish to continue acting as he had at the beginning of the relationship felt unacceptable to Mike. Their relationship seemed to some extent to be defined by its 'openness' and I wondered what else was important to them or whether, if this 'openness' was threatened, the relationship itself might not survive. In any case, it appeared that they were no longer in agreement about what they wanted from their relationship, and they had not found a way to communicate successfully with one another about this. I remarked that what at first appeared to be a very relaxed and flexible way of being in a couple now looked surprisingly rule-bound and brittle. I suspected that I was taking a gamble in offering them this feedback so early in our encounter, but it seemed important to give them a sense of how I was experiencing them, even if this might feel challenging, so that they could correct me if they needed to. In fact, they both agreed that my observations did indeed feel accurate. I reflected back to them that this agreement about the situation might give us a useful platform for further discussion, and we ended the session with their enthusiastic agreement to continue to work with me.

After they left my office I checked that my recorder had worked and made my customary brief notes in the ten-minute interval before the next session. I noted down my impression of the couple-construct which Luke and Mike had created. It seemed to me this was characterised by an agreement to have an open relationship. At this point it was not clear to me the extent to which Luke and Mike shared the same motivation for this, or were equally happy about how this worked in practice. I was struck by how easily Luke's status as the high-achiever in the couple seemed to have been undermined by Mike's growing confidence in his own career. I wondered about the extent to which their couple-construct could embrace change, and whether Luke and Mike would be willing to change. It seemed significant that their interactions in the room with me had been mostly conflictual, and they had not evidenced much appreciation of each other's worldview. My sense was that both were more heavily invested in following their own interests rather than finding new ways to be a team, and, if my hunch was correct, our meetings might allow them to recognise that and decide whether to continue as a couple or end their relationship.

Session two

At the end of the previous session we had agreed that Luke would come alone for the next meeting. He seemed very eager to express his feelings about being in couple therapy, saying immediately 'You know I really hate that it's come to this, that we end up talking to a therapist. It's so far from where we started'. I asked him to tell me more about where they started and how now was so different, and our conversation began.

Luke explained that in the beginning they had a lot in common: 'You wouldn't have thought it looking at it from outside. I suppose I had a relatively privileged upbringing with private schooling and university. I went straight into a good job and I've been financially successful. He had a tougher time and fewer advantages, but he's really bright and successful in his own way. I work hard and play hard and he's the same. As it happens he's more sociable than me – in fact it's surprising how well he gets on with anyone, he has a gift for making friends. People think I'm gregarious but really I've always been wary of ties. I never had any hang-ups about drugs and getting about, and the good thing about Mike when we met was he was up for anything. We had a pretty open relationship from the start and it worked well for a long time. I think it's only really the last year or so he's become clingy and possessive. I don't like it when he's possessive: I feel like I'm being controlled and that really presses my buttons!'

I reflected that it sounded as though when they met Mike very much complemented his lifestyle; he fitted in well and they had fun together, but over time he developed more of his own interests, created his own career, and, it seems, made more demands on him. Luke agreed. He described how he was very supportive of Mike's efforts to improve his qualifications but had not foreseen the extent to which it would involve Mike in a new circle of friends from the hospital and the college. It sounded, I said, as though he felt excluded from this new circle of friends.

> Luke: Yes, in a way. I feel Mike keeps them away from me and on the odd times I've met them I feel they judge me; I'm just the guy who earns the money, while they take the moral high ground with all their psychobabble. Which is crazy really, given I got a degree years ago.
>
> Me: It sounds like you feel they disapprove of you?
>
> Luke: Well they don't exactly say it, and Mike doesn't say it, but I get the sense they look at me as some sort of reprobate! Some middle-aged druggie! And since Mike got involved with this addiction course he's been different too. I mean he's still up for a drink but we do less of the drugs now. And when I get home on a Friday night there are always these sort-of questions in the air: Where did you go? Who were you with? What did you do? Not just interested, but more like I'm reporting to matron! So that's when I decided to push back and I raised the idea of opening up our relationship more. I figured if I'm feeling stifled let's let some air in, let's bring a third guy in, not just play away. We talked about 'threesomes' right at the start when we met, but decided against it. But this seemed like the right moment to raise it again.
>
> Me: So in response to Mike getting closer to you …
>
> Luke: More taking me over!
>
> Me: OK, so in response to that, you propose bringing in a third person with the aim of reducing the pressure on you?
>
> Luke: Yes, but it backfired big time. He really didn't go for it, started shouting at me that I couldn't handle intimacy, that I was a sex addict, that I didn't care about anyone except myself … and then he came right back and said if I really cared we would get a civil partnership! Really didn't see that one coming – smart move!

I reflected to Luke that listening to him talking about his relationship, and especially his last remark about Mike making a smart move, I had the image of two boxers in a ring sparring. I said this sat oddly for me alongside the close relationship he had described at our first meeting.

> Luke: That feels really sad ... and I get the mental image of keeping back from him so I don't get punched. It feels important somehow, this sense I've always had of holding myself back. With Mike I thought I could get involved just enough to keep us ticking fine, but it seems like he wants more of me. And he wants to box me in now with this talk of a civil partnership. Not sure either is an option!

He looked crestfallen and sat silently for a while. It felt as if we had reached a serious point, but we were also nearly at the end of our time so I reflected that I felt he had helped me get a much fuller picture of his experience of being in a relationship with Mike. I also felt we had been able to reflect together on what being in any intimate relationship meant to him, and I had the impression he found it challenging to let others get close. His use of drugs and 'playing away' seemed to fit with this in the sense that they functioned to keep him busy and stimulated, but did not make emotional demands on him. All the time Mike was happy to be part of this way of being, Luke could see him as a 'buddy', but now that he wanted a more exclusive relationship Luke did not know how to respond, other than to withdraw. Luke agreed that this was broadly accurate, and also said that it helped just to get his difficulties out in the open so he could have a look at them: 'I don't know where to go from here, but at least it's a relief to let it all out!' I wondered if Luke might be able to share some of these thoughts with Mike in a future session – could he, as it were, be 'open' with Mike? Luke looked uncomfortable at this prospect, but said he would think about it.

Session three

Mike needed little prompting from me to begin talking. He had clearly used the time since our first session to come to some conclusions, and he hit the ground running:

> Mike: You know, I've been thinking a lot since our first meeting and it seems to me we never really have been a proper couple. I mean, call me old-fashioned if you want, but it's never really been like

> the song – just the two of us. There's always been the dope, or the coke, or the booze. I can't remember more than the odd couple of days when we haven't been high on something, or coming down off something, or planning the next party.

He went on to say one of the things he found most attractive about Luke in the early days was there was never a dull moment. Being with Luke was 'a real roller-coaster of fun' and in the first couple of years he just enjoyed the ride. 'It was a change for me to go with the flow. My background is all hard graft and money was tight when I was growing up, so being with Luke was a real contrast. And then over the next couple of years I started to find it hard to keep up. I mean there were my studies, and I needed to take them seriously if I was going to move up the nursing ladder and not get stuck at the bottom. So I had to make time and devote the energy to them. But it was still pretty much fine because Luke was travelling most weeks so we partied hard at the weekends, and every weekend was like starting over together. But eventually I realised the weekends for him were just an extension of the week – don't get me wrong, he's very professional, very good at what he does, but in the evenings wherever he is he hits the bars and so far as he's concerned I'm nowhere and he does what he wants, takes what he wants. So the weekends really aren't that special, just more of the same, except I'm there to keep the flat tidy and do all the food and the cleaning and that.'

He paused for a few minutes and then continued: 'God, I sound like a golf widow, don't I? And I hate hearing myself sound like this – it isn't really me. Luke's favourite saying is something from Warhol: 'One's company, two's a party and three's a crowd'. I'm not sure what Warhol meant, but I think Luke says it to emphasise how much he likes a good time! But it hasn't been a good time for me, not for a long while.'

I reflected that this catchphrase sounded rather ambiguous since the more usual phrase might be 'two's company, three's a crowd'. If you say 'one's company' perhaps it means you're self-sufficient? I wondered how he understood it?

> Mike: That's weird, I never thought of it before. It sounds like the exact opposite of how he is – I mean he just never behaves as though he's self-sufficient, he always seems to have someone in tow … if not me then some casual pick-up. And he's always in a crowd in the sense that he's never happier than when he's in a disco or a nightclub.

I said that I was feeling a bit puzzled too, but one of the things I was picking up, one of the things this sense of puzzlement underscored, was that perhaps there were some aspects of Luke he didn't know a lot about, just as there were aspects of Mike that Luke wasn't aware of. I felt a bit surprised since, when I thought about an 'open relationship', I imagined there would be a lot of discussion about how each partner was feeling.

> Mike: did not pursue this but continued: And I'm not just having a selfish moan here. I'm also worried for him. I mean he doesn't see it this way, but I think he's running all kinds of risks. He tells me he's in control, but it's obvious to me that if he's on his own and taking God knows what, and in any kind of combination, and then going off with people he's never met in his life ... And when I say any of this to him direct he just says, 'Oh this is your nursing training coming out, you used to be so much more chilled', so I feel he's pushing me away and trashing me as a professional at the same time.

I asked Mike how he felt about Luke meeting other people when he was away on business.

> Mike: Well, I used to be pretty much OK with it, and in fact we prided ourselves on not being jealous and being able to have a kind of open relationship.
>
> Me: You used to ...?

This seemed to pull Mike up short, and he reflected that, thinking about it now, their open relationship was increasingly more Luke's ideal than his:

> Mike: I mean, I didn't object and we were going around with a group where that was the norm. We were very clear about boundaries: no sex with friends, and no overnight stays. But Luke always took advantage of this arrangement more than me. I never said anything because I liked the feeling that I could play around a bit if I wanted, but I rarely did. And Luke's always had more confidence than me. He can pick people up without trying, so on some level I thought this was a good deal – better to agree to some playing away than risk losing him altogether. But frankly I think he's become a bit of a sex addict, on top of everything else.

> Me: I have a sense, listening to you, that you have been unhappy about at least some aspects of your relationship with Luke for quite a while. And you say, in a jokey way, that you sound like a 'golf widow', and you don't recognise yourself. Then you say that actually you're worried for him and you think he is a sex addict. But I don't hear you saying clearly to Luke what it is you want and don't want in a straightforward way, in an open manner. It seems a little as though you assume that there is something about being in an 'open relationship' which automatically allows each of you to know what the other wants, but my sense is that this type of relationship can only thrive if both parties invest time and effort into checking in with each other and making decisions about how they want it to evolve. I imagine it's even more hard work than a monogamous relationship!

Mike looked very thoughtful at this, and then reflected that he had taken to assuming that, as it was 'open', Luke would 'see' what was going on for him, without having to be told. I reflected that it sounded like a kind of magic – that the very fact of calling it 'open' somehow automatically meant each could see what the other wanted without the need for discussion.

> Mike: Yes, in a way. I feel very 'adult' and 'serious' now with the idea we need to keep talking about the relationship. And it's not that we didn't talk about what we wanted at the beginning; then it felt rather daring and revolutionary – the opposite of what my parents stand for. But the idea of talking about it now feels frightening because we probably want different things.

I asked Mike if he could imagine sharing these thoughts with Luke in our next session, and he left the session saying he would think about it.

Session four

I generally use this session to meet with the couple together, reflect with them on their experience of the previous two sessions, and relate what was explored in each session to their couple-construct. Rather to my surprise, given their limited level of interaction in our first session, I discovered that they had spent a considerable amount of time during the past two weeks discussing what had happened in their individual sessions with me. It seemed their curiosity about these sessions had enabled them to move away, at least to a degree, from their recent conflictual way of relating.

I reflected that it seemed they had managed to talk about some quite sensitive issues in a constructive way, and I wondered how they had done this. They responded that it was only in our sessions that they had realised how close they were to breaking up and this realisation encouraged them to risk being more honest with each other than they had been previously. Mike said that he discovered how angry he was with Luke over their open relationship, but that this had been quickly replaced by the realisation that he had agreed to it, and so was equally responsible for their situation. Luke told Mike that he increasingly felt judged for his drug and alcohol use, but he also reflected that part of his anger about this was that he feared he was increasingly using substances to help him cope on a daily basis. He had been able in our individual session to acknowledge the extent to which he used drugs and recreational sex to avoid intimacy.

> Mike: I mentioned that odd thing about 'One's company, two's a party and three's a crowd' to Luke and we figured out it really should be 'Three's company, two's a crowd'.
>
> Luke: I don't feel great admitting this, but I'm happiest on my own – or maybe not happiest, but least stressed. I'm not good at intimacy, so if it's not just me, then the next best thing is a crowd, and the most challenging thing of all is being a couple. There, I've said it and I'm not proud of it. But I can't take it back! A lot of the time two really is a crowd so far as I'm concerned!

I shared my sense of them as a couple, saying that it seemed they had initially agreed to create a relationship that provided them both with a measure of freedom. This freedom was expressed in terms of a relaxed attitude to drugs and recreational sex. The relationship was 'open' in the sense that they maintained a fairly flexible boundary and did not impose rules on each other. For a while this agreement seemed to work well for both of them, but my sense was that such flexible boundaries needed to be regularly discussed and renegotiated, and required more attention than more rigid boundaries where there was greater clarity about what could be inside a relationship, and what must be excluded. I wondered whether, for an 'open' relationship to endure, they needed to ensure they nurtured their couple-construct, since this was the base to which they would return having played away. It seemed to me that their initial notion of an 'open' relationship had not included agreement about what to do if either member of the couple pushed the boundaries. At the same time, they seemed to assume that each knew what the other wanted, without detailed discussion. In the absence of regular consideration of their individual beliefs, values and assumptions about their relationship – a willingness to regularly enter each other's worldview – they had each adopted an increasingly rigid view of the other: Mike increasingly saw Luke through the lens of 'addiction', and rejected him since a relationship with an addict did not fit with his new sense of self as a responsible professional; Luke, meanwhile, increasingly viewed Mike as an authority figure who had reneged on their open relationship and was now busy setting him up as an 'addict'. It seemed, paradoxically, that each felt limited, even imprisoned, by their open relationship; what had been intended to be open to what life had to offer was now experienced by both of them as closed to possibilities, including, perhaps, the possibility of change. Neither was able to see their couple-construct from the position of the other.

Luke and Mike agreed that my description of their relationship did broadly capture their own sense of the situation. At this point, and given that we were approaching the end of our session, I thought it would be helpful to encourage them to share their reaction to hearing each other's understanding of their couple-construct, and I asked them to address each other directly. The act of turning to each other and the request that they speak directly to each other was cathartic: both were visibly shaken and moved. Mike spoke first and said he had not realised before the extent to which he had withdrawn from Luke, and was shocked to hear how different his image of them as a couple was from Luke's image. He said he couldn't believe how powerful it felt to say this to Luke, and have him listen rather than walk away. Luke responded that he felt for the first time that he had an accurate picture of their relationship, and it was not how he had imagined it.

Session five

This session felt rather more sober and less energised than the previous session. In session four I felt that Luke and Mike were reporting to me on the extent to which they had found new motivation to talk to each other, and were recounting to me how the experience of sharing their emotional lives together again had given them a sense of being a couple once more. They had discovered, and were shocked by, the extent to which they had come to hold different expectations of being in relationship, and they had left the session optimistic that this, in itself, might be enough to enable them to get past their difficulties and move on. I was pleased that both recognised that they had made a start on reinventing their relationship, but I was concerned to check with them at the beginning of this session whether they were still in this optimistic place, since I felt that there was considerably more work ahead if they were to continue as a couple. They both acknowledged that they did not know if they would be able to refashion their relationship to the extent that would offer them enough reason to stay together.

Luke seemed to have moved quite a long way already, though, as he said that he felt motivated for his own sake on reaching a deeper understanding of his use of drugs and recreational sex; at this point he could not tell how this might impact on his relationship with Mike. Mike, for his part, recognised that he had to some extent excluded Luke from his new life, and acknowledged that he had fallen into the habit of relating to him in the way he related to substance users in his workplace. He felt shocked that he had done this, and, at the same time, was not sure how Luke could be part of this new life; if Luke really did think 'two was a crowd', perhaps he did not actually want to be with Mike at all.

Though both were clearly daunted by the issues their new perspective on their relationship threw up, they agreed at the end of the session to contract for five more meetings. I was not particularly surprised at our next meeting that Mike attended alone. He told me that they had agreed to take a break from their relationship and they both intended to pursue individual therapy. As he explained, they had come to the realisation in the course of their work with me that their relationship no longer provided them with the freedom which they had initially sought. The fact that they had taken their relationship for granted seemed, on reflection, indicative of the way they had fallen into the habit of taking each other for granted. In couple therapy they had first thought that this realisation alone might provide a solution to their dilemma, but when they discovered that this insight was the beginning of a journey rather than the destination, they realised they were not motivated enough to continue.

The experience of couple therapy had, though, provided them with motivation to continue in individual therapy. Luke had no previous experience of therapy and now wanted to work on his reliance on drugs and recreational sex. Mike had been shocked to discover the extent to which he had distanced himself from Luke and had attributed all their difficulties to

Luke's 'addictions'. With regard to their relationship, it seemed both had arrived at an enhanced appreciation of the challenges of creating a flexible couple-construct, and a greater understanding of what each meant by the word 'freedom'.

Concluding reflection

I have outlined my way of working with couples (and in this case a couple presenting with issues of addiction) in the hope that this may assist other existential-phenomenological practitioners to clarify their own approach in this area. I have drawn on theory and practice which I have developed over a number of years (2000, 2002, 2007; du Plock & Fisher, 2005). I am indebted to Spinelli (1997/2006, 2007) for his investigation of relational dimensions of therapeutic encounter. My own approach in this area is grounded in the understanding that it is only in the course of careful clarification of their couple-construct that the members of a couple can obtain the sense of agency which will enable them to decide whether they wish to continue or change their way of being in relationship. This clarification can enable the couple to generate a more sustaining couple-construct, but it may also, as it did for Luke and Mike, lead them to decide that their individual needs cannot be met within the existing couple-construct. We might conclude, in this case, that the therapy has in some sense 'failed', but this would be a mistake, since the realisation by the partners of the ways in which their current couple-construct is untenable can also provide them with the possibility to part on the basis of greater insight which may provide a resource for future personal relationships. Privately I reflected that while much of our work had focused on their different views on addiction, perhaps the true addiction was a shared one: an addiction to the concept of an open relationship that never really existed.

References

Cohn, HW (1997) *Existential Thought and Therapeutic Practice: An introduction to existential psychotherapy*. London: Sage Publications.

Du Plock, S (2000) Gifts of life: An existential-phenomenological approach to shopping addiction. In A Baker (Ed) *Serious Shopping: Essays on consumerism and psychotherapy* (pp. 73–94). London: Sage Publications.

Du Plock, S (2002) Some reflections on an existential-phenomenological approach to addiction. *Existential Analysis*, *13*(1), 83–90.

Du Plock, S (2007) The world of addiction. In E van Deurzen & S Young (Eds) *Existential Perspectives on Supervision. Widening the horizon of psychotherapy and counselling* (pp. 67–77). Basingstoke: Palgrave Macmillan.

Du Plock, S & Fisher, J (2005) An existential perspective on addiction. In E van Deurzen & C Arnold-Baker (Eds) *Existential Perspectives on Human Issues: A handbook for therapeutic practice* (pp. 67–77). Basingstoke: Palgrave Macmillan.

May, R (1983) *The Discovery of Being. Writings in existential psychology*. New York: WW Norton & Co.

May, R, Angel, E & Ellenberger, HF (Eds) (1958) *Existence: A new dimension in psychiatry and psychology*. New York: Basic Books.

Sartre, J-P (1943) *Being and Nothingness: An essay on phenomenological ontology* (HE Barnes, Trans). London: Methuen.

Spinelli, E (1994) *Demystifying Therapy*. London: Constable. (Republished 2006, PCCS Books)

Spinelli, E (1997) *Tales of Un-knowing: Therapeutic encounters from an existential perspective*. London: Duckworth. (Republished 2006, PCCS Books)

Spinelli, E (2007) *Practising Existential Psychotherapy. The relational world*. London: Sage Publications.

Van Deurzen, E & Iacovou, S (Eds) (2013) *Existential Perspectives on Couple Therapy*. London: Palgrave Macmillan.

16

Family Therapy and Sexuality: Liminal possibilities between systemic and existential approaches

– Dr Alex Iantaffi –

This chapter is an exploration, from a systemic perspective, of how existential themes might be useful in family therapy, especially when approaching issues of sex and sexuality. I am using sex and sexuality as distinct terms here to indicate acts and behaviours with the first, and identities with the latter. It is, of course, impossible to fully extricate one from the other, as identities can also be linked to acts and behaviours, yet it remains useful to at least distinguish where the primary focus might be at any given discussion point.

Unlike some of the other chapters in this book, this one does not take a purist existential perspective. I am a systemic psychotherapist, working under the large professional umbrella of family therapy, and I have been influenced by existential perspectives. I believe the body of work on existential family therapy is yet to be more fully developed. I hope that the book in its entirety will provide the reader with a multifaceted understanding of existential therapy, and its intersection with other approaches, such as family therapy. Nevertheless, I hope this chapter will be of use to both existential therapists working with families, and to family therapists looking at integrating existential perspectives.

Locating family therapy

Family therapy could be defined as an interdisciplinary approach, since it was born from, and influenced by, a range of therapeutic schools

(Goldenberg, Goldenberg & Goldenberg, 2012). The influence of these schools, and the various perspectives within them, varies by geographical context, historical moment, cultural heritage and political climate. It would be beyond the scope of this chapter to provide a detailed and comprehensive history of family therapy. Nevertheless, before considering how existential perspectives might inform family therapy, I would like to spend some time introducing what I consider to be key characteristics of family therapy. I will also discuss how sexuality has, or has not, played a major role in this field so far.

One of the major innovations of family therapy was to consider relational and systemic issues. How those issues might be theorised and addressed varies significantly between theoretical schools, yet the emphasis on system remains. Many approaches consider both micro systems, within individual family systems, and macro systems within which families form and operate. For example, gender, race and class systems might be considered within the therapy room by exploring both the influence of those macro stories on a family and its members, and the way that families and individuals contribute to actively shaping stories about those macro systems. The relationship between macro and micro, outer and inner systems, is often seen as moving in both directions, and the influence of those systems can be considered to be circular.

As family therapy became influenced by feminist and social constructionist perspectives, the issue of what systems are considered has also been discussed in the field. Hare-Mustin (1994) uses the analogy of a therapy room as a mirrored room. Within a mirrored room what is reflected back is what is present. Therefore, usually, views, identities and systems of privilege present in the mainstream culture are also most influential in the therapy room, if we are not watchful and intentional. Within social constructionist approaches to family therapy, reflexivity becomes central, as systems are approached critically both inside and outside of the therapy room. Reflexivity in this context is not just individual, but also relational (Burnham, 2005).

This systemic, critical, and relationally reflexive approach to family therapy has the potential to accommodate a broad range of views and stories, and it was personally what attracted me to train in systemic psychotherapy (still labelled marriage and family therapy in the US). Nevertheless, family therapy was also born within specific geographical, racial, and historical perspectives, which privilege a certain construct of 'family' (Cecchin, Lane, & Ray, 1994). Within this construct, which I would argue is a heteronormative one, family therapy has traditionally not included a broad range of perspectives on sex and sexualities (Iantaffi,

2010), despite the fact that these could be considered to be key components in many families.

In fact the field of sex therapy seems to have developed into its own domain and, although there are some family therapists who specialise in it, this is not a widespread occurrence. My hypothesis is that a heteronormative view of family does not leave much space for sex and sexualities. Heteronormativity in fact is more than just the systemic supremacy of a heterosexual orientation in many societies, such as in the UK and the US. As Warner (1993) explains, it includes constructs of whiteness, class, and education privilege, and gender as a binary where masculinity and femininity are their own, distinct domains. Within this view, sexualities become homogenous and invisible, and sex is reduced to reproduction and relegated within the realm of medicine and more mechanistic approaches to sexual health.

I would argue that generally family therapy as a discipline has so far failed to embrace the possibilities for bringing sex and sexualities into the therapy room. It seems to be unacceptable to place constructs such as 'family' and 'sex' into the same arena. The former has been politicised and idolised as a unit within which issues of sex and intimacy are discussed only if what is considered to be 'pathology' arises (e.g. low desire, erectile dysfunction). When those issues are discussed it is usually within dyadic systems, as couples are considered to be the only acceptable location for sex and sexualities within families. Sex and sexualities as macro systems, as well as micro systems affecting all family members including children are rarely, if ever, discussed in family therapy. In fact, I believe that family therapy training does not generally provide a solid foundation for therapists to be able to work with adults, young people, or children around issues of sex and sexuality.

As well as only discussing sex when something is 'not working', which assumes a norm and creates pathology rather than encouraging a range of diverse stories and possibilities (Barker, 2011, and this volume), sexualities are usually only brought into the family therapy room when they are seen as 'other'. For example, parents might bring up their child's sexuality if said child is suspected to be, or comes out as anything other than heterosexual. Similarly, gender is often discussed in a way that reinforces binary, biological and psychological differences (e.g. women's and men's differing communication styles), unless someone in the family systems has a transgender and/or gender non-conforming identity.

Those conversations often reflect back who is present in the room as a therapist, since family therapists are also sexual beings, with their own experiences, stories, and embodiments. I believe it is often in this intersection between the therapist's own sexuality and those of the family systems in the room that possibilities for existential approaches become most clearly manifested.

On being a family therapist

Family therapists often see systems in moments of crisis. In a paper discussing existentialism and family therapy, Haldane and McCluskey describe families who come to therapy as 'trapped in repetitive patterns of behaviour and relationships which maintain the status quo and inhibit development, maturation and individuation' (Haldane & McCluskey, 1982: 122). The description goes on in a similar pessimistic fashion, perpetuating both the assumption that families only come to therapy when in pain, and that there is a 'healthy', and 'correct' way of being a family, that is, being able to develop, mature and individuate. However, they also highlight that an existential approach to family therapy is focused on relational reflexivity, negotiating goals with the family, rather than diagnosing either the individual or the system. These descriptions seem to be paradoxical: assuming there is a universal model of 'healthy family' on one side, and wanting to move away from pathologising individuals or family systems. I believe such paradox is embedded in how many of us are trained, and how we are asked to practise on a day-to-day basis. Most therapists are given models of what a 'healthy' individual or family looks like. Even though we might be presented with multiple models, most of those are still informed by dominant discourses, such as heteronormativity, white privilege, ableism, and so on. Furthermore, those discourses inform the professional systems we interact with: licensing bodies, health insurance, and diagnostic matrices (e.g. *ICD*, *DSM*). At the same time, most therapists, especially those educated within systemic and/or existentialist perspectives, learn to privilege relational reflexivity, and usually have a genuine desire to move away from externally defined pathology models and towards client-defined wellness models. Before a client or therapist has even moved into the therapy room, there is a complex, paradoxical context in existence, which influences the ways in which they can meet with one another, in a therapeutic manner.

The steps of an existential approach to family therapy that is focused on relational reflexivity and negotiating goals with the family, rather than diagnosing either individual or the system, require the therapist to *be with* the family rather than *work on*, or for the family. This can be a challenge given that many approaches to family therapy include interventions and ways to interact with family systems to disrupt habitual patterns and behaviours. Being with a family during moments of crisis and/or change requires the capacity to be present with both ourselves and the clients. If we are still making sense of our own reactions to what is being talked about in the therapy room, our capacity to be present with our clients can be affected. I believe this can often be the case when sex and sexuality are brought up in the therapy room, since therapists are not often invited to reflect on their own positions in relation to their sexual behaviours, identities, and experiences. This seems to be part of the paradoxical context where part of the normative discourse is that sex and sexuality are assumed to be heternormative, monosexual, and private. This can be best illustrated with an example. At a workshop given as part of a conference for marriage and family therapists in the US, I invited participants to explore their own life journeys with regard to their beliefs about sex and sexuality. They were invited to individually map influences on their current belief system through a visual technique called 'rivers of experience' (Iantaffi, 2011). Although everyone engaged in the exercise, there was some discussion of how this approach 'felt like therapy'. It seems that trainee therapists are more willing to turn their lens on clients than on themselves, especially when it comes to matters of sex and sexuality, which are considered to be personal and private within the mainstream culture we live in. Eventually, most participants seemed to be engaged with exploring their own journeys, and how those might have shaped their presence with clients in the therapy room. However, this was not something they had often, if ever, been invited to consider before.

If we accept that our knowledge is always situated (Shotter, 1993; Spinelli, 2007), and that our embodied experiences (Merleau-Ponty, 2002; Shotter & Katz, 1998) shape who we are and how we interact with others, exploring our own position in relation to sex and sexualities become paramount for our development as therapists. This means not only exploring our position in relationship to other people's sex lives and sexualities, but also rather becoming increasingly aware of our own, embodied experience of sex and sexuality. From this perspective, we hold the paradox of recognising our common humanity, through our desire to make meaning of our lives (Frankl, 1978), while also being prepared not to make assumption about our clients, whether we regard them to be similar or different from us. This can be far more challenging than it seems at first sight. The assumption of heteronormativity, which includes as discussed earlier a range of other constructs such as whiteness, class, education, ableism, and gender as a binary, is so ingrained in the mainstream culture that it manifests in our very being (Griffin, 2007). For example, over the past few years, most conversations I have been involved in, or witnessed, about disclosure of sexual orientation with clients have always been centred on disclosure of non-heterosexual orientations. It seems to be rare for heterosexual therapists to consider their daily, routine acts of disclosure, such as wearing a marriage band, or possibly having a picture of their child in their office, or embodying gender in a way that conforms to societal expectations. Yet queer or transgender therapists might self-scrutinise, as well as being scrutinised by colleagues, employers, and possibly clients, especially when working with children or young people, since the latter are often seen as people who need to be 'protected' from sex and sexuality, and especially from queer sex and sexualities.

Even in a field generally as progressive as that of therapy, it seems that Rubin's model of sexual legitimacy (1984), which identifies some identities and behaviours as belonging to an 'inner, charmed circle' of legitimacy, and some to be outside of that circle and therefore being seen as deviant, can still be a way of making sense of many interactions in the family therapy room. What is considered to be within the circle and outside the circle might have shifted slightly in the past two decades, yet the confines of the circle seem to be far narrower than human experiences. In similar ways, the confines of what is considered to be a family have somewhat shifted, but the therapeutic tools used by therapists, such as genograms, are mainly based on particular systems. For example, even though recently genogram symbols have been revisited to include a symbol for transgender identities, this still seems to reinforce the gender binary by implying that there are 'men', 'women', and 'transgender people'. The latter becomes a catchall category, within which there is not much room for gender identity and expression beyond the process of being othered as not cisgender.[1] To stay with the example of the genogram, this tool is also challenging when mapping non-monogamous relationships and families, as well as larger family systems, both of origin and of choice.

Beyond the confines of mainstream culture, legitimacy, and therapeutic tools, lie, in my opinion, what Yalom, arguably one of the most prominent, contemporary US existential therapists, (1980) defines as the 'givens' of

---

1. 'A cisgender person is a person who is content to remain the gender they were assigned at birth – thus if you identify as the gender on your birth certificate then you are cisgender' (Richards, this volume).

human existence: our mortality, isolation, meaninglessness, and freedom. How families deal with those givens is also a systemic issue. Both micro and macro systems shape how we interact with those givens, our beliefs about them, and the way we make meaning individually, and as family systems. For example, our faith system might make meaning of mortality and freedom in particular ways, and those might come into tension with an individual or even a whole family system's experience in times of crisis. Similarly, family therapists have their own personal relationships with those givens, which shape their professional interactions in the therapy room. Family therapists' intimacy with their own meaning-making around those givens, especially in relation to sex and sexualities, and an awareness of the variety of meaning-making stories and divergent experiential realities clients inhabit, hold potential for transformative therapeutic encounters, where therapists can sit together with families, and be fully present.

Existential invitations to address sex and sexuality in family therapy

Other, more experienced authors have written about existentialism in family therapy (Haldane & McClusky, 1982; Lantz, 1993; Lantz & Gyamerah, 2002; Whitaker, Greenberg & Greenberg, 1981). They highlighted how both existentialism and family therapy are influenced by a range of perspectives, and how they have intersected historically in various ways. I would now like to reflect on what opportunities there might be for family therapists when adopting an existential framework in their discussions of sex and sexuality with their clients.

First of all, existential therapists have a role to play in challenging the medical model of diagnosing and labelling parts of human existence, including sex and sexualities, that might be seen as being located 'outside the charmed circle' of legitimacy (Barker, 2011, this volume). This stance, of privileging the client's meaning-making over the meaning-making of dominant discourse, offers possibilities for the family therapist to approach families from a range of lenses. For example, as a queer, gender non-conforming person I have often listened to straight couples and families from a slightly different perspective. My very embodiment in the room tends to challenge easy alignments around gender for many clients, which can open possibilities for new dialogues to emerge. For example, when working with couples I have found myself listening to clients talk about how oppressive gendered expectations have been in their sexualities and their sex lives. When working with families, especially families with transgender, and/or gender non-conforming children and young people, my being in the room and asking everyone what their preferred gender pronouns are displaces the assumption that there is no choice around gender, and opens up freedom of choice around everyone taking a position in relation to gender and language. My being in the room as a family therapist with these same families also reflects back a slightly different reality from that promoted by mainstream culture's values, and can both challenge and soothe some of the anxieties families bring to the therapeutic table.

From an existential perspective, the *Umwelt*, the physical dimension (Binswanger, 1963; van Deurzen, 2001), experienced in the present, in the therapy room was shifted in some of those cases. However, those shifts are not only possible through embodying identities outside the circle, even though this can be powerful in some therapeutic encounters. They are also possible through literally opening up space through therapeutic questioning and listening. For example, asking age-appropriate questions around sex and sexualities in family therapy settings can be a powerful way of exploring new existential possibilities for clients. Acknowledging that sex and sexualities are experiences that are with us throughout the life course, and that our embodied experiences of them will change over time, and that those experiences impact our family dynamics in a range of ever-changing ways, can be a powerful way to expand the family's perceptions of what is happening for them on both individual and systemic levels. When working with families where an older sibling is coming out as queer and/or transgender, for example, families tend to leave out individuals who are considered 'too old' or 'too young' to understand what is happening. However, these people are often sharing space with the same family system and are affected by the conversations happening, as well as by the changes in these systems. Inviting clients to acknowledge the physical reality of sharing space with those family members usually leads to more explicit choices as to whether to include them or exclude them from those conversations. In my experience, often families choose to include those family members and find that their relationships improve once the physical reality of change in their family system is acknowledged.

On the *Mitwelt*, the social dimension (Binswanger, 1963; van Deurzen, 2001), family therapy has much to offer when approaching sex and sexualities. A systemic perspective can invite both therapist and client to explore how they position themselves in relation to both macro stories shaping their experiences of sex and sexualities, and to each other. This dimension is for me one of the places to hold the paradox of interconnectedness and individuality. Personally, accepting the limitations of my humanity, as well as the unavoidable feeling of separateness at times help me to feel connected to others through our shared experience of these existential stories. One of the ways in which this can manifest when discussing sex and sexuality in family therapy is in conversations about individual agency and embodiment, and relational negotiations. Moving away from the mainstream culture's tendency to see sex and sexuality as deeply personal as well as 'normative' can reveal possibilities for mutual listening in family systems, and contribute to the creation of shared meanings, which can be continuously renegotiated as our individual and relational experiences grow. For example, when working with families where there might be a high level of stress due to the recent birth of a child, exploring societal, gendered, cultural, and individual expectations about sex and sexuality can support families in choosing a preferred position in relation to these expectations, and in creating stories in which there can be a higher degree of felt freedom.

In existential terms, the *Eigenwelt*, the psychological dimension (Binswanger, 1963; van Deurzen, 2001), invites therapists and clients to explore the sense of self and any attachments to individuality. In this dimension the focus is personal and private. When considering family therapy around sex and sexuality, this plane is about the moments where clients might be making sense of their own feelings, reactions, thought processes and stories around relational issues. For example, parents who have come out to teenage or adult children as queer or transgender might need some time to make sense of their children's reaction, whatever this might be, and explore the impact of those reactions on their sense of self. When exploring this dimension I find Harré's ideas (1998) around the self as situated, and therefore not singular, to be supportive of processes of personal transformation. The latter might be related to a deepening relationship of clients and therapists with themselves, or simply to changes occurring due to ageing, which also have an impact on our experiences of sex and sexuality.

The *Überwelt*, the spiritual dimension (van Deurzen, 2001), can be challenging when discussing sex and sexualities in family therapy if rigid or dogmatic views are held in a way that closes possibilities for dialogue. Yet it can also be a rich dimension for intimacy and growth. For example, when working with a range of young Christian couples facing various barriers to sexual intimacy, paying attention to this dimension was essential for the therapeutic encounter to be possible in the first place, and to truly listen to the meaning-making occurring individually, relationally, and at a faith-community level. Using family therapy tools, such as bringing key informants into the room, either literally, or through the use of narrative techniques, allowed the emergence of concerns and experiences on the other dimensions, which could then be listened to in a way that felt welcoming and authentic. Many of those couples in fact might have approached therapy as a place where they feared being asked to do something uncomfortable and contradictory to their spiritual beliefs. Once they realised that their spiritual dimension was being given space and attention, they were able to explore the challenges that had brought them to therapy more fully and with increased openness to self-determined possibilities.

Conclusion

These dimensions are not separate from each other, and as therapists we do not come into contact with them in a linear fashion or in neat boxes. Families and individuals are complex systems, operating in circular and multilayered dynamics. Both existential approaches and family therapy tools can help therapists in making sense of what happens in the therapy room. Traditionally, neither one of those approaches, nor the philosophical schools within them, might have approached sex and sexualities directly. However, I believe that both approaches have the potential to create new realities for therapists, therapy training, and therapeutic relationships when considering many of the values underlining them. Family therapy can certainly help us to better understand the relational dimensions of sex and sexuality, the macro and micro stories shaping them on individual and systemic levels, and privilege relational reflexivity lenses to ensure a dialogue between therapists and clients, where the latter feel a degree of agency and freedom. Existential approaches to family therapy can enhance these tools by providing a theoretical framework for those dialogues in which therapists can listen for both dissonance and resonance, recognising the paradox of diverging realities and common human processes of meaning-making. When used together those can be powerful tools for liberation, enhancing the capacity of the therapy room to no longer be a purely mirrored room that reflects back a limited number of possibilities, but rather a spacious locus for a transformative therapeutic encounter.

References

Barker, M (2011) Existential sex therapy. *Sexual and Relationship Therapy*, *26*(1), 33–47.

Barker, M (2014) Existential sex therapy. In M Milton (Ed) *Sexuality: Existential perspectives* (pp. 285–304). Ross-on-Wye: PCCS Books.

Binswanger, L (1963) *Being-in-the-World: Selected papers of Ludwig Binswanger.* New York: Basic Books.

Burnham, J (2005) Relational reflexivity: A tool for socially constructing therapeutic relationships. In C Flaskas, B Mason & A Perlesz (Eds) *The Space Between: Experience, context and process in the therapeutic relationship* (pp. 1–17). London: Karnac Books.

Cecchin, G, Lane, G & Ray, WA (1994) *The Cybernetics of Prejudices in the Practice of Psychotherapy.* London: Karnac Books.

Frankl, V (1978) *The Unheard Cry for Meaning: Psychotherapy and humanism.* New York: Simon & Schuster.

Goldenberg, H, Goldenberg, I & Goldenberg, SM (2012) *Family Therapy: An overview.* Belmont, CA: Brooks/Cole.

Griffin, P (2007) Sexing the economy in a neo-liberal world order: Neo-liberal discourse and the (re)production of heteronormative heterosexuality. *The British Journal of Politics & International Relations*, *9*(2), 220–38.

Haldane, D & McCluskey, U (1982) Existentialism and family therapy: A neglected perspective. *Journal of Family Therapy*, *4*(2), 117–32.

Hare-Mustin, RT (1994) Discourses in the mirrored room: A postmodern analysis of therapy. *Family Process*, *33*(1), 19–35.

Harré, R (1998) *The Singular Self: An introduction to the psychology of personhood.* London: Sage Publications.

Iantaffi, A (2010) Queer family therapy: A contradiction in terms? In L Moon (Ed) *Counselling Ideologies: Queer challenges to heteronormativity* (pp. 51–70). Farnham: Ashgate.

Iantaffi, A (2011) Travelling along 'rivers of experience': Personal construct psychology and visual metaphors in research. In P Reavey (Ed) *Visual Psychologies: Using and interpreting images in qualitative research* (pp. 271–83). London: Routledge.

Lantz, JE (1993) *Existential Family Therapy: Using the concepts of Viktor Frankl.* Upper Saddle River, NJ: Jason Aronson.

Lantz, J & Gyamerah, J (2002) Existential family trauma therapy. *Contemporary Family Therapy*, *24*(2), 243–55.

Merleau-Ponty, M (2002) *The Phenomenology of Perception.* London: Routledge.

Richards, C (2014). Trans and existential-phenomenological practice. In M Milton (Ed) *Sexuality: Existential perspectives* (pp. 217–30). Ross-on-Wye: PCCS Books.

Rubin, G (1984) Thinking sex: Notes for a radical theory on the politics of sexuality. In C Vance (Ed) *Pleasure and Danger: Exploring female sexuality* (pp. 267–319). New York: Routledge.

Shotter, J (1993) *Conversational Realities*. London: Sage Publications.

Shotter, J & Katz, AM (1998) Creating relational realities: Responsible responding to poetic 'movements' and 'moments'. In S McNamee & KJ Gergen (Eds) *Relational Responsibility: Resources for sustainable dialogue* (pp. 151–61). London: Sage Publications.

Spinelli, E (2007) *Practising Existential Psychotherapy. The relational world*. London: Sage Publications.

Van Deurzen, E (2001) *Existential Counselling and Psychotherapy in Practice*. London: Sage Publications.

Warner, M (1993) *Fear of a Queer Planet: Queer politics and social theory*. Minneapolis, MN: University of Minnesota Press.

Whitaker, CA, Greenberg, A & Greenberg, ML (1981) Existential marital therapy: A synthesis, a subsystem of existential family therapy. In G Pirooz Sholevar (Ed) *The Handbook of Marriage and Marital Therapy* (pp. 181–217). New York: Spectrum.

Yalom, ID (1980) *Existential Psychotherapy*. New York: Basic Books.

Epilogue

– Prof. Martin Milton –

I hope that, like me, the reader will have found this volume stimulating, unsettling and thought-provoking. I am delighted with this volume and with the individual efforts of all the authors and I think it has the potential to be an important contribution to the field of existential psychotherapy and to the wider fields that engage critically with our efforts to understand sex and sexuality. I look forward to the debates as they unfold and the new and critical thinking that may progress our understandings of these most intimate of experiences. Because progress we must. While we have become clearer and treat people's sexuality with more respect and understanding than we used to, we must not be complacent. So this is not the final word, this book is but a modest contribution to an ongoing debate in relation to sexuality.

While existential perspectives are being drawn upon to explore and enrich our understanding of a range of topics, due to limits of time and space and the wider cultural *Zeitgeist*, there are many experiences and phenomena that we could not explore in this volume. We therefore hope that this book will function as encouragement to those thinkers and practitioners who are interested in these and other topics.

Some of the topics we have not covered have long been of interest to sexologists, and so are ripe for an existential contribution. For instance, we were not able to include a chapter on being homophobic; while some authors have made mention of it, this volume does not include a whole chapter on the meaning and uses of 'pornography'; nor does it explore the relationship of pleasure to pain nor of the practices associated with BDSM. The volume was also not able to consider some of the more existential-sociological manifestations of sexual identities such as 'butch', 'femme', 'fairy' nor social phenomena associated with sexuality, such as 'camp'.

Another area we have only touched on briefly contains topics more usually associated with forensic psychologists, topics such as the relationship between sex and violence whether that be rape, intimate partner abuse, intergenerational sexual abuse or sex as an instrument of war. These are important topics in their own regard but they are also important because we are currently in a *Zeitgeist* that assumes aggression and sexual desire are mutually exclusive phenomena, yet we know of course that much fruitful and creative sexuality has components of both. To leave this unconsidered runs the risk of pathologising even consensual and loving sexual intimacy when the aggressive aspect is recognised.

Sexuality is not a static experience, neither personally nor culturally. Some of the other topics we could not attend to are relatively new phenomena, topics such as people's experiences with technologically mediated relationships and online sexuality, for example, Internet dating, 'sexting', telephone and forum sex, etc. These are already offering people exciting and creative ways of interacting as well as us hearing about people's responses of shame, guilt and anxiety.

These are not simply topics of interest to those in some academic ivory tower; these are issues that concern the clients who consult us and the services in which we work. These are topics that require as wide a reflection as is possible and not to contribute may well be to limit our clients, our culture and ourselves to an impoverished understanding of a central and crucial aspect of being. So whether it is a contribution to existing topics or potential contributions to new and poorly understood experiences, we hope that this book plays its part in that ongoing exploration.

Contributors

The Editor

Prof. Martin Milton is a chartered psychologist and registered existential psychotherapist. He is director of counselling psychology programmes at Regent's University London School of Psychotherapy and Psychology. Martin's two recent edited books are *Therapy and Beyond: Counselling psychology contributions to therapeutic and social issues* (Wiley-Blackwell, 2010) and *Diagnosis and Beyond: Counselling psychology contributions to understanding human distress* (PCCS Books, 2012). In addition he has published in a range of academic journals that focus on sexuality and is on the editorial board of *Existential Analysis* and *Psychology of Sexualities Review* (formerly *Lesbian and Gay Psychology Review*). He was one of the recipients of the 2012 British Psychological Society awards for the Promoting of Equality of Opportunity.

Contributors

Dr Meg-John Barker is a senior lecturer in psychology at the Open University and a UKCP accredited existential therapist working in sex and relationship counselling. Meg has published co-edited collections on non-monogamies and sadomasochism with Darren Langdridge and the two of them also co-edit the journal *Psychology & Sexuality* through Taylor and Francis. Meg's research on sexualities and relationships has been published in many journals and books and has culminated recently in a general audience book called *Rewriting the Rules* (www.rewriting-the-rules.com). Meg regularly provides training for counsellors, therapists and other practitioners on working with people in openly non-monogamous relationships, and has written a chapter covering this in *Sexuality and Gender for Counsellors, Psychologists and Health Professionals: A practical guide* (with Christina Richards, Sage Publications, 2013).

Contributors – 339

Dr Hans W Cohn (1916–2004) was an existential psychotherapist and poet. He originally trained in group analysis and went on to be a longstanding contributor to the Society of Existential Analysis, having been on its editorial board from the very first issue in 1990. Over time he published 10 papers in the journal. He is also well known as the author of *Existential Thought and Therapeutic Practice: An introduction to existential psychotherapy* (Sage Publications, 1997) and *Heidegger and the Roots of Existential Therapy* (Continuum, 2002).

Prof. Simon du Plock is Head of Post-Qualification Doctorates at the Metanoia Institute, London, where he directs joint doctoral research programmes with Middlesex University. He is an existential psychotherapist and counselling psychologist who has published widely and lectures internationally on aspects of existential-phenomenological therapy. He has edited *Existential Analysis*, the leading UK journal for existential practitioners, since 1994.

Marcia Gamsu is a UKCP registered existential psychotherapist and BACP accredited counsellor having trained at the School of Psychotherapy and Psychology at Regent's University. Marcia has worked in the NHS, in a primary care setting, in a tertiary psychotherapy setting and in the voluntary sector. She currently works as a counsellor/psychotherapist in private practice and as a tutor at the New School of Psychotherapy and Counselling.

Dr Alex Iantaffi is an Assistant Professor with the Program in Human Sexuality, Department of Family Medicine and Community Health, at the University of Minnesota. He is also a licensed marriage and family therapist, who originally trained in the UK as a systemic psychotherapist. He is Editor-in-Chief for the *International Journal of Sexual and Relationship Therapy*. His therapeutic work is currently focused on transgender and gender non-conforming youth, and their families. Alex has conducted research, and published on gender, disability, sexuality, deafness, education, sexual health, HIV prevention, and transgender issues. His scholarly work has been increasingly focused on issues of intersectionality and sexual health disparities.

Prof. Darren Langdridge is Head of the Department of Psychology at the Open University, UK, Honorary Professor of Psychology at Aalborg University, Denmark and a UKCP accredited existential psychotherapist working in private practice. His research and writing have focused on the critical application of ideas from phenomenological and hermeneutic philosophy to social psychology and psychotherapy within the substantive context of the social scientific study of sexualities. His books include *Existential Counselling and Psychotherapy* (Sage Publications, 2012); *Safe, Sane and Consensual: Contemporary perspectives on sadomasochism* (with Meg Barker, Palgrave Macmillan, 2007); *Phenomenological Psychology* (Pearson, 2007); *Understanding Non-monogamies* (with Meg Barker, Routledge, 2010). He founded and co-edits the journal *Psychology & Sexuality* and is currently working on his next book *Sex–Sexuality–Citizenship*, which will be published by Oxford University Press.

Dr Marc Medina is a BACP accredited and UKCP registered psychotherapist and supervisor in private practice. He is also a clinical supervisor for Mind. Marc is an ACAS trained and qualified mediator and an experienced executive coach. He has also worked as a psychotherapist and supervisor in the NHS at Broadmoor Psychiatric Hospital and is an associate lecturer at the Contemporary College of Therapeutic Studies at Birkbeck, University of London. He has published papers on human sexuality, everyday courage, family therapy and leadership and more recently has carried out research in the area of long-term recovery from addiction and the reciprocity of ideas that may exist between existential psychotherapy and twelve-step recovery.

Richard Pearce is a UKCP registered, and BACP Senior Accredited psychotherapist having previously worked as a development economist in universities, research institutes and international organisations. He is a member of Higher Education Academy (HEA). He worked for many years in a university student counselling service, and currently has a thriving psychotherapy practice in the Bath area, as well as working as an affiliate counsellor for the BUPA Employee Assistance Programme. Recent publications include 'On Being a Person: Sartre's contribution to psychotherapy', *Existential Analysis, 22*(1) and 'Escaping into the Other: An existential view of sex and sexuality', *Existential Analysis, 22*(2).

Christina Richards is Senior Specialist Psychology Associate at the Nottinghamshire Healthcare NHS Trust and West London Mental Health NHS Trust (Charing Cross) Gender Clinics. She works in this capacity as an individual and group psychotherapist and psychologist conducting psychotherapy, assessment and follow-up clinics as part of a multidisciplinary team. She is an accredited psychotherapist with the British Association for Counselling and Psychotherapy (BACP) and is an Associate Fellow of the British Psychological Society (BPS). She lectures and publishes on trans, sexualities and critical mental health, both within academia and to third-sector and statutory bodies. She is the co-author of a clinical guidebook on sexuality and gender with Meg Barker, *Sexuality and Gender for Mental Health Professionals: A practical guide* (Sage Publications, 2013) and is a co-editor of the *Palgrave Handbook of the Psychology of Sexuality and Gender*, which is due to be published in 2014.

Dr Paul Smith-Pickard, MEd, MA(dist), DPsych, is an existential analyst/psychotherapist in private practice. He is a doctoral supervisor for New School of Psychotherapy and Counselling, visiting lecturer at the Gignesthai Centre for Existential Psychology, Athens, Greece, and external examiner at the Dartmoor Centre for Counselling and Psychotherapy. Dr Smith-Pickard has published on a range of topics including: Sexuality in supervision, *Therapy Today* (March, 2009) and Transference as existential sexuality, in the *Journal of the Society for Existential Analysis*; Smith-Pickard, P & Swynnerton, R (2005) The body and sexuality, in E van Deurzen & C Arnold-Baker (Eds) (2005) *Existential Perspectives on Human Issues*. London: Palgrave; Existential sexuality and the body in supervision, in E van Deurzen & S Young (Eds) (2009) *Existential Perspectives on Supervision in Counselling and Psychotherapy*, London: Palgrave; and The role of psychological proximity and sexual feelings in negotiating relatedness in the consulting room: A phenomenological perspective, in M Luca (Ed) (2014, forthcoming) *Sexual Attraction in Therapy*, London: Wiley-Blackwell.

Prof. Ernesto Spinelli is a Fellow of the British Psychological Society (BPS) and in 2000 was awarded the BPS Division of Counselling Psychology Award for Outstanding Contributions to the Advancement of the Profession. He is also a United Kingdom Council for Psychotherapy (UKCP) registered existential psychotherapist as well as Fellow and Senior Accredited member of the British Association for Counselling and Psychotherapy (BACP). In 1999, Ernesto was awarded a Personal Chair as Professor of Psychotherapy, Counselling and Counselling Psychology. He was Chair of the Society for Existential Analysis (1993–1999) and remains an active Life Member. Currently, Ernesto is the Director of ES Associates, an organisation dedicated to the advancement of psychotherapy, coaching, facilitation and mediation through specialist seminars and training programmes. Author of numerous papers and texts on existential phenomenology, the second edition of *Practising Existential Psychotherapy: The relational world* (Sage Publications, 2007), which has been widely praised as a major contribution to the advancement of existential theory and practice, is being prepared for publication in 2014.

Index

A

Aanstoos, CM 297, 300
abnormal/ity x, 4, 25, 26, 28, 29, 37, 43, 46, 47, 65, 124, 126, 285 (*see also* normality)
Acton, H 21, 32, 36, 58
Adam, BD 201, 214
Adams, LG 286, 292, 297, 298, 300
Adams, M 40, 61, 180, 195, 208, 214, 218, 230
Adams, N 289, 301
adolescence 186, 225
    lack of distinction between, and adulthood 190, 192
    second, 222
adolescent/s
    fantasies 106
    sexual abuse of, 177
'adultification' of children 190–2
aesthetics, being sexual as an expression of 52–6, 192
aetiology
    biological, 221
    psychogenic/organic, 297
affirmation 34, 87, 107, 161, 162, 167
affirmative therapy xi, 6, 208, 296 (*see also* gay affirmative therapy)
    ethical, 161–2
    LGBQ, 161–2
    power, politics and, 164–6
    in practice 166–71
aggression 337
    'benign'/'malignant', 73
Alderson, K 141, 158
Algren, Nelson 204, 207
Ally, M 107, 114
ambiguity ix, xi, 95
    embodiment and, 255
    philosophy of, 85, 86 (*see also* Merleau-Ponty)
    sexual, 262
    subject/object, 86

American Psychiatric Association 285, 301
American Psychoanalytic Association 5
Anderson, T 99, 114
Angel, E 323
Anti-Homosexuality Act (2014, Uganda) 3
anus 69, 70
anxiety ix, 27, 57, 73, 99, 105, 191, 226, 285, 286, 294, 295, 307, 337
    existential, 98, 99, 152, 241
    of freedom 206, 211
Arendt, Hannah 259
Asch, SE 270, 282
asexuality 7, 32, 122, 242, 265, 289
'as-if' dimension 119
assimilation 48, 165
assumptions
    cultural, 10, 22, 57, 292
    of difference 45
    existentialist critique of sexual, 24–34
    gender, 50, 52, 202
    health service, 10
    positivistic, 10
    reductionist, 10
    socio-cultural, 63
atmosphere, sexuality as, 23, 24, 81, 83, 84, 235, 261, 310 (*see also* Merleau-Ponty)
attunement 9, 51
Attwood, F 285, 301
authenticity 144, 217, 221, 223, 240, 243
    and bad faith 94–9
    and sex 103–4
authority 45, 95, 145, 146, 172, 261, 320
autonomy ix, 239, 244
    client, 234, 237, 238

B

BACP (*see* British Association for Counselling and Psychotherapy)
bad faith 93–114, 143, 152, 165, 206, 212, 219, 221, 222, 225, 266, 279
Bagemihl, B 30, 58
Baker, CD 287, 290, 304
Bao, AM 221, 228
Barker, M vi, vii, 1, 4, 7, 10, 13, 14, 47, 48, 49, 58, 198–216, 218, 222, 224, 227, 228, 229, 265, 266, 276, 278, 281, 282, 283, 285–304, 326, 330, 334, 338, 340, 341
Barnes, H 128, 136, 153, 154, 158
Barrett, J vi, 217, 221, 227, 228
Bartlett, A 4, 14
Bass, BA 290, 301
Bataille, G 235, 246, 247, 248
Bauer, GR 228, 282
Baur, S 236, 248
BDSM (bondage and discipline, sadism and masochism) 29, 336
beauty 53–5
Beauvoir, S de 48, 49, 58, 80, 82, 148, 198–216, 221, 228, 258, 282, 299, 301 (*see also* Sartre)
   and Sartre's philosophy of relating 205–8
   and Sartre's relationships 202–5
Beck, AT 5, 14
behaviourist/s 5, 71, 120, 141
Being and Nothingness 62, 84, 85, 94, 99, 103, 205, 305
Being and Time 38, 240
being-in-the-world 93, 96, 98, 108, 122, 222, 240
   as a couple 307
   homosexually 132
   sexually 62–74, 122, 123, 125, 133, 135, 155
   with others x, 240, 281
Bell, S 144, 158
belonging 211
Bennett, C 144, 158
Berelowitz, S 177, 195

Berglund, H 122, 128, 138
bestiality 56, 70
bias/es 12, 24, 28, 49, 53, 56, 85, 149, 153, 187, 224, 306, 309
Bible, the 34
Bidell, M 4, 14
binary
   gender as, 50, 326, 329
   opposition ix
   sexual orientation as, 43, 44
bi-negativity 165
Binswanger, L 240, 241, 242–4, 245, 247, 248, 280, 331, 332, 334
biology/biological
   homosexuality as, 38, 45, 66, 125, 126, 128, 132
   left-handedness as, 46–7
   sexuality as, 25–7, 62, 66, 122, 124, 127, 133, 221
      rejection of, 103, 126
   transsexuality as, 221, 225
bisexual/bisexuality 30, 43, 44, 63, 66, 67, 122, 124, 127, 128, 131, 132, 135, 164
Black, DA 1, 14
Bloch, S 283
bodily felt experience 89, 101, 254, 255
body, the
   childhood experiences of, 184, 185, 189
   and desire 87–8, 134, 188, 256
   double sensation of, 85–7
   image 100, 293
   listening with, 260, 261
   lived experience of, 85, 112, 257
   /mind
      integration 297
      split 85, 297
   relation to consciousness 26, 27, 298
bonding 40, 189, 191
   and sex 26, 30
Borchers, S 96, 114
Boss, M 5, 14, 63, 67, 68, 74, 129, 136, 181, 195, 196
Bost, Jacques-Laurent 203
Boulet, DB 293, 303
Bouman, WP 10, 14, 226, 228, 269, 282

Bourdieu, P 253, 262
Boyle, M 288, 289, 290, 301
BPC (*see* British Psychoanalytic Council)
BPS (*see* British Psychological Society)
Brabant, E 236, 249
bracket/ing 9, 143, 147, 148, 152, 162, 208, 234, 292, 294
Braun, V 290, 304
Brewaeys, A 226, 228
bricoleur 81–4
Briod, M 180, 196
British Association for Counselling and Psychotherapy (BACP) 129, 136, 234, 249
British Broadcasting Corporation (BBC) 3, 14
British Psychoanalytic Council (BPC) 5, 14
British Psychological Society (BPS) 6, 14, 15, 129, 136, 234, 249, 278, 282
Buber, M 207, 215, 225, 228, 243, 269, 282
Buddha, the 35
Buggery Act (1533) 31
Burnham, J 325, 334
Butler, C 296, 301
Butler, J 39, 50, 51, 58, 85, 90, 258, 278, 282
Butler, P 177, 196
Byrne, A 296, 301

C

Camus, Albert ix, xii, 205
Cannon, B 128, 136, 155, 158
Carey, MP 288, 300, 304
Carlson, TS 160, 173
Carroll, L 23, 58
Cartesian division of mind and body 85, 100, 253, 297
castration 64, 71
Catalano, J 93, 107, 114
Cavarero, A 258, 259, 262
Cecchin, G 325, 334
Cheung, WCJ 221, 228
childhood 180–5

and sexuality 177–80, 185–8
children
 being sexual 187–90
 'adultification' of 190–2
cisgender 217, 218, 220, 221, 222, 224, 225, 265, 329
civil partnership 131, 314, 315
Clark, A 269, 282
Clark, D 142, 143, 144, 145, 158, 162, 172
Clark, RD 270, 283
Clarke, V 144, 158
class 49, 53, 97, 183, 184, 251, 325, 326, 329
Clausen, B 284
Cohn, HW x, 7, 11, 12, 15, 35, 58, 62–75, 121, 124, 125, 126, 127, 136, 267, 269, 270, 272, 273, 277, 282, 306, 323, 339
'coming out' 122, 130, 145, 147, 148, 149, 152, 274, 317, 331
competition 29, 99, 206
condom use 146, 277
Connell, RW 300, 301
consent 71, 72, 131, 190, 224, 233, 234, 236
'conversion' therapy 129
Cooper, M 225, 228, 238, 249 270, 282, 292, 301
Council for Healthcare Regulatory Excellence 234, 249
Counter-Reformation movement 183
couple
 construct 306, 307–9, 312, 313, 318, 320, 322
 therapy 212, 233, 305–23
 sex 289, 296
Cox, G 217, 228
Coyle, A vi, 4, 5, 6, 16, 17, 141, 144, 157, 158, 159
Crabtree, C 21, 32, 36, 42, 51, 58
Cree, V 177, 196
criminal offence 55, 224
Croissant, JL 290, 301
Cross, MC 161, 162, 172
cross-dressing 31, 276

D

Dahlberg, H 171, 172
Dahlberg, K 171, 172
Daily Mail 2, 15
Daily News Live 2, 15
Dalle Pezze, B 133, 136
Dasein 38, 119, 121, 122, 240, 242, 269
D'Augelli, AR 4, 15
Davies, D 6, 15, 141, 142, 143, 145, 146, 148, 149, 150, 151, 158, 159, 162, 172
Da Vinci, Leonardo 65
death ix, xii, 7, 12, 21, 84, 97, 178, 223, 241, 273, 280, 294
  being-towards-, 62
  instinct 72, 73
  penalty 3
Dempsey, BJ xi, xii
Denman, C 28, 29, 58, 126, 136, 235, 246, 249, 276, 282, 288, 289, 301
Derrida, J 130, 136
De Saussure, F 82, 83
descriptive exploration 67, 265, 271, 278, 309
de-sedimentation 32 (*see also* sedimentation)
desire 5, 9, 27, 51, 84, 87–90, 98, 124–7, 131–2, 134, 165, 186, 326
  and shame 255–6
determinism 122, 181
  biological, 103, 133
  sexual, 40
developmental arrest 65, 66, 68
deviation 25, 26, 69, 212
De Vries, GJ 221, 228
diagnosis 4, 271, 286–92 (*see also* medical diagnosis)
  critical existential approach to, 286–92
diagnostic criteria 4
Diagnostic and Statistical Manual of Mental Disorders (*DSM*) 3, 4, 285, 287, 288, 289, 291, 298, 327
Diamond, L 39, 40, 58

difference/s 34, 47, 48–53, 110, 141, 166, 209, 244
  anatomical, 45
  as the aim of desire 87, 89
  cultural, 296
  denial of, 6, 160, 164, 166
  gender, 32, 33, 48, 50, 51, 52, 65
  labelling, 42, 44, 45, 46, 47
  politics of, 164–5
  sexual, 48, 49, 63–5, 66, 124
discourse analysis 4
discrimination 5, 51, 151, 219, 224
discriminatory psychotherapeutic practice 160
  non- xi, 5, 6
dissociation 32, 193–5, 309
diversity xi, 30, 31, 50
  cultural, 161
Doan, RE 298, 301
dogging 200
dominance and submission 305
domination 87, 125, 164, 241, 242, 243, 244, 247, 306
Donovan, JM 1, 15
DSM (*see Diagnostic and Statistical Manual of Mental Disorders*)
Dumbledore, Professor Albus 2
du Plock, S xi, 6, 9, 13, 15, 21, 32, 33, 36, 58, 122, 128, 129, 136, 141–59, 160, 161, 162, 172, 305– 323, 339
dynamical systems theory 10, 182

E

Easton, D 198, 215
Eigenwelt 298, 332
Elkaïm, A 204
Ellis, H 123, 132, 137
embodied inter-experience 253–5
embodiment 26, 35, 37, 85, 87, 108, 134, 217, 226, 252, 254, 256, 327, 330, 332
  and existential dimensions 297–300
  lack of sense of, 255
empowerment 34, 133, 187

encounter 99–101
endocrinologist 218
epoché 119, 224
Epstein, D 1, 15
equality 47, 129, 131, 132, 201, 224
erectile dysfunction 105, 271, 286, 287, 289, 293, 298, 326
erotic experiences, children's 188–90
eroticism 245, 246, 247, 248
erotogenic zones 69
Etherington, K 224, 228
ethical 64, 90, 94, 112, 144, 146, 161, 162, 251, 261
    codes 234, 248
    practice 129, 142, 161, 245
eugenics 127
Evans, K 171, 172
exclusion 33, 47, 160
exhibitionism 70
existential theory 124–9
    dilemmas 121–3
'expert/s' 53, 54, 237, 273
    difficulties and dangers of being 22, 146, 152, 279, 288
    who are? 23
exploitation 165, 237
    sexual, 177, 237
expression, sexual and social 110–12

F

facticity 35, 57, 95, 102, 103, 107, 108, 281
Faderman, L 130, 137
Falzeder, F 249
family 97, 169, 272
    therapy 324–33
Fausto-Sterling, A 289, 301
feminine 63, 64, 66, 68, 148, 278, 295
feminism 63, 85, 166
feminist 38, 50, 85, 145, 164, 210, 258, 325
Ferenczi, Sandor 236
fetish 71, 105
fetishism 70, 71, 268
Fine, C 37, 50, 58

Finlay, L 171, 172, 224, 228
Finn, M 201, 215
Firmin, C 195
Fisher, J 322, 323
Fishman, JR 288, 301
fixedness 25, 32, 44, 120, 123, 132, 135, 151, 193
Fleming, D 287, 302
Flemons, D 287, 302
flesh 26, 27, 135, 278
Fletcher, R 10, 15
Flowers, P 171, 173, 269, 282
for-itself, the 80, 128, 153
formulation 10, 90, 120, 125
Foucault, M 24, 31, 58, 80, 88, 90, 129, 130, 131, 137, 155, 251–62, 278, 279, 282, 288, 301
Foulkes, SH 265, 267, 268, 269, 272, 273, 282
Frankl, V 293, 301, 328, 334
Freud, S 5, 15, 12, 15, 63, 64, 65, 66, 67, 69, 70, 71, 72, 73, 74, 75, 82, 83, 84, 87, 124, 127, 137, 154, 166, 173, 185, 186, 194, 196, 236, 294
Frie, R 241, 242, 243, 244, 247, 249, 254, 262
'friends-with-benefits' 201
Fromm, E 72, 73, 74, 75, 236
'fuckbuddy' 201
Fullbrook, E 199, 202, 203, 205, 207, 215
Fullbrook, K 199, 202, 203, 205, 207, 215

G

Gabriel, L 235, 249
gag reflex 289
Gamsu, M 13, 233, 280, 339
Garcia-Falgueras, A 221, 228, 229
Garland, Judy 217
Gauntlett, D 278, 282
Gay, P 185, 196
gay
    affirmative therapy 141–59, 160–72

(see also affirmative therapy)
    the case for, 161–3
    in practice 166–71
gene, 44, 45
gaze, the 151, 164, 255
Gelder, K 31, 59
gender 4, 30, 32, 33, 38–40, 47–52, 80, 121, 217–19, 221–5, 227, 265, 278–9, 325–6, 329–32
    difference (see difference, gender)
    identity disorder 10
    transitioning 217
Gender Recognition Act (2004) 224
genital/s 69, 71, 80, 84, 186, 187, 188, 189, 192, 218, 257, 266, 290, 297
    configuration 217
    surgery 217
genogram 209, 329
Gijs, L 226, 228
Gilbert, K 1, 17
Gill, R 285, 302
Goldenberg, H 9, 15, 161, 162, 172, 325, 334
Goldenberg, I 325, 334
Goldman, J 188, 196
Goldman, R 188, 196
Goldner-Vukow, M 267, 283
Gonsiorek, JC 6, 15
Gopnik, A 180, 196
Gough, B 224, 228
Grace, V 290, 302
Green, R 220, 228
Green, S 287, 302
Greenberg, A 330, 335
Greenberg, M 180, 196
Greene, B 6, 15
Griffin, P 329, 334
Gross, Otto 236
group therapy, existential 265–84
    task of the group 270–40
    sex and sexuality, talking about in, 276–80
guilt 104, 106, 162, 170, 209, 220, 233, 234, 235, 297, 337
    -inducing injunctions 184
Gyamerah, J 330, 334

H

Haider-Markel, DP 126, 137
Haldane, D 327, 330, 334
Hall, M 296, 302
Halley, J 38, 59
Halperin, D 39, 59
Hamer, D 44, 59
Hardy, J 198, 215
Hare-Mustin, RT 325, 324
Harper, AL 300
Harré, R 332, 334
Head, S 4, 16
Heaton, J 7, 16
Heidegger, M 22, 35, 38, 56, 59, 62, 82, 83, 90, 95, 121, 122, 133, 134, 137, 149, 158, 181, 196, 240–2, 243, 249, 269, 279, 283
Henley, Don 265
Herdt, G 221, 229
Herek, GM 6, 15
hermaphrodism of the soul 31
Hershberger, SL 4, 15
heteronormativity 208, 220, 224, 278, 325, 326, 327, 328
heterosexism 161, 165, 167
heterosexist 2, 12, 33, 85, 162, 168, 170, 172, 258
heterosexual normative bias 85
Heywood, C 237, 244, 245, 249
Hill, DB 226, 229
Hinitz, BF 183, 184, 197
Hitchings, P 6, 16
Hite, S 289, 302
HIV 147, 152, 162
Hofman, MA 230
homonegativity 5, 162, 172
homophobia 162, 336
homosexual/ity 31, 43, 44, 65–9, 80, 119, 124, 127, 129–30, 136, 142, 145, 152–3, 268
    identity 129–35
Hopcke, M 152, 158
horizontalisation 119, 213, 225, 270, 278
Horney, Karen 236
Hoshiai, M 226, 229

humanistic therapies/therapists 5, 7, 141, 142, 149, 150
Humpty Dumpty 23, 24
Hunter, J 4, 17
Husserl, E 37, 82, 83, 119, 163

I

Iacovou, S 307, 323
Iantaffi, A 10, 13, 324–35, 339
identification
   group, 45
   with the father/mother 64, 65, 66, 68
I–It relating 207, 225, 269
imagination 36, 55
   aesthetic, 55
   erotic, 288
   public, 55
impotence 73
incongruence 95, 149
individuality 35, 123, 243, 244, 247, 268, 332
inequality 9, 165, 171, 172, 248
infantile sexuality 69, 70, 185
'infantilisation' of adults 190–2
Ingham, H 273, 283
instinct 72–3, 84, 125
Institute of Medicine (IOM) 4, 16
intentionality 82, 84, 85, 86, 87, 97, 128, 154, 155
intercourse, sexual 31, 55, 186, 233, 287, 288, 289, 290, 296
interiorisation 107, 108
intimacy, distrust of 105–7
intersubjectivity 23, 26, 27, 33, 35, 42, 48, 51, 81, 89, 126, 129, 133, 153, 182, 205, 234, 242, 256, 265, 273
Iraq 126
Irigaray, L 48, 49, 51, 52, 59
Irvine, JM 291, 302
isolation x, 37, 69, 89, 96, 97, 101, 105, 126, 235, 238, 240, 330
I–Thou relating 144, 207, 242, 268–70, 277

J

Jackson, S 177, 178, 183, 184, 185, 188, 195, 196, 289, 290, 302
Jagger, Mick 265
Jagose, A 38, 39, 59
jealousy 66, 209, 297
Jehu, D 234, 236, 249
Jiang-Ning, Z 229
'Johari Window' 273, 274
Johnson, M 100, 114
Johnson, VE 288, 289, 303
Jones, Bridget 48
Jones, E 64, 65, 75, 236
Jopling, D 96, 114
Jordan-Young, R 50, 59
Joseph, A 21, 48, 49, 59
Joslyn, MR 126, 137
judgements
   normative, 68
   value, 45
Jung, CG 186, 187, 196, 236
Jungian analyst 152

K

Kaeser, F 186, 196
Kaplan, HS 288, 289, 302
Kaschak, E 287, 302
Katz, AM 328, 335
Katz, JN 43, 59
Kaufman, G 255, 262
Kaye, J 34, 59
Keane, H 291, 302
Kemp, R 133, 137
Kessler, SJ 289, 290, 302
Kierkegaard, S ix, x, xii, 119, 124, 125, 134, 137, 223, 227, 229, 279, 283
King, MB 4, 5, 14, 16
Kinsey, A 127, 137
   research 127
kinship 97
Kirby, S 180, 181, 196
Kirk, SA 4, 16, 288, 302
Kissane, DW 267, 283
Kitzinger, C 4, 16, 158

Klein, F 127, 137
Klein, M 12, 186, 196, 236
Kleinplatz, PJ 286, 287, 288, 290, 292, 293–5, 297, 298, 302
Knorr-Cetina, K 34, 59
Knowlson, T 5, 16
Koran, the 34
Kosakievicz, Olga 203, 205
Krege, S 222, 229
Kruijver, FPM 221, 229
Kurtz, E 119, 123, 137
Kutchins, H 4, 16, 288, 302

L

labelling 92–6
Labriola, K 200, 215
Lacan, Jacques 82
'lads' mags' 285
Lage, E 270, 283
Laing, RD 80, 252, 258, 262, 287, 293, 302, 303
Lambert, M 239, 249
Lane, G 325, 334
Langdridge, D xi, 6, 9, 13, 16, 38, 59, 160–72, 180, 182, 196, 198, 199, 200, 208, 209, 210, 214, 215, 269, 277, 282, 283, 289, 298, 301, 303, 338, 339
Långström, N 122, 128, 137
Lantz, JE 330, 334
Lanzmann, Claude 204
Laplanche, L 69, 75
Laumann, EO 285, 303
Lawrence, AA 222, 229
Lebolt, J 160, 173
Le Bon, Sylvie 204
Leck, G 43, 59
Le Coin, Elisabeth 205
left-handedness 46–8
Legg, C 5, 6, 16
lesbian and gay
  affirmative therapy 6, 141–57, 160–72, 296
  studies 5, 6, 38
  experience 7, 10–11, 120, 123, 127, 130, 133, 135
Lescariges, C 183, 184, 197
Le Vey, S 44, 59
Levi-Strauss, Claude 81, 82
liberal 10, 164, 166
libido 72, 84
listening, maieutic 260, 261
Loewenberg, H 222, 229
Lombardi, EL 224, 226, 229
love 3, 39, 73, 96, 130, 131, 162, 200, 201, 202, 203, 206, 211, 214, 233, 234, 236, 239, 242, 243, 244, 245, 246, 247, 248, 280
lovers, the world of 258–61
Luft, J 273, 283

M

Maass, A 270, 283
'macho society' 151
Madison, GB 62, 75
Maheu, René 202
Mahrer, AR 293, 303
male, ejaculatory 86
marriage, same-sex 3, 34, 131
Marriage Act (2013) 3
Marshall, BL 290, 303
Martinot, S 99, 114
Marx, Karl 82, 166
Marxism 81, 83, 107
masculine 63, 66, 68, 164, 295
Masters, WH 288, 289, 303
masturbation 26, 70, 170, 184, 188, 288, 296
Matsumoto, Y 229
May, R 293, 303, 306, 323
Maylon, A 142, 158
McCluskey, U 327, 330, 334
McGeorge, C 160, 173
McKenna, W 290, 302
medical
  diagnosis 267, 271, 286, 287, 297
    (see also diagnosis)
  discourse ix
  insurance 10
  intervention 183, 287

model 288, 294, 297, 330
profession 53, 289–90
technologies 221
Medina, M 7, 8, 12, 21, 32, 33, 36, 38, 59, 119–38, 340
Mercer, C 285, 303
Merleau-Ponty, M xi, 8, 12, 23, 24, 26, 27, 62, 75, 79–90, 102, 114, 119, 121, 132, 133, 134, 137, 182, 197, 223, 229, 253, 254, 256, 258, 261, 262, 297, 303, 328, 334
'metamours' 202
Michelangelo 65
micro systems 325, 326
Milton, M xi, 1–18, 21, 42, 60, 141, 144, 152, 157, 158, 159, 161, 173, 296, 303, 336–7, 338
minority/minorities
   group 34, 226
   sexual, xi, 3, 161, 162, 164, 167
   stress 4, 226, 269
Miracle, AW 285, 303
Miracle, TS 285, 303
Mirvish, A 96, 114
Mitchell, K 295, 303
'Molly Houses' 31
'monogamish' 201
monogamous relationship/s 13, 198, 169, 201–2, 208, 209, 210, 213, 318
monogamy 169, 198, 201, 208, 213, 310
   non- 198–216 (*see also* open relationships, and polyamory)
mononormativity 208, 209, 211, 213, 214
monosexual 328
Morris, K 94, 96, 107, 114
Morris-Roberts, C 1, 17
Moscovici, S 270, 283
mother 48, 64, 65, 66, 68, 69, 71, 155, 185, 205, 225, 236, 297, 298
Mugabe, Robert 3
murder 2, 33, 71

N

Nardi, PM 1, 17
National Health Service (NHS) 10, 266, 267, 275
'natural'
   assumptions 22, 28, 50, 52, 56, 66, 83, 121, 208
   condition of being 162, 178
   expression of sexuality 25, 27, 30, 32, 33, 50, 56, 126, 129, 288, 290
   selection 28, 29
   world 98, 108
Neal, C 6, 15, 141, 142, 143, 145, 148, 149, 150, 158, 159
Newman, M 234, 249
NHS (*see* National Health Service)
Nietzsche, F ix, x, xii, 120, 134, 137, 166, 279, 283, 306
Nigeria 126
non-discriminatory therapy xi, 5, 6 (*see also* gay affirmative therapy)
non-monogamous relationship/s 198–216 (*see also* open relationships, and polyamory)
   non-consensual, 198
   open, 198–213
Norcross, J 239, 249
normality 21, 25, 27, 28, 29, 43, 55, 58, 69, 70, 110, 157, 185, 208, 266, 274, 285, 289
normative/normativity 4, 68, 80, 85, 143, 145, 150, 165, 170, 212, 216, 258, 268, 328, 332
   non-, 2, 208

O

Obama, Barack 3
objectification xi, 85, 86, 87, 207, 212, 244
Oedipus complex 64, 65, 66, 67
Office of the Children's Commissioner 177
Ogden, G 289, 298, 303
omnipotence ix, 73

ontic 8, 12, 13, 93, 103, 121, 122, 241, 258
ontological 8, 9, 12, 13, 84, 86, 93, 121, 122, 128, 156, 240, 258
open relationships 169, 200, 203, 296, 310, 312, 313, 317, 318, 319, 320, 322 (*see also* non-monogamies)
oppression 9, 131, 148, 164, 165, 171
   'five faces of', 165
orgasm 69, 70, 87, 88, 98, 179, 189, 285, 288, 289, 290, 295, 298
orientation, sexual (*see* sexual orientation)
otherness x, 32, 34, 41–2, 48, 52, 55, 57, 89

P

paediatrics 183
paedophilia 70, 99, 179, 190, 191, 192
Paik, A 285, 303
Panopticon 279
pan-sexualism 63
paraphilias 286
parenting 145, 151
Parker, A 38, 59
Parker, H 44, 60
PDE5 inhibitors 287, 293, 295
Pearce, R x, xi, 8, 12, 21, 27, 36, 60, 92–118, 340
peer pressure 39, 191
penis 225, 290, 293, 295, 297
   Freudian theory 64, 71
persecution 68, 126
perverse xi, 28, 70, 126, 153, 179
   polymorphously, 70
perversion/s x, 5, 43, 67, 69–71, 129, 141, 268
phallocentrism 12, 48, 49, 52, 258
phenomenological
   attitude 37, 162, 163
   descriptions 85, 89, 209
   enquiry 119, 129, 224, 253
   exploration 219, 222-224, 226, 278
   method 9, 166, 208, 253, 279
   perspective 66, 142, 180

reduction 83, 163
   stance 63, 170, 171, 208–10, 234
   theory 124, 141, 153, 305
Phenomenology of Perception 62, 79, 83, 84, 85, 132
physiology 63, 94, 102, 104, 108, 113
Pixton, S 160, 173
plasticity 28, 128
   of sexual experience 122, 131
Plato 65
Plummer, K 32, 60, 278, 283
polyamorous relationships 7, 200, 203
polyamory 200, 213
polygamy 199
Pomeroy, W 127, 137
Pontalis, JB 69, 75
Pope, K 234, 235, 250
pornography 55, 103, 105, 336
   child, 179, 190
positive regard 142, 145, 146, 149, 151
Potts, A 290, 302, 303, 304
power ix, xi, 28, 44, 45, 46, 48, 52, 54, 55, 71, 89, 130, 155, 161, 162, 165, 181, 188, 190, 236, 257, 258, 275, 277, 280, 288, 295, 305
   differentials 167, 171, 237
   politics and affirmative practice 164–6
   'will to', 220
powerlessness 73, 74, 165, 235, 293
'practico-inert' 108, 110, 112
pre-adolescent sexuality 186, 191
premature ejaculation 287, 289
promiscuity 99, 105, 106
psychiatry 3, 4
   anti-, 287
psychoanalysis 5, 7, 21, 67, 81, 82, 84, 163, 166, 186, 267
psychoanalytic
   circles 5
   literature 5, 141
psychodynamic 142, 149, 268, 273
psychoeducation 267, 277
psychology 1, 13, 49, 64, 144, 180, 183, 185, 288
   abnormal, 4
   behavioural, 288

child/children's, 180, 183,
  Gestalt, 81, 82
  lesbian and gay, 144
psychopathology 226, 269
psychosexual clinics 289, 300
Pugh, T 2, 17

Q

queer affirmative therapy 160
queer theory 38–9, 166
Quist, RM 126, 137

R

race 45, 325
Rae, G 95, 114
Rahman, Q 44, 61, 137
Rambukkana, N 200, 215
Ramsay, R 43, 44, 61
Rancière, J 53, 60
randomised controlled clinical trials 238
rape 2, 71, 99, 105, 177, 185, 271, 276, 337
Rayner, E 5, 17
Rechtin, A 96, 114
reciprocity 86, 88, 90, 101, 109, 207, 211, 213, 242, 243, 257, 259
reductionism, challenge to 10–11
reflexivity, relational 325, 327, 333
Reformation movement 183
regressive-progressive method 107
Reich, Wilhelm 178
Reid, LL 278, 284
relationship
  anarchy 202
  ethics 212, 213, 214, 233–5
  existential perspective on, 239–44
religious
  beliefs 66
  leaders 23
reparative therapy 129
reproduction 25, 26, 27, 28, 29, 30, 54, 102, 184, 218, 219, 226, 326
retirement 211, 294
Richards, C vi, 4, 9, 10, 13, 14, 17, 109, 208, 209, 215, 217–29, 265–83, 329, 335, 338, 340
Ricoeur, P 160, 163, 166, 173, 277, 284
Ritchie, A 199, 215, 216
Ritter, KY 168, 173
Rivers, I 4, 17
rivers of experience 328
Rogers, CR 6, 17
Rotherum-Borus MJ 4, 17
Roughgarden, J 29, 30, 50, 60
Rowley, H 202, 212, 213, 216
Rowling, JK 2
Rozanski, C 229
Rubin, G 288, 304, 329, 335
Rubin, R 199, 216
Russell, J 234, 235, 236, 250
Russia 3
Rutter, PA 160, 173, 234, 237, 250

S

sadism 29, 73, 89, 99
sado-masochism 55, 62, 70, 72, 289
Sakalli, N 126, 137
Samuels, A 165, 173
Sanders, SG 1, 14
Sartre, J-P x, xi, xii, 8, 12, 34, 38, 60, 62, 75, 80, 81, 82, 84, 85, 86, 88, 89, 90, 92, 93, 94, 95, 96, 97, 99, 103, 107, 108, 109, 110, 112, 113, 114, 115, 121, 128, 143, 148, 153, 154, 156, 159, 165, 173, 178, 198–214, 216, 220, 223, 224, 229, 242, 250, 257, 258, 270, 284, 299, 304, 305, 306, 323 (see also Beauvoir, S de)
and de Beauvoir's philosophies of relating 205–8
and de Beauvoir's relationships 202–5
Savic, I 122, 128, 138
Sawubona 252
Scalzo, C 180, 197
scapegoating 272, 276
Scherrer, KS 208, 304

Schrock, DP 278, 284
science/s 4, 180, 267
   cognitive, 180
   human, 11, 226, 227
   neuro-, 254
scientist 23
   political, 3
   -practitioner stance 218
Sears, T 21, 22, 23, 24, 60
sedimentation/s 32, 120, 193–5, 247, 274, 309
sedimented
   biases 56
   ideas 266, 274, 278
   limitations 32
   self-concept 151
   self-construct 247
seduction 261
   'hypothesis' 186
Semlyen, J 16
sensate-focus 285, 289
sensation/s 86, 89, 188, 289, 293, 295, 297
   double, 85–7
sex
   the dark shimmer of, 257–8
   oral, 289, 296
   role reversal 30
   roles 30
   safer, 146, 147, 169, 170
   -talk 293
   therapy 4, 13, 267, 285–300, 326
Sex and the City 286
sexologists 130, 336
   Victorian, 24, 25, 124
sexology 22, 25, 53, 54, 56, 124
sexual
   being,
      and biology 25–7
      existence precedes essence 38–41
      existential choice 34–7
      as an expression of aesthetics 52–6
      and gender 47–52
      and identity 30–4
      issues of normality/abnormality 27–30
      and otherness 41–7
   difference 63–5
   dysfunctions 4, 10, 105, 288, 291
   exclusivity 206
   exploitation 177, 237
   feelings 42, 66, 134, 167, 193, 194
   fluidity 39–42, 46
   harassment 105
   intercourse 233, 290
   labelling 42–6
   orientation 5, 6, 25, 43, 51, 93, 128, 131, 133, 142, 153, 155, 161, 170, 326, 329
   potential 94, 102–3, 108, 109, 112, 113, 195
   predators 179
   preferences 33, 103, 121, 122, 126
   selection 29, 30
   violence 179
Sexual Fluidity: Understanding women's love and desire 39
sexualisation 186
   hyper-, 285, 300
sexuality
   defining human, 22–4
   existential theory and practice 7–10
   landscapes of, 2–5
   permeates existence 84–5
   pre-adolescent, 186, 191
   and violence 71–4
sexually
   aversive 287
   open relationship 169
Shakespeare, T 289, 304
shame xi, 64, 89, 99, 101, 123, 162, 184, 293
   and desire 255–6
Sheppard, A 53, 60
Shernoff, M 146, 147, 159
Sherrod, D 1, 17
Shotter, J 328, 335
Singer, I 246, 250
Single Equality Act (2010) 224
'singular universal' 92, 94, 107–10, 112–13, 164
situatedness 9

Smith, G 5, 14
Smith, JA 171, 173
Smith-Pickard, P xi, 7, 8, 12, 13, 17, 23, 24, 60, 79–91, 121, 138, 251–62, 341
Socarides, CW 5, 17
Society for Existential Analysis 7, 21, 153
sociologists 3
sodomite 31, 130
sodomy 31
Spinelli, E x, xii, 7, 8, 10, 12, 13, 17, 21–61, 102, 121, 124, 125, 126, 127, 128, 130, 138, 149, 150, 153, 159, 177–97, 222, 229, 238, 239, 240, 242, 247, 248, 250, 265, 271, 274, 277, 278, 284, 287, 292, 304, 305, 306, 307, 309, 322, 323, 328, 335, 341
spiritual (see Überwelt)
Star Wars 190
Stawarska, B 82, 91
Steinbeck, J 89, 91
Stern, D 254, 262
Storr, M 286, 304
Stotts, A xi, xii
Strand, DA 1, 18
stress, minority related 4
structural inequalities 171
structuralism 81, 83
Strupp, Hans 239
subjectivity 49, 74, 85, 97–9, 104, 239
　female, 49, 52
　male, 49
　phallocentric, 52
suicidal ideation 146
suicide 100, 130, 235
Sullivan, A 131, 138
Sulloway, FJ 185, 186, 197
super-ego 64, 66
supervision 7, 261, 280
Swaab, DF 221, 228, 229
swinging 200
Swynnerton, R 7, 17, 23, 24, 60, 121, 138, 341
systemic approach 324–33
Szasz, T 7, 18, 269, 284, 287, 304

T

taboo xi, 56, 84, 192, 234, 235, 257, 260, 261, 276, 293
Taormino, T 198, 216
Tatchell, P 119, 127, 130, 131, 138
temporality x, 35, 37, 70, 223
Terndrup, AI 168, 173
Thelen, E 181, 197
theory
　critical social, 163, 166,
　dynamical systems, 181–2
　evolutionary, 29
　existential, 7, 21, 34, 42, 50, 58, 153, 305
　family systems, 324–33
　post-colonial, 166
　psychoanalytic, 66, 73
　queer, 38–9, 166
　sexological, 31
therapeutic
　alliance 142, 152, 273, 307
　factors 271
　relationship 13, 143, 144, 146, 167, 233–48, 334
therapy
　affirmative, 6, 141–73, 208, 296
　conversion, 129
　couple, 305–23
　existential, 62, 63, 120, 123, 134, 144, 145, 149, 156, 157, 208, 247, 265, 270, 286, 287, 292–3
　family, 324–35
　feminist, 145
　group, 265–84
　pink, 141, 142
　psychoanalytic, 63
　relationship, sexuality in the 233–50
　reparative, 129
　sex, 285–304, 326
　sexuality and, 233
　a technical approach to, 237–9
　termination of, 235, 245
Theunissen, Michael 242
'thing-ify' 41
third sex 130
Thorne, B 233, 234, 250

Three Essays on the Theory of Sexuality 63, 66, 67, 124
threesomes 169, 200, 203, 314
Tiefer, L 287, 290, 302, 304
Tiemersma, D 81, 91
Tillich, P 133, 138
Tisdale, S 44, 61
Tobin, RD 130, 138
torture 33, 46
totalisation 94, 108, 109, 111
touching 85, 86, 143, 245, 289, 296
    self-, 296
transgender 13, 31, 141, 217–18, 225, 296, 326, 329, 331, 332
    and existential practice 217
    general issues 226
transgressive sexuality 28, 55, 56, 276
transitioning 219–23
transphobia 218, 220, 223–6
transvestism 70
Tremblay, P 43, 44, 61
Trotter, JK 3, 18
Twitter 2

U

Überwelt 298, 332
Uganda 3, 126
Umwelt 297, 298, 331
UK Council for Psychotherapy (UKCP) 234, 250
United Kingdom 3, 200
universal
    position 164
    singular, 107–10, 112–13
Ussher, JM 287, 290, 304

V

vaginismus 48, 287, 289, 290, 293, 296, 298
van Deurzen, E vi, 18, 40, 61, 123, 138, 143, 159, 218, 230, 241, 250, 292, 297, 304, 307, 323, 331, 332, 335
van Deurzen-Smith, E 7, 18, 68, 75, 120, 126, 134, 138, 145, 146, 150, 159, 270, 284, 292, 297, 304
Vanetti, Dolores 204, 207
Vares, T 290, 304
Vasquez, M 234, 250
Ventegodt, S 267, 284
Viagra 288, 300
Vian, Michelle 204
victim/s 12, 36, 57, 150, 151, 152, 177, 235
    blaming 9
Victor, Pierre 205
Victorian sexology/sexologists 24, 25, 30, 124
Vidal, G 42, 43, 61
violence 165, 184, 225, 337
    anti-gay, 3
    sexuality and, 71–4
    towards children 179
voyeurism 70

W

Wallace, DL 2, 17
Warner, M 326, 335
Weatherall, A 290, 304
Weber, J 95, 115
Weeks, J 22, 24, 61, 124, 130, 138
Whitaker, CA 330, 335
Wider, K 96, 115
Wiegand, DM 126, 137
Wilberg, P 260, 262
Wilchins, RA 229
Wilde, Oscar xi
Wilson, GD 44, 61
Wincze, JP 288, 300, 304
Wooler, Stuart 46
worldview, development and maintenance 193–4

Y

Yalom, I 240, 250, 265, 267, 271, 273, 279, 280, 281, 284, 286, 287, 292, 293, 294, 304, 329, 335

Young, IM 164, 165, 173, 258
Young, S 7, 18

Z
Zhou, JN 221, 230
Zilbergeld, B 290, 295, 304
Zimbabwe 3
Zulu culture 252